Alastair Sawday's

SPECIAL
PLACES TO STAY
IN
SPAIN
AND
PORTUGAL

Typesetting, Conversion & Repro:	Avonset, Bath
Maps:	Bartholomew Mapping Services (a division of HarperCollins Publishers, Glasgow)
Printing:	Jarrold Book Printing,
Design:	Springboard Design, Bristol
UK Distribution:	Portfolio, London
US Distribution:	St Martin's Press, New York

First published in 1999 by Alastair Sawday Publishing Co. Ltd
44 Ambra Vale East, Bristol BS8 4RE, UK.

Alastair Sawday has asserted his right to be identified as the author of this work.
ISBN 1-901970-03-5 Printed in the UK

Alastair Sawday's

SPECIAL PLACES TO STAY
IN
SPAIN
AND
PORTUGAL

"There is a great deal of Spain which has not been perambulated. I would have you go thither . . ."

Dr Johnson to Boswell

ASP

Alastair Sawday Publishing

ACKNOWLEDGEMENTS

Guy Hunter-Watts is a rare phenomenon, an Englishman who has taken deep root in his new soil and maintained both a sense of humour **and** an easy-going worldliness, too. He makes contact in the easiest way and is a colourful and well-loved figure in his adopted village near Ronda. When I arrived, late, to stay with him the village mayor had willingly waited for my arrival, in vain, and the assembled girls who were due to sing me a *sevillana* had lapsed into rehearsal. But I succeeded in cajoling them into performance, and the village boys gleefully showed me the way to 'la casa de Guillermo'. Everyone seems to celebrate his presence in the village.

(The inclusion of his house in this book is, of course, entirely unconnected to Guy's regular gifts to this office of the fine local *manchego* cheese. But such generosity does go a long way in this cynical world.)

Guy has researched, administered and written the Spanish part of this book, and much of the Portuguese part, too. He has faithlessly abandoned his old CV for a machine more likely to get him there on time, but is nevertheless heroically willing to tolerate the very rough with the smooth. I will always be in his debt; he works hard, loyally, and with unerring good taste... of the **Special Places** variety.

Carol Dymond did much of the research in Northern Portugal; her progress from one magnificent house to the next was a miracle of self-discipline, and I am hugely grateful to her. (She lives in the Alentejo, by the way, and would welcome visitors who are happy to work hard and help her clear land and plant trees. Contact us.)

Series Editor:	Alastair Sawday
Editor:	Guy Hunter-Watts
Production Manager:	Julia Richardson
Administrative support:	Emma Baverstock, Carol Dymond, Annie Shillito, Lisa (Pea) Saunders
Accounts:	Sheila Clifton, Maureen Humphries
Cover design:	Caroline King
Symbols:	Celia Witchard,
Photographs:	Quentin Craven, Guy Hunter-Watts, Lisa (Pea) Saunders
Constant support:	The whole team at Alastair Sawday's Tours has provided constant support: Annie Shillito, Dave Kelly and Eliza Meredith.

Thanks to: Jemma Markham, Else Denninghof-Stelling, María Sanchís Pages and Caro Wallace-Davis for recommending new places; to Richard Church and Tony Rounthwaite for help with mail-outs; to Joaquín the postman for making it up the hill; to all the readers who took the trouble to write; to Diana Paget for her inspired introduction and to Leica, Lucy and Poppy for canine connivance.

Even if you plan to spend your Spanish holiday on the Costa del Sol then you should buy this book! We have managed to find delicious places to stay even there... no mean achievement.

However, most of our *Special Places* are in more salubrious areas far from the tanning crowds; in mountain hamlets, hill-hugging white villages, ancient quarters of ancient towns, remote country spots where eagles soar and silence softens the landscape. But the 20th century has not been ignored; we reach deep into big cities and many of our favourite places are thoroughly modern.

Every editor claims that each edition is better than the previous one. But it is TRUE in this case! We have paid attention to every criticism, every letter which recounted tales of disappointment. The photographs of swallows nesting atop a bathroom cabinet were enough to let us know that the tales of bird-droppings were true, after all. Any hint of a cold welcome, a casual remark about awful food... and we were off to take another look. So this new book is bereft of the few places that were imperfect and filled with newly discovered houses and hotels that are genuinely special.

We remain implacably opposed to the worst excesses of modern tourism, to the chain hotels, the corporate hospitality tendency, the grim blocks that masquerade as hotels, the cultural insensitivity of most hotel building. We celebrate those foreigners who strive to integrate, the devoted souls who pour their hearts into restoration and rebuilding, the talented designers who bring a fresh eye to old places and the people who band together to bring new life to their communities.

If your travels in Spain and Portugal are to go as deep as you dare hope, if you are to meet good people in their interesting homes and hotels, then do use *Special Places* as a basic tool. It will transform your Spanish and Portuguese holiday.

Alastair Sawday

The existence of this book reflects a new awareness in both Spain and Portugal that there is life and interest beyond the beach. 'Turismo rural' has entered the vernacular; Brussels is funding developments through its CEDER programme and in both countries people are discovering the joys of their interiors and that jobs can be created there, too. Walking is in vogue and whichever of Iberia's remote mountain ranges you choose for your rambling you can now find a good place to lay your head at the end of the day. Just five years ago this was unthinkable.

The really good news is that these changes are being better managed than in the past; the lunatic development of the sixties and seventies left a butchered coastline. A lesson has been learned. People have begun to reaffirm rather than renounce their roots: time-tried country cooking is being exalted, buildings are being restored rather than bulldozed, local craftsmens' order books are full and forgotten mountain pathways are being rediscovered.

We need to support and celebrate this change in attitude because parallel to it runs the trend towards globalisation and standardisation. Walk down Seville's delightful Calle Sierpes and you now find Virgin, C&A, M&S, Body Shop and McDonalds. Every provincial town has some half a dozen big supermarkets selling Irish butter, French cheese, German beer and English biscuits. Folk south of the Pyrenees are embracing the European ideal with open arms and you don't need the poetic sensibility of Laurie Lee to realise that whatever the benefits of the new Europe something is being lost.

The Spain we love so dearly is different; anyone who has witnessed the spontaneity of a village *feria*, drunk coffee first thing in a worker's bar, been touched by flamenco's deep mystery or travelled through the Meseta's open spaces would surely agree. We hope that this book, in its own small way, can be instrumental in helping to preserve regional difference by extolling all that which is local, home-spun, family and friendly. In both Spain and Portugal people still tend to feel a deep attachment to their *patria chica* or home town or village. And it is this love of all that is local, singular and different which offers so much hope for the future.

However, Spain has few of those quirky and cosy B&B-type places which make a stay in England or France such a treat (see our books!). So we have widened our net and included a number of places whose owners are neither Spanish nor Portuguese. We DON'T deliberately search out ex-pats. But some of them have created marvellous hostelries and those we include have a proven track-record of commitment to their adopted land and people. Most have 'gone native', are keen hispanophiles and you will profit from their love of their host culture.

We DO admit to our nostalgia for the Iberia of Morton, Brennan and Lee, of Ford, Byron and of Irving but we nevertheless would suggest that there has never been a better time to visit the Peninsula. You get a fistful of pesetas for your dollar or pound, you can sleep and eat well for half of what you could back home and - armed with this book - you have a short-cut to the loveliest hotels, most beautiful regions and the kindest of people. You'd be barmy to head South without a copy!

HOW DO WE CHOOSE OUR HOTELS

Each one has to be special in some way or another. If it is modern, it will be run by good people, or have wonderful views or be in the best part of town, or even be a really successful modern building. If it is kitsch in places then its redeeming features might be the best food in town and vast beds. Or it may be the only place to sleep in a an area of really glorious countryside.

We ignore unfriendly hotels, noisy ones too, or those that are over-priced or bad value. We flee from the ugly, the dreary and from plain bad taste. And we give a wide berth (with just a few exceptions) to the chain hotels. This means that the state-run Posadas of Spain and the Pousadas of Portugal are not included here. Some of them are as magnificent as ever but we believe that, by and large, they lack the warmth and personality of our smaller hotels. However glorious they might be they are run by the state and they tend to show it.

So in the countryside we look for lovingly-converted farms, barns, abbeys, monasteries, inns and manor-houses. We seek out quiet country, long views and nature at her best. We find places that set us alight, rekindle our faith in humanity's capacity for creating beauty. Flashes of originality, exotic taste, plain honesty of style... all these things help.

In the cities and towns we have found quiet places to hide in, hotels of panache and style, an amazing place in Seville which is more house than hotel. There are country B&Bs run by devoted families, simple little pensions and all of the places we have chosen have far more character than the chain hotel which may be just across the way.

And we hold dear to our right to be utterly subjective in these matters. Please tell us when you think we may have got things wrong; thanks to your help and comments this third edition of *Special Places* is a better book than its predecessor.

A WORD ABOUT THE BALEARICS

We are delighted that Mallorca, Ibiza and Menorca are included for the first time in this book - and the places we have chosen are every bit as special as their mainland cousins. But a word of warning; expect to pay about 50% more than in the rest of Spain. We promise that we haven't deliberately sought out expensive places!

ANDALUSIA

Again, the large number of places in this guide in Andalusia reflects an undeniable fact: this is, by far, the most visited part of Spain.

SUBSCRIPTIONS

You should know that we charge owners a small sum to appear in this book: without it this guide would not exist. But we do NOT include hotels and houses simply because they are prepared to pay: we visit them, select and then invite subscription. Clearly, one or two drop away but they are mercifully few. The book now has a reputation and people ask us if they can come in. Those which make it in are the ones we LIKE.

HOW TO USE THIS BOOK

Abbreviations:
C/	calle=street	
s/n	sin número = unnumbered	
Pts	Pesetas	
Esc	Escudos	

The spelling of proper names in Spain In those parts of Spain where there are two official languages (eg Galicia, the Basque Country, Catalonia) - the names of people and places will often have two different spellings. We have tried to use the ones that you, the traveller, are most likely to SEE in each instance: this may mean one version in the address, another in the directions on how to get there.

Coding and Prices
S=single, D=double, Tw=twin, Tr=triple, Q=quadruple, Ste=suite, Apt=apartment, Hse=house
M=Set menu, C=approx price for a 3 course meal with wine à la carte.

Prices are given for the room unless otherwise specified, ie p.p.=per person.

All prices exclude VAT unless otherwise stated. Despite our best efforts some prices may be slightly higher than those quoted in this book.

MEALS

Times   The Spanish eat much later than we do: breakfast often doesn't get going until 9am, lunch is generally eaten from 2pm onwards and dinner is rarely served before 8.30pm.
In Portugal things get going slightly earlier. Lunch is normally eaten between 1pm and 2pm, dinner between 7pm and 10 pm - NOT later. If you have picked up Spanish habits be careful when you cross the border if you don't want to go hungry to bed.

Breakfast   The universal 'Continental' offering tends to be uninspired in both Spain and Portugal: coffee, toast (perhaps cakes), butter and jam. Marmalade is a rare sight in spite of all those lovely oranges, and freshly squeezed juice is the exception rather than the norm. But few places would object if you supplement your meal with your own fruit.

Remember, in Spain especially, that many local folk breakast on patés and olive oil, perhaps with garlic and certainly with tomato if you're in Catalonia. Your hotelier will often assume that you would prefer a blander, more northern-European offering. So do ask if you prefer a more authentic breakfast.

Tea tends to be poor so if you can't do without it we would recommend that you take a few tea bags with you. Most places would be only too happy to supply you with hot water. *Té* in Spain and *chá* in Portugal normally is served plain. Ask for *con leche/com leite* if you like it with milk or *con limón/com limão* for a slice of lemon. In Spain the bars always serve camomile tea (*manzanilla*) - it can be a useful evening drink because coffee is nearly always very strong.

Coffee in Portugal comes in three sizes: small black expresso - *uma bica* or *um café*; small white - *um garoto*; large white - *um galão*. This last is nearly all milk with just a smidgin of coffee so for a more normal black coffee ask for *um café duplo com um pouco de leite* (a double black coffee with a dash of milk).

Lunch and Dinner - Spain   The daily set meal - *el menú* - is normally available at lunch and dinner although you are not always told so. Ask for it - it tends to be much cheaper than dining à la carte. Many restaurants serve only à la carte at weekends.

In general you don't get the delicate flavours and sauces that you might in France or Italy. But more and more places are serving *cocina de autor* - the chef's own more elaborate creations. It goes without saying that it makes good sense to try anything which is local/regional.

Tapas and *raciones* are an essential part of eating out in Spain and can be great fun. A *tapa* is a small plate of hot or cold food served with an aperitif before lunch or dinner. It could be a small plate of olives, anchovies, cheese, spicy chorizo suasage, fried fish, a slice of potato omelette... portions vary as does the choice. It is a delicious way to try out the local specialities and even if your Spanish is poor, don't worry - tapas are often laid out along the bar for you to gesticulate at.
A choice of four or five could be a delicious meal in itself - and a very cheap meal at that. If you would like a whole plateful of any particular tapa then ask for *una ración de* e.g. *queso* (cheese). Most bars will also be happy to serve you a half portion - *una media ración*.

Tipping is still the norm here. At the bar you are generally presented with your change on a small saucer; just leave a couple of small coins. When it comes to paying for lunch or dinner 5-10% is the norm but you would rarely be made to feel emabarrassed if you don't tip. Similarly, your taxi driver does not automatically expect a tip.

Lunch and Dinner - Portugal   It is surprisingly inexpensive to eat out in Portugal. The set meal - *ementa turistica* - may offer a small choice while à la carte - *á lista* - is a full choice. The dish of the day - *prato do día* - is usually a local speciality and helpings can be enormous. It is perfectly normal to ask for a *media dose* - half portion - or for two adults to ask for *uma dose* - a portion - to share between two.

When you sit down at virtually any restaurant in Portugal you will be given things to nibble before your meal arrives - olives, *chouriço* (spicy suasage), sardine spread. Do remember - you will be charged for whatever you might eat.

Bacalão - salt cod - is the national dish: there are said to be 365 different ways of preparing it! Pork (like in Spain) is also much used but we would advise fish rather than meat as a rule of thumb; and don't despise the humble sardine - it is often the cheapest item on the menu and can be very good. The basic mix for the ubiquitous *salada mista* is tomatoes, onions and olives. You can ask for it *sem ólio* - without oil. Puddings are normally very sweet.

In general a cover charge is added to the bill and there is no need to tip. In some of the smarter restaurants a 10% service charge may be added or you are expected to leave a little something.

The Iberians are not yet very vegetarian-conscious. Indeed, vegetables rarely appear and when they do they are often boiled beyond recognition. So be prepared to increase the salad and fruit intake to compensate!

SPANISH AND PORTUGUESE HOTELS - THINGS TO KNOW

Seasons   When we give a price range the lower is the Low Season, the higher the High Season. There may also be a Mid Season price between the two! In MOST of Spain, High Season includes Easter, Christmas, public holidays and the summer. In skiing resorts, High Season includes the snowy months. Some hotels (especially those in and around the big cities) classify weekends as High and weekdays as Low. If in doubt, ring, fax or e-mail to check prices.

Public Holidays   In both countries everything closes down on:
January 1st, Good Friday, May 1st, Corpus Christi, August 15th, November 1st, December 8th, December 25th.
In addition Spain feasts on January 6th, Easter Monday, June 24th, July 25th, October 12th, December 6th.
Portugal on April 25th, June 10th, October 5th, December 1st.
Easter week 1999 is from Sunday March 28th-Sunday April 4th.
Easter week 2000 is from Sunday April 16th - Sunday April 23rd.

Paying   The most commonly accepted credit cards are Visa, Mastercard and Eurocard. Many hotels take Eurocheques though sometimes an additional charge is levied for this. Larger places will probably take Diner's Club and Amex. You will often find a cash dispenser close at hand; again Visa, Mastercard and Eurocard are the most useful. As we go to press the Euro is being introduced into both countries and at first will operate in parallel with the peseta and the escudo. By 2002 it should be fully operational.

Checking out of your hotel   As in the rest of Europe most hotels will expect you to vacate your room before 12am. Remember, too, that if you arrive at a hotel in the early afternoon your room may still not be made up.

Booking   We would always advise booking well ahead if you plan to be in Spain or Portugal in the summer or at Easter. August in both countries tends to be a month of overcrowding and is best avoided unless you are heading for one of the more remote places. At the end of this book we include bilingual booking forms for sending or faxing your reservation. Readers have found these to be very useful though some hotels have been slow to reply. Hotels will often send you back a signed or stamped copy of your fax so you have a written confirmation of your booking.

Bathrooms   Those of you who like your bath should know that the length of baths in both countries can vary from half to full length. In the South where water is such a precious commodity you may prefer to shower. Most of the places in this book have bidets. And when you are packing for your holiday do put in a bar of soap; the more simple 'hostal' type places occasionally don't give you any and many of the hotels will only have those minute throw-away soaps which are so difficult to find when you drop them in the bath.

In Portugal don't pull the cord which dangles above your bath unless you are in dire straits. It is an alarm and may bring your friendly receptionist rushing to your side.

Slippers!   Winters in both countries can be very cold and buildings often have marble or tiled floors which take ages to warm up. So we would always recommend packing a pair of warm slippers to make your nocturnal perambulations more comfortable.

Plugs   Virtually all sockets now have 220/240 AC voltage but they are nearly always 2-pin. Remember to pack an adaptor.

Registration   It remains law that you should register on arrival in a hotel. Hotels have no right, once you have done so, to keep your passport.

ALL THOSE NAMES

These pages reveal a plethora of different terms to describe the various hostelries. We include no star ratings in our guides; we feel they are limiting, rigid and often misleading. We prefer to guide with our description at any particular place. This list serves as a rough guide to what you might expect to find behind each name.

Can	A farmhouse in Catalonia or the Balearic Islands. Often quite isolated.
Casona	A grand house in Asturias (many were built by returning émigrés).
Cortijo	A free-standing farmhouse, generally in the South.
Finca	A farm; most of those included here are of the working variety.
Fonda	A simple inn. It may or may not serve food.
Hacienda	A large estate. A South American term, it is sometimes used in Spain, too.
Hostal	Another type of simple inn where food may or may not be served.
Hostería	A simple inn which tends to serve food.
Mas	Another term for a farmhouse in the Northeast of Spain.
Mesón	First and foremost a restaurant; rooms have often been added later.
Posada	Originally it meant a coaching inn. Beds and food available.
Pousada	The same as the above, but in Galicia.
Parador	Originally another term for an inn. The one included here is not state-run.
Pazo	A grand country or village manor in Galicia or Portugal
Venta	A simple restaurant; rooms have often come later.
Quinta	A large Portuguese manor house. Often quite grand.

HINTS AND TIPS FOR TRAVELLERS IN SPAIN AND PORTUGAL

Passport   The British Visitor's Passport is no longer accepted; a full EC/British passport is now required. Keep it with you at all times; many museums offer free entry to EC citizens but you will need to show it as proof.

Security   A degree of caution is necessary in the larger cities especially in the narrow side streets. Best not to carry ostentatious bags or cameras.

Telephoning   Since we last went to press both countries have made changes to their systems of dialling. We apologise if you have had difficulty in contacting any of the numbers in our previous book.

From Spain or Portugal to another country:
Dial 00 then add the country code and then area code without the first 0.
Eg ASP in Bristol from Spain: UK No. 0117 9299921 = 00 44 117 9299921

Within Spain:
All 9 figures are now always required whether intra or inter-provincial.

Within Portugal:
From one province to another the full area code is required including the first 0. Within a province you don't need the three figure regional dialling code.

Calling to Spain or Portugal from another country:
From the USA
To Spain: 011 34 then the 9 figure number
To Portugal: 011 351 then area code without the first 0 and remaining
                     numbers

From the UK:
To Spain: 00 34 then the 9 figure number
To Portugal: 00 351 then area code without the first 0 and remaining
                     numbers

In Spain all mobile numbers now begin with a 6. This is your best clue as to when you're dialling an (expensive) mobile number. In Portugal mobile phone numbers begin with a 0931 or 0936. But the world of mobiles is changing fast and there will doubtless be more changes on the way.

In Spain and Portugal telephone cards are easily available; buy one at the beginning of your holiday from a tobacconist or post office because coin operated boxes are few and far between. In both countries the cheapest starts at about £5 (US$7.5).

Driving   The worst time to drive in both countries is on any of the public holidays listed earlier when there is a massive exodus towards the country and the beach. And the whole of the month of August is best avoided when returning émigrés rush homewards in overloaded cars: they are hot, tired, in a hurry to get home and can be very dangerous.

In both countries it is compulsory to carry with you in the car: a spare set of bulbs, a warning triangle and, in Portugal, a fire extinguisher and basic first aid kit.

DON'T FORGET YOUR DRIVING LICENCE: if you are hiring a car you will need it and in both countries it is a (fineable) offence to drive without it.

Both countries have remarkably good terms for car hire. At the time we go to press a small car can be hired for about £100, or $150 US, for a week.

And remember that foreign number plates attract attention in the big cities. Never leave your car unattended with valuables inside. Use a public car park; they are cheap and safe and a few pounds/dollars could save you from a nightmare visit to the local constabulary.

Maps   Driving in northern Portugal, especially, requires patience as does finding some of the rural hotels in Galicia. The maps at the front of this book are to give you an approximate idea of where places are but do take a detailed road map with you eg Michelin 1/400000 series Nos 440-446 or the Hildebrandt ones. Both series are available in the UK from Stanfords (0171 836 1321) or in the USA from The Complete Traveller Bookstore (212 685-9007).

GETTING THERE

Ferries to Spain from England
P&O sail to Bilbao twice a week from Portsmouth: a visit to the Gugenheim Museum makes this sailing an obvious first choice.
Tel: 0870 2424999
Brittany Ferries sail to Santander twice a week from Plymouth.
Tel: 0990 360360
(Sample fare for both of above accompanies: Car + 2 adults + cabin for a one month break costs £800-£850 in mid summer with both companies).

Flights to Spain and Portugal
It can be remarkably inexpensive to fly to Spain and Portugal from the UK: the popularity of package/golfing holidays means that there are charters most of the year. The travel sections of the Sunday broadsheets, your local travel agent or the Internet are the best places to get to grips with a really wide choice. Even at busy times of the year you can pick up bargains if you book late.
There are also scheduled flights from the UK with the following companies (amongst others):

Iberia	Tel: 0171 8300011
British Airways	Tel: 0345 222111
Go Airlines	Tel: 0845 6054321
TAP	Tel: 0171 8280262
Easyjet	Tel: 0870 6000000
British Midland	Tel: 0845 6071628
Monarch Airlines	Tel: 01582 400000

Public Transport
Trains, buses and taxis are very cheap in both countries, compared to the UK. You meet more people, are under less stress than when you're driving and you get much more of a feel for the country by travelling this way. You can take an overnight sleeper from London, wake in the South of France and take in all of the view as you cross the Meseta! Spain has a high-speed rail link between Madrid and Sevilla which gets you all the way down South in under two and a half hours. And some of the smaller regional lines would bring a tear to any rail buff's eye; the journey between Ronda and Algeciras is particularly memorable.

Spanish Tourist Offices
UK   57/58 St. Jame's Street, London SW1A 1LD
        Tel: 0171 486 8077
USA   665 Fifth Avenue, New York 10022
        Tel: 212 759 8822

Portuguese Tourist Offices
UK   PNTO, 22/25 Sackville Street, London SW1A 1DE
        Tel: 0171 494 1441
USA   PNTO, 590 Fifth Avenue, New York 10036-4704
        Tel: 212 354 4403/4/5/6/7/8

YOUR COMMENTS

We need your comments and suggestions; thanks to the many letters which you have sent to us over the past years the quality of this guide book has greatly improved. A huge thank you to all of you for the time and effort you have taken in sharing your opinions with us. Please use the form for your comments at the back of this book with abandon; we will offer a free night at one of our Andalusian B&Bs to the wittiest hotel report. ¡Gracias!

Explanations of symbols

 Your hosts may speak any form of English, from pidgin to perfect.

 Pets are welcome although at times would be housed not in your rooms but in an outbuilding. Check when booking if restrictions/small supplement apply.

 Garden with shady area for sitting out and where meals can normally be taken.

 Hotel has its own swimming pool though not necessarily in use all year round.

 Good **country** walks close by the hotel.

 At least a part of the building is more than a hundred years old.

 Some or all of the buildings have air-conditioning.

 Credit cards accepted; most commonly Visa and Mastercard.

 Vegetarians catered for with advance warning.

 You can garage your own bike here or hire one locally.

DISCLAIMER

We make no claims to pure objectivity in judging hotels. They are here because we LIKE them. Our opinions and tastes are ours alone and this book is a statement of them; we cross our fingers and hope that you will share them.

We have done our utmost to get our facts right but apologise unreservedly for any mistakes that may have crept in. Sometimes, too, prices shift, usually upwards, and 'things' change. We would be grateful to be told of any errors or changes, however small.

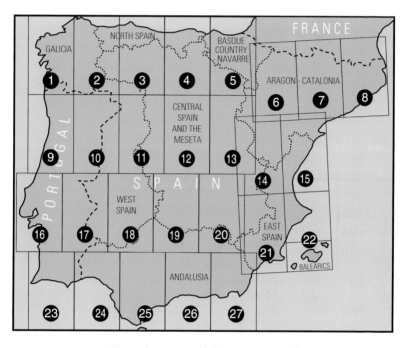

Spain and Portugal
General Map

CONTENTS

Central Portugal

Southern Portugal

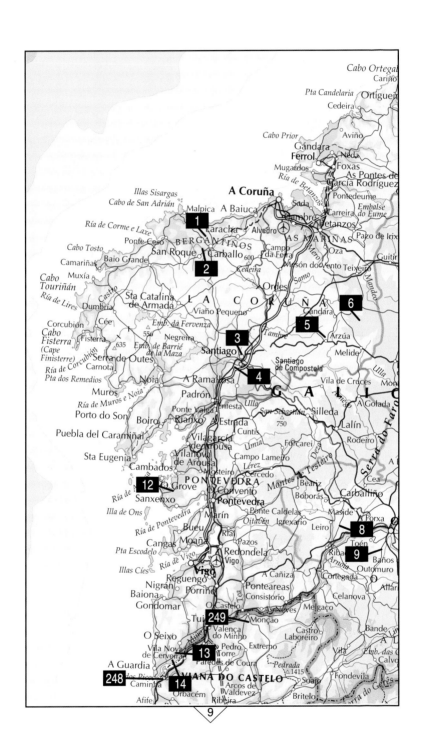

Map scale 1cm : 13km

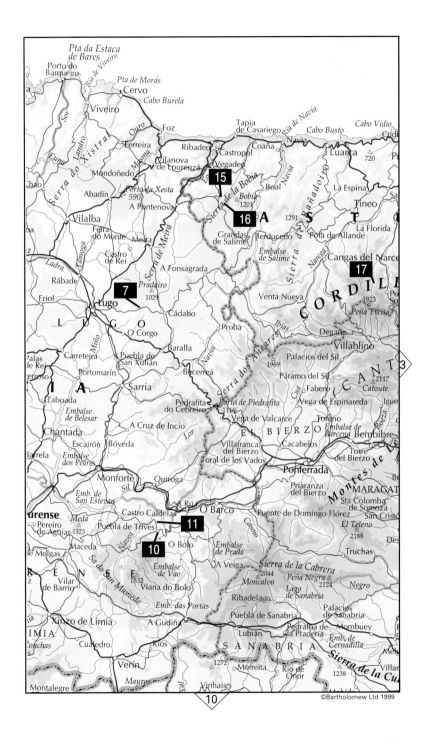

©Bartholomew Ltd 1999

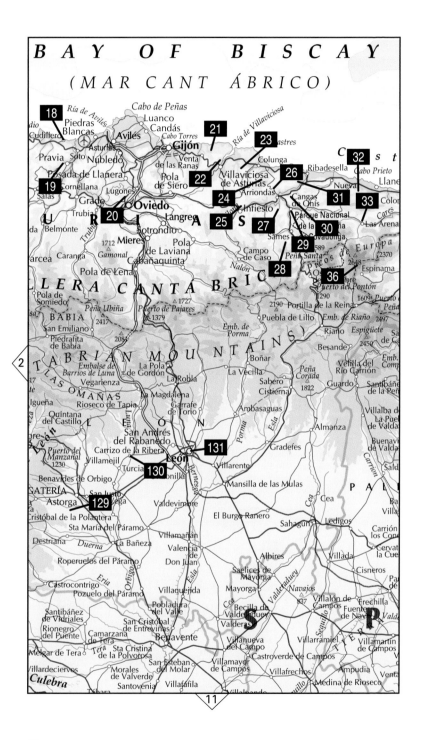

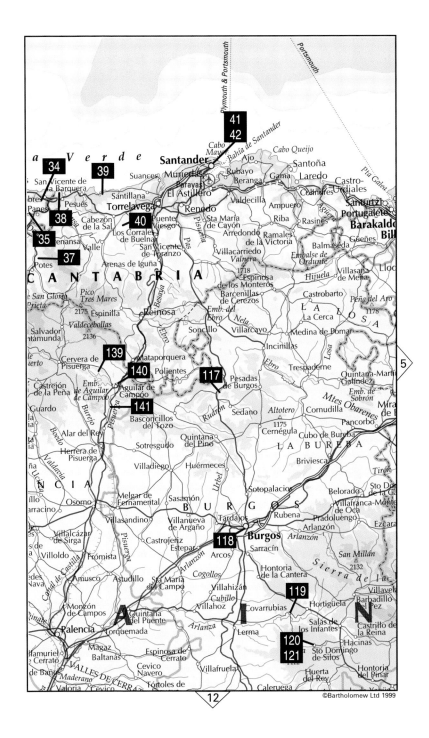

a Verde

34

San Vicente de la Barquera
bres
Panes
38
Pesués

Cabezón de la Sal
Los Corrales de Buelna
35
enansal
Valle
37
Potes

San Vicente de Toranzo

Arenas de Iguña

39

Suances
Santillana
Torrelavega
40
Puente Viesgo
Renedo

Cabo Mayor
Santander
Murïedas
Parayas
El Astillero

Ajo
Rubayo
Beranga
Gama

Cabo Queijo

Santoña
Laredo
Castro-Urdiales

41
42

Bahía de Santander

Valdecilla
Ampuero
Riba
Rasines

Sta María de Cayón
Arredondo
Ramales de la Victoria

Balmaseda

Colindres
Santurtzi
Portugalete
Barakaldo
Bil
Güeñes

Pta Galea

C A N T A B R I A

Villacarriedo
Valnera
1718
Espinosa de los Monteros
Barcenillas de Cerezos

Embalse de Orduñte

Villasana de Mena

Llo

Castrobarto
Peña del Aro
1178

Pico Tres Mares
e San Glorio
Prieta
2175 Espinilla
Valdecebollas
2136

Reinosa
Emb. del Ebro
Nela
Soncillo
Villarcayo
Medina de Pomar

L A L O S A

La Cerca

Salvador
tamunda

Cervera de Pisuerga
uerto

139
Mataporquera
Polientes

Trespaderne
Quintana-Marti
Galíndez
Emb. de Sobrón

5

Pesadas de Burgos
Sedano
Mira
de l

140
Aguilar de Campóo

117

Castréjon de la Peña
Emb. de Aguilar de Campóo
141
Basconcillos del Tozo

Altotero
1175
Cernégula

Cornudilla
Pancorbo

L A B U R E B A

Mtes Obarenes

Cubo de Bureba

Alar del Rey
Sotresgudo
Quintana del Pino
Huérmeces

Briviesca

Tirón

Herrera de Pisuerga
Villadiego

Sotopalacios

Belorado
Sto Do
de la C
Villafranca-Montes de Oca

N C I A
Osorno
Melgar de Fernamental
Sasamón
B U R G O S
Villanueva de Argaño
Tardajos
Rubena
Pradoluengo
Arlanzón
Ezcar

arracino
Villasandino
Castrojeriz

118
Burgos
Sarracín
Arlanzón
San Millán
2132

S i e r r a d e l a

s de
Villalcázar de Sirga
Villoldo
Frómista
Estepar
Arcos

Hontoria de la Cantera

Villavela

edes
Nava
Amusco
Astudillo
Sta María del Campo

Cogollos
Villahizán
Cubillo
Villahoz
Covarrubias

119
Hortigüela
Salas de los Infantes

Barbadillo
Pez
Castrillo de la Reina

Monzón de Campos
Quintana del Puente
Arlanza
Lerma

120
121
Sto Domingo de Silos

Hacinas

Palencia
Torquemada

Hontoria del Pinar

hamuriel
e Cerrato
de Baños
Magaz
Baltanás
Espinosa de Cerrato

Villafruela

Huerta del Rey

Caleruega

V A L L E S D E C E R R A
Maderano
Valoria
Cevico
Tórtoles de

12

©Bartholomew Ltd 1999

4

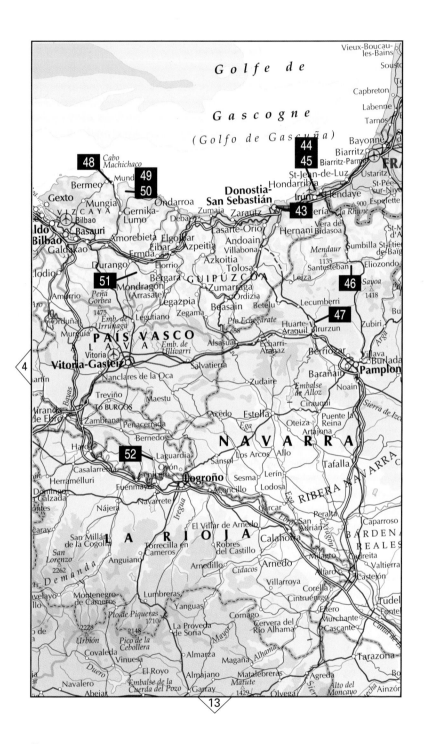

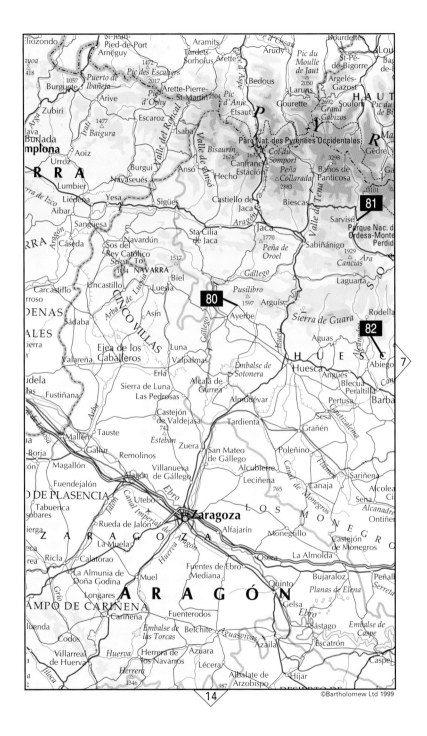

©Bartholomew Ltd 1999

6

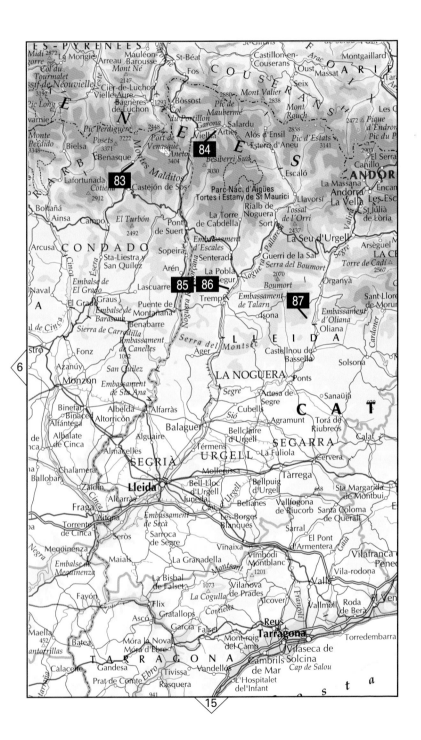

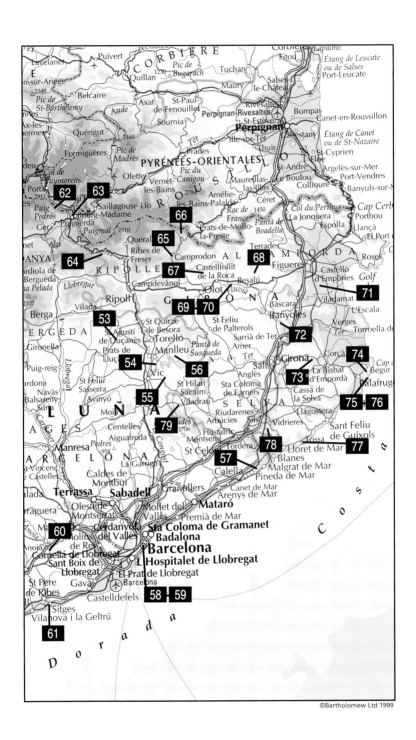

©Bartholomew Ltd 1999

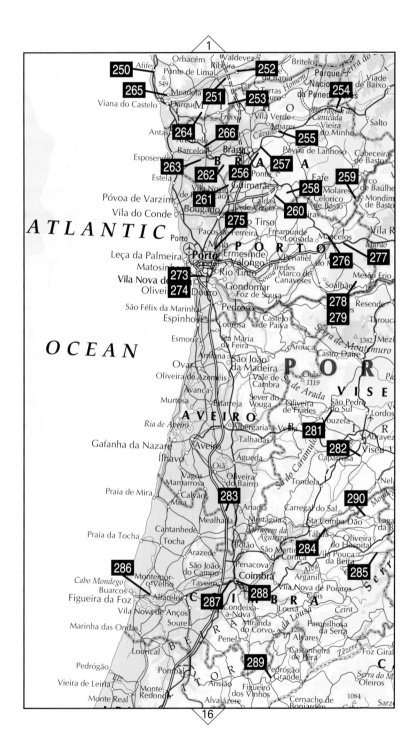

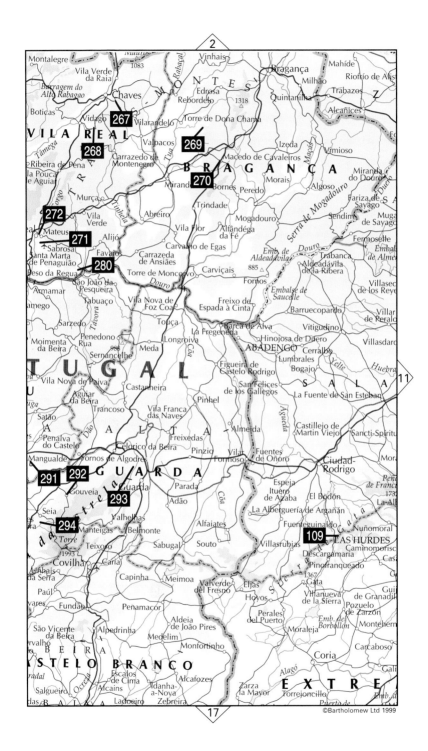

©Bartholomew Ltd 1999

11

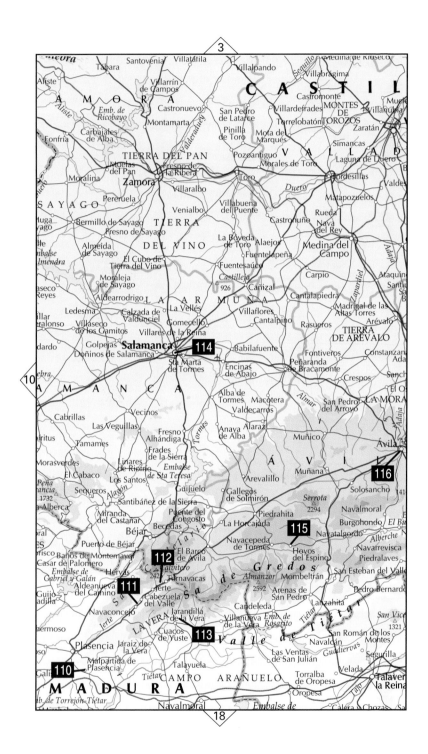

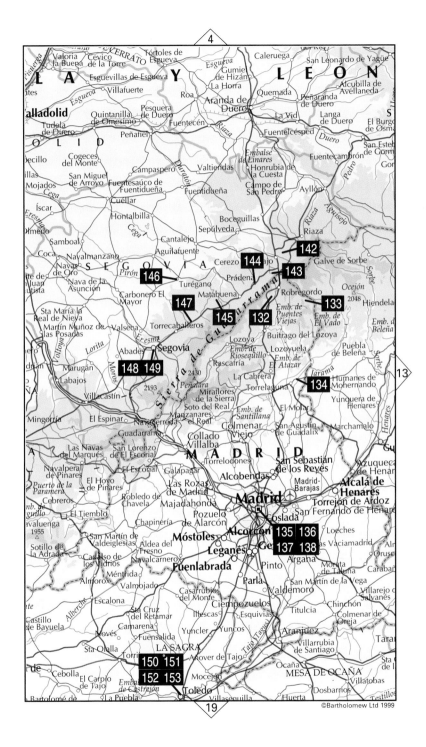

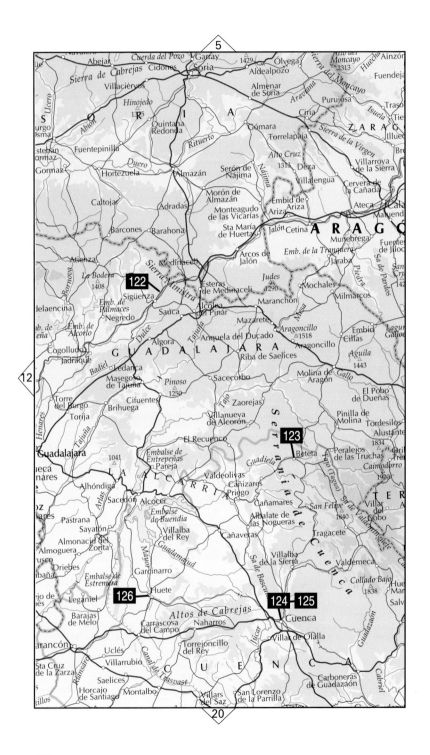

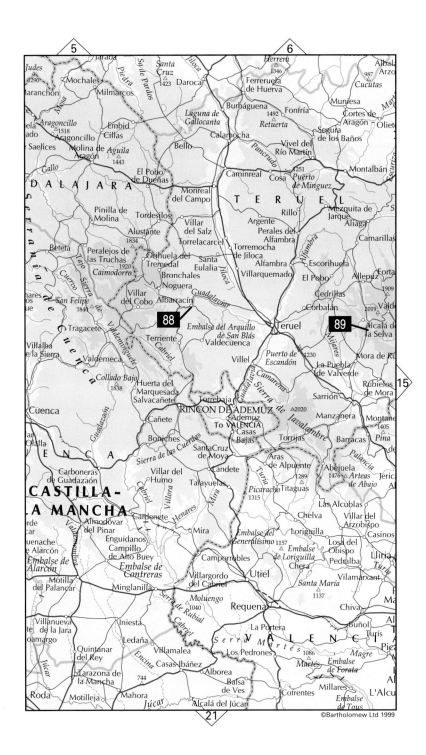

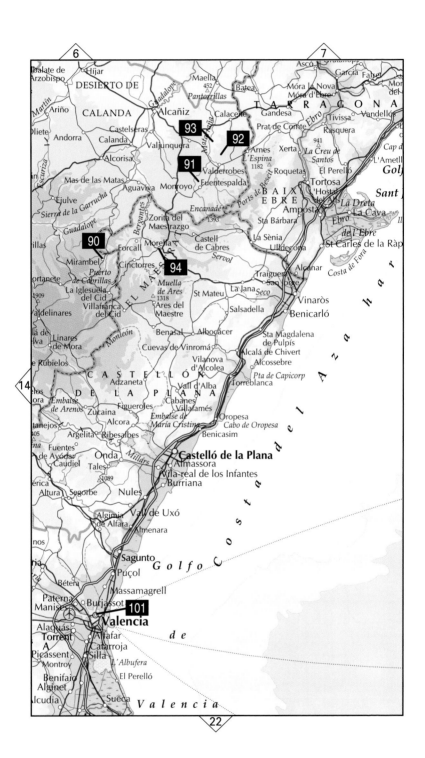

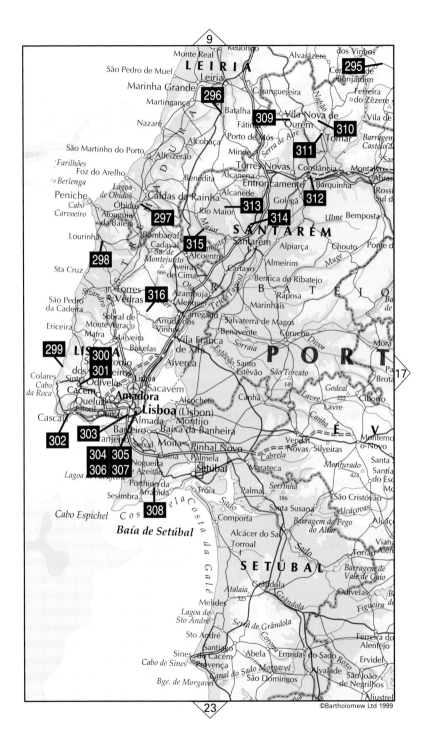

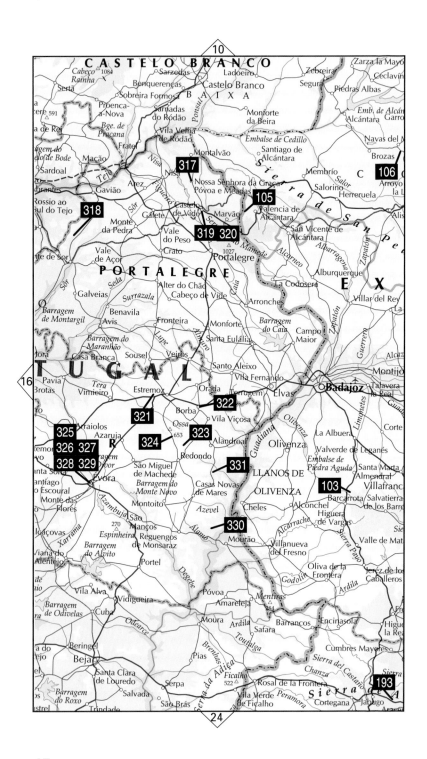

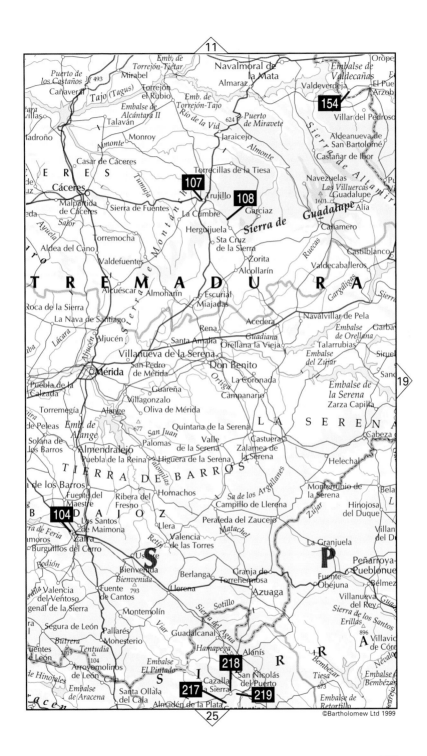

Puerto de los Castaños
Cañaveral
Emb. de Torrejón-Tiétar
Mirabel
Torrejón el Rubio
Navalmoral de la Mata
Almaraz
Valdeverdeja
Oropesa
Embalse de Valdecañas
El Pue
Arzob
Tajo (Tagus)
Talaván
Embalse de Alcántara II
Emb. de Torrejón-Tajo
Río de la Vid
624
Puerto de Miravete
Villar del Pedroso
Villas
Madroño
Monroy
Jaraicejo
Almonte
Aldeanueva de San Bartolomé
Castañar de Ibor
Casar de Cáceres
Torrecillas de la Tiesa
Navezuelas
Las Villuercas
1601
Guadalupe
Alía
Cáceres
Trujillo
Garciaz
Cañamero
Malpartida de Cáceres
Sierra de Fuentes
La Cumbre
Herguijuela
Sta Cruz de la Sierra
Sierra de Guadalupe
Castilblanco
Torremocha
Valdefuentes
Zorita
Alcollarín
Valdecaballeros
Roca de la Sierra
Alcuéscar
Almoharín
Escurial
Miajadas
Gargáligas
Navalvillar de Pela
Embalse de Orellana
Garba
La Nava de Santiago
Aljucén
Santa Amalia
Acedera
Rena
Guadiana
Orellana la Vieja
Talarrubias
Siruel
Villanueva de la Serena
San Pedro de Mérida
Don Benito
Embalse del Zújar
Sanc
Mérida
La Coronada
Embalse de la Serena
Puebla de la Calzada
Guareña
Campanario
Zarza Capilla
Torremegía
Alange
Villagonzalo
Oliva de Mérida
de Peleas
Emb. de Alange
677
San Juan
Quintana de la Serena
LA SERENA
Solana de los Barros
Almendralejo
Palomas
Valle de la Serena
Castuera
Cabeza
Puebla de la Reina
Higuera de la Serena
Zalamea de la Serena
Helechal
TIERRA DE BARROS
Hornachos
Monterrubio de la Serena
Bela
de los Barros
Fuente del Maestre
Ribera del Fresno
Sa de los Argallanes
Campillo de Llerena
Hinojosa del Duque
Villan
del D
Los Santos de Maimona
Llera
Peraleda del Zaucejo
Zafra
Valencia de las Torres
La Granjuela
Burguillos del Cerro
Bodión
Usagre
Bienvenida
Berlanga
Granja de Torrehermosa
Fuente Obejuna
Peñarroya-Pueblonue
Valencia del Ventoso
Fuente de Cantos
Llerena
Azuaga
Bélmez
genal de la Sierra
Montemolín
Villanueva del Rey
Sierra de los Santos
Erillas
896
Segura de León
Pallarés
Monesterio
Viar
Guadalcanal
Sotillo
Villavic
de Cór
Butrera
1104
Tentudía
Embalse El Pintado
Hamapega
Alanís
Arroyomolinos de León
Cala
Cazalla
la Sierra
San Nicolás del Puerto
Tiesa
673
Embalse de Bembéza
Embalse de Aracena
Santa Ollala del Cala
Almadén de la Plata
Embalse de Retortillo

154
107
108
104
218
217
219

©Bartholomew Ltd 1999

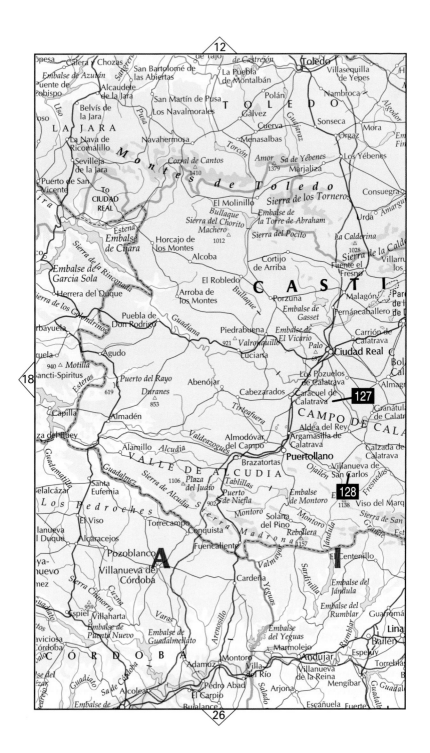

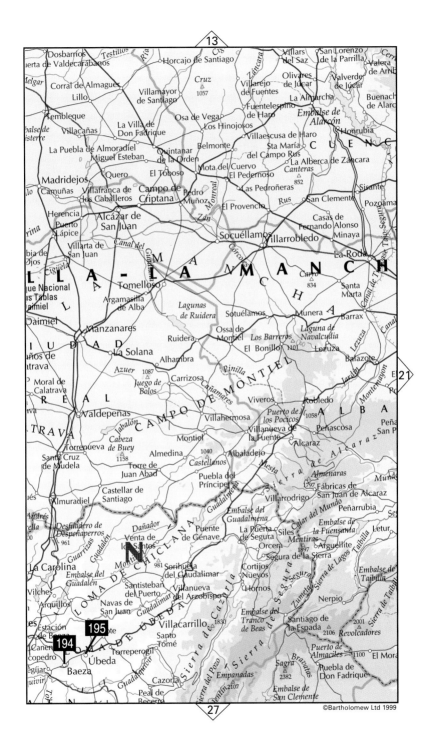

Dosbarrios
uerta de Valdecaråbanos
Testillos
Rła
Horcajo de Santiago
Villars
del Saz
San Lorenzo
de la Parrilla
Cerro
de Arri

Melgar
Corral de Almaguer
Lillo
Cruz
1057
Villarejo
de Fuentes
Olivares
de Júcar
Valverde
de Júcar
Buenach
de Alarc

Tembleque
Villacañas
Villamayor
de Santiago
Osa de Vega
Los Hinojosos
Fuentelespino
de Haro
Villaescusa de Haro
La Almarcha
Embalse de
Alarcón
Honrubia

La Villa de
Don Fadrique
Belmonte
Sta María
del Campo Rus
CUENC

balse de
isterre
La Puebla de Almoradiel
Miguel Esteban
Quintanar
de la Orden
Mota del Cuervo
Canteras
La Alberca de Zancara
852

Madridejos
Quero
El Toboso
El Pedernoso
Sisante

llo
Camuñas
Villafranca de
los Caballeros
Campo de
Criptana
Pedro
Muñoz
Las Pedroñeras
San Clemente
Pozoama

Herencia
Puerto
Lápice
Alcázar de
San Juan
Zán
El Provencio
Rus
Casas de
Fernando Alonso
Minaya

rina
Villarta de
San Juan
Canal del
Guadal
Socuéllamos
Villarrobledo
La Roda

bia de
ljos
Cigüela
Corco
M
A
N
Santa
Marta

LLA-LA
L
MANCH
Cano
834

ue
Tablas
aimiel
Tomelloso
Argamasilla
de Alba
Munera
Barrax

Daimiel
Manzanares
Lagunas
de Ruidera
Sotuélamos
Laguna de
Navalcudia
Lezuza

ños de
atrava
La Solana
Ruidera
Ossa de
Montiel
Los Barreros
El Bonillo
N101
Lezuza
Balazote

I U D A D
Alhambra
Azuer
1087
Carrizosa
Pinilla
Canal

Moral de
Calatrava
Juego de
Bolos
Cañamares
M
O
N
T
I
E
L
Viveros
Puerto de
los Pocicos
Robledo
1038
A L B A

R E A L
CAMPO DE
Villahermosa
Villanueva de
la Fuente
Peñascosa
Peña
San P

TRAVA
Valdepeñas
Montiel
Albaladejo
Alcaraz

Torrenueva
Cabeza
de Buey
1158
Almedina
Castellanos
1040
Mesta
Sierra de Alcaraz
Almenaras
797
Mund

Santa Cruz
de Mudela
Torre de
Juan Abad
Puebla del
Príncipe
Fábricas de
San Juan de Alcaraz
Peñarrubia

Castellar de
Santiago
Villarrodrigo
Embalse de
la Fuensanta

és
Almuradiel
Andrés
ella
Desfiladero de
Despeñaperros
00
961
Dañador
Venta de
los Santos
Puente
de Génave
La Puerta
de Segura
Siles
Orcera
Mentiras
1897
Arguellite
Letur

La Carolina
Embalse del
Guadalén
N
981
Sorihuela
del Guadalimar
Cortijos
Nuevos
Segura de la Sierra
Embalse de
Taibilla

Vilches
Arquillos
Santisteban
del Puerto
Villanueva
del Arzobispo
Hornos
Nerpio

Estación
de Baeza
Navas de
San Juan
Villacarrillo
1830
Embalse del
Tranco de Beas
Santiago de
la Espada
2001
2106
Revolcadores

copedro
194
Torreperogil
Santo
Tomé
Puerto de
Almaciles
1100
El Mora

egijar
Úbeda
Cazorla
Sagra
2382
Puebla de
Don Fadrique

uivir
Baeza
Peal de
Becerro
Empanadas
2107
Embalse de
San Clemente

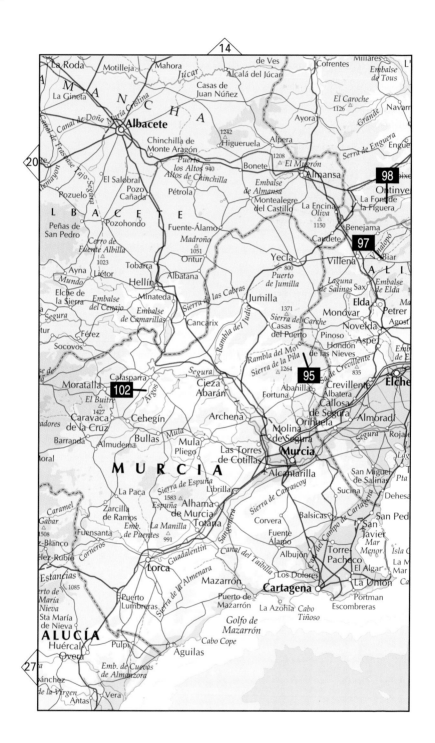

Alcudia
Sueca
Valencia
Algemesi
Cullera
Alzira
Carcaixent
Tavernes de la Valldigna
99
Llosa de Ranes
Gandía
Xàtiva
Quatretonda
Alquería de
Canals
Castelló
la Condesa
Clariano
de Rugat
Oliva
100
Albaida
Embalse
Pego
Denia
Muro de Alcoy
de Beniarrés
Ondara
Montgó
△753 *Cabo de San Antonio*
Cocentaina
Gorgos
Jávea
96
Parcent
Gata de Gorgos
Cabo de la Nao
Alcoy
966
Tárbena
Benissa
Puerto
Callosa
Calpe
Ibi
de Ares
d'En Sarria
Peñón de Ifach
△1558
La Nucía
Jijona
Altea
Embalse
Pta de la Escaleta
de Tibi
Benidorm
San Vicente
Villajoyosa
del Raspeig
Campello
San Juan de Alicante
Cabo de las Huertas
M E D I T E R R A N E A N
Lorellano
Alicante
Bahía de
S E A
Alicante
Alicante
Cabo de
Sta Pola
Sta Pola

C   A   N   T   E

Costa Blanca

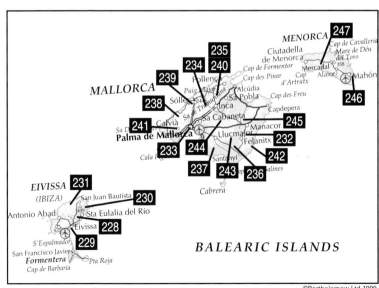

MENORCA **247**
Cap de Cavalleria
Mare de Déu
235
Ciutadella
del Toro
de Menorca
△358
234 **240**
Cap de Formentor
Mercadal
Alaior
Mahón
239
Pollença
Cap des Pinar
Cap
d'Artrutx
MALLORCA
Puig Major
Alcúdia
Cap des Freu
Sóller
Sa Pobla
246
238
Inca
Sa Trismuntana
Sa Cabaneta
Capdepera
241
Calvià
Manacor
245
Palma de Mallorca
Llucmajor
Sa D
Felanitx
232
233
244
Santanyí
242
Cala F
237
243
236
Salines
Cabrera

EIVISSA **231**
(IBIZA)
San Juan Bautista **230**
Antonio Abad
409
Sta Eulalia del Río
S'Espalmador
Eivissa **228**
229
San Francisco Javier
478
Formentera
Pta Roja
Cap de Barbaria

B A L E A R I C   I S L A N D S

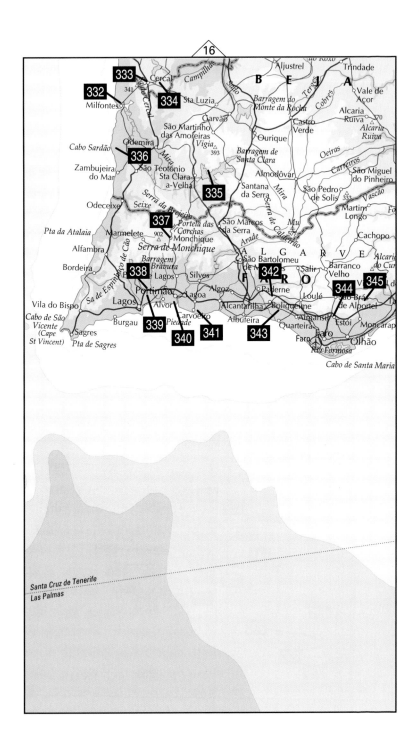

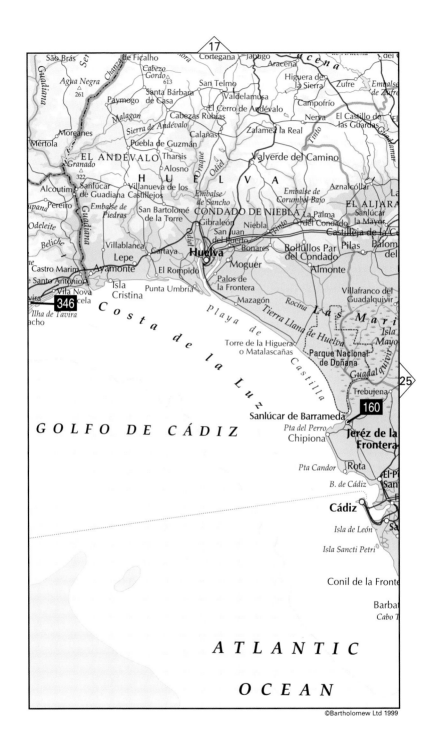

São Brás
Agua Negra
△ 261
Guadiana
Moreanes
Mértola
Alcoutim
Pereito
upana
Odeleite
Beliche
ne
Castro Marim
Santo António
vira
Ilha de Tavira
acho

Charca de Ficalho
Cabezo Gordo △ 613
Páymogo
Malagon
Sierra de Andévalo
Granado △ 322
Sanlúcar de Guadiana
Embalse de Piedras
Villablanca
Lepe
Ayamonte
Isla Cristina
Vila Nova
cela

346

Santa Bárbara de Casa
Cabezas Rubias
Puebla de Guzmán
EL ANDÉVALO
Tharsis
Alosno
Villanueva de los Castillejos
San Bartolomé de la Torre
Cartaya
El Rompido
Punta Umbría

Cortegana
San Telmo
Valdelamusa
El Cerro de Andévalo
Calañas
H   U   E   L   V   A
Embalse de Sancho
CONDADO DE NIEBLA
Gibraleón
San Juan del Puerto
Huelva
Moguer
Palos de la Frontera
Mazagón

Jabugo
Aracena
Higuera de la Sierra
Zufre
Campofrío
Nerva
Zalamea la Real
Valverde del Camino
Aznalcóllar
Embalse de Corumbel Bajo
La Palma del Condado
Niebla
Bollullos Par del Condado
Almonte
Rocina
Tierra Llana de Huelva
Torre de la Higuera o Matalascañas
Parque Nacional de Doñana

c e a n a
Higuera de la Sierra
Zufre
Embalse de Zufre
El Castillo de las Guardas
Tinto
EL ALJARA
Sanlúcar la Mayor
Castilleja de la C
Pilas
Palom
del
Villafranco del Guadalquivir
Las   M a r i
Mayo
Guadalquivir

Costa   de   la   Luz

Playa   de

Castilla

25

Trebujena

160

G O L F O   D E   C Á D I Z

Sanlúcar de Barrameda
Pta del Perro
Chipiona

Jeréz de la Frontera

Pta Candor
Rota
El-Pı
San
B. de Cádiz
Cádiz
Isla de León
Sa
Isla Sancti Petri

Conil de la Fronte

Barba
Cabo T

A T L A N T I C

O C E A N

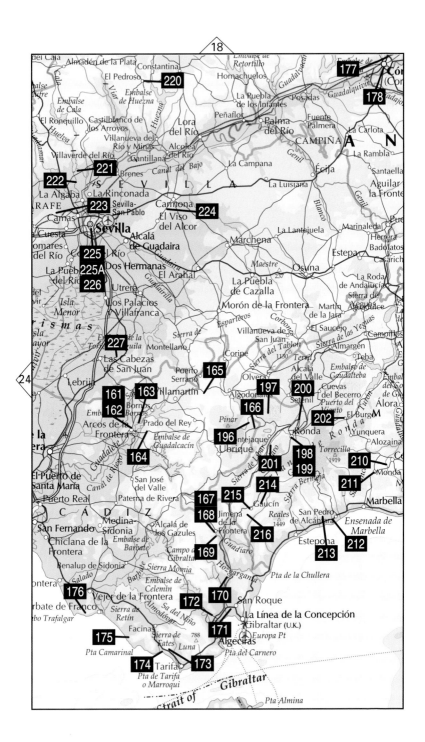

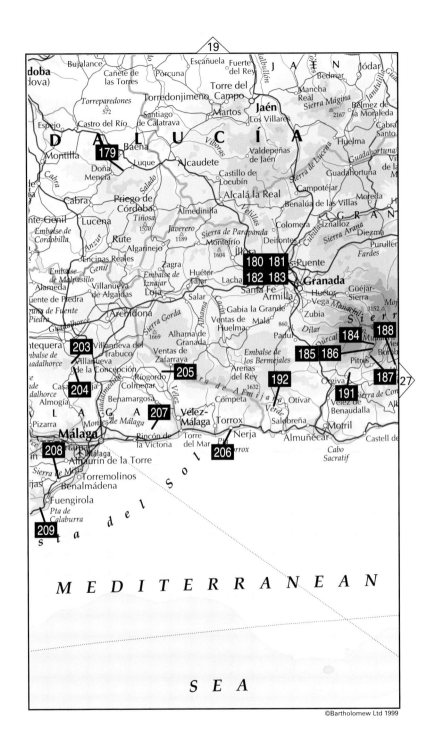

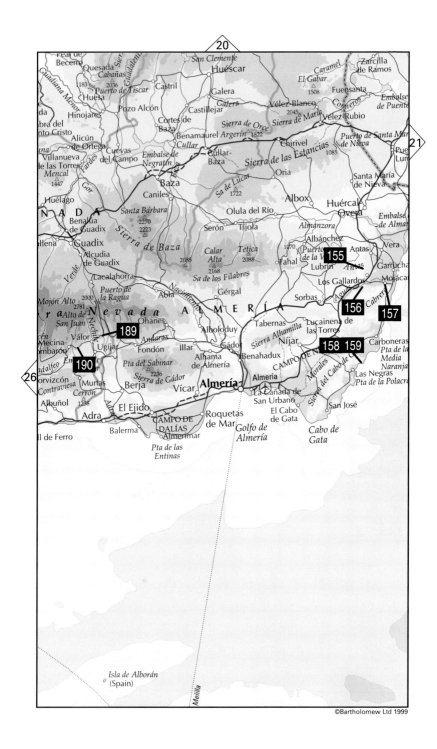

*"For centuries there were miracles
and apparitions to be seen at every
turn of the road to Santiago; you
could meet angels, beggars, kings
and status-seekers – the
Plantagenet King Edward I on
horse-back, St. Francis of Assisi
walking barefoot and a certain
Flemish wayfarer who is reputed to
have carried a mermaid around
with him in a tub."*

FREDERIC V. GRUNFELD - *Wild Spain:
A Traveler's and Naturalist's Guide*

Galicia

Casa Entremuros

Cances Grandes 77
15107
Carballo
La Coruña

Tel: 981 757099 or 639 555440
Fax: 981 757099
E-mail: entremuros@finisterrae.com/turural
www: www.finisterrae.com/turural/emuros.htm

Management: Santiago Luaces de La-Herrán

The wild, indented coastline of the Rías Altas is little known beyond Galicia. But here are long stretches of fine, sandy beaches, hidden coves and a number of old fishing villages where the sea food is among the best in Spain. Santiago and Rosa will help to unlock the region's secrets for you if you stay at their solid old granite house which they have recently opened to their first paying guests. They have created four bedrooms and very handsome they are, too: shining parquet-clad floors, fitted wardrobes, lovingly restored antique beds and good bathrooms. Number three is the best, we felt, with its antique trunk and two large wardrobes. There is a large, light-filled lounge with a wood-burner in the huge *lareira* (inglenook) and dresser. You breakfast in the old kitchen which still has the original granite sink; Rosa makes fresh fruit juices and there is local cheese and honey and cake. A warm, quiet and unassuming place to stay: no meals apart from breakfast but Casa Elias is only a mile away — you can have a memorable meal there at any time of year.

Rooms: 4 with bath & wc.
Price: D/Tw 6000-8000 Pts.
Breakfast: 500 Pts.
Meals: None available.
Closed: Never.

How to get there: From Santiago de Compostela, by the Alameda, take the road for 'Hospital General', continue on to Carballo, then on towards Malpica to Cances. House is signposted by petrol station.

Pazo de Souto

Torre 1
15106
Sisamo/Carballo
La Coruña

Tel: 981 756065
Fax: 981 756191
E-mail: pazo@redestb.es
www: www.personal.redestb.es/pazo

Management: Carlos Taibo Pombo

It is hard to find more charming or kinder hosts. Carlos and his father José have recently opened their fine old Galician manor house to guests. It has stood here for 300 years near the rugged north coast, lost among fields of maize. The vast sitting room has a *lareira* (inglenook) fireplace, exposed stonework and heavy old beams. The dining area, similarly designed, has tables up on a gallery, all subtly lit. Outside is a large garden and from the terrace there are fine views across the surrounding farmland. A splendid granite staircase leads up to the guestrooms — we preferred those on the first floor to the rather smaller attic ones. It is all spick and span, the furnishings are new and lots of locals were dining there when we visited (fresh fish daily from the nearby fishing village of Malpica). If you fancy cooking for yourself, you can use the guest kitchen for a small supplement. All this and the wild beauty of the north coast besides. Carlos is most helpful and has impeccable English.

Rooms: 11 with bath & wc.
Price: D/Tw 9000 Pts.
Breakfast: 500 Pts.
Meals: Lunch/Dinner 1500-1750 Pts (M), 3000-3500 Pts (C).
Closed: Never.

How to get there: From La Coruña C552 (or A9) towards Finisterre to Carballo. From here take road towards Malpica; hotel is signposted to the left.

Hostal Hogar San Francisco

Campillo del Convento San Francisco 3   **Tel:** 981 572564/572463
15705   **Fax:** 981 571916
Santiago de Compostela
La Coruña

Management: Aniceto Gómez Nogueira

Few hostelries can be quite as appropriate as the San Francisco if you´ve followed the Way to Santiago. This old monastery, parts of it nearly five centuries old, is very near the cathedral and the medieval heart of Santiago. It may not be quite as grand as THE hotel on the Obradoiro square but its cloister (now a lovely meditative space with palm trees, roses and fountain), its very fine old refectory and the almost monastic peace that envelops you once you pass the gate, are powerful enticements to stay. The guestrooms, up a couple of good old granite staircases, are mostly at the front of the building and some have views across to the cathedral. They are simply furnished; religious prints adorn the walls and the floors are marble. So close to a high point of religious fervour, their rather austere décor doesn't seem out of place. And forgive the size of the singles: they were once monks' cells. Dine in the cavernous refectory with both Santiago and San Francisco looking on from their respective altars; the menu is a mix of Galician and traditional Spanish with fish a speciality.

Rooms: 71 with bath & wc + 1 suite.
Price: S 6100-7000 Pts; D/Tw 8500-10300 Pts; Ste 15000-16000 Pts.
Breakfast: 650 Pts.
Meals: Lunch/Dinner 2000 Pts (M).
Closed: Never.

How to get there: Take 'Salida Norte' from motorway. Follow signs to centre and Cathedral. Hotel next to Monumento de San Francisco, close to the Faculty of Medicine just 150m from Cathedral.

Casa Grande de Cornide

Cornide (Calo-Teo)
15886
Santiago de Compostela
La Coruña

Tel: 981 805599
Fax: 981 805751
E-mail: casagrandecornide@abonados.cplus.es

Management: María Jesús Castro Rivas

This very special B&B just 15 minutes' drive from Santiago is surrounded by exuberant Galician green. Casa Grande might be likened to a good claret: refined, select and worth paying a bit more for. José Ramón and María Jesús are both lecturers (he writes books, including one on *The Way to Compostela*) and a love of culture is evident throughout their home. It has a large collection of modern Galician paintings, a huge library and decoration that is a spicy cocktail of old and new: exposed granite, designer lamps, wooden ceilings, and — all over — the paintings. A place to come to read, to paint in the beautiful mature garden or to ride out from the house (four bikes free of charge for guests). The studied décor of the lounges and library is also to be found in the bedrooms and suites, some of which are in a separate building. They have all mod cons and the same mix of modern and old furnishing; there are books, ornaments, more paintings and little details, like handmade tiles in the bathrooms, that all help create a special feel.

Rooms: 6 with bath & wc + 4 suites.
Price: D/Tw 11000-13000 Pts, Ste 13000-15000 Pts.
Breakfast: 950 Pts.
Meals: None available.
Closed: 20 December-10 January.

How to get there: From Santiago N550 towards Pontevedra. After 7km, just after Cepsa petrol station, turn left and follow signs.

Pazo de Sedor

Castañeda
15819
Arzua
La Coruña

Tel: 981 193248
Fax: 981 193248

Management: María Jesús Saavedra Pereira

One of a number of Galician *pazos* open to guests, Pazo de Sedor is a delectable place to stay if you're on the road to or from Santiago — or anywhere, come to that. It is an imposing, 18th-century country house surrounded by wooded hillsides and fields of maize and grazing cattle. Inside, you get a definite sense of its aristocratic past: the rooms are cavernous and a broad balustraded staircase joins the two floors. The building's most memorable feature is the enormous open fireplace (*lareira*) that spans one whole wall of the dining room with a bread-oven at each side. The bedrooms are a real treat; they are high-ceilinged, decorated with family antiques, have embroidered bedcovers and curtains and shining parquet floors; half of them have their own balcony. One room has beautiful Deco beds; all are big enough to take an extra bed and the apartment has full facilities for the disabled. Meals are as authentic as the house: all the flavours of Galicia with many of the vegetables home-grown. Try the local cheese and cold sausage. We loved it.

Rooms: 6 with bath & wc + 1 apartment.
Price: Tw 9000 Pts; Apt 12000 Pts inc. VAT.
Breakfast: 500 Pts.
Meals: Lunch/Dinner 2000 Pts (M).
Closed: Never.

How to get there: From Lugo N540, then N547, towards Santiago de Compostela. At km57 post right to Pazo.

Hotel San Marcus

Plaza Porta Sobrado de los Monjes   **Tel:** 981 787527
15132   **Fax:** 981 787680
Sobrado
La Coruña

Management: Manuel Carreira.

Manuel's welcome is effusive... and genuine. He loves Spain but after years in London loves the English and their language as dearly. He has now come home to create his Shangri-La beside the pilgrim's path to Santiago and opposite one of the oldest Cistercian monasteries in Europe. It is a smart, modern hotel of human proportions. Manuel treats every guest with the personal attention that he considers basic to the art of hostelry. His rooms are like wedding cakes — some of you might not choose the rather showy flourishes but few would fail to appreciate their comfort. Manuel thought long and hard about every last detail when he was designing and furnishing the hotel. Furniture was specially made, bathrooms were carpeted and the Laura Ashley fabrics hark back to his days in Albion. Room 16 is particularly grand with a great canopied bed whilst another four rooms have a sitting area in the covered gallery. But the cherry on this cake is the fabulous prize-winning food — lots of Galician specialities with fish to the fore; those map-book people rate it and our readers do, too.

Rooms: 12 with bath or shower & wc.
Price: S 3500-5500 Pts; D/Tw 5500-6000 Pts; D 'Special' with water bed 8000 Pts.
Breakfast: 500 Pts.
Meals: Lunch/Dinner 2200 Pts (M), approx. 4000 Pts (C).
Closed: January & February,

How to get there: From Lugo NVI west towards La Coruña. At La Castellana, left onto LC231 to Tejeiro, and then Sobrado. Hotel opposite monastery.

Pazo de Villabad
Villabad
27122
Castroverde
Lugo

Tel: 982 313000/313051
Fax: 982 312063

Management:
Luis Abraira and Teresa Arana

Opened in 1994 in a delectably quiet corner of Galicia, the Pazo de Villabad is the kind of place where you sigh and say "If only there were more like this...". You are welcomed by mother and son into a very grand family home — NOT a hotel. All the furniture and paintings that decorate bedrooms, sitting and dining rooms are family heirlooms. There are stacks of lovely pieces in the big, airy bedrooms — old brass or walnut beds, dressers and old tables; in the corridors there are statues, a *chaise longue* and family portraits above the grandest of stairwells. Endearingly, the rooms are named after beloved family members — Aunt Leonor, Great-grandmama. But most seductive is the lovely breakfast room with a gallery and an enormous *lareira* (inglenook) fireplace where you can feast on cheeses, home-made cakes and jams and pots of good coffee. The heart and soul of it all is Señora Teresa Abraira, a hugely entertaining and sprightly lady, so determined to get it right that she studied rural tourism in France before opening her own house. Do go and meet her and share a truly wonderful home and gardens.

Rooms: 6 with bath & wc.
Price: S 10000 Pts; D/Tw 12000-14000 Pts.
Breakfast: 800 Pts.
Meals: Dinner on request approx. 2500 Pts (M) exc. wine.
Closed: 15 December-15 March.

How to get there: From Madrid towards La Coruña on the A6. Exit to Castroverde. There C630 towards Fonsagrada, and after 1km left to Villabad(e). House next to church.

Map No: 2

Pazo Viña Mein

Lugar de Mein-San Clodio
32420
Leiro
Orense

Tel: 988 488400 or 608 887059
Fax: 988 488400

Management: Javier Alen

Here, far off the beaten track and cradled amongst the steeply banked Ribeiro vineyards, an almost monastic silence and peacefulness await you. But expect no cell for the night here: the guestrooms are among the largest we saw in Spain, with beds and bathrooms to scale, terracotta floors, antique furniture and carefully chosen fabrics and prints. One has a double door onto the terrace where you can sit and soak up the quiet beauty. The living room and dining area work as well as the guestrooms. Wood and granite complement one another; in the enormous lounge there is a traditional *lareira*, a huge fireplace large enough to seat a whole family on its side benches during cold winters. Nowadays central heating means you won't feel the need to huddle in your inglenook but you can expect a fire in the hearth. There are lots of books, too — Javier Alen owns a bookshop in Madrid. In the warmer months you can dine out on the terrace; with regional dishes and wines from the state-of-the-art *bodega* next to the *pazo*. Bikes are there for exploring the surrounding countryside and there is a pool, too. This is good value and there's nothing to explode your lullaby.

Rooms: 5 with bath & wc + 2 two bedroom apartments.
Price: D/Tw 7000 Pts; Apt 10000 Pts.
Breakfast: Included.
Meals: Lunch/Dinner 3000 Pts (M), 3000-4000 Pts (C) (on request, minimum 4 persons).
Closed: Never.

How to get there: From Orense N120 towards Vigo. At km596 post right towards Carballiño. Continue for 10km, then right towards San Clodio, then on to Viña Mein.

Palacio Bentraces

Bentraces
32890
Barbadás
Orense

Tel: 988 383381
Fax: 988 383381
www: www.edigital.es/rusticae

Management: Angeles Peñamaría Cajoto

The old granite stones of Bentraces are steeped in history; built for a Bishop this delectable *palacio* was passed on to a noble Galician family who in turn sold it on — and so on: there are no fewer than six different coats of arms on different parts of the building! Angeles Peñamaria will unravel the web of its history and tell of the three long years of restoration which have resulted in one of the most sumptuous and elegant manor-house hostelries in Spain. The elegance within is hinted at by a rather Florentine southern façade and the gorgeous formal gardens that lap up to the building; push aside the heavy doors to discover an elegant world of books, rugs, engravings, parquet floors, marble staircases, all set off by the warmth of the colour schemes. Anyone with an interest in antiques would love it and no-one could fail to enjoy the choice of lounges, the enormous breakfast room in the palace's old kitchen and the sumptuous guest bedrooms: marble and bathrobes in bathrooms, top-of-the-range mattresses and bed linen, suites with room for a cocktail party. Romanesque chapels and monasteries are nearby and Santiago is an hour to the west. Book a suite, dine, and just luxuriate.

Rooms: 5 with bath & wc + 2 suites.
Price: D 14000 Pts; Ste 20000 Pts.
Breakfast: 1000 Pts.
Meals: Dinner 4000 Pts (C).
Closed: 20 December-20 January.

How to get there: From Orense towards Madrid on N525, then (just past km7 post) N540 towards Celanova to Bentraces. Here at 'Bar Bentraces' turn right and Pazo is beside the church. Ring bell at main gate.

9

Casa Grande de Trives

Calle Marqués de Trives 17   **Tel:** 988 332066
32780   **Fax:** 988 332066
Poboa de Trives
Orense

Management: Adelaida Alvarez Martínez.

Sometimes grand family homes converted to receive guests cease to be either 'grand' or 'family'. Not so Trives; here the balance between caring for you and respecting your intimacy is just right. This noble old village house (it has its own chapel) was one of the first in Galicia to open to guests. Like good claret it has improved with time. The rooms are in a separate wing of the main building, big and elegantly uncluttered with lovely wooden floors and the best of mattresses. There is a sitting room where you can have a quiet drink, and a truly enchanting garden beyond for the warmer months. Breakfast is taken in an unforgettable dining room; here the richness of the furnishings, the cut flowers and the classical music vie with the grand buffet breakfast — a real feast. There are home-made cakes, fruit, big pots of coffee, croissants, and it all makes its way up from the kitchen via the dumb waiter. Fine bone china adds to the elegance of the meal. A marvellous place and a most gracious welcome by mother and son. *Grand Cru* Galicia!

Rooms: 7 with bath & wc.
Price: S 6200 Pts; D/Tw 7700 Pts.
Breakfast: 750 Pts (buffet).
Meals: None available.
Closed: Never.

How to get there: From Madrid A6 towards La Coruña, then N120 towards Orense to just past A Rua where you turn left (by filtering off right) onto C536 to Puebla (Poboa) de Trives. House in centre of village on left.

Map No: 2

10

Pazo Paradela

Carretera Barrio km 2
32780
Pobra de Trives
Orense

Tel: 988 330714 or 608 777637
Fax: 988 330714
E-mail: phparadela@tpi.informail.es

Management: Mañuel Rodríguez Rodríguez

You are at the heart of Galicia's green interior, a short drive from the sleepy village of Trives. Your home for the night is a 17th-century manor house with long views of the surrounding hillsides. Your host, Manuel, is a cheery fellow who speaks superb English: he grew up in the States where he dreamed of returning to his native soil and restoring these imposing old granite stones of the house his father bought some thirty years back. His natural generosity (and optimism) is reflected in the way the building has been restored and decorated; no corners have been cut here: "you have to be proud of your work," he says. So bedrooms were given only the best: chestnut floors and beds, marble-topped tables, rugs, beautiful antique mirrors and chairs, state-of-the-art heating and air-conditioning and Portuguese marble in the bathrooms. Views are long and green. The treats continue at table: in the vast granite-hearthed dining room, try the home-made honey at breakfast and for dinner expect the best of Galician country cooking with many of the veg freshly dug up from Paradela's kitchen gardens. This is real hospitality: share a *Queimada* with your hosts, the local hot brew that keeps the evil spirits at bay.

Rooms: 8 with bath or shower & wc + 1 'special room'.
Price: S 6000 Pts; D/Tw 7500 Pts + 7% VAT; 'Special' 10000 Pts + 7% VAT.
Breakfast: 750 Pts.
Meals: Dinner 2000 Pts (M).
Closed: 23 December-2 January.

How to get there: From Leon on the NVI to Ponferrada, then N120 into A Rua Petin and from here C536 to Trives. Through the centre of the town, cross bridge, then first right. Follow signs.

11

Hotel Pazo El Revel

36990
Villalonga
Pontevedra

Tel: 986 743000
Fax: 986 743390

Management: Luis Ansorena Garret

The caring eye of Don Luis Ansorena Garret, owner of this lovely old *pazo*, has watched over the Revel for the last three decades. This was one of the first palace-style hotels to open in Galicia and its reputation has grown with the years. The stately façade and huge gates greet you on arrival; and the surrounding gardens are a feast in themselves with exuberant stands of hydrangea. The palm, plum and citrus trees add an exotic touch and there's a bracing whiff of sea air penetrating this rich greenery. You enter the house via a grand entrance hall; here, as throughout the Revel, the granite, the beams and the tiled floors are warmly authentic. Sitting and dining rooms are large and airy and there is an attractive terrace with wicker furniture. The bedrooms are properly equipped, have tiled floors and 'rustic' furnishing, and are good value. Both staff and owner will bend over backwards to look after you but are mindful of your intimacy. There is bar service here and plenty of good seafood restaurants just a short drive away, and at breakfast there is bread hot from the oven. But book ahead.

Rooms: 22 with bath & wc.
Price: S 6650-7650 Pts; Tw 10650-11650 Pts.
Breakfast: Included — buffet.
Meals: None available.
Closed: October-May.

How to get there: From Pontevedra, Vía Rápida to Sanxenxo. There, towards A Grove and A Toxa. Through Villalonga; at end of village turn left following signs to El Revel.

Finca Río Miño

Las Eiras
36760
O Rosal
Pontevedra

Tel: 986 621107
Fax: 986 621107

Management: Tony & Shirley Taylor-Dawes

The green hills and rivers of northern Portugal and Galicia are dear to Tony and Shirley Taylor-Dawes. They know the people, villages, food and wines like few others; they even write books about them. Perhaps their passion for fine wine led them to this 250-year-old farm with its terraced vineyards and *bodega* carved in solid rock. And what a position, up on the bank of the Miño with views across to Portugal. In the vast garden are two pine-clad lodges built by Tony. They are simply furnished, have their own small kitchen (although breakfast can be provided), lounge and two bedrooms. Best of all are the terraces which have the same wide view over the river. In the main house there is another room with bathroom, a sitting room with pretty Portuguese furniture, a breakfast room and an unforgettable terrace with a rambling passion fruit providing extra shade. Don't miss dinner where port is king, whether in sauces for meat or in puddings like 'sozzled apricots' or 'Duero lemon haze'. There's a pool-with-a-view, or river beaches at the end of the farm track and the Atlantic just five miles away. *Minimum three night stay in July/August for lodges. No VAT on listed prices.*

Rooms: 1 with bath & wc + 2 lodges sleeping up to 4 with bath & wc.
Price: Tw 8500 Pts; Lodge (for 2) 10000 Pts, (for 3) 12000 Pts (for 4) 15000 Pts.
Breakfast: 700 Pts.
Meals: Gourmet dinner from 4000 Pts (M) inc. port tastings.
Closed: Never.

How to get there: From Vigo N550 to Tuy. La Guardia exit then C550 for about 15km. Just after km190 post, left at 'Restaurante Eiras' sign, over next crossroads, signposted to left after 1.5km.

Map No: 1

Hostal/Restaurante Asensio

Rua do Tollo 2   **Tel:** 986 620152
36750   **Fax:** 986 620152
Goian
Pontevedra

Management: Dolores Martínez González and Fernando Asensio

Special it most certainly is even though at first glance at the photos you may wonder how this simple hostelry earns its place in the pages of this guide. But there are two very good reasons for booking a room here. One: so you can meet Dolores ('Loli') and Fernando. They lived for many years in the UK and just love to receive English-speaking guests. Two: Fernando's gourmet cooking. It's no idle boast when Fernando claims he can "satisfy even the most demanding of palates". With the Minho just a spit away his art inevitably gravitates towards fish: lamprey and elvers are house specials, sea food too and to accompany there is a quality-rather-than-quantity wine list (the wine from the village is superb). Tables are beautifully laid up in the small, pine-clad dining room which leads off from the bar area where you breakfast (see main photo). With food this good rooms could be just an afterthought but they're as spruce as spruce can be, and comfortable rather than memorable — our favourites are certainly the two new ones just recently grafted on to the original building. But oh what food!

Rooms: 6 with bath or shower & wc.
Price: D/Tw 6500 Pts.
Breakfast: 375 Pts.
Meals: Lunch 1200 Pts (M); dinner 3000-4000 Pts (C). Closed on Wednesdays and Sunday evenings.
Closed: 15 September-10 October.

How to get there: E1 from Vigo to Tuy then exit at km172 post onto N-550 towards La Guardia/A Guarda. Continue for 15km and Asensio on left as you pass through Goían.

"From my first visit, simply being in Spain has always occasioned in me a kind of joy, a physical tingle which comes from a whole crop of elements: its light, its landscape and, most of all, its human rhythm, a manner of being that graces the place."

ALASTAIR REID - *Whereabouts: Notes on Being a Foreigner*

Northern Spain

Hotel Rural Casa Pedro

33776
Santa Eulalia de Oscos
Asturias

Tel: 98 5626097
Fax: 98 5626097

Management: María del Mar Fernández López and Pedro Martínez Rodríguez

The Oscos are a group of high mountain villages in western Asturias that have only recently attracted walkers in search of new pastures. It is a lovely, deepest green land of gorse, heather, rushing streams and long views. In one of the area's more attractive villages, the Casa Pedro provides a safe port of call if you're planning to explore the area. Modern it may be but this stone and slate house blends well with the village architecture; only traditional local building materials were used. The hotel sits high up above the road and has wonderful views. The young owners greeted us with genuine friendliness and we think you´ll agree that the rooms are worth every last peseta. They are medium-sized with smart, walnut furniture and good bathrooms; those at the front have the best views but all look out to the green beyond. The food is good, traditional fare (try the hake in cider) and eating here won't break the bank. There are wonderful walks straight out from the village and bikes available at the hotel.

Rooms: 6 with bath or shower & wc.
Price: D/TW 5000-6500 Pts.
Breakfast: 400-600 Pts.
Meals: Lunch/Dinner 1500 Pts (M), 2000-2500 Pts (C).
Closed: Never.

How to get there: From Oviedo A66/A8 to Aviles then N632/634 along coast to Vegadeo. Here AS11 to Puerto de la Garganta; right at top to Santa Eulalia. Hotel in centre of village.

Hotel La Marquesita

Carretera General s/n
33654
San Martín de Oscos
Asturias

Tel: 98 5626002/621252
Fax: 98 5626002

Management: María Carmen Gutiérrez Mosquera

Your easy-mannered hosts are passionate about their area, its history, archaeology and ravishing natural beauty. Few can know it better (a son is a mountain guide) and they ensure you get the utmost out of your visit. The hotel is small, unpretentious and utterly authentic. After difficult times during the Asturian depression of the last decades, the building was renovated and returned to its original purpose of receiving guests (*hospedería*) in 1994. You´ll enjoy the restaurant which has the local slate used to handsome effect and a fine old grandfather clock; very snug and welcoming. It is one of the very best places to eat — just count the number of locals. Three of the bedrooms look onto the street, three onto the garden. These are small, impeccably clean, with simple wooden furniture (the beds were in the family before they opened the hotel), lithographs by the owner and nice touches such as fresh apples (this is Asturias) and a few flowers. Such simple genuine hospitality will make your heart sing long after you leave.

Rooms: 6 with bath & wc.
Price: D/Tw 8000 Pts.
Breakfast: 700 Pts.
Meals: Lunch/Dinner 1500 Pts (M).
Closed: Never.

How to get there: From Gijón A8, N632, N634 along coast to Vegadeo. There AS11 to Puerto de la Garganta, and then AS13 through Villanueva de Oscos and on to San Martín de Oscos.

Map No: 2

La Corte
33843
Villar de Vildas
Asturias

Tel: 98 5763131

Management: Adriano
Berdasco Fernández

Villar de Vildas is a tiny hamlet, literally at the very end of the road. At the western flank of the Somiedo park — where some of the last bears in Europe roam free — you could find no sweeter place from which to discover some of the many beautiful walks of the Pigüeña valley. Your inn is a 19th-century farmhouse of wood and stone, carefully reconverted by Adriano to create a small guesthouse and restaurant. You enter by a small courtyard and up old stone steps to a handsome wood-floored guest lounge (spot your host as a young boy in the photos). There are books, a handsome hearth and a galleried balcony that catches the afternoon light. A narrow wooden spiral staircase brings you up to your rooms; ask Adriano should you need a hand getting cases up. There are only five rooms (there's also an apartment next door) and they are just right. They vary in size; two have dormer windows looking to the stars and peaks, all have good bathrooms and comfy beds. There are durries, pine furniture; all of it sparkling clean. The restaurant is just as welcoming; low-ceilinged: beamed and with basket lamps. Expect to meet the locals who come for the Asturian cooking — or just a drink. If you like the Alps, but think that they are over-walked, this is for you.

Rooms: 5 with bath & wc + 1 apartment.
Price: D/Tw 6500 Pts; Apt 10000 Pts inc. VAT.
Breakfast: 525 Pts.
Meals: Lunch/Dinner 1350 Pts (M), 2000 Pts (C).
Closed: Never.

How to get there: From Oviedo take N634 west. Just before Cornellana left on AS15 to Puente de San Martín. Here AS227 south to Aguasmestas. Here, right to Pigüeña and climb on up via Cores to Villar de Vildas.

La Casona de Pío

Riofrío 3
33150
Cudillero
Asturias

Tel: 985 591512
Fax: 985 591519

Management:
Manuel Alfredo Valle

Don't miss Cudilleros: this is one of the prettiest little fishing villages of the Asturian coast, a huddle of houses around a sheltered cove where you can still watch the catch being landed first thing in the morning. When you enter this elegant little hotel (just one street back from the pretty main square), it is hard to imagine that Pio, a well-known local personality, once had his fish-salting factory here! But in a way fish is still the focus: this is one of the area's very best fish restaurants and it would be hard to fault it — beautifully presented tables and food, an extraordinarily crafted wooden ceiling, and a chef who is making waves. When I visited I was ushered through to the kitchen to see its snazzy equipment and all kinds of good things were on the go in boiling pots and sizzling pans. Come out of season and Pio's charming owners will let you choose your bedroom, no easy task. Ours might be 104 because of its private terrace or one on the top floor which gets more light. Most of the furniture is chestnut; here are crocheted linen curtains, beautiful taps and hydro-massage tubs. These rooms were among the smartest we saw in the area and are amazingly good value at any time of the year. A picnic can be prepared for walks and other sorties.
One of this edition's very best new entries!

Rooms: 10 rooms with bath & wc + 1 suite.
Price: D/Tw 7000 — 9000 Pts; Ste 10000-13000 Pts.
Breakfast: 800 Pts.
Meals: Lunch/Dinner 2800 Pts.
Closed: End of January. Please check.

How to get there: From Oviedo take the A66 motorway to Aviles; then on towards Luarca. Turn right off the road for Cudillero. The hotel is in the town centre, just off the main square.

18

Hotel Casa del Busto

Plaza del Rey Don Silo 1
33120
Pravia
Asturias

Tel: 98 5822771
Fax: 98 5822772

Management: Alberto Mencos Valdés

This very fine old nobleman's mansion, which once belonged to the famous liberal politician Jovellanos, was restored and converted just five years ago into a small hotel by its two sophisticated young owners. They spent years doing it and now run courses in furniture restoration — many of their lovely pieces come from their own workshop. Ceilings are high, floors are rustically tiled or wooden, the staircase is marble and, a most unusual feature, some walls are original *tabique* (wattle and daub). Elsewhere you'll find tapestries, sculptures and chandeliers and, despite so much grandness, a relaxed atmosphere. The dining area is in the delightful interior courtyard and the guestrooms give onto the gallery above, each room with its own special touch (the suite has a jacuzzi too). The decoration is a harmonious potpouri of the noble and the simple. The owners will help you organise your visits, even occasionally go with you, and there are occasional 'gastronomic days'. A high-class yet friendly place to stay.

Rooms: 26 with bath & wc + 2 suites.
Price: Tw 6500-9450 Pts; Ste 8500-10500 Pts.
Breakfast: 750 Pts; English breakfast also served.
Meals: Lunch/Dinner 1200 Pts (M), 3000 Pts (C). Restaurant closed on Fridays.
Closed: Never.

How to get there: From Oviedo, N634 to Grado. There take AS237 to Pravia. In village centre.

Map No: 3

Casa Camila

Fitoria 28
33194
Oviedo
Asturias

Tel: 985 114822
Fax: 985 294198
E-mail: guru@asturnet.es

Management: Antonieta Domínguez Benito

Oviedo is a city which is often missed as one journeys on to more spectacular parts of Asturias and Spain. Yet there is one very good reason for coming; to visit the exquisite churches of Santa Maria del Narranco and San Miguel de Lillo, built on a thickly-wooded hillside by the Asturian king Ramiro I in the ninth century. Visit and you will understand why these diminuitive buildings have a grandeur far beyond their modest dimensions. Casa Camila shares the same magic mountain and has enormous views out across the surrounding meadows all the way to the distant Picos. Asturias has a long tradition of innovative architecture (returning emigrants have always wanted to be noticed!) and the modern lines and rich pomegranate colour of this building strike a bold note of welcome. Within is a light, modern edifice; most memorable is a beautiful crafting of wood throughout the building, especially in the oak parquet of second-storey bedrooms (but all of them are good-looking). Camila's cuisine is a match for its rooms; Asturias is its main inspiration but the Mediterranean tradition is also there, salads are interesting and the veggie side of things hasn't been neglected (stuffed onions and aubergines are specialities). This is an utterly peaceful spot; do come, take a path straight out from the hotel for a mile and a half or so and wonder at these early Romanesque churches.

Rooms: 6 with bath & wc + 1 suite.
Price: S 10000 Pts; D/Tw 12500 Pts; Ste 20000 Pts.
Breakfast: Included.
Meals: Lunch/Dinner 2000 Pts (M).
Closed: Never (Restaurant closed on Mondays).

How to get there: From Oviedo, in area known as Pulmarin, towards Monte Narranco following signs for Fitoria. Hotel 1.5km after leaving town.

Map No: 3

La Quintana de la Foncalada

Argüero
33314
Villaviciosa
Asturias

Tel: 98 5876365 or
609 976325
Fax: 98 5876365

Management: Severino García and Danièle Schmid

You will be welcomed with unaffected simplicity at this honeysuckle-clad farmhouse at the heart of the coastal *mariña* area of Asturias. Severino and Danièle are keen that their guests should learn about the people and traditions of their land; they encourage you to try potting (potters worked here in the 18th century) and help with the Asturian ponies or the organic veg patch. Nearly everything is home produced: honey, cheese, juices and jams. The inside of the house is what you might expect from such people; bedrooms are light, cheerful and uncluttered, with smallish bathrooms. Many of the fittings, like the unusual table lamps, were made by Severino. The atmosphere is relaxed; make yourself a hot drink in the large kitchen whenever the mood takes you. Upstairs there is a guest lounge with wicker furniture and masses of information on walks and visits. Severino will happily guide you towards some delectable beaches, good eateries and the best excursions from La Quintana by bike or pony. A perfect place for a family holiday.

Rooms: 5 with bath & wc + 2 suites.
Price: S 4500 Pts; D/Tw 6000 Pts; Ste 9000 Pts .
Breakfast: 500 Pts.
Meals: Dinner 2000 Pts (M).
Closed: Never.

How to get there: From Gijón N632 towards Santander. At Venta de las Ranas left onto AS256 towards Tazones. After 5km, in Argüero, Foncalada is signposted.

Hotel Casa España

Plaza Carlos I
33300
Villaviciosa
Asturias

Tel: 98 5892030/5892682
Fax: 98 5892682

Management: María José Lorda

When rich emigrants came home after working in Central and South America many of them built grand houses with their earnings — these are the *Casas de Indianos* that you stumble across in far-flung corners of green Asturias. Casa España is one of them. It catches the eye with its display of colonial wealth in arched stone doorways, balconies and projecting eaves. It stands at the heart of the busy little town of Villaviciosa, looking out onto the main square, and was opened for paying guests in 1995. The rooms are on two floors, reached by the wide central staircase. They are mostly large, high-ceilinged and have lovely wooden floors. The furniture is nearly all made of wood, too; many of the pieces are original, period antiques and there are original oils in some of the rooms. Bathrooms are big, all with full-length baths. The bar downstairs is lively throughout the day; this is where (continental) breakfasts are served as well as snacks at other times. Although there is no restaurant there are lots to choose from close by.

Rooms: 12 with bath & wc + 2 suites.
Price: D/Tw 6000-10000 Pts; Ste 8000-12000 Pts. *In August minimum stay 6 days.*
Breakfast: 600 Pts.
Meals: Snacks and light meals available in hotel bar.
Closed: Never.

How to get there: From Santander A67/N634 towards Oviedo. Just after Infiesto (about 40km before Oviedo) right on AS255 to Villaviciosa. In centre of town.

Map No: 3

El Correntiu

Sardalla 42
33560
Ribadesella
Asturias

Tel: 98 5861436
Fax: 98 5861436

Management: María Luisa Bravo Toraño

Certainly one of the most original conversions we have come across in Spain: how do you fancy spending the night in a converted grain silo? The buildings are off to one side of a traditional Asturian farm house that stands in nine acres of grounds. If you're wondering about the abundance of fruit trees (even bananas) it's because this part of Spain has a microclimate and nearly everything seems to thrive. A stream babbles by just behind your dwelling: *escorentia* means 'place that collects rain water'. The renovation works surprisingly well: elegantly simple, rather Scandinavian in the crisp use of wood, ochre tones to impart warmth, discreet lighting and lots of space. Each apartment even has its own kitchen garden from which you may pick to your heart's content. One has a sitting room and fireplace; all have books, games, sheets and towels... everything you might need. If you're more of a traditionalist there is also a little cottage in the grounds, fully equipped for self-caterers. You are very close to the lovely little fishing village of Ribadesella at the mouth of the river Sella, there are magnificent beaches and Maria Luisa (her English is excellent) will advise on all things local and can supply you with eggs and milk fresh from the farm.

Rooms: 1 cottage for 4 and 2 apartments for 2/3.
Price: Apt (for 2/3) 7000-9000 Pts; Cottage (for 4) 10000-12000 Pts.
Breakfast: None — self catering.
Meals: None — self catering.
Closed: Never.

How to get there: From Ribadesella head for Gijón on N632. After bridge turn left for 'Cuevas-Sardalla'. From here it is 2km to El Correntiu.

Hotel Posada del Valle

Collia
33549
Arriondas
Asturias

Tel: 98 5841157
Fax: 98 5841559
E-mail: posadadelvalle@asturvia.cajasur.es

Management: Nigel and Joann Burch

Nigel and Joann Burch's love of Spain is more than a passing romance; they lived and worked in eastern Spain for the best part of twenty years. But they longed for greener pastures and after two long years of searching the hills and deep valleys of Asturias they found the home of their dreams — a century-old farmhouse just inland from the rugged north coast with inspirational views out to rock, wood and meadow. And already they are nurturing new life from the soil whilst running a small guesthouse; the apple orchard is planted, the flock grazing on the hillside and the first guests delighting in the sensitive conversion that has created one of the area's most beguiling small hotels. Rooms are seductive affairs with polished wooden floors below, beams above and carefully matched paint and fabric. Perhaps most memorable is the glass-fronted dining room — here the menu pays homage to the best of things local. You are close to the soaring Picos, the little-known beaches of the Cantabrian coast and some of the most exceptional wildlife in Europe. Do book a second or third night here.

Rooms: 8 with bath & wc.
Price: D/Tw 6800-9000 Pts.
Breakfast: 750 Pts.
Meals: Dinner 1900 Pts. Lighter meals also available.
Closed: 16 October-14 March.

How to get there: N634 Arriondas, take AS260 signposted Mirador del Fito. After 1km right turn signposted Collia/Torre. Straight through village of Collia (don't take righthand turn to Ribadesella). The hotel is 300m on the left after village.

24

Palacio de Cutre

La Goleta s/n
Villamayor-Infiesto
33583 Villamayor-Infiesto
Asturias

Tel: 98 5708072
Fax: 98 5708019
E-mail: palacio-de-cutre@hotelesasturianos.com
www: www.hotelesasturianos.com/palacio-de-cutre

Management: Alejandra Iglesias and Javier Álvarez

Javier worked for one of Spain's largest hotel chains but is now a firm convert to the 'small is beautiful' school of hostelry. He and his wife Alejandra have lavished energy and care on this intimate yet luxurious small hotel. Part of the spirit is captured by the leaflet describing the hotel: it's written as if all were seen by the magnificent old oak which towers gloriously over Cutre's lovely gardens. It tells that it was born in the same century as the palace — the sixteenth — and from its branches can look in on beautifully decorated guestrooms where no detail is lacking: it sees flounced and beribboned curtains, cushions on beds, Tiffany-style lamps, antique bedsteads, luxurious bathrooms and only the very best fabrics. It can also glimpse the cheerful dining room with its chequered table cloths and rush-seated chairs. But we give Alejandra herself the final word: she insists that what makes the place so special is Cutre's cuisine, an innovative mix of traditional Asturian dishes with more elaborate dishes. And we would add that the wonderful Costa Verde coast is very close.

Rooms: 11 with bath & wc + 1 suite.
Price: S 8500-10950 Pts; D/Tw 9950-14850 Pts; Tr 12650-19750 Pts; Q 14850-22450 Pts.
Breakfast: 950 Pts.
Meals: Lunch/Dinner 3500 Pts (M).
Closed: 25 January-15 March & 24-25 December.

How to get there: From Santander towards Oviedo N634. At km356 post right towards Borines/Colunea. Cross railway line, then river, then turn right towards Cereceda and follow signs for 2km to Palacio.

Map No: 3

25

Hotel Halcón Palace

Cofiño s/n
Carretera AS260 Arriondas-Colunga
33548 Cofiño-Arriondas
Asturias

Tel: 98 5841312 or 606 411209
Fax: 98 5841313

Management: Leo Benz

This is a soul-stirring area of Spain cradled between the mighty Picos mountains to the South and the rugged coast to the North. Amazingly, a few years ago this building was abandoned, overrun with vegetation and doomed to ruin... until this Spanish-Swiss couple arrived with the energy and conviction to create their dream hotel. The chief protagonist here is the incomparable view that claims all your gaze as you sit on the terrace or at your bedroom window. There are century-old trees in gardens dripping with colour — this part of Asturias enjoys a micro-climate. Indoors, the gentle good manners of your two hosts communicate themselves to the very building. The dining rooms are elegant but still conducive to long, lazy meals and here, as in other communal areas, antique and modern furnishings combine well. The rooms are smart, sparkling clean and guests are spoiled with the very best mattresses and that view from every room. Finally, there is a cosy bar for an aperitif before dinner. "Leo is a super host" enthused a reader.

Rooms: 14 with bath & wc + 1 suite.
Price: S 7000-9500 Pts; D/Tw 9000-13000 Pts; Ste 12000-16000 Pts.
Breakfast: Included.
Meals: Lunch/Dinner 1600 Pts (M), 3000-4000 Pts (C).
Closed: February & 24-26 December.

How to get there: From Arriondas take SA260 towards Colunga. After 5km turn left following signs for hotel.

Map No: 3

La Quintana

Granda de Arriba
33546
Parres-Arriondas
Asturias

Tel: 98 5922320

Management: Marta Iglesias

This gorgeous Asturian farmhouse is more than 200 years old and... Simón Bolívar's nanny might have lived here! There are other reasons for staying at La Quintana however. It is tucked away in the prettiest of hamlets, a heavenly setting in the rolling green of the hinterland. Marta and Marcelino's restoration work to create four guestrooms shows total respect for the building's past. The rooms are a delight: heavy beams, stone, antique furniture and one truly splendid wrought-iron bedstead. The doubles share a massive bathroom; the twin has its own, separate from the room. One of the bathrooms is specially designed for disabled guests. There are enticing views through the fruit orchards that surround the farm to the hills beyond — you may see deer or wild boar; you will hear owls at night. The former kitchen is now a cosy wooden-floored sitting room — the old bread oven is in one corner. A dream place for walkers — paths lead straight from the house to connect with routes towards Covadonga and both rooms and food are marvellous value. "An unforgettable place and people" wrote one reader.

Rooms: 3 sharing bath & wc + 1 with private shower & wc.
Price: D/Tw 4500-5000 Pts.
Breakfast: 350 Pts.
Meals: None available: can use kitchen.
Closed: Never.

How to get there: From Arriondas N634 towards Oviedo; after 2km in Ozanes left towards Tospe and Llerandi. Signposted on right after 3.6km.

La Casona de Mestas

Las Mestas
Carretera Taranes-Ponga
33557 Mestas de Ponga
Asturias

Tel: 98 5843055
Fax: 98 5843092

Management: Nieves Uzal Alvérez and Jorge Luis González

Surrounded by soaring peaks, set beside a mountain torrent, Casona de Mestas is at the heart of one of Spain's most beautiful mountain ranges. Because it is friendly, comfortable and fairly priced it is fast acquiring a reputation among the walking community. But even if you prefer just gazing at these glorious mountains it is a fine place to put up for the night. The rooms are smallish, unpretentious but just right; they are light with simple wooden furniture and most of them have writing desks. Really good mattresses and the sound of water guarantee a blissful night's rest and you won´t be disturbed by the sound of football commentary from the next room because TVs are absent. Water is the essence of Mestas; it is built beside a hot spring whose 30°C waters are channelled directly to the hotel's pool and hydro-massage baths. From the glass-fronted restaurant there is a tremendous view and, to cap it all, excellent regional cooking with a definite slant towards game-based dishes. Jorge and Nieves, the hotel's young owners, are thoughtful hosts and it's worth spending a night here for the scenery alone.

Rooms: 14 with bath & wc.
Price: S 5400 Pts; D/Tw 8000 Pts inc.
VAT.
Breakfast: 600 Pts.
Meals: Lunch/Dinner 1500 Pts (M), 3000
Pts (C).
Closed: 20 January-1 March.

How to get there: From Cangas de Onís
N625 towards Riaño/Puerto del Pontón.
After 10km right towards Beleño on AS261. Hotel on right after 13km.

Map No: 3

Hotel Peñalba

La Riera
33589
Cangas de Onís
Asturias

Tel: 98 5846100
Fax: 98 5846100

Management: Roberto González González

Peñalba stands just beside the road that leads from Cangas up to the lakes of Covadonga, an attractive old village house that in 1989 won a prize for its conversion from private home to hotel. The traditional elements of local architecture — wood, slate and heavy beams — have been successfully married to more innovative features like the spiral staircase that leads up to rooms on the first floor and then up again to the converted attic. The rooms are smallish but attractive and all the better because of their (studied) simplicity. Ochre colours, wooden floors (and wooden ceilings in the attic rooms) and bouquets of dried flowers have been carefully combined to create a mood of warmth and welcome. The same sense of intimacy pervades the bar and restaurant and dining à la carte or from the set menu will please both your palate and purse. It would be a treat to be here in autumn when the valley is dressed in russet, red, green and gold, perhaps to ride into the mountains in the company of the young owners. We enjoyed Roberto's ebullience.

Rooms: 8 with bath & wc.
Price: D/Tw 5000-7000 Pts; Q 8000-12000 Pts.
Breakfast: 550 Pts.
Meals: Lunch/Dinner 1800 Pts (M).
Closed: Never.

How to get there: From Ribadesella N634 towards Oviedo. In Arriondas N625 to Cangas de Onís, then AS114, AS262 towards Covadonga. Hotel in La Riera on right.

Hotel Aultre Naray

Peruyes
33547
Cangas de Onis
Asturias

Tel: 98 5840808
Fax: 98 5840848
E-mail: aultre@hpr2.es
www: www.hotelesasturianos.com/aultre-naray

Management: Pilar Celleja and Fernando Mateos

Asturias' grand *casonas* date from a time when returning emigrants invested the gains of overseas adventures in fine and deliberately ostentatious homes. The transition from grand home to fine hotel has been an easy one at Aultre Naray. The name means, "I'll have no other" — as *hidalgos* would declare to their heart's desire and what Pilar and Fernando would have you exclaim after a visit. Amid the greenest green, looking up to the high peaks of the Escapa sierra, this is a splendid base for exploring Asturias. Furnishing and decoration is 90s-smart; you may not have heard of interior designer Paco Terán, but those in fashionable Madrid society certainly have. Here he has lovingly married print, fabric and furniture with the more rustic core elements of beam and stone walls. No expense has been spared; ever slept beneath a Christian Dior duvet before? We marginally prefer the attic rooms but all are design-mag memorable. Perhaps the biggest treat is breakfasting out in milder weather on the terrace, with a choice of crêpes, home-made cakes, or even eggs and bacon. And there are lots of good places to eat nearby.

Rooms: 10 with bath & wc.
Price: S 6500-9500 Pts; D/Tw 8000-12000 Pts.
Breakfast: 850-1200 Pts.
Meals: Dinner 2000 Pts (C).
Closed: Never.

How to get there: From Oviedo towards Santander on motorway, then N634. After passing Arriondas at km335 post turn right towards Peruyes. Climb for 1km and the hotel is on left just before village.

Hotel El Carmen

El Carmen s/n
33567
Ribadesella
Asturias

Tel: 98 5861289
Fax: 98 5861248
E-mail: hcarmen@green-soft.com
www: www.green-soft.com/hcarmen

Management: José Ruisánchez Rodrigo

Two enthusiastic Sandras are your delightful hostesses should you stay a night at El Carmen. In the tiniest of hamlets (but there is a cheap and cheeerful restaurant right next door) the hotel faces south towards the Sierra de Santianes: all the guest rooms were designed to catch the view when the building recently made the leap from farm to hostelry. The decoration has been a labour of love; one Sandra plied the antique shops in Madrid in the knowledge that her finds could be expertly restored by the other. Their combined female sensitivities have created the prettiest of bedrooms where stencilling and crocheted lace curtains perfectly complement the old dressers, trunks and wardrobes. Bathrooms and heating, on the other hand, are all state of the art. The sitting room and dining room have an open hearth, stone walls and terracotta floors; we enjoyed our breakfast here with choral music to accompany the home made cake and excellent coffee. This would be an ideal place to stop for two or three nights and head either for the unspoilt beaches of the Asturian coast or up towards the magnificent Picos. And make sure to try a *fabada* at the restaurant next door.

Rooms: 8 with bath & wc.
Price: S 5400-7000 Pts; D/TW 6500-8900 Pts; Tr 8500-11100 Pts.
Breakfast: 600 Pts.
Meals: None available.
Closed: Never.

How to get there: From Ribadesella N632 to the west. After 1km turn left on small road to El Carmen. Follow signs for 3km to hotel.

Casería de San Pedro

Carretera Caldueño-Llanes   **Tel:** 98 5406213 or 608 471174
33507
Caldueño-Llanes
Asturias

Management: José Manuel and Mari Paz Amieva Pandal

If you are loathe to repack your cases every morning and are looking for a deeply restful holiday at the heart of 'green' Spain — perhaps with friends or children — why not book in for a longish stay at San Pedro? Its position could hardly be better: cradled on a green hillside between the unspoilt beaches of the Asturian coast and the mighty Picos range. Mari Paz and José Manuel are dairy farmers: they once lived in this gay, flower-bedecked stone house before they built themselves a larger one next door. Although this is a self-catering set-up you'll get to know and like this amiable couple: they enjoy their visitors and both are keen to show you around the farm and can supply you with milk and eggs, honey from their own hives and home-made cider. The house has been beautifully decked out: the kitchen-lounge-diner downstairs has a comfy four-piece suite, a table to seat six and nearly all the kit you'd find in your own kitchen. All of it is spotless. Lots of chestnut has been used in stairs, beams and floor and the three bedrooms have a really cosy feel: they share two bathrooms and two lead onto the balcony of the photo. If you don't fancy cooking there's a restaurant within walking distance which will even give you a takeaway if you prefer. Or you could use the barbecue.

Rooms: 3 bedroom house with bath & wc.
Price: 15000 Pts per night regardless of number of people.
Breakfast: None — self-catering.
Meals: None — self-catering.
Closed: Never.

How to get there: Coming from west on the N634 exit for Posada. Here take A5-115 towards Covadonga. From km7 post left at signs. House on left after 1km.

Hotel Torrecerredo

Barrio Vega s/n
33554
Arenas de Cabrales
Asturias

Tel: 98 5846656/40
Fax: 98 5846640

Management: Pilar Saíz Lobeto

Torrecerredo is just outside the busy town of Arenas de Cabrales, a hub for walkers and sightseers visiting the Picos. If you are searching for that 'room with a view' look no further. The views are stunning — more so even than the photograph suggests — a 'double glory for hearts and eyes'. The hotel is a rectangular, modern building on a hillside just outside the town. The bedrooms are spartan but perfectly adequate; we preferred those on the first floor at the front. What we liked most here was the pine-clad dining/sitting room where guests are treated to simple home cooking — the perfect thing when you return from a day in the mountains. Walking is the main activity here; Jim, Pilar's partner, is a mountain guide and walkers come from all over to walk with him. Few know the area as intimately as he and Pilar; they are generous with time and advice on routes and can help plan excursions including nights in mountain refuges, canoeing, riding, climbing or caving. Good value: no frills and an excellent special offer in the low season: 3000 Pts per person, room and half board!

Rooms: 16 with bath & wc.
Price: S 5000 Pts; D/Tw 7000 Pts.
Breakfast: 500 Pts.
Meals: Lunch/Dinner 1200 Pts.
Closed: Never.

How to get there: From Santander N634 towards Oviedo then left on N612 towards Potes. In Panes C6312 (AS114) to Arenas de Cabrales. Through town and right after Hotel Naranjo de Bulnes. Signposted.

La Casona de Villanueva

33590
Villanueva de Colombres
Asturias

Tel: 98 5412590
Fax: 98 5412514
E-mail: casonavillanueva@abonados.cplus.es

Management: Nuria Juez and Angel Gascón

Angel and Nuria left successful city careers in search of their rural idyll. First they found the right building, a grand old 18th-century village house in the quietest of hamlets close to the Cantabrian coast. Next came a year of external restoration work and then the interior decoration. Rooms vary in size and configuration as you'd expect in an old house; each and every corner has been carefully studied, there are warm pastel colours on the walls, paintings and etchings, antiques everywhere. There are exposed granite lintels, heavily-shuttered windows, attractive fabrics and lots of plants. And a host of smaller details, like home-made jams at breakfast, cut flowers to grace the table or classical music to accompany your meal, show your hosts' eagerness to make your stay a memorable one. Nuria is passionate about her walled garden; it has fish ponds, flowers and vegetables. Both your hosts speak good English and gladly help you plan your visits: Romanesque churches, fishing villages and the soaring Picos de Europa are all close by.

Rooms: 6 with bath & wc + 2 suites.
Price: S 6000-7000 Pts; D/Tw 7500-9000 Pts; Ste 13000-15000 Pts.
Breakfast: 650-900 Pts.
Meals: Dinner on request approx. 3000 Pts (C).
Closed: Never.

How to get there: From Santander N634 towards Oviedo. At km283 post left towards Colombres. Through village then 2km to Villanueva. Signposted in village.

Map No: 4

La Tahona de Besnes
33578
Alles
Asturias

Tel: 98 5415749
Fax: 98 5415749
E-mail: latahona@ctv.es
www: www.unionhoteleraasturias

Management:
Sarah and Lorenzo Nilsson

In a valley of chestnut, oak and hazelnut with a crystalline brook babbling by, the Tahona de Besnes is a number of old village houses which have been carefully converted into a country hotel. The main building was once a bakery, another a corn mill, a third a stable. At the heart of it all, the bakery-restaurant is prettily decorated with dried flowers, chequered table cloths and old farm implements. Choosing from the menu will be hard; mention should be made of the *pote* (Asturian bean stew), regional cheeses, wild mushrooms and dishes cooked in cider. There is also a terrace up above the brook, a perfect place for a cool glass of cider after your journey or a pre-dinner drink. Rooms and apartments are decorated to match their rustic setting; there are comfy beds, good bathrooms and nothing too fancy. The hotel has plenty of literature on the area and can arrange for you to ride, walk, canoe, fish or take trips out by jeep. And when you finally drag yourself away, make sure you take a local cheese and a bottle of honey-liqueur, or other goodies from the bakery.

Rooms: 13 with bath & wc.
Price: D/Tw 6800-8800 Pts.
Breakfast: 750 Pts.
Meals: Lunch/Dinner 1850 Pts (M), 3000 Pts (C).
Closed: Never.

How to get there: From Santander N634 towards Oviedo; after 67km left to Panes. In Panes right after bridge towards Lagos de Covadonga to Niserias. Here towards Alles and then follow signs.

Hotel Rebeco

Carretera Fuente Dé s/n
Fuente Dé
39588 Camaleño
Cantabria

Tel: 942 736600/01
Fax: 942 736600

Management: Ottomar Casado

What the photograph doesn't show are the mountains that rise sheer behind the hotel. The setting is spectacular enough to defy description but just imagine walking on wild paths at over 1,000 metres up through yew, beech and oak woods where brown bears used to roam and the 'chamois' antelope is still protected. The hotel, which is just next to the cable-car, is a heavy old mountain house of stone and great timbers with balconies, geraniums, arches and beams — stacks of character and an appropriately uncluttered interior. The rooms are all slightly different, the emphasis being on plain walls, rich-textured materials, rugs and polished wood furniture. Those with mezzanines are ideal for families with children. It is all impeccable and simple and would be equally pleasing in winter or summer. There are three dining rooms — others know this is a good eating house — and the Rebeco is justifiably proud of its cooking, based on the very varied list of regional specialities such as local trout, meats, sausages and cheeses — delicious!

Rooms: 30 (including 11 duplex) with bath & wc.
Price: S 5500-6500 Pts; D/Tw 7500-8800 Pts.
Breakfast: 600 Pts.
Meals: Lunch/Dinner 1600 Pts (M), 3500 Pts (C).
Closed: Never.

How to get there: From Santander A67/N634 towards Oviedo. Left at Unquera onto N621 to Potes. In Potes follow signs to Fuente Dé.

36   Map No: 3

Casa Gustavo Guesthouse

Aliezo
39584
Tama-Potes
Cantabria

Tel: 942 732010
(Bookings UK 01629 813346)

Management: Lisa and Michael Stuart

In the beautiful Liébana valley lies the tiny hamlet of Aliezo where you will find an old farmhouse — Casa Gustavo. Your young English hosts are not typical ex-pats; Lisa and Mike love their adopted land, have learned its language and know its footpaths like few others. Within the thick stone walls of their house are low timbered ceilings and wood-burning stoves; this is home with a heart. For home it is; don't expect hotelly trimmings like hairdryers, television sets or telephones here. They believe that what visitors like best is a hot meal, a hot shower and a good bed at the end of a day. The house is deliciously organic; some rooms are small, some large, some have balconies, one an en-suite bathroom and all are shuttered. Redstarts nest beneath the eaves just outside. There are dogs and cats, a cosy lounge, magazines and books. But Mike and Lisa agree that no matter how lovely their home, the real reason to be here is Nature herself and her Picos mountains. A superb place for ornithology, botany and walking. And free transport to the beginning of your walks!!

Rooms: 1 with bath & wc; 2 twins, 1 double and 1 quad sharing bathroom.
Price: S 2000-3000 Pts; D 2500-3000 Pts; Tw 2500-3500 Pts.
Breakfast: Included.
Meals: Dinner 2000 Pts (M); packed lunch 500 Pts.
Closed: Never.

How to get there: From Santander A67/N634 towards Oviedo. Left at Unquera onto N621 towards Potes. Shortly before Potes, through Tama, and then after 200m left to hamlet of Aliezo.

Hotel Don Pablo

El Cruce
39594
Pechón
Cantabria

Tel: 942 719500
Fax: 942 719500

Management: Pablo and Magdalena Gómez Parra

Don Pablo enjoys a beguiling spot between the two estuaries on the outskirts of the hamlet of Pechón. The sea is just a few hundred yards away and a track snakes towards it through green fields from the hotel. This is all the creation of kindly ex-banker Pablo and his wife Magdalena who never faltered in their conviction that 'it could be done'. Theirs is a well-dressed hotel; downstairs is a very spick and span little dining room where breakfasts include fresh fruit juices and Cantabrian cakes. Stone, antiques and oak beams decorate the inside, greenery adorns the outside where there is a terrace for sitting out when it's warm. There is a large sitting room with an oversized television. The bedrooms, medium sized, have good wooden beds, chests, bathrooms and splendid oak ceilings. We especially liked the attic rooms looking out to the Cantabrian Sea. This is a modern hotel with looks — and a heart.

Rooms: 35 with bath & wc.
Price: S 5900-7900 Pts; D/Tw 7900-9800 Pts; Tr 9500-12500 Pts inc. breakfast in high season.
Breakfast: Included.
Meals: None available; restaurant next door.
Closed: Never.

How to get there: From Santander A67/N634 towards Oviedo. 9km after San Vicente de la Barquera right to Pechón. Hotel on right as you leave Pechón.

Hotel Esmeralda

Calle Antonio López 7
39520
Comillas
Cantabria

Tel: 942 720097/720015
Fax: 942 722258
www: www.masistencia.es/esmeralda

Management: Gilberto Fernández

A short drive from Santillana, between the towering Picos de Europa and the rugged northern coast of Cantabria, Comillas is an endearing little place. Right at the top of the town the bright awnings and handsome façade of the Hotel Esmeralda beckon you in. This is every inch a family hotel; the ever-amiable Gilberto Fernández and his mother would have you feel, as they do, that this is your home. The inside of the building retains the atmosphere of a grand 19th-century village house. To one side of the main hallway is a small bar; the dining room leads off from here. Meals are memorable affairs; red peppers stuffed with hake might not be on the menu when you stay but expect the food to be GOOD. And there is a small but carefully put-together wine list, too, with good Riojas to the fore. Across the way from the restaurant there's a small sitting/reading area from where the original staircase leads up to the rooms; and most attractive they are, too, with their original tiled floors and cavernous bathrooms. Some rooms at the front of the building have balconies. Gilberto also has a whole farm for rent nearby: call him if you're interested.

Rooms: 17 with bath & wc.
Price: S 5000-7000 Pts; D/Tw 7000-10000 Pts; D 'Specials' & Tr 9000-13000 Pts.
Breakfast: 600 Pts.
Meals: Lunch/Dinner 2000 Pts (M), 3000 Pts (C).
Closed: February.

How to get there: From Santander A67 towards Oviedo, then C6316 via Santillana to Comillas. Second building on right as you enter old part of town.

Posada La Casona de Cos

Cos Mazcuerras
39509
Mazcuerras
Cantabria

Tel: 942 802091
Fax: 942 802091

Management: Natalia Sanmartín

In an all but unknown village of Cantabria, just a short drive from Santillana this could be a super place to stay before or after you take the ferry. This is my very favourite type of hostelry: small, family-run, unpretentious and a place where locals still far outnumber foreign visitors; in short, Spanish to the core. Bright-eyed, ever-smiling Natalia has built the reputation of the place over the past 33 years and what is so refreshing is not only her pride in her four-(possibly five-) hundred-year-old home but also the relish with which she greets you as hostess. Enter by way of a busy bar (where would the Spanish be without them?): beyond is the dining room. It feels as if it has always been there: low and beamed, it has marble-topped tables, a fire in the hearth and has a little of the atmosphere of a French bistro. The reader who discovered this place for us enthused about Natalia's home cooking and waxed more lyrically still about the delicious fruit juices at breakfast (e.g. a mix of apple, pear, grapefruit and lemon). Upstairs you'll find simple, spotless guest bedrooms: no frilly extras but it all feels just right. There's also a quiet little lounge along the corridor from your room.

Rooms: 12 with bath or shower & wc.
Price: D/Tw 7000 Pts.
Breakfast: 500 Pts.
Meals: Lunch approx. 2750 Pts; dinner approx. 1750 Pts (M) inc. wine.
Closed: Never.

How to get there: From Santander towards Oviedo, first on A67 and then on N634. In Cabezón de la Sal left onto C625 towards Reinosa, and then left at Puente de Santa C. to Cos. Posada on right in village.

Hotel Central

Calle General Mola 5   **Tel:** 942 222400
39004   **Fax:** 942 363829
Santander
Cantabria

Management: Cristina Vélez

'Something different' is the Central's motto — and it certainly is engagingly different.
Its leitmotiv — and its delight — is BLUE, echoing from the blue façade to the blue
and white suite to the height-of-fashion partly-blue doors and views out (from the top
floor) to the blue sea. In an old building with the occasional uneven floorboard, it is at
the hub of the fine old town of Santander, on a pedestrian street for nocturnal peace,
just 200m from the ferry. It was completely restored, in Art Deco style, five years ago.
One of the owners is an interior designer and the bar area is a work of art in itself,
decorated with 'foreign' objects (moose head, sledge, hockey stick for Canada, cricket
bat for Britain, jazz instruments for New Orleans), old cabin trunks and an ancient
hotel switchboard, a *centralita*. The management team is as light-hearted and travel-
minded as the décor. King Alfonso XIII and his large family spent pre-war summers
here that were unsurpassed in elegance and high living. Modernity and memories are
well married at the Central.

Rooms: 40 with bath & wc + 1 suite.
Price: S 7250-10150 Pts; D/Tw 11000-
15900 Pts; Ste 22000-33000 Pts.
Breakfast: 350 Pts or 750 Pts (buffet).
Meals: Lunch 1500 Pts; dinner approx.
2500 Pts (C). Closed on Sundays.
Closed: Never.

How to get there: Head to main P.O
('Correos Central') and from there to Plaza
Porticada. Unload outside hotel and staff will show you where to park.

Hostal Mexicana

Calle Juan de Herrera 3
39002
Santander
Cantabria

Tel: 942 222350/54
Fax: 942 222350

Management: María Eufemia
Rodríguez and Caridad Gómez
Rodríguez

The photograph says it all: at the Mexicana you feel you are in a different era. This modest little hostal first opened its doors in 1955 (when the picture was taken!) — and has been run by the family of María Eufemia ever since. A kinder and more gentle family you could not hope to meet. You would probably not write home about the rooms but you WILL have a comfortable night here. The rooms are simple and the furniture is unmistakably Spanish, the bathrooms spick and span. The hostal is excellent value considering that you are right in the town centre. But what we liked most about the Mexicana was its tiny restaurant; it reminded us of an English seaside B&B with its cornices, deliciously dated 50s furniture and sense of timelessness. As you might expect, the food is simple home cooking. Do consider the Mexicana if you are looking for something not too grand. Santander has the charm of a slightly down-at-heel port; watch boats on the quay, admire the Cantabrian Cordillera on a clear day, eat fish-of-the-day in authentic sailors' restaurants.

Rooms: 27 with bath & wc.
Price: S 2400-4300 Pts; D/Tw 3800-6200 Pts.
Breakfast: 375 Pts.
Meals: Lunch/Dinner 1800(M).
Closed: Never.

How to get there: In town centre very close to Plaza del Ayuntamiento (town hall); underground parking in square; reduction for Mexicana clients.

"The best fish in Spain - the best fish in Europe! Basque cooking lets the quality of the ingredients shine through undisguised and what we have available to us is remarkable... fish from the Cantabrian sea, mushrooms and game from the Pyrenees, vegetables from the Navarra valley and wines from the Rioja..."

JUAN MARI ARZAK - *Basque chef*

Basque Country – Navarre – La Rioja

Hostal Alemana

Calle San Martín 53
20007
San Sebastián
Guipúzcoa

Tel: 943 462544
Fax: 943 461771
E-mail: halemana@adegi.es

Management: Luis and
Roberto Garagorri Esnoz

If visiting the North of Spain do spend at least one night in San Sebastián; the locals insist this is the most beautiful town in Spain. La Concha, a sweep of golden sand, is the centre of life and, just one street back from the promenade, Hostal Alemana is ideal if the grander hotels are not your thing. The hostal occupies the upper floors of an elegant turn-of-the century townhouse. The Garagorri family has run a hostal here for more than thirty years and it was given a thorough face-lift in 1992. The rooms have been designed with business people in mind, with credit-card keys and trouser presses that you might not need. But we do appreciate their generous proportions, good beds and large bathrooms. The breakfast room is a lovely place to start your day: the light pouring in from the three windows in its curved wall will take your mind off the taped music pouring in from elsewhere. It would be tempting to use this as a last stop before the ferry and have a final dinner at one of the seafront restaurants.

Rooms: 21 with bath & wc.
Price: S 6000-8000 Pts; D/Tw 8000-10500 Pts.
Breakfast: 600 Pts.
Meals: None available.
Closed: Never.

How to get there: From motorway take exit 9 for Ondarreta; continue towards town centre. Hostal is 2km from motorway exit.

Iketxe

Apartado 343
20280
Hondarribia
Guipúzcoa

Tel: 943 644391
Fax: 943 644391

Management: Patxi Arroyo and Fátima Iruretagoiena

Another enchanting B&B in the rolling green Basque country. Very near the lovely town of Hondarribia yet entirely rural, Iketxe is a house that matches its owners: quiet, unpretentious and utterly Basque. You can only wonder at the energy of Patxi who built his home virtually single-handed and made much of the furniture too. He finished it all just four years ago but you might not guess that Iketxe is a new house, so faithfully has local building tradition been respected. The rooms are beautiful; first there are the views and then the decoration — wood floors, bright kilims, handsome bathrooms and no two of them alike. Floors are terracotta and two of the upstairs rooms have their own balcony. It would be hard to choose but ours would probably be number 1. We were glad that there was no television to break the spell. Fátima will happily help at breakfast time when it comes to planning your visits or recommending one of the many restaurants in Hondarribia. Hats off to Patxi for realising his dream and sharing it with us.

Rooms: 5 with bath & wc.
Price: D/Tw 6000-7000 Pts.
Breakfast: 500 Pts.
Meals: None available.
Closed: Never.

How to get there: From Irún towards Hondarribia. Just before airport left towards Arkoll, then follow signs to Iketxe.

Maidanea

Barrio Arkoll
Apartado 258
20280 Hondarribia
Guipúzcoa

Tel: 943 640855
Fax: 943 640855

Management: Rosamaría Ugarte Machain

Maidanea, one of the first B&Bs to open in this beautiful corner of the Basque country, is a chalet-style farmhouse on a hill looking over the river to France. It is a traditional Spanish home with a mix of old and new furnishing, tiled floors, lace curtains, a collection of old plates, plants and books, and religious images over some of the beds. It has been much restored — you probably wouldn't guess it was more than 400 years old. There is a big, galleried sitting/dining room for breakfast, a relaxed meal served as late as you like; the silence of the place and good mattresses encourage late starts. The bedrooms, on the first and attic floors, are modern and medium-sized. Señora has lavished much care on details such as her dried flower arrangements and her hand-embroidered sheets and cushions. Some rooms have the view across to France and number 4, our favourite, has its own balcony. The whole house is utterly spotless, there is a good mature garden and the old streets of nearby beautiful Hondarribia to discover. *Owners speak French.*

Rooms: 6 with bath & wc.
Price: D/Tw 6000-7000 Pts.
Breakfast: 500 Pts.
Meals: None available.
Closed: Never.

How to get there: From Hondarribia take Irún road and turn right just past airport. Through Amute, on towards Bekoerrota; signposted.

Map No: 5

Venta de Donamaría

Barrio deVentas 4
31750
Donamaría
Navarre

Tel: 948 450708
Fax: 948 450708
E-mail: donamariako@jet.es

Management: Elixabet Badiola & Imanol Luzuriaga

A mouth-watering address! Donamaría is tucked away off to one side of a pass through the mountains between France and Spain, within striking distance of Pamplona. Your hosts are sophisticated, amusing folk whose love of the finer things in life is given ample expression in their guesthouse. These two old village houses (guestrooms in one, restaurant in the other) are packed full of objets d'art, antiques, old toys, dried flowers and a few surprises to boot; it all creates an intimate, relaxed atmosphere, much of it tongue in cheek. This is most certainly a place to linger over lunch or dinner; connoisseurs rave about the food: traditional Navarre dishes with 'a French touch and modern elements'. The tradition is long: there has been a restaurant here for almost 150 years. The rooms are all that you'd expect — big, with antique furniture, timbered ceilings, lots of dried flowers and richly-coloured fabrics. Mother, father and daughter welcome you most graciously into their home. It is, by the way, set among old oak forests where the heart soars at every turn.

Rooms: 5 with bath or shower & wc.
Price: D/Tw 8800 Pts.
Breakfast: 500 Pts.
Meals: approx 1700 Pts (M), 3750 Pts (C). No meals on Sundays or Mondays.
Closed: Never.

How to get there: From San Sebastián take motorway towards France, then N121 to San Esteban (Doneztebe). Here NA404 towards Saldías. Venta in village of Donamaría on right.

Map No: 5

46

Venta Udabe

Valle de Basaburúa
31869
Udabe
Navarre

Tel: 948 503105 or 608 977538
E-mail: pb17602@autovia.com

Management: Laura Ganuza Tudela and Javier Fernández

On the edge of a tiny Navarrese village, Venta Udabe is the creation of two dedicated young folk who have revived its 300-year-old tradition of hostelry. It is a beautiful little inn, every detail designed for aesthetic appeal. The large timbered dining room has ochre walls, a fireplace and antiques lovingly restored by Laura. There are two sitting rooms, one downstairs with a fireplace and one upstairs with peace and quiet. There are dried flowers everywhere and masses of old farm implements. The bedrooms have been designed with the same affection, books and flowers echoing the warmth of the wooden furniture and floors. Rooms at the front are slightly smaller and give onto a (quiet) road. Javier describes Udabe's cuisine as "Navarrese, with imagination". Its reputation is spreading and it is generously priced. Breakfast is a feast of fruits, yoghurt and home-made jams, after which you may ride out, on a bike or a horse, into the deepest green of the Navarre hills.

Rooms: 8 with bath & wc.
Price: D/Tw 8000 Pts.
Breakfast: Included.
Meals: Lunch/Dinner 1700 Pts (M), 2600 Pts (C).
Closed: 20 December-1 February.

How to get there: From Pamplona N240A towards San Sebastián. Then N130 still towards San Seb. and at km117 post in Latasa Uriza, take 2nd right following signs to Udabe. On left as you pass through village.

Map No: 5

Atalaya Hotel

Passeo de Txorrokopunta 2
48360
Mundaka
Vizcaya

Tel: 94 6177000/6876888
Fax: 94 6876899

Management: Maria Carmen Alonso Elizaga

Atalaya has one of the friendliest and most 'family' of Vizcaya's small hotels; the Spanish daily *El País* gives it no less than 10 out of 10 for service! You couldn't better its position, tucked away at the heart of the village of Mundaka, a stone's throw from the lively fish market and just yards from a beach at the edge of a deep inlet carved by the Cantabrian sea. The house speaks of the optimism of the early years of the century; its open, galleried frontage lets in the ever-changing light and lets you contemplate sand, sea and the adjacent church tower of Santa María. The owners — kind, straightforward folk — care deeply for their hotel; you'll probably meet them when you arrive and they'll find time to help you plan visits. We would choose a room with a sea view, but they're all worth a night; medium-sized, carpeted and with modern prints, they are spick-and-span, quiet and comfortable — and have more gadgets than you need, plus king-size beds. Atalaya would be a marvellous place to spend a last night before the ferry (car and belongings safe in the free car park); there are simple meals on offer in a recently opened restaurant or there are good fish restaurants within walking distance.

Rooms: 11 with bath & wc.
Price: S 9000-1000 Pts; D/Tw 11300.12500 Pts.
Breakfast: 950 Pts.
Meals: Tapas & light meals throughout the day.
Closed: Never.

How to get there: From Bilbao BI-631 via Mungia to Bermeo. There, right on BI-635 to Mundaka; left into village centre. Hotel near Santa María church.

Urresti

Barrio Zendokiz
48314
Gautegiz Arteaga
Vizcaya

Tel: 94 6251843
Fax: 94 6251843
E-mail: urresti@nexo.es

Management: María Goitia

One of the very latest Basque B&Bs to open, this is a dream come true for María and José María, Urrresti's two young owners, who launched themselves wholeheartedly into the restoration of the old farmhouse which was near to ruin when they first arrived. Outside it still looks like a 17th-century farmhouse; inside it is more modern. Breakfast is served in the large sitting/dining room, and good value it is too; cheese, home-made jam, fruit from the farm and plenty of coffee. For other meals guests have free rein in a fully-equipped kitchen. The smart, impeccably clean bedrooms upstairs have parquet floors and new, country-style furniture; some have their own balcony and number 6 is especially roomy with a sofa-bed. The house stands in lush green and lovely countryside with the sea not far away — and Guernika, too. There are old forests of oak and chestnut to be explored, perhaps on the three bikes available for guests. The whole area is a Natural Park and many come here just for the birdlife (visitors are constantly astonished by the birdlife in Spain).

Rooms: 6 with bath & wc.
Price: D/Tw 5000-6000 Pts.
Breakfast: 500 Pts.
Meals: None available; use of kitchen 600 Pts.
Closed: Never.

How to get there: From Guernika take road towards Lekeitio; after 6km left towards Elanchobe. House on right after 1.2km.

Txopebenta

Barrio Basetxetas
48314
Gautegiz-Arteaga
Vizcaya

Tel: 94 6254923/6257448
Fax: 94 6254923/6257448

Management: Juan Angel Bizzkarra

Between Guernika and the rugged north coast, in an area of great natural beauty, Txopebenta is one of the most remarkable of a growing number of first-class B&Bs in the Basque country. The house bears witness to the boundless energy and optimism of its owner Juan 'Txope' Bizzkarra. He decided that to create a guesthouse at his 19th-century farmhouse he would have to add another floor; and he did so by careful use of old railway sleepers as good sound lintels, stairs, benches and roof supports. The whole house now breathes an air of solid well-being. The sitting/breakfast room is ideal for a convivial breakfast with delicious local cheese and fresh fruit juice. The rooms at the top are low-ceilinged and particularly cosy. There is a terrace where you can sit in summer. Your hosts certainly love their land; they will want you to visit it all. Don't miss the 'painted forest' in the Oma valley and the Biosphere Reserve of Urdaibai with its spectacular birdlife — and there are beaches within walking distance.

Rooms: 6 with bath & wc.
Price: D 6000 Pts; Tr 7500 Pts.
Breakfast: 500 Pts.
Meals: None available.
Closed: Never.

How to get there: From Guernika take road towards Lekeitio and after 6km left towards Elanchobe. House on right after 0.8km.

Mendi Goikoa

Barrio San Juan 33
48291
Axpe-Atxondo
Vizcaya

Tel: 94 6820833
Fax: 94 6821136

Management: Agurtzane Telleria and Iñaki Ibarra

"Donde el silencio se oye" — (where you can hear the silence) — is the way the owners like to describe their hotel. Peaceful it is, and utterly beautiful. Mendi Goikoa is one of a new breed of chic country hotels which provide *Cordon Bleu* cooking and a bed to match. The hotel is two 19th-century farms — big, handsome buildings in a huge meadow with panoramic views from every room. The main restaurant is vast and high-ceilinged — it was the old barn — and absolutely packed with antiques. The emphasis is on traditional Basque dishes with a few of the chef's own innovations. There is a smaller breakfast room and a real gem of a bar in the other building. It is a popular venue for the suit-and-tie brigade though you won't feel uncomfortable if you are not one of them. A wedding-feast place, in fact, but don't be put off. The guestrooms are as good-looking as the dining room with beams, exposed stones, some lovely old pieces, lots of carpet — and utterly seductive views. And there are lovely walks up to (or towards!) the surrounding peaks to work up an appetite for dinner.

Rooms: 12 with bath & wc.
Price: S 8925 Pts; D/Tw 13125 Pts.
Breakfast: 900 Pts.
Meals: Lunch/Dinner 2500 Pts (M). No meals on Sundays or Mondays.
Closed: 22 December-8 January.

How to get there: From A8 exit 17 for Durango. From there BI-632 towards Elorrio. In Atxondo right to Axpe; house up above village, signposted.

Antigua Bodega de Don Cosme Palacio

Carretera de Elciego s/n
01300
Laguardia
La Rioja

Tel: 941 121195
Fax: 941 600297
E-mail: cosme@bodegaspalacio.com

Management: Carmen Enciso

So you like the best in food and wine? Then don't miss out on this double treat. Don Cosme Palacio is one of Rioja's most reputed *bodegas*: the tempranillo grape has been working its magic here, in casks of French oak, for more than a century. Visitors have been coming from all over the world to taste and buy the wine and it seemed right and proper that they should be offered food as delicious as the wine itself. Thus was born the restaurant where Jean-Pierre, Don Cosmé's French-Basque cook (what better credentials?), works his alchemy: he can turn the base elements (always fresh, always local) into such gourmet delights that the price seems almost a token payment. I had one of the most delicious meals of my ten years in Spain. Before or after dinner head down to the cellars where there is a bar for tastings and the main wine stores which have recently been decorated with a remarkable series of frescos depicting all things oenological: Dionysius, Noah (an early wine-buff), harvest time and so on. Visit the winery in the company of the delightful manager, Carmen. And the rooms: each is named after a different grape variety and all are beautifully decorated and kitted out. In short, superb: an obligatory stopover if visiting La Rioja.

Rooms: 13 with bath & wc.
Price: Tw 9900 Pts inc.VAT.
Breakfast: 850 Pts inc.VAT.
Meals: Lunch /Dinner 4000 Pts inc. VAT (M).
Closed: 23 December-7 January.

How to get there: From A68 exit 10 for Lenicero. Through village and then left to Elciego and on to Laguardia. Hotel on right as you enter the village.

Map No: 5

"Among my happier memories of Spain will be Barcelona and the Ramblas on a summer evening. A little way down, near the flower stall, was one of those beautiful Spanish markets where fish and fruit rivalled each other in colour. I never became tired of walking round, delighted by the easy good manners of the market people and their sense of beauty – of the beauty of common things . . .'"

H. V. MORTON - *A Stranger in Spain*

Aragon –
Catalonia

La Tria

08589 **Tel:** 93 8530240
Perafita **Fax:** 93 8530240
Barcelona **E-mail:** la_tria@seker.es

Management: Maite Tor Pujol-Galcerán

This area of the Pyrenean foothills remains puzzlingly 'undiscovered'; as you wander through beautiful old Perafita you'll meet few visitors. But it is lovely. Snug in the green countryside just a short walk from the village, this 17th-century Catalan *mas* will quicken your passion for the natural world. Gentle-mannered Maite is a painter and her sensitivity is reflected in the simple, country-style decoration; rooms are fresh, light and uncluttered. The place is really more geared to self-catering lets — there are two kitchens — but Maite will happily prepare you a Catalan (or continental) breakfast if you wish, and there are two cheap-and-cheerful restaurants in Perafita. In the main farmhouse are an enormous wooden-floored dining room and two lounges, one very cosy with open hearth. The whole place is blissfully quiet and would be ideal for families; there's an enormous, carefully tended garden and a dairy farm to explore — Maite and husband Lluís enjoy showing guests round. Central heating means you'll be comfortable at La Tria in the cooler months, too. The area is known for its many Romanesque churches.

Rooms: 1 with bath & wc; 7 sharing 2 bathrooms.
Price: D/Tw 6000-6500 Pts inc. VAT.
Breakfast: 750 Pts, or self-catering.
Meals: None available.
Closed: First fortnight in July.

How to get there: From Barcelona N152 to Vic. Bypass town to west then turn off for Sant Bartolomeu del Grau. There towards Perafita; La Tria signposted to left before arriving in village.

Mas Banús — Casa Rural

El Banús
Tavérnoles
08519 Osona
Barcelona

Tel: 93 8122091
Fax: 93 8887012
E-mail: banus@redestb.es

Management: Antonio Banús

This grand Catalan farmhouse, nearly five centuries old, has always been the seat of the Banús family — their family tree proudly graces a corner of the sitting room, taking the lineage back to 1214. It is a noble but sympathetic house, with an overgrown garden, lots of mature trees and the farm estate beyond. A very grand old arched doorway leads you into the house where there are vaulted ceilings, great flagstones and a solid staircase leading up to the guestrooms. And what lovely rooms they are! Low, beamed and decorated with the family heirlooms, they are in what once was the granary to the main house. No matter that a couple share bath or shower rooms; Antonio Banús insists that the last thing he wanted was to create a hotel atmosphere. We liked the corner room best — number 8. On the same floor there is a large sitting room and the dining room below is a treat: there are farm-fresh eggs for breakfast and for dinner there is good Catalan country cooking. There are boating, cycling and riding nearby and any number of Romanesque churches and chapels. Antonio also has an adjacent house for rent: weekends 30000 Pts, weekly 85000 Pts.

Rooms: 3 with bath or shower & wc + 2 sharing bath & wc.
Price: D/Tw 6000 Pts.
Breakfast: 600 Pts.
Meals: Dinner 1750 Pts (M).
Closed: One week in September. Please check.

How to get there: From Vic C153 towards Roda de Ter. After approx. 5km turn right towards Tavérnoles (signposted for Parador); El Banús on right after 2km.

54

Mas Pratsevall

Mas Pratsevall s/n
Apartado de Correos123
08522
Taradell
Barcelona

Tel: 93 8800880
Fax: 93 8850566

Management: Ramón Godayol
Vallmitjana

A number of fine old buildings in the village of Taradell are testimony to a once thriving weaving industry; the arrival of the big mechanised looms put an end to its golden years but you still meet a number of well-heeled Catalans here. Nowadays they use the village as a hill-station during the hot summer months, a place where they can escape the noise and pollution of Barcelona. This imposing edifice — these Catalan farmhouses always look as if they were built to last — sits proud on a hill looking out over the village. In summer, window boxes of geraniums lighten a rather sober façade; the mood of restraint is carried over into the cool and uncluttered interior of the two guest apartments — they are the result of the renovation of two old granaries. Both are large enough for a family or group of friends (each has two double bedrooms and one single) and have all the necessary bits and pieces for a comfortable week or two of self-catering — in addition to fridges, ovens and hobs, each has a washing machine and central heating. What brings them into the 'special' league is their lovely turn-of-the-century furniture which matches the beams and terracotta floors. Shuttered windows look to the large surrounding garden; beyond it is a stand of old oak and pine trees, a shady spot to wander or picnic on sunny days.

Rooms: 2 self-catering apartments each sleeping up to 6.
Price: Apt (for 2) 12500 Pts. *Minimum stay 2 nights.* Weekly 75000 Pts for 2.
Breakfast: None — self-catering.
Meals: None — self-catering.
Closed: Never.

How to get there: From Barcelona towards Vic on N152. Exit for Taradell/Centre Comercial. After approx. 4km right at junction then left into Calle Catalunya. Right at end then right again to Pratesevall.

El Jufré

08511	**Tel:** 93 8565167
Tavertet-Osona	**Fax:** 93 8565167
Barcelona	

Management: Josep Roquer

The medieval hilltop villages of this part of Catalonia rival some of those in Provence. Simply driving up to Tavertet past craggy limestone outcrops and stands of forest is memorable; once you arrive and look out over the plain far below you can only gasp at the magnificence of what lies before you. Stay with Josep and Lourdes and their two young children in their very old house: parts of it date back to 1100. It was rebuilt in the 1600s and then refurbished to create the guesthouse. You'll like your room; there are eight and they happily marry the old (beams, exposed stone) and the new (good beds, lighting and bathrooms). We would choose one that looks straight out over the craggy ledge on which El Jufré is perched. There is a terrace on which to linger over an aperitif and a restaurant next to the house; it's a friendly place with good, simple fare and a special reduction (it's not expensive anyway!) for guests of Josep and Lourdes. For lovers of utter tranquility and high places and those glad to trade car for foot.

Rooms: 8 with bath & wc.
Price: D/Tw half-board only: 5500 Pts p.p inc. VAT.
Breakfast: Included.
Meals: Dinner included (M).
Closed: Christmas & New Year, 6 January & 1st week of September.

How to get there: From Vic C153 towards Olo/Roda de Ter to L'Esquirol/Santa María Corco. Here, right to Tavertet. House on left as you enter village.

Can Rosich

Apartado de Correos 275
08398
Santa Susanna
Barcelona

Tel: 93 7678473
Fax: 93 7678473

Management: Mateu Valls and Montserrat Boter

You could hardly ask for a better position: you are very close to the beach, Barcelona and Figueres are an easy drive away and yet you're hidden away up a thickly wooded valley in 20 hectares of bucolic loveliness. You wouldn't think that this old *masía* is more than two centuries old: it's been completely rebuilt in recent years. To one side of the large hallway is a beamed dining room with six tables decked out in bright chequered cloths. We vouch for the cooking: it is wholesome, delicious and amazing value when you consider that the price includes a good Catalan wine. Among Montserrat's specialities are rabbit, pork from the farm and (order in advance!) *Asado de Payés*, a thick stew with three different meats, plums and pine nuts. Breakfast, too, is a hearty meal: cheese and cold meats, fruit and orange juice. Can Rosich's bedrooms are large and comfy and are named after different birds and animals of the region. Beds are antique but mattresses brand new and you'll find a beribboned, neatly ironed bundle of towels on your duvet, a nice touch. Most of the rooms have plenty of space if you should wish to add a third bed: a good choice for one night or for a longer stay.

Rooms: 5 with bath or shower & wc.
Price: D 5800 Pts.
Breakfast: 600 Pts.
Meals: Dinner 1500 Pts incl. wine.
Closed: Never.

How to get there: From the A7 take Maçanet exit. Then N2 towards Barcelona to Santa Susanna. Here, right at first roundabout for 'nucleo urbano', then follow signs for Can Rosich.

Hotel Adagio

Calle Ferran 21
08002
Barcelona
Barcelona

Tel: 93 3189061
Fax: 93 3183724

Management: Tomas Medina

In a lively narrow street of the 'Gothic' quarter, hard by the Ramblas, the Adagio is an excellent choice if you are visiting Barcelona and don´t want to spend too much on your hotel. The building is 1900s but you might think it newer; like many of the city's hotels it was given a very thorough face-lift for the 1992 Olympics. It is a tidy little place — the reception is clean and light with young and smiling staff; those we met spoke very good English and obviously enjoyed working there. Downstairs there is a bright sitting/dining area with simple tables and chairs and modern paintings; the buffet breakfasts are served here. Rooms are surprisingly well-equipped for their price; spotlessly clean, most of them have a small balcony onto the street. The hotel is deservedly popular with younger travellers and there is masses of information (and help) at reception on what to do and see. This is the sort of place for striking up friendships with fellow travellers; it is intimate, family-run, and with many of the city's more interesting sights a short walk away.

Rooms: 38 with bath & wc.
Price: S 8500 Pts; D/Tw 10500 Pts.
Breakfast: Included.
Meals: None available.
Closed: Never.

How to get there: From South up Ramblas to Plaça del Teatre then right to Plaça Sant Miquel. Here left into Carrer de Ferran and hotel on left. For the car: Parking Intelligente on Rambla dels Caputxins.

Hotel Gran Vía

Gran Vía Corts Catalanes 642   **Tel:** 93 3181900
08007   **Fax:** 93 3189997
Barcelona
Barcelona

Management: José Luis García Picazo

At the heart of the city on one of its liveliest arteries, the Gran Vía, is an old and much-loved institution; you really get a feel here for the optimism that was in the air during Catalonia's remarkable 'Belle Époque'. It looks nothing from the street but go through the canopied portal and the place captivates with its air of frayed decadence. A grand carpeted stairway sweeps you up to the drawing room: it would be a perfect place to film a period costume drama with its parquet floors, immense chandelier, oils, gilt mirrors and globe in one corner. The dining room is rather more workaday but we would duck out of the hotel and breakfast instead in one of the many lively cafés nearby. Out to the back of the building is a patio with palms and aspidistra. The bedrooms are mostly large and have recently been given a thorough face-lift: we liked the high ceilings and parquet floors (some are now carpeted). Double glazing means that you can have a room looking onto the Gran Vía and still sleep. A reliable hotel and right in the centre.

Rooms: 54 with bath & wc.
Price: S 9000 Pts; D/Tw 12500 Pts.
Breakfast: 650 Pts.
Meals: None available.
Closed: Never.

How to get there: From the north to Barcelona on A7 then follow 'Ronda Litoral'. Exit 23 onto Diagonal/Passeig de Gracia to Gran Vía. Nearest parking is in Calle Caspe, just one street south of hotel. Metro: Plaza de Catalunya.

Map No: 8

El Trapiche

Can Vidal
Els Casots
08739 Subirats
Barcelona

Tel: 93 7431469
Fax: 93 7431469

Management: Marcela and Michael Johnston

A dream really: imagine waking up from a deep slumber to see the crags of Montserrat silhouetted against a blushing dawn and vineyards all around... *cava* vineyards at that. It takes no leap of imagination to see what drew this couple to this old Masia. Michael is front of house and will probably be cook: he is gregarious, multilingual and fun and knows all the local lore that would be of interest to you. You'll probably meet the whole family because the focus of El Trapiche is relaxed and wholesome meals are eaten around the large dining room table: your hosts are generous with the wine! All the bedrooms are large: two are twin-bedded with showers and the best, the Blue Room, is enormous with a table and chairs from where you can contemplate the lovely view. They have simple pine furniture, warm colours, darkened beams and wooden floors, all with central heating for the colder months. Try to visit the Codorniu cellars which are just down the road and if wine is really your thing there's the wine museum at Vilafranca, just five miles away. And if you fancy a walk you can be picked up at the far end by this ever-obliging couple.

Rooms: 2 with bath or shower & wc.
Price: Tw 7500 Pts; Blue Room 10000 Pts.
Breakfast: Included.
Meals: Lunch/Dinner 1500 Pts incl. wine.
Closed: Never.

How to get there: From A7 exit 27 for Sant Sadurni. As you leave motorway immediately left towards Ordal. Continue for 3km to Els Casots, and take first track on left 600m beyond hamlet.

Hotel La Santa María

Paseo de la Ribera 52
08870
Sitges
Barcelona

Tel: 93 8940999
Fax: 93 8947871
E-mail: reservas@lasantamaria.com
www: www.lasantamaria.com

Management:
Ute Voigt and Antonio Arcas

The charms of Sitges are many; no surprise that it was for many years a fashionable resort town with wealthier Catalans. The crowd is more international now but the town has kept its intimacy and life centres on the promenade and beach. At the heart of it all is the Santa María. There is a bright awning and a terrace; within is the dining room, a small sitting and bar area and the bedrooms — all under the caring eye of Señora Ute, the hotel's indefatigable owner-manager. The rooms with their own balconies and a view across the palm trees to the bay beyond are well worth the extra. They are well furnished with mostly wooden beds, tables and desks; one or two have their original tiled floors and old furniture and some are large enough for a whole family. All of them have prints of Sitges; there may well be fresh flowers. But let's not forget the food; as you'd expect, lots of seafood and fish from the day's catch... and much more besides. Certainly a place where you should book ahead, especially in the season. The hotel has its own car park.

Rooms: 75 with bath & wc.
Price: S 8300 Pts; D/Tw 10920 Pts;
D/Tw (facing sea) 14000 Pts.
Breakfast: Included — buffet.
Meals: Lunch/Dinner 2800 Pts (M), 3000 Pts (C).
Closed: 12 December-12 February.

How to get there: From Barcelona A16 motorway through Tuneles de Garaf. Take the SECOND exit for Sitges center, follow signs to Hotel Calipolis. The Santa María is on sea-front.

Map No: 8

Can Borrell

Retorn 3
17539
Meranges-La Cerdanya
Gerona

Tel: 972 880033
Fax: 972 880144
E-mail: info@canborrell.com
www: www.canborrell.com

Management: Antonio Forn Alonso

Can Borrell was once the shelter of mountain shepherds who brought their flocks up to the high slopes of La Cerdanya for the rich summer grazing. High up to one side of a valley, this two-hundred-year-old farmhouse of granite and slate is tucked away in the tiniest of villages with meadows in front and mountains beyond. Within wood is all about you in beam, shutter and furniture while slate floors mirror the buiding's exterior. Its restoration and conversion from home to hotel have been sensitively accomplished; not over-pretty, but nevertheless inviting and with the warmth and intimacy of a little Cotswolds pub! The rooms welcome you with fabulous views and excellent beds. They vary in size because they follow the idiosyncrasies of an old house and they are uncluttered by all those gadgets that you get in grander hotels. And expect something out of the ordinary at your (small) dinner table. The cooking here is, in the owner's words, "traditional Catalan — with a special touch". Hardly surprising that Can Borrell should have been making waves since it opened and we include it here wholeheartedly.

Rooms: 8 with bath & wc.
Price: S 8000-9000 Pts; D/Tw 10000-11000 Pts.
Breakfast: Included.
Meals: Lunch/Dinner 3000 Pts (M), 3000-5000 Pts (C). Closed Monday nights and Tuesdays.
Closed: 7 January-30 April, except weekends.

How to get there: From Barcelona A18 via Terrassa and Manresa then C1411 to Berga. Through Tunnel del Cadí then on towards Andorra. After approx. 5km right towards Puigcerdá. In Meranges village, signposted.

Hotel del Lago

Avenida Dr Piguillem 7
17520
Puigcerdà
Gerona

Tel: 972 881000
Fax: 972 141511

Management: Bartolomé Pascual Tubau

In such a quiet setting, just beside the lake from which it takes its name, this pretty rose-coloured hotel has been run by the Tubau family for more than fifty years; this place would be a perfect choice for the big relax. There is a large flower-filled garden, shady spots beneath the trees and an unusual hexagonal dining room that is built almost entirely of wood; a light and a cheery place for breakfast in the cooler months. Although no dinners are served, there are bags of restaurants just a short walk from the hotel. The faithful (most of them Spanish and French) return here year after year, many of them during the skiing season because you are within easy reach of some of the best Catalan runs and some of the French slopes, too: you are less than a mile from the border. The guestrooms are carpeted and prettily decorated with floral prints — pinks and salmons mostly — for bedcovers and curtains. They are smaller than average but honestly priced. It all has a home-from-home feel and your hosts will treat you as family friends.

Rooms: 13 with bath & wc + 3 suites.
Price: Tw 9000-10000 Pts; Ste 12500-13500 Pts.
Breakfast: 800 Pts (buffet).
Meals: None available.
Closed: Never.

How to get there: From Barcelona A18 via Terrassa and Manresa then C1411 to Berga. Through Tunnel del Cadí then right to Puigcerdà. Hotel signposted in town; next to the lake.

Cal Pasto

Calle Palos1
17536
Fornells de la Mutanya-Toses
Gerona

Tel: 972 736163
Fax: 972 736163
E-mail: ramongasso@logiccontrol.es

Management: Josefina Soy Sala

Josefina and Ramón are quiet, gentle folk. Their family has farmed in this valley for generations and they are devoted to it. Two rooms next to their house were opened to guests and more recently Ramón's parents' former home was converted to create a further six guestrooms. These are spotlessly clean and simply furnished; all have tiled floors, a very Spanish choice of fabric and good beds. Our favourites were those in the attic where wooden ceilings create a cosier feel. The breakfast room is slightly soulless but don't be put off; you will be served a grand breakfast and afterwards will probably be asked to visit the *Museo del Pastor* (shepherd's museum) — a testimony to the work of four generations of Ramón's family on the surrounding mountainsides. The trans-Pyrenean, Mediterranean-to-Atlantic footpath runs right by the house and you may feel inspired to do part of it. In the evening, choose between Josefina's cooking and the quiet little restaurant next door.

Rooms: 6 with bath or shower & wc.
Price: D/Tw 5500 Pts.
Breakfast: 800 Pts.
Meals: Dinner 1700 Pts.
Closed: Never.

How to get there: From Barcelona N152 towards Puigcerd via Vic and Ripoll. Just past Ribes de Freser turn left at km133.5 post and then 2km to village. House by restaurant.

Hotel Grèvol

Carretera Camprodón a Setcases s/n
Vall de Camprodón
17869 Llanars
Gerona

Tel: 972 741013/130130
Fax: 972 741087
E-mail: INFO@hotelgrevol.com
www: www.hotelgrevol.com

Management: Antonio Sole Fajula

Less than two hours drive from Barcelona, close to ski slopes, mountain trails and a whole series of Romanesque churches, El Grèvol will at first sight make you wonder if you aren't in the Swiss Alps. Carved pine balconies, exposed stonework, slate and wood floors and wooden furniture all provide the perfect setting for the après-ski. But there are no cuckoo clocks here; instead there are high ceilings, a free-standing central hearth and lots of glass to bring in the light. As you'd expect of a hotel with four-star status the guestrooms (each named after a different alpine flower) come with all the trimmings. The ones on the first floor give onto the balcony that runs round the building; attic rooms have pine ceilings and dormers and smaller stand-up balconies. The whole hotel has a warm, enveloping feel; food is regional/international/haute-cuisine — "it tastes good and looks good" says Antonio (there is more snacky food in the bar if you prefer). In season the hotel fills with people heading off for the ski slopes in Vallter. And the hotel has an indoor swimming pool and a bowling alley — less seductive, perhaps, than the mountains which tower about you.

Rooms: 34 with bath & wc + 2 suites.
Price: D/Tw 15600-18850 Pts; Ste 25700-32100 Pts.
Breakfast: 1425 Pts.
Meals: Lunch/Dinner 3975 Pts (M), 5000 Pts (C).
Closed: Never.

How to get there: From Barcelona A7 towards France then N152 via Vic to Ripoll. There C151 to Camprodón. Hotel is 1500m from Camprodón on the road to Setcases.

Map No: 8

65

Hotel Calitxó

Passatge el Serrat s/n
17868
Molló
Gerona

Tel: 972 740386
Fax: 972 740746

Management: Josep Sole Fajula

A second hotel close to Camprodón with more than just a hint of the Tyrolean chalet. Entering this pretty mountain village, over 3,000 feet up in the Pyrenees, you'll see the Calitxó set back from the road. It has an attractive balconied façade brightened by the pots of geraniums adorning each and every balcony. You enter through the restaurant; the day we visited there was a merry atmosphere and nearly all the diners were local — always a good sign. The menu is a mix of Catalan/trad Spanish and ingredients come fresh from the market. Ours might be the fillet steak in cream sauce with wild mushrooms; prices here are more than reasonable. The rooms are all you need: generous-sized with locally-made wooden furniture, and each has a view of the surrounding mountains. Some have their own balconies; when booking ask for one *con balcón*. Señora's friendly welcome, even though she was very busy attending her restaurant clients, melted our reserve and we liked her small, unpretentious hotel. Lovely local walks through orchid-strewn fields, skiing and the beautiful Romanesque churches close by – they are all irresistible.

Rooms: 26 with bath & wc.
Price: S 5900 Pts; D/Tw 7100 Pts; Ste 10600 Pts.
Breakfast: 1050 Pts (buffet).
Meals: Lunch/Dinner 2600 Pts (M), 3700 Pts (C). Restaurant closed on Mondays.
Closed: Never.

How to get there: From Ripoll C151 to Camprodón, and continue on C151 to Molló.

Map No: 8

Mas el Guitart

Santa Margarida de Bianya
17813
La Vall de Bianya
Gerona

Tel: 972 292140
Fax: 972 292140
www: www.turismerural.com.

Management: Lali Nogareda

El Guitart is right up with the avant-garde of a new, dynamic approach to rural tourism that has been gripping Spain for the last couple of years. Lali and Toni are young and enthusiastic hosts; he left television, she left designing, to launch themselves with gusto into the restoration of this old dairy farm. Thanks to their hard work (and their good taste) they have succeeded in creating one of Catalonia's very best small B&Bs. We loved the rooms; each is decorated in a different colour with Lali's stencilling to match; there are wooden floors and beams, old beds and washstands, rugs, decent bathrooms and good views. We especially liked the Blue room. The breakfast and sitting rooms are decorated in similar vein; breakfast is Catalan, with juice, jams and home-made sausage there are good things awaiting at dinnertime, too. There are also two fully-equipped kitchens if you want to prepare your own meals. This would be an excellent choice for a longer stay. From here you could set out to explore the surrounding mountains but look to Toni for advice; he has researched and marked new walking routes in the valley. Exceptional hosts, home and countryside.

Rooms: 4 with bath & wc + 2 two bedroom apartments.
Price: D/Tw 6000 Pts; Apt 10000 Pts inc. VAT. *Minimum stay 2 nights.*
Breakfast: 600 Pts.
Meals: Dinner on request 1400 Pts.
Closed: Never.

How to get there: From Gerona C150 to Besalú. Continue on C150 to Castellfollit de la Roca. Here follow signs Ripoll/Camprodón. House signposted in Vall de Bianya.

Mas Salvanera

17850
Beuda
Gerona

Tel: 972 590975
Fax: 972 590975
E-mail: salvanera@interbook.net
www: www.girona/soft.com/salvanera

Management: Rocío Niño Ojeda and Ramón Ruscalleda

In a blissfully quiet part of the lovely wooded Pyrenean foothills, Mas Salvanera — a solid 17th-century Catalan farmhouse — was recently transformed into the smartest of country hotels. The guestrooms, in an old olive mill next to the main house, are named after signs of the zodiac. Rocio´s flair for decoration has found an outlet here; beneath lovely old darkening beams the antique pieces (most of them restored by her), carefully arranged flowers and colour-coordinated fabrics have been sensitively combined. Bathrooms are big, too, with all the extras. Our favourite room was Cancer but they are all large and elegant. The main building has an old well, vaulted ceilings and open hearths, more antiques and lots of exposed stone. Upstairs there is the guest dining room, dominated by the grand 18-place dining table. Breakfast here is a big buffet, taken at any time you choose. Lunch and dinner are also an occasion for Rocío to spoil you once again; *paella* and rabbit are two of her regional specialities. There is a quiet walled garden with a pool among the olives — the right place for a siesta. Or there are six bikes if you're feeling more energetic.

Rooms: 8 with bath or shower & wc.
Price: D/Tw 11000 Pts.
Breakfast: 1000 Pts.
Meals: Lunch/Dinner 3000 Pts.
Closed: 1-17 September & 1-10 January.

How to get there: From Gerona NII towards Figueres, then C150 via Banyoles to Besalú. Here right on N260, then left for Maià de Montcal and then follow signs to Beuda; Mas Salvanera after 1.6km.

Can Jou

La Miana
17854
Sant Jaume de Llierca
Gerona

Tel: 972 190263
Fax: 972 190444
www: www.turismerural.net/canjou

Management: Rosa Linares and Michael Peters

You will remember arriving at Can Jou: all the way up the track to the farm you sense you are leaving the mundane, the ordinary, behind you. Round a final bend and there it is, high on a hill looking out over miles and miles of thick forest of oak and beech. Small wonder that Mick and Rosa were inspired to revive this old Catalan farm; first by working the land, then by giving the house a family (they have four children), thirdly by restoring the old barn so they can now share the beauty of it all with their guests. The guestrooms are simple, furnished with a mix of old and new; six have their own balcony and bathrooms while four larger rooms share three bathrooms. This would be a fine place for a family holiday; there is the farm to explore (ducks, turkeys, cattle and sheep), horses to ride (a perfect place for learners and there are marked forest bridle-ways for experienced riders). Rosa's regional cooking will have you dining in every night and many of the ingredients come straight from the farm. Close to the house is a spring-filled rock pool — if you´re heading back to Nature, head here.

Rooms: 8 with bath & wc + 4 family rooms sharing 3 bathrooms.
Price: B&B 4500 Pts p.p; half board 5900 Pts p.p; full board 6900 Pts p.p.
Breakfast: Included.
Meals: Lunch and/or dinner included, if full/half board.
Closed: Never.

How to get there: From Figueres N260 to Besalú and to Sant Jaume de Llierca. Left into village, and then 2nd left into Calle Industria. Continue for 6km along track to house, marked at all junctions.

Map No: 8

69

Rectoria de la Miana
17854
Sant Jaume de Llierca
Gerona

Tel: 972 190190

Management: Frans Engelhard
and Janine Westerlaken

At the heart of a vast stand of beech and oak, at the end of 6km of rough and winding track, La Miana sits in a setting of incomparable beauty. History is very present here: in the Middle Ages there was a fortified manor-house; in the 1300s a rectory was built complete with vaulted ceilings, escape tunnel and chapel. It took courage and vision for Frans Engelhard to embark on its restoration. But his dream of a house open to all, a place for theatre and workshops where the creative impulse could be given free rein, is fast being realised and from the ruins has emerged an extraordinary and beautiful — if simple — hostelry. No two rooms are alike. They have pastel walls, they are furnished almost exclusively with antique furniture, there are bright kilims and each old handmade floor tile is a work of art. In the vaulted dining room downstairs you will have a genuine Catalan breakfast, and regional dishes for lunch or supper. The walking here is wonderful, there is riding at a nearby farm and La Miana has bikes. Or just abandon yourself to the hushed loveliness of it all. Perhaps better for walkers than for those seeking easy comfort.

Rooms: 6 with bath/shower & wc.
Price: D/Tw half board 4500 Pts p.p; full board 6000 Pts p.p inc. VAT.
Breakfast: Included.
Meals: Lunch and/or dinner included.
Closed: Never.

How to get there: From Figueres N260 to Besalú and Sant Jaume de Llierca. Left into village, then 2nd left into Calle Industria. 6km along track to house following signs to Can Jou (marked at all junctions). Rectory just past Can Jou farmhouse.

Map No: 8

El Molí

Mas Molí
17469
Siurana d'Emporda
Gerona

Tel: 972 525139
Fax: 972 525139
www: www.svt.es/unio/agroturisme/elmoli.htm

Management: Maria Sanchís Pages

Unusually for this guide, El Molí is a modern building; but it more than earns a place in the 'special' category alongside its older Catalan neighbours. Although open for just over a year, it has already been awarded a Diploma for B&B excellence. Its position couldn't be better; you are just 7km from wonderful Figueres and the Dalí museum, while just a half hour drive will bring you to the beach. The house is modelled on the traditional Girona *mas*; inside, its tiled floors, wooden furniture and big rooms with views across the farm are ample compensation for sharing a bathroom (although at the time we go to press, more are on the way). But the heart of the house is Maria; don't miss the chance to share dinner (wonderful value) and conversation with her and husband Josep; veg, chicken and beef come straight from the farm and there's an infusion of *hierbas* to end your feast. At breakfast, try the home-made yoghurt and jams. Ask to see the old ice-well in the garden; it was built in Roman times. This would be a good place to break the journey travelling north or south, Maria will even prepare dinner earlier for her guests and can help organise cycling routes out from the farm.

Rooms: 2 with bath & wc; 2 sharing bath & wc.
Price: D/Tw 5000-6000 Pts.
Breakfast: 600 Pts.
Meals: 1400 Pts (M).
Closed: Never.

How to get there: Coming from the North on A9 take exit 4 towards La Escala, then turn right to Siurana d'Emporda. Arriving in village El Molí is signposted.

Can Fabrica

17844
Santa Llogaia del Terri
Gerona

Tel: 972 594629
Fax: 972 594629

Management: Marta Casanovas

On top of a gentle hill with wide, inspirational views all around sits the 17th-century farmhouse that Marta and Ramón have restored and brought back to life, not least by planting trees and farming their 17 acres of land. They have created a blissful corner of peace and quiet whence to explore the nearby villages and Romanesque churches. If you are here in summer, do visit the Dali museum by night! Ramón is an engineer, Marta a designer. They are an exceptionally friendly young couple with environmentalist leanings and want you to discover the treasures of their area; there are four bicycles for hire and a wealth of walking and cycling routes. The bedrooms are smallish, simply furnished with old pieces and lamps, while soft materials set off the bare stone walls. The food is good home cooking, often with produce from the farm, and you will have Can Fabrica honey on the breakfast table as well as the traditional Catalan ingredients of tomato, oil and garlic. A lovely place and lovely people; stock up on farm produce before you move on.

Rooms: 6 with bath or shower & wc.
Price: S 3550 Pts; D/Tw 7100 Pts; Tr 10050 Pts inc. VAT.
Breakfast: Included.
Meals: Dinner 1950 Pts (M).
Closed: November-Easter (but open for Christmas).

How to get there: Leave A7 at exit 6 onto C150 towards Banyoles. After approx. 8km bear right towards Cornellà del Terri then at roundabout towards Medinya. After 2.5km left to Santa Llogaia; through village, 400m of track to house on left.

Map No: 8

Can Massa

Calle Vell s/n   **Tel:** 972 488326
17120   **Fax:** 972 488326
La Pera   **E-mail:** jmassa@teleline.es
Gerona   **www:** www.svt.es/unio/agroturisme/massa.htm

Management: Josep Massa Roura and Irene do Carmo Pires Lopes

Two hundred years or so ago this building served as a carriage shed. It was acquired by the Massa family some 50 years ago. At this most congenial B&B, as guests of the quiet-mannered Josep and Irene, you will be keenly aware of the past: in the photos of loved members of the families captured in black and white (spot Josep as a boy), in the soporific tock of the grandfather clock, in the dresser with its collection of old glass and china — the very antithesis of a chain hotel. So too is the feel of the bedrooms: there is the 'parents' room, the 'grandparents' (with the suite they bought as newly-weds) and our favourite, the blue room, which has its own terrace and a beautiful geometric tiled floor. Your hosts have restored many of the pieces of furniture themselves. From the kitchen come family recipes: starters, main courses and puds are all home-made. Eating here is a genial affair around one large table with your fellow guests. Stay a couple of days and visit the Castell Gala Dalí (open 15 March-30 Sept) or perhaps go for a bike ride with a map and explanations provided. The beach is just half an hour away...

Rooms: 4 with bath or shower & wc.
Price: D 5500-7000 Pts; Tw 7000-8500 Pts.
Breakfast: 600 Pts.
Meals: Dinner 1700 Pts inc. wine.
Closed: Never.

How to get there: From A7 exit for Gerona Nord and follow signs towards Pálamos. At km15 post right to La Pera where house is signposted just past phone box

Hotel Aigua Blava

Playa de Fornells
17255
Begur
Gerona

Tel: 972 622058/624308
Fax: 972 622112
E-mail: hotelaiguablava@aiguablava.com
www: www.aiguablava.com

Management: Joan Gispert-Lapedra

The Aigua Blava is something of an institution. It is a largish hotel which, thanks to careful and friendly management and clever design, makes the place feel both welcoming and half its size. This is reflected in the bedrooms; they're all decorated differently and ranged on several terraced wings which look over the gardens and down to a delicious hidden cove below — so rugged a piece of coast is almost unspoilable. Run by the same family (the manager started at 15), nourished by the same chef (his son is training to take over), tended by the same gardener for 45 years, the hotel has a strong tradition of personal attention. Señor Gispert cares deeply for his guests. Breathe deeply in the sweet-smelling pinewoods, bask beside the huge pool, enjoy fresh lobster in the dining room while delighting in the sight of the small fishing port or sip a cool drink at the smart snack bar on the uncrowded beach. The sense of hospitality comes naturally to the family and their staff and you are constantly made to feel that you are a special guest; no groups are taken and customer loyalty is strong. The village, too, is one of the prettiest on the Costa Brava, so you should book ahead if planning a stay at Aigua Blava.

Rooms: 85 with bath & wc + 5 suites.
Price: S 9000-11500 Pts; D/Tw 11400-19500 Pts; Ste 17000-23500 Pts.
Breakfast: 1600 Pts.
Meals: Lunch/Dinner 3650 Pts (M), 4500-5500 Pts (C).
Closed: 7 November-22 February.

How to get there: From Gerona C255 to Palafrugell. From there GE650 to Begur. Signposted on entry to village.

Map No: 8

Hotel Llevant

Francesc de Blanes 5
17211
Llafranc
Gerona

Tel: 972 300366
Fax: 972 300345
E-mail: hllevant@arrakis.es

Management: The Farrarons Puic family

On the pedestrians-only sea front in a busy little village, Llevant is a family-run hotel with many a devotee returning year after year; they come both for the hostelry and also for the hosts. The building is 60 years old but you could never tell; everything sparkles here from bathroom to crockery to the sea that almost laps its way to the door. The Puic family are proud of their creation, constantly improving and refurbishing; the bedrooms are very smart, with every mod con. But what makes it all special enough to earn a place in this guide is the restaurant/terrace. The promenade here is always animated, highly so at the evening *paseo* time, and beyond all this the sea is a constant backdrop; what better place to watch the world go by than this terrace, with the hotel's prize-winning cooking as an accompaniment? The beach at Llafranc is sandy, clean and safe — we walked from end to end in September without seeing a scrap of paper! Good value at any time of the year, particularly so in the low season. Note that higher prices listed are for half-board, obligatory in high season (Easter, June-Sept).

Rooms: 24 with bath & wc.
Price: S 4125-6900 Pts; D 6750-8900-12500 Pts; Tw 9300-17500 Pts.
Breakfast: 950 Pts (buffet).
Meals: Lunch/Dinner 2200-2450 Pts (M).
Closed: November.

How to get there: From Barcelona A7 north to exit 9 (San Feliu); past San Feliu and Palamos to Palafrugell. Here follow signs to Llafranc; hotel in centre of village right on sea-front. Park in street.

Map No: 8

Hotel Sant Roc

Plaça Atlàntic 2
17210
Calella de Palafrugell
Gerona

Tel: 972 614250/615286
Fax: 972 614068/617012
E-mail: santroc@grn.es

Management: Teresa Boix and
Bertrand Hallé

If only there were more hotels like Sant Roc on the Costa Brava. For it remains, in many parts, a stunning stretch of coastline and this quiet little hotel could restore your faith in seaside holidays in Spain. It is very much a family affair — not just family-owned and run but also a place where guests are valued like old friends (some return year after year). The setting is marvellous: a perch at the edge of a cliff amid pine, olive and cypress trees. From terrace and dining room there are views across the bay and its brightly-painted boats to the pretty village beyond. The sea is ever with you at Sant Roc, its colours changing with every hour. The best rooms are those with seaward terraces, of course, but we liked them all, their most striking feature being hand-painted beds and an abundance of original oil paintings. With Franco-Catalan owners you would expect something special from the kitchen and justifiably — the food is good and Bertrand and Teresa are charming hosts. There is a path from the hotel down to the beach and longer walks around the bay.

Rooms: 46 with bath or shower & wc + 3 suites.
Price: S 9400Pts; D/Tw 13600 Pt; Ste 26000 Pts.
Breakfast: 1000 Pts.
Meals: Lunch/Dinner 3000 Pts (M).
Closed: 2 November-15 March.

How to get there: From Barcelona A7 north to exit 6 (Girona Norte) then follow signs for La Bisbal via Palamos then on to Palafrugell; from here to Calella; hotel signposted.

Hotel Diana

Plaza de España 6
17320
Tossa de Mar
Gerona

Tel: 972 341886/341116
Fax: 972 341886/341103

Management: Fernando
Osorio Estarra

Although long ago discovered by the sun-and-sea brigade, Tossa de Mar still retains some of its charm, especially in the *Vila Vela*; wander up for wonderful views at sunset or sunrise. Visit out of season and stay at the Diana. The building is said to have been built by one of the Gaudí school; it certainly is a beautiful example of Spanish Art Nouveau. The hotel is surprisingly luxurious, considering such modest prices; chandeliered, bannistered and columned — the building hasn't forgotten its youth. There are old pieces in public rooms, like grandfather clocks, oils, gilt mirrors and the original tiled floors. Although some are modern, most bedrooms have period furniture; our favourites are those with a terrace looking across the bay. Bathrooms have recently been revamped and thoroughly modernised. The hotel's patio looks out across the beach to the dancing waves but breakfast inside is just as much fun, amid ferns and wicker tables and chairs; the windows and doors would make any artist sigh!

Rooms: 16 with bath & wc + 5 suites.
Price: D/Tw 8700-12400 Pts; Ste (sea views) 10700-14400 Pts.
Breakfast: 1100 Pts (buffet).
Meals: None available.
Closed: November-Easter.

How to get there: From Barcelona A7 towards France. Exit 9 towards Lloret de Mar; on past Lloret north to Tossa de Mar. Here follow signs for Vila Vella/Playa. Hotel on sea front.

Map No: 8

77

Oriol Riera

Veïnat Pibiller 1
17412
Maçanet de la Selva
Gerona

Tel: 972 859099
Fax: 972 851316

Management: Dolors Bosch Llinás

A special place, for those who are happy to forego some minor comfort in order to enjoy an authentic Catalan home. If you're happy to share a shower room and conversation at table, then stay as a guest of Dolors at her 200-year-old Catalan farmhouse. It is, she rightly points out, *"una casa muy bonita"*. This is the antithesis of those credit-card hotels we so dislike; pull in off the busy NII and the ivy-clad frontage of Oriol Riera offers rest for sore eyes. Inside, decoration is as personal as in any family home: pictures of Dolors' family, sporting trophies on a shelf above a lace-clad dresser, dried flowers hanging down from the old beamed and planked ceiling. There are two dining rooms; dressers display the family china, there's a highchair for younger children and, in one corner, a stone staircase leads up to the bedrooms which are large enough to accommodate extra beds should the need arise. You'd be a fool to miss dinner; again we leave the last word to Dolors who describes it as, *"familiar — calidad de primera clase"*.

Rooms: 4 sharing bathroom & wc.
Price: D/Tw 5000 Pts.
Breakfast: 650 Pts.
Meals: Lunch/Dinner 1400 Pts (M).
Closed: Christmas.

How to get there: From A7 take exit 9 for Massanet de la Selva. Towards Barcelona on NII; 500m after marker for km691 turn left at sign (careful-brow of hill!) and you'll see Oriol Riera to the right.

Map No: 8

Xalet La Coromina

Carretera de Vic 4   **Tel:** 93 8849264
17406   **Fax:** 93 8848160
Viladrau
Gerona

Management: Gloria Rabat

Once here, you will wax as lyrical as the Coromina's staff do about the stunning Parque Natural del Montseny: its woodlands are grandiose, water flows and falls everywhere, indigenous trees and rare plants flourish. It is a place for a back-to-nature walking holiday. The building dates from the turn of the century when wealthy Catalan families first built themselves summer retreats away from the sticky city. It has kept its elegant exterior while being thoroughly modernised inside. The ancient/modern mix is visible in the decoration too: the little sitting room has an old fireplace; all bedrooms have their own personality with an antique in each, English and French prints for curtains and bedcovers, good bathrooms and yet more stupendous views. The Coromina prides itself on its food and on using local produce in season. You can expect delicious mushroom dishes made with local *setas* just as they spring up after the rain. And the car rally memorabilia? Gloria's husband, Antonio Zanini, was one of Spain's most successful drivers. A gentle small hotel in a spectacular setting which won its Michelin star for good cuisine in its very first year.

Rooms: 8 with bath & wc + 1 suite.
Price: S 8600 Pts; D/Tw 11000 Pts; Ste 12750 Pts.
Breakfast: 1000 Pts.
Meals: Lunch/Dinner 2500 Pts (M), 3700 Pts (C).
Closed: 3-28 January.

How to get there: From Barcelona A2 towards Girona/France and exit for Vic/Puigcerdá. Then N152 to Tona then right on BV5303 for Selva/Viladráu.

Map No: 8

Hospedería de Loarre

Plaza Miguel Moya 7
22809
Loarre
Huesca

Tel: 974 382706
Fax: 974 382713
www: www.pirineo.com

Management: Jorge Valdés Santonja

This fine old 17th-century building graces the prettiest of main squares in the little village of Loarre. It has recently been restored and given new life thanks to a local government initiative: no corners were cut nor pesetas spared in this complete face-lift (cheering to see that the hotel has full facilities for the disabled). You'd probably mention the food before the rooms on the postcard home: Aragonese and French Basque cooking, seasonal veg and the best cuts of meat; autumn's a good time to stay when wild mushrooms and game dishes are on the menu. To accompany your meal try one of the local Somantano reds (let yourself be guided by your waiter): they are all reasonably priced and honest, robust wines. Loarre's bedrooms are comfortable, clean and tastefully furnished with pine beds and tables and the occasional antique. The best of them (three in all) have balconies giving onto the square whilst those at the rear get a view out over the rooftops to the almond groves beyond. Do come to visit the 12th-century castle (see photo) and the fabulous rock formations (and griffon vultures) of the nearby Mallos de Riglos range of mountains. Jorge and wife Anna are young and friendly: they'll advise on what to do.

Rooms: 12 with bath & wc.
Price: S 4100-5100 Pts; D/Tw 6200-8200 Pts.
Breakfast: Included.
Meals: Lunch/Dinner 1800 Pts (M), approx. 4000 Pts (C).
Closed: Never.

How to get there: From Huesca take N240 to Ayerbe. Here right on the HU311 to Loarre. Hotel is in main square (with garage space for 3 or 4 cars).

Casa Frauca

Carretera de Ordesa s/n
22374
Sarvisé
Huesca

Tel: 974 486353/486182
Fax: 974 486353

Management: Carmen Villacampa

So close to the border, this delightful little roadside hotel could very well be a French townhouse with its neo-classical pilasters, symmetrical design and pale pink wash, but inside it is faithful to its Spanish Pyrenean environment and has all the right timbers, tiles, sloping ceilings and pieces of rustic furniture. We especially took to the round window with its two semicircular shutters. The owners are a kind and gentle couple who like caring for their guests and keep their house clean and warm. There is an intimate, rather smoky little bar for close encounters with the locals and a dining room where regional dishes will nourish the active visitor — lots of salads and vegetables, good stews and roasts, and plenty of everything. Sarvisé is in an extraordinary valley of abandoned villages that was due to be dammed... and never was, thank heavens! Enjoy the wooded hillsides, rugged rocks and rushing streams, or the snow and ice in winter.

Rooms: 12 with bath & wc.
Price: S 3000-5000 Pts; D/Tw 4000-6000 Pts.
Breakfast: 475 Pts.
Meals: Lunch/Dinner 1600 Pts (M), 3000-4000 Pts (C).
Closed: Never.

How to get there: From Lérida N240 towards Barbastro then N123/C318 to Ainsa. Then N260 towards Biescas to Sarvisé. Hotel on left in village.

La Choca

Plaza Mayor 1
22148
Lecina de Bárcabo
Huesca

Tel: 974 343070 or 608 633636
Fax: 974 343070
www: www.staragon.com/hhu/hshu012.htm

Management: Ana Zamora and Miguel Angel Blasco

Lecina de Bárcabo is for lovers of high places: a tiny hamlet in a rugged, wild part of Huesca perched at the edge of a limestone outcrop. Miguel Angel and Ana left teaching to restore this lovely old fortified farmhouse and... to farm rabbits. But glorious La Choca cried out to be shared so they opened the house as a farm-school and later as a guesthouse. You will be captivated by the indescribable beauty of the views, the utter tranquillity of the hamlet. We fell asleep to the hooting of an owl and awoke to the sound of a woodpecker! The public rooms have stone walls and ancient timbers; the bedrooms are also rustically simple... and television-free. Three of them are big enough for a family and one has its own terrace. And you'll eat well here (often to the strains of classical music): home-made jams at breakfast, regional dishes with a French influence at other meals — and Ana's own recipes, too. Cave paintings nearby, bikes to be rented in the hamlet and gorgeous walks straight out from the house into the Sierra de Guara National Park.

Rooms: 9 with bath & wc.
Price: S 3500 Pts; D/Tw 5350 Pts inc. VAT.
Breakfast: 550 Pts.
Meals: Dinner 1600 Pts (M); lunch 2500-3000 Pts (C). (Except Thursdays).
Closed: November & 24-27 December.

How to get there: From Huesca on N240 towards Barbastro. 2 km after village of Angües left towards Colungo. 15km after Colungo left towards Lecina de Bárcabo. House first on left entering village.

Hotel San Marsial

Carretera Francia s/n
22440
Benasque
Huesca

Tel: 974 551616
Fax: 974 551623
E-mail: hotel.sanmarsial@pirineo.com
www: www.pirineo.com/hotel.san.marsial

Management: The Garuz family

Benasque is a pretty place in the Aragonese Pyrenees, a centre for winter sports or for walking once the snows melt. The San Marsial is an immensely warm, friendly little hotel with a smile at reception and rooms of human proportions, all lovingly created thanks to a combined family effort. A successful combination of slate floors, beamed wooden ceilings and rustic furniture makes it feel like a home from home, a place to linger over dinner or a good book. Wood is the basic material: many of the pieces were made or installed by the carpenter owner. The bedrooms are very smart — many have attractive hand-painted bedheads; there are wooden floors and ceilings and matching curtains and bedcovers. Ten rooms have their own small terrace; all of them are light, medium-sized and have good bathrooms. In corridors, sitting and dining rooms there is a veritable museum of old farm implements, skis, chests... and in the middle a lovely hearth diffusing yet more warmth. The nearest ski stations are only 5km away.

Rooms: 23 with bath & wc + 2 suites.
Price: S 5800-8500 Pts; D/Tw 8500-11800 Pts; Ste 18000 Pts.
Breakfast: 1100 Pts.
Meals: Lunch/Dinner 2100 Pts (M), approx. 3800 Pts (C).
Closed: 10-20 November.

How to get there: From Lérida N240 to Barbastro then N123 to Graus. From here C139 to Benasque. Through village and hotel on left.

Besiberri

Calle Deth Fort 4
25599
Arties-Valle de Aran
Lérida

Tel: 973 640829
Fax: 973 640829

Management: Carmen Lara Aguilar

Besiberri is our favourite place to stay in this neck of the woods: it is small, intimate and managed by the friendliest of families. This pretty, flower-clad building certainly looked to the Alps for its inspiration and the first sight of it might remind you of sojourns in Switzerland or Germany. You enter through a small sitting room which has the dining area off to one side. There's an open hearth, beamed ceiling, Carmen's dried flower arrangements and a collection of old pewter jugs. Wonderful to warm yourself in front of a blazing fire after a day on the ski slopes. Upstairs there are sixteen bedrooms which are, like that porridge, 'just right': cheerfully decorated, clad throughout in wood, they have deeply comfy beds and window boxes brimming with geraniums (in season). At the end of each floor there is a balcony with chairs looking out to the river which runs fast and deep. You might like to splurge and take the suite at the top of the building; it has windows to both sides, its own balcony and a small lounge. There are no meals served here apart from breakfast but you are just yards away from one of the best restaurants in the Pyrenees. We still remember Carmen's kindly smile and natural ebullience.

Rooms: 16 with bath & wc + 1 suite.
Price: D/Tw 8000-11000 Pts; Ste 14000-16000 Pts.
Breakfast: Included.
Meals: None available.
Closed: May & November.

How to get there: From Lérida N230 to Viella then C142 to Arties. Signposted to right as you enter village.

Casa Guilla

Santa Engracia
Apartado 83
25620 Tremp
Lérida

Tel: 973 252080 or 606 333481
Fax: 973 252080
E-mail: casaguilla@c1313.es
www: www.web-show.com/casaguilla/

Management: Richard and Sandra Loder

This is a matchless position, a veritable eagle's nest. As you soar higher and higher to the tiny hamlet perched high on a rocky crag you can only wonder at the courage of Santa Engracia's earliest inhabitants. Richard and Sandra Loder have a head for heights and after returning from Africa patiently set about restoring the buildings that make up Casa Guilla — a fortified Catalan farmhouse parts of which are nearly 1,000 years old. The house is a labyrinth: it twists and turns on many different levels. There are two sitting rooms — one large with an open hearth, another smaller with books and local info. The bedrooms are simply but cosily furnished; there are terracotta tiles, heavy old beams, low ceilings... all deliciously organic. And there are big breakfasts with home-baked bread, generous dinners with lots of game and that incomparable view from both dining room and terrace to accompany it. Caring and informative hosts in a fascinating part of Catalonia; geologists, lepidopterists, ornithologists and botanists are in their element here! A superb place.

Rooms: 1 double, 3 twins + 1 triple sharing 3 shower rooms.
Price: Half-board only: 6500 Pts p.p inc. VAT.
Breakfast: Included.
Meals: Dinner included, packed lunches 700 Pts.
Closed: Never.

How to get there: From Pobla de Segur C147 towards Tremp. After 5km right into Salás de Pallars, then right at school following signs to Santa Engracia. After 5.6km fork left for village. House near church.

Map No: 7

Casa Mauri

Santa Engracia
25636
Tremp
Lérida

Tel: 973 252076

Management: Anne and Mike Harrison

Few villages in Spain can match spectacular Santa Engracia for setting; from its rocky ledge you look across to hill, gorge and mountain — all of it changing with each passing hour. Just arriving here you feel a sense of adventure, of discovery. The heady magic of the place soon worked its spell on Anne and Mike who have gradually restored and renovated a group of 200-year-old houses. Guests can choose between the house and the *apartamento*. Either would be perfect for a family — or the house for a group of friends. Rooms come with radiators and wood-burners, attractive wooden furniture; pine and beam and pointed stone walls, rugs and bamboo lamps lend warmth. A place where you'd want to stay several nights. To do? — if you should tire of that grandest of views you could follow dinosaur footprints, visit Romanesque churches, bird-watch or, most obviously, choose between any number of fabulous walks in the area — you may see wild horses and boar. Rooms and dinner are both excellent value, Mike and Anne happy in their role of hosts. *From May to October weekly lets preferred.*

Rooms: 1 house with 3 bedrooms sharing 2 shower rooms; 1 apartment with 2 bedrooms sharing 1 bathroom.
Price: D/Tw 6000 Pts inc. VAT. Houses: (for 4) 37000-65000 Pts; (for 6) 45000-78000 Pts weekly.
Breakfast: 500 Pts; 750 Pts (cooked).
Meals: Lunch/Dinner 1700 Pts (M) or self-catering.
Closed: Never.

How to get there: From Tremp north towards La Pobla de Segur on C147. After garage (on the right) turn left to Talarn. After bends, left for Santa Engracia. Under railway; 10km of good track to village. Park and walk up to house; house last on left.

Can Boix
Can Boix s/n
25790
Peramola
Lérida

Tel: 973 470266
Fax: 973 470266

Management: Joan Pallarés

No fewer than ten generations of the Pallarés family have lived and worked at Can Boix; three of them have turned this seductively located inn into something of an institution in Catalonia. But this is not a family to sit back on its laurels; as you'll see from the photo, innovation and renovation have led Can Boix solidly into the 90s thanks to the unflagging enthusiasm of Joan. Come, if only for the food; it is a celebration of what is locally grown or raised. Presentation is superb, and even if the dining room is big enough for a banquet the accompanying views are as scrumptious as the meal and it still feels welcoming. Guest bedrooms are big and modern, yet nevertheless cosy, thanks to the wooden floors and furniture; they all have terraces (see photo) — large, mirrored, fitted wardrobes and every mod-con. Bathrooms are marbled, double-sinked, plush; tubs will hydro-massage you if the sauna and high pressure showers of the gym have not worked their magic. This is a blissfully peaceful spot; cycle or ride into the spectacular foothills of the Pyrenees. An immensely friendly and comfortable hotel which cares equally for both business people and travellers.

Rooms: 20 with (hydromassage) bath & wc.
Price: D/Tw 16000 Pts.
Breakfast: 1000 Pts (buffet).
Meals: Lunch/Dinner 2800 Pts (M), 4800 Pts (C).
Closed: 2 weeks in November & 2 weeks in January. Please check.

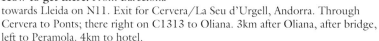

How to get there: From Barcelona towards Lleida on N11. Exit for Cervera/La Seu d'Urgell, Andorra. Through Cervera to Ponts; there right on C1313 to Oliana. 3km after Oliana, after bridge, left to Peramola. 4km to hotel.

Los Palacios

Calle Palacios 21
44100
Albarracín
Teruel

Tel: 978 700327
Fax: 978 700358

Management: Valeriano Saez Lorenzo

Albarracín is one of Teruel's most attractive walled towns; its narrow streets tumble down the hillside beneath the castle and eventually lead you to a lovely main square and the medieval cathedral with its ceramic-tiled tower (a later addition). Los Palacios is a tall, balconied and handsome building just outside the city walls; its earthy colours seem to fix it to the hillside on which it stands. The 50-year-old building was just recently thoroughly refurbished and so was born this small hostal. The bedrooms are furnished with workaday wooden furniture; floors are decked in modern tiles. The fabrics are a shade satiny but forgive this little lapse: these are utterly Spanish rooms, impeccably clean and the views from their small balconies are second to none. It is good to escape from telephone and television; the owners are keen not to disturb their guests' utterly silent nights. The little breakfast room/bar area has views, too, and while busy preparing your breakfast the owners will happily chat about trips from the hostal. This little inn has few pretensions, is amazingly cheap and we recommend it wholeheartedly.

Rooms: 16 with bath or shower & wc.
Price: S 2500 Pts; D/Tw 4500 Pts inc. VAT.
Breakfast: 250 Pts.
Meals: 1300 Pts (M).
Closed: Never.

How to get there: From Teruel N234 north towards Zaragoza. After approx. 7km left on TE901 to Albarracín. Here through tunnel and right after 150m and Hostal is first house on right.

Map No: 14

Hotel Esther

44431 **Tel:** 978 801040
Virgen de la Vega **Fax:** 978 801059
Teruel

Management: Miguel Andrés Rajadel García

The high mountains and hilltop villages of the Maestrazgo have only recently begun to awaken the curiosity of those in search of new pastures to walk and ski. At the heart of this wild and beautiful area the modern little Esther is one of our favourite places. It is a purely family business — father, mother and son look after bar, reception and restaurant. The focus is the dining room; it is modern but a timbered roof, mounted ceramic plates and a lovely tiled picture of Jaca help to create intimacy. You can expect a memorable meal here; specialities are roast lamb and kid as well as jugged meats like turkey and rabbit. Try the junket with honey for dessert. There is a good choice of wines and you can trust Miguel's recommendations. Decoration is the same upstairs and down: tiled floors, simple wooden furniture. The bedrooms have small bathrooms and are irreproachably clean. Hotel Esther is another of the small hotels included here which prove that modern hotels can have a heart, too. Honest prices for rooms and food.

Rooms: 19 with bath & wc.
Price: S 4000 Pts; D/Tw 7500 Pts.
Breakfast: 650 Pts.
Meals: Lunch/Dinner 1800 Pts (M), 2750-3500 Pts (C).
Closed: 8-25 September.

How to get there: From Valencia towards Barcelona; at Sagunto left on N234 towards Teruel. TE201 to Mora de Rubielos then TE201 towards Alcalá de la Selva. 2km before Alcalá on right.

Map No: 14

Fonda Guimera

Calle Agustín Pastor 28   **Tel:** 964 178269
44141   **Fax:** 964 178293
Mirambel
Teruel

Management: Pedro Guimera

Mirambel is one of the most beautiful of the hilltop villages of the Maestrazgo, a place so well preserved that when Ken Loach came to film *Land and Freedom* it sufficed to move a few cars and the cameras were up and rolling for his 1930s drama. A lovely arch leads you through the town walls and straight into the village's main street; just along on your left is Fonda Guimera. The inn is just seven years old but you would never guess it; it is a lovely stone building that is utterly faithful to local tradition and fits perfectly between much older houses on both sides. On the ground floor are the bar and the restaurant which serves simple home-cooking. Upstairs the rooms are as unpretentious as the hosts but they lack nothing and are impeccably clean with simple wooden furniture and shutters. Bathrooms are smallish but have good-quality towels. The rooms at the back look out over terracotta roofs to the mountains beyond; a few have their own terrace. When leaving you may be tempted to question your bill; can it really be so little?

Rooms: 18 with bath & wc.
Price: D/Tw 3500 Pts inc. VAT.
Breakfast: 300 Pts.
Meals: Lunch/Dinner 1100 Pts (M), 1800 Pts (C).
Closed: Never.

How to get there: From Valencia A7 towards Barcelona; exit for Vinarós. Here N232 to Morella; just before Morella, CS840 to Forcall. Here road to La Mata de Morella, then Mirambel. Under arch and Guimera along on left.

La Torre del Visco

Apartado 15   **Tel:** 978 769015
44580   **Fax:** 978 769016
Valderrobres
Teruel

Management: Piers Dutton and Jemma Markham

Bajo Aragón is one of Spain's best-kept secrets: beautiful, wild, unspoilt by tourism and stacked with natural and man-made treasures. Stay with Piers and Jemma and renew body and spirit in their superbly-renovated medieval farmhouse. Standards of comfort, decoration and food are high, as is their gift for creating a relaxed atmosphere. Their farmland and forests protect the house from modern noise and nuisance in this exceptional walking country; peace is total inside and out — neither telephone nor television to disturb you in your room. After a day of discovery — your hosts will advise you, they have been here for years — settle with one of their 7,000 books in front of a great log fire, delight in their eclectic taste where each piece of furniture, be it antique, modern or rustic, Art Deco or Nouveau, fits with the old tiles, beams and exposed brickwork. Dinner is a feast of own-farm produce, the Visco's *bodega* offers a fine choice of wines, breakfast in the great farmhouse kitchen is renowned. One of the most exceptional hostelries in Spain.

Rooms: 10 with bath & wc + 4 suites.
Price: D/Tw 25000-28000 Pts; Ste 38000 Pts (half-board).
Breakfast: Included.
Meals: Lunch approx. 4000 Pts; dinner included.
Closed: Never.

How to get there: Fom Barcelona A7 south towards Valencia. Exit junction 38 for L'Hospitalet de L'Infant y Móra. Follow signs to Móra la Nova, then Gandesa. There towards Alcañiz, but left in Calaceite to Valderrobres. There left towards Fuentespalda, and after 6km right. Follow track to house.

Map No: 15   **91**

Mas del Pi

44580   **Tel:** 978 769033
Valderrobres
Teruel

Management: Carmen and Ramón Salvans

This is the stuff of which back-to-nature dreams are made. High on a hilltop Mas del Pi is literally at the end of the road — your arrival will be a memory to savour. Ramón and Carmen have worked their 70-hectare farm for 12 years; there are vines, olives and almonds, ducks and chickens and a beautiful big vegetable patch. What better way for them to meet new people and share their love of the place than by setting up a small B&B? And thus an old tradition has been rediscovered: 200 years ago this was a coaching inn. Things here are definitely rustic; hosts and house are utterly unaffected. The Salvans are proud of their simple guestrooms with their tiled floors, old furniture and views across the farm. At breakfast there are home-made jams and cakes and newly-laid eggs. We have fond memories of sharing dinner and easy conversation; nearly everything from meat to veg to wine to liqueur is home-produced. Outside there is the farm to explore and glorious walks, with the Pyrenean sheepdog to accompany you if you want; children love it here. "We would readily stay here again" enthused one reader; "the perfect escape" wrote another. And a pool has just been finished.

Rooms: 6 with bath & wc.
Price: 4500 Pts p.p (half-board).
Breakfast: Included.
Meals: Lunch 1200 Pts; dinner included.
Closed: Never.

How to get there: From Barcelona A7 south to exit 40 for L'Aldea-Tortosa. C235 to Tortosa, then C230 towards Mora la Nova. After 16km left to Valderrobres. Just before village turn right towards 'Ermita de los Santos'. Follow road for 4km then good track for 3km to reach Mas del Pi.

Hotel La Parada del Compte

Antigua Estación del Ferrocarril
44597
Torre del Compte
Teruel

Tel: 97 8769072/73
Fax: 97 8769074
www: www.openclick.com/rusticae

Management: José María Naranjo and Pilar Vilés

The old railway station of Torre del Compte, tucked away in the valley below the village, has recently been given a new lease of life thanks to the dynamism of its young owners. At the very end of the road that cuts down from the village a highly original ochre-and-Bordeaux-coloured hotel awaits you: José and Pilar were convinced that rural tourism and modern design and innovation could be happy bedfellows. Look for designer furniture, a bold use of glass and metal, and state-of-the-art bathrooms and beds rather than rustic-style nostalgia. And it works. Each bedroom's colour and decoration is inspired by a different town in Spain; thus Madrid is about classical elegance, Mérida inspired by Roman motifs, Valencia's whites and blues evoke the Mediterranean. It's hard to choose a favourite but we might go for França because it gets the sun first thing. All fittings and furnishings are top of the range throughout the hotel, from taps to beds to sofas. Relax in a light, airy reading room, dine on innovative and beautifully presented 'contemporary Mediterranean' cuisine then head out (perhaps along the old railway track) to discover the wilderness and wonder of this part of Spain.

Rooms: 7 with bath & wc + 2 suites.
Price: D 15000 Pts; Tw 12000 Pts; Ste 20000 Pts inc. breakfast.
Breakfast: Included.
Meals: Lunch/Dinner 3500 Pts (M). Not available on Mondays.
Closed: 10-31 January.

How to get there: A7 exit for Hospitalet Del Infante/Mora de Ebru. From Mora N420 towards Alcañiz. Just after Calaceite turn left to Torre del Compte.

Map No: 14

Hotel Cardenal Ram

Cuesta Suñer 1
12300
Morella
Castellón

Tel: 964 173085
Fax: 964 173218

Management:
Jaime Peñarroya Carbo

The whole of the town of Morella is a listed *patrimonio artístico nacional* and you'll see why when you first catch sight of this fortress town girt about with its unbroken wall. In one of its grandest mansions you find a hotel as remarkable as the town. Just to one side of the colonnaded main street the proportions and upper storey of arched windows give the Cardenal Ram a Venetian air (when it was built there was a constant cross-cultural exchange between the Genoese and the Eastern Spaniards). Enter through the 15th-century arched doorway beneath the coat of arms of the Ram family and you may well be greeted by Jaime Peñarroya: he's passionate about his hotel and wild horses wouldn't drag him away. A wonderful vaulted stairwell sweeps up to the guestrooms — and what rooms! They are big, with polished parquet floors; bedheads, writing desks and chairs are all of carved wood. Bright bedcovers and rugs add a welcome splash of colour and the bathrooms are superbly appointed. You'll have a special dinner as guests of Jaime: truffles are a speciality and there are delectable home-made puddings. And both food and rooms are amazingly good value. Come and discover the wild beauty of the Maestrazgo: there's a long distance pathway (GR route) which links a series of these hilltop villages. Visit before it gets well known!

Rooms: 17 with bath & wc + 2 suites.
Price: S 4500 Pts ; D/Tw 7500 Pts;
Tr/Ste 9500 Pts.
Breakfast: 800 Pts.
Meals: Lunch/Dinner 1750 Pts (M),
approx. 4500 Pts (C).
Closed: Never.

How to get there: From Valencia A7 towards Barcelona; exit for Vinarós. Here N232 to Morella. Up into old town (if lost ask for Puerta de San Miguel); hotel in main street 200m from cathedral.

"The light is brilliant, the atmosphere is preservative, the colours are vivid, so vivid that sometimes this seems like a painted country as the mauve and purple shadows shift across the hills, as the sun picks out a village here, a crag there, as the clouds scud idly across the candlewick landscape of olives or cork oaks and the red soil at your feet seems to smoulder in the heat."

JAN MORRIS - *Spain*

Eastern Spain

El Fraile Gordo

Apartado 21
03650
Pinoso
Alicante

Tel: 968 432211
Fax: 968 432211

Management: David Bexon

Multi-talented David Bexon — singer, interior designer, upholsterer and actor — has recently moved on to a new career as innkeeper and chef-in-residence of El Fraile Gordo. He needed to draw on more of his Renaissance talents when he set about restoring this old farmhouse. Why *El Fraile Gordo* (the fat Friar)? The house stands where Brothers of the Franciscan order once lived and worked. Hard to imagine what confronted David when you see dining and sitting rooms, kitchen and bedroom; everything feels much older, thanks to the many antiques and old materials that he searched out when nursing the building back to life. But this is more than a simple farmhouse; stained-glass windows, grand piano, statues, and original sculptures have added sophistication to lowly origins. Guestrooms are fresh and welcoming, with beds for big sleeps and glorious wrap-around views. There's a delightful walled garden, a terrace that captures the morning sun, inspired cooking (do buy David's cookery book!) and a host whose hospitality and kindness run far beyond the call of duty. *Specialíssimo.*

Rooms: 4 with bath & wc.
Price: D/Tw 7000-8000 Pts; Tr 'family room' 10000 Pts.
Breakfast: Included.
Meals: Dinner 3000(M). Just snacks on Mondays.
Closed: 2 weeks in January after Epiphany.

How to get there: From Alicante towards Valencia on A7; first exit on N330 for Madrid. Exit to Novelada. In centre left at lights and at top A403 towards Algueña At end of road, left onto C3223 towards Fortuna. After 4km right towards Cañada del Trigo; house in hamlet after 700m.

Map No: 21

Hotel Els Frares

Avenida del País Valencià 20
03811
Quatretondeta
Alicante

Tel: 96 5511234
Fax: 96 5511200
E-mail: elsfrares@logiccontrol.es
www: www.holidaybank.co.uk.elsfrares/

Management: Patricia and Brian Fagg

Brian and Pat left successful careers in the UK to head for the Spanish hills; their Herculean efforts have borne fruit at their village inn and restaurant, 5 years ago a hundred-year-old ruin. But now the attractive pastel frontage of the building, and a constant flow of visitors, are adding life and colour to the village. Just behind the village, the jagged peaks of the Sierra Serella rise to almost 5,000 feet — the hotel takes its name from them. There are rooms with private terraces looking out across surrounding almond groves to those lofty crags. Good mattresses ensure good sleep, fabrics are bright, there are framed photos of the Sierra Serella, and some rooms have their original floor tiles. We thought the cosy dining and sitting rooms just right for the hotel; you'd look forward to returning here after a walk, perhaps under the guidance of Brian who now knows the surrounding mountains better than the locals themselves. At table, choose from a menu that celebrates local dishes and *tapas* yet still finds a place for imaginative veggie alternatives; many ingredients — from olive oil, to fruit, to herbs — are home-grown. Here you have two immensely likeable hosts who have made many Spanish friends.

Rooms: 9 with bath & wc.
Price: D (with terrace) 7500 Pts; Tw 6500 Pts inc. VAT.
Breakfast: Included.
Meals: 1600 Pts (M), 3000 Pts (M-gourmet), 2500-3500 Pts (C).
Closed: 2 weeks in January & 14 June-10 July 1999.

How to get there: From Alicante N340 to Alcoy. Here AP3313 towards Callosa de Ensarria; after Benilloba left to Gorga. Here sharp right along unmarked road for 5km to Quatretondeta (on map spelt Cuatretondeta).

Map No: 22

96

Hotel Vila de Biar

C/San José 2
03410
Biar
Valencia

Tel: 96 5811304/5810055
Fax: 96 5811312
E-mail: hotelbiar@cvt.es

Management: Begoña Miró

This hilltop village is worth a long detour. Its monuments chart the history of the land and people; Moorish tower on top of its rocky pinnacle and below, among streets of lime-washed houses, several surprisingly ornate churches and chapels from the Christian period. Wander its streets for those cameo shots and stay a night at this newly-opened hotel. The façade is all that is left of the nobleman's house. Behind its salmon-coloured frontage you find a hotel for both tourist and business person alike: maybe this explains the muzak in reception and a slightly anodyne feel to bedrooms and dining area. We'd book one of the attic rooms: their wood-clad ceilings give them a cosier feel than those on the floor beneath. From here you can lap up the tranquility of the place: open your window wide to catch birdsong, the sound of church bells and views out across the garden. A large pool among pine and cypress trees could be the place to put a long, hot drive behind you. We were won over by the friendliness of the staff and the slant of the menu towards local Alicante fare. Climb up to the castle for a stunning sunset and do try to be here for the extraordinary festival when the Crescent and the Cross once more do battle and the whole town goes medievally mad!

Rooms: 39 with bath or shower & wc + 2 suites.
Price: S7500-8250 Pts; D/Tw 8800-9900 Pts; Ste 11800-12900 Pts.
Breakfast: 800 Pts.
Meals: Lunch/Dinner 2290 Pts (M).
Closed: Never.

How to get there: From Alicante towards Madrid on A7, exit for Villena then Biar is signposted on the right. Hotel signposted in Biar.

Bodega Los Pinos

Casa Los Pinos
46635
Fontanares
Valencia

Tel: 96 2222090
Fax: 96 2222090
E-mail: pinos @jet.es

Management: Madeleine and Manuel de Olaechea

The province is called Los Alhorines. The word comes from the Moorish period and means corn chamber: the rich agricultural lands have always provided bountiful produce. It seemed the perfect place for Madeleine and Manuel when they came to Spain in search of a house and land where they could farm organically. Just a few years on this is one of a small number of organic vineyards in Spain and a visit here is a must for anyone who enjoys good wine. "The best organic wine in Spain," writes the magazine Vinum. The house has a truly Mediterranean feel: cypress trees suggest Provence, the elegant frontage evokes Tuscany. On the ground floor is the guest lounge with a huge wrap-around settee by the hearth and a collection of hand-painted plates and copper saucepans beneath the beams. Next door is a vaulted dining room and beyond the courtyard with an enormous bay, yuccas and palms. Choose between high-ceilinged guest bedrooms — you cross the corridor to your bath or shower room — and the enormous self-catering apartment. You can swim, play tennis, ride and visit the *bodega*. But do find time for a stroll through the vines with the dogs and do eat in: "I cook very well," says Madeleine matter-of-factly!

Rooms: 3 with bath or shower & wc + 1 apartment.
Price: D/Tw 10000 Pts; Apt 15000 Pts inc. breakfast and VAT.
Breakfast: Included.
Meals: Lunch/Dinner 1500-2000 Pts incl. wine.
Closed: 15 December-15 January.

How to get there: From Alicante towards Madrid on N330. Exit for Fontanares (approx. 70km from Alicante). Los Pinos is 800m before Fontanares. Signposted on the right.

Hostería de Mont Sant

Subida al Castillo s/n
46800
Xátiva (Játiva)
Valencia

Tel: 96 2275081
Fax: 96 2281905
E-mail: montsant@servidex.com
www: www.servidex.com/montsant

Management:
Javier Andrés Cifre

The Arab castle is above and red-roofed city below, mountains and Mediterranean beyond, terraced gardens groaning with orange trees and 700 newly-planted palm trees. There is fascinating archaeology (Iberian and Roman shards, Moorish fortifications, Cistercian monastery walls — the history of Spain in a nutshell) and a Moorish irrigation system that has guaranteed water in all seasons since the 12th century. The mountain streams are channelled, refreshing the air as they go, into a 250,000-litre cistern under the garden. Señor Cifre's old family house has cool, beamed living areas with unexpected nooks, charmingly undecorated guestrooms (just natural materials, old tiles, antique furniture and no pictures "because the windows frame pictures enough") and a see-through kitchen! Pity the exposed cooks but enjoy the delicious food. Enjoy, too, the balconies, terraces and quiet corners. There is a marquee for receptions and a few log cabins are to be built under the pines but it will surely remain as friendly and peaceful as ever.

Rooms: 6 with bath or shower & wc + 5 suites.
Price: S 12000 Pts; D/Tw 15000 Pts; Ste 20000 Pts.
Breakfast: 1200 Pts.
Meals: Lunch/Dinner 3500 Pts (C).
Closed: Never.

How to get there: From Valencia N340 towards Albacete. X(J)átiva exit and here follow signs for 'Castillo de Xátiva'. Signposted.

Map No: 21

La Casa Vieja

Calle Horno 4
46842
Rugat
Valencia

Tel: 96 2814013
Fax: 96 2814013
E-mail: lacasavieja@xpress.es

Management: Maris and Maisie Andres Watson

This most peaceful of hideaways — discovered by Maris and Maisie just two years ago — combines 400 years of old stones with a very contemporary idea of volumes and shapes. There are original arches, columns and capitals (it was probably a nobleman's house), vast twisty beams, ancient floor tiles and a well in the courtyard. In a more recent vein the swimming pool occupies most of the remaining patio space and there are views beyond to the orange grove-clad hillsides. A double-height sitting area faces an immense fireplace where deep sofas hug you as you sip your welcome *fino* before dining, indoors or out. The many antiques have been in Maris' family for as long as she can remember; for example, the 16th-century grandfather clock, Persian rugs, hand-carved mahogany table and the many oil paintings. Bedrooms are equally full of character, the beds firm, the night-time village-quiet; kettles, tea and coffee remind you of home. Maris' cooking follows the seasons; expect market-fresh produce with interesting veggie alternatives but if there's some dish you'd particularly like to try, just ask. And the new restaurant (it has lovely hand-crafted terracotta tiles) is just the place for your feast: expect to rub shoulders with locals as well as with visitors.

Rooms: 6 with bath & wc + 1 suite.
Price: D/Tw 9000-11000 Pts; Ste 15000 Pts inc. VAT.
Breakfast: Included.
Meals: Lunch 2500 Pts; dinner 3500 Pts (M/C).
Closed: 2nd & 3rd week of January & last 3 weeks of September.

How to get there: From Valencia A7 south then exit 60. N332 towards Gandia/Alicante. Exit onto CV60 towards Albaida. Exit for Terrateig/Montechelvo/Ayelo de Rugat/Rugat. Through Montechelvo; Rugat is 2nd village to left, signposted.

Ad Hoc

Boix 4
46003
Valencia
Valencia

Tel: 96 3919140
Fax: 96 3913667
E-mail: adhoc@nexo.net
www: www.sercotel.es

Management: Eva de Roqueta

Valencia is a vibrant city, its old quarter brimming with fine old baroque-fronted mansion houses and its streets buzzing with life until the early hours: come for some of the best bar life in Spain. Ad Hoc is in a brilliant position at the heart of the old quarter in a quiet street and it's by far the best of the town's small hotels. The owner is in the art business and he lavished much care — and many of the paintings from his collection — on the building's restoration. Warmth is what Ad Hoc is about: in the way you are greeted, the choice of colour scheme and the general feel of the place. Wafer-bricking is the décor's leitmotiv: then there are handsome original floors, gilded mirrors, stencilled ceilings and barrel vaulting. The dining room is as intimate as they come with just a dozen tables: only breakfast is served at the moment, but the plan is to serve lunches and dinners (and right next door is one of the city's better restaurants). The bedrooms are as carefully manicured as the rest of the hotel: rugs, writing desk and the same sensitive lighting. Do make sure you visit the cathedral where you can see what Valencians claim to be the the chalice used by Christ at the Last Supper: the Holy Grail!

Rooms: 28 with bath & wc.
Price: S 11900 Pts; D/Tw 16700 Pts.
Breakfast: 850 Pts — Continental.
Meals: soon to be available.
Closed: Never.

How to get there: Situated in historic centre of Valencia. On interior ring road, pass Torres de Serranos, Boix is third on the right.

Map No: 15

Molino Sahajosa

Carretera Calasparra-Cehegin s/n
30420
Valentín
Murcia

Tel: 968 720170
Fax: 968 721290
E-mail: sahajosa@paralelo40.org
www: www.netvision.es/sahajosa

Management: Vicente Lópes

The López family has been here for nearly two hundred years; they were millers and every corner of this place must hold some treasured memory for Vicente. Water is the life-giver and decorative element; the Sahajosa is the fast-flowing stream which powered the mill; it now rushes joyfully past the building, untamed. First floor bedrooms give onto a wide, central corridor where there is a museum dedicated to the building's past. The old grain measures are there, as are esparto mats, threshing platforms, 'Roman' scales which were once so much a part of country life and even the old village cinema projector. Your room will be large, with high ceilings and a Casablanca-style fan, brass bedsteads, a sweep of panelling and with old lamps that remind you of those who once lived here. Downstairs the dining room is large, light and looks out to a large expanse of orange grove (its fruit, freshly squeezed, will be yours at breakfast). Do stay for dinner; Antonia's cooking incorporates the best local dishes and ingredients — and her own preserves. You can swim most of the year and the surrounding hills are easily negotiated on mountain bikes, or you could simply think of that old Andalusian adage: "How wonderful to do nothing... and then rest".

Rooms: 10 with bath or shower & wc + 2 houses.
Price: D/Tw 6000 Pts; House 8000-12000 Pts.
Breakfast: Included.
Meals: Lunch 1700 Pts (M); dinner approx. 2000 Pts.
Closed: Never.

How to get there: From Murcia towards Almería. Exit at km651 post towards Caravaca de la Cruz on C415. Just past Cehegín right towards Calasparra and after approx. 12km right to Valentín.

Map No: 21

Western Spain

Rocamador

Apartado de Correos No. 7
06160
Barcarrota
Badajoz

Tel: 924 489000
Fax: 924 489001
E-mail: mail@rocamador.com
www: www.rocamador.com

Management: Elena Manzano

The monastery of Rocamador, long forgotten amid the wide spaces of Estremadura, has recently had new life breathed into its old, old stones by its remarkable owners, Carlos Tristancho and Lucia Bosé. Lucia is loathe to have it classified as a hotel: it is home and hostelry and much more besides and, as for star ratings, "the stars are up above us here," she quips. The labyrinthine buildings fan out around the cloister and chapel which is now the setting for dinners where music and candlelight may accompany you into the early hours. You may recognise some of your fellow guests: it's that kind of place. Bedrooms are among the most extraordinary and romantic we've come across in Spain: most are vast, so are the bathrooms (some with shower heads four metres up, some with a *chaise longue* next to the bath!). There are hand-painted tiles, enormous beds, enticing views, three-piece suites, rich fabrics, wafer-bricking, vaulted ceilings, open hearths. Each room is quite different from the next. The Rocamador is luxurious, daring and unique and feels a long way away from the world in which we normally live. *Note: the above address is for correspondence. The actual address of the hotel is: Ctra. Nacional Badajoz-Huelva km 41, Almendral.*

Rooms: 23 with bath & wc + 3 suites
Price: S 10000-15000 Pts; D 14000-18000 Pts; Ste 25000 Pts.
Breakfast: 1200 Pts.
Meals: Lunch/Dinner 5500 Pts (Gourmet M), 7000 Pts (C). Closed on Mondays.
Closed: Never.

How to get there: From Madrid take N5 and exit for La Albuera (km382 post). Into village of La Albuera, then towards Jerez de los Caballeros. At km41 post turn right, cross bridge and follow drive to Rocamador.

Map No: 17

103

Hotel Huerta Honda

Avenida López Asne s/n
06300
Zafra
Badajoz

Tel: 924 554100
Fax: 924 552504

Management: Antonio Martínez Buzo

If you travel through Western Spain then do make a detour to visit Zafra; there is a castle with a stunning Renaissance patio, a beautiful arcaded main square and any number of churches to visit. And the Huerta Honda should be your hotel for the night. It is an unmistakably southern-Spanish hotel: geraniums, bougainvillaea and fountains in abundance. The décor is a trifle kitsch in places but it speaks of years of caring from its owner, Antonio Buzo. There is a guest lounge with wicker furniture, open log fires in winter and a superb hotchpotch of ornamentation — balsa parrots, geometric tiles, a mounted deer's head, statue-lamps. Next door are the dining rooms — the atmosphere is intimate, with ochre walls and heavy beams above beautifully laid tables. Huerta Honda is famous for its hams and you might be tempted to splurge here (always worth it when the cook is Basque!) but there is a cheaper menu if you prefer. And the bedrooms are fun, too. With balconies onto the plant-filled patio they have an eclectic mix of original paintings, hand-painted furniture, rugs and wickerwork. And all around you are the unforgettable wide and open landscapes of Estremadura.

Rooms: 40 with bath & wc.
Price: S 7920 Pts; D 9900 Pts.
Breakfast: 1000 Pts.
Meals: Lunch/Dinner 3500 Pts (M), 4500 Pts (C).
Closed: Never.

How to get there: From Mérida south to Zafra. The hotel is in the city centre, near the Palacio de los Duques de Feria.

Map No: 17

Casa Salto de Caballo

La Fontañera
10516
Valencia de Alcántara
Cáceres

Tel: (00 351) 45 964345
Fax: (00 351) 45 964345

Management: Eva Speth

Another one of these amazing spots in Spain where it would be hard to say which is more beautiful: the journey there or the being there. Follow a narrow road across glorious, open, rolling hills to this furthest reach of the province of Cáceres and of Spain too: you are slap bang on its border with Portugal. This was where smugglers would ply their trade, their saddlebags brimming with bread, coffee and garlic. In these days of pan-european markets you now walk straight out from the house (or ride) into Portugal's glorious São Mamede Natutral Park along those same secret pathways — with not a thought for border patrols. Eva and Joaquín were so taken by it all they left their native Germany and restored this elegant village house seeking good, solid comfort rather than gadgets and gimmickry. The old floor tiles are still there and "it is beautifully clean" (wrote an enthusiastic reader) and Eva's vegetarian cuisine is as delicious as it is imaginative (she is a nutritionist and dietician). Generous hosts, generous prices and as far from the madding crowd as you could hope to get. *Note: you're in Spain (just!) but phone/fax number is Portuguese. So phone 00 351 45 964345 from Spain or England.*

Rooms: 3 with bath & wc + 2 sharing bath & wc.
Price: D/Tw 5000 Pts.
Breakfast: Included. Special brunch: 750 Pts.
Meals: Lunch/Dinner 1300 Pts.
Closed: Occasionally during the winter. Please check.

How to get there: From Cáceres N521 towards Portugal. Through Valencia de Alcántara, then right towards San Pedro. After 2km right again for La Fontañera. Last house on left in this village; signposted.

Map No: 17

105

El Vaqueril

Avenida de Alemania 8
10001
Cáceres
Cáceres

Tel: 927 191001/223446 or
608 101710
Fax: 927 191001

Management: Beatriz Vernhes de Ruanu

The big skies and cork-oaked hillsides of Estremadura make it one of Spain's grandest visual feasts. Reached by a tree-lined drive, and at the heart of 320 hectares of cattle ranch, this old farmhouse stands amid carob, olive and palm trees. Its ochre and white frontage gives it a very southern face; the row of crenellations that top its façade look not a bit warlike. The house is classic *cortijo*; things gravitate towards a large central patio — the South's most effective technique for ensuring shade at any time of the day. No two bedrooms are the same; they are big, with domed ceilings and decorated with bright fabrics and the family antiques. There are pretty hand-painted tiles in bathrooms, framed etchings and prints, open hearths. You sense a designer's hand has been involved. Downstairs is a vaulted lounge with a riotous ceramic hearth and a cavernous, beamed dining room; beef comes from the farm, of course. Breakfast is as generous as the evening meal — there may be home-made cake — and, you may, once replete, cycle or walk out into the estate. Cáceres and Mérida are an easy drive. *Note: address above is for correspondence and not that of farm.*

Rooms: 6 with bath & wc + 1 suite.
Price: Tw 8500 Pts; Ste 11000 Pts.
Breakfast: 600 Pts.
Meals: Dinner 3000-4000 Pts (C).
Closed: Never.

How to get there: From Cáceres towards Alcántara on C523. Just before village of Navas del Madroño turn left at sign for El Vaqueril and follow long track (have faith!) to the farmhouse.

Mesón La Cadena

Plaza Mayor 6   **Tel:** 927 321463
10200   **Fax:** 927 323116
Trujillo
Cáceres

Management: Juan V. Mariscal Mayordomo

La Cadena (the Chain) was a privilege granted by Felipe II whereby, like embassy status, those staying here had right of asylum from the *guardía*. The privilege no longer holds but this unpretentious little place remains an excellent inn. It is right on the beautiful arch-rimmed Plaza Mayor; Pizarro, the town´s most famous export, looks sternly down from his horse in one corner. The rooms are all on the second floor and are refreshingly simple: medium-sized with tiled floors, bright locally-woven rugs and twin beds. We would choose a room looking onto the square but from the rooms at the back you can see the mountains. The restaurant specialises in good solid Extremeño cooking; any remaining fried-food fans should try the *Migas Extremeñas*. There are wonderful *chorizo* sausages and other delicious things porky. You can eat outside under the arches while in cooler weather eat in the Cadena's old dining room with its heavy old roof beams and tiled floors. Storks come to land here and just a short drive to the south is the Monfragüe Park where there is bird-watching galore.

Rooms: 8 with bath & wc.
Price: Tw 5500 Pts.
Breakfast: 800 Pts.
Meals: Lunch/Dinner 1500-3000 (M).
Closed: Never.

How to get there: Follow signs for 'Centro Ciudad'. The hotel is on the main square.

Finca Santa Marta

Pago de San Clemente
10200
Trujillo
Cáceres

Tel: 927 319203 or 91 3502217
Fax: 927 319203 or 91 3502217
E-mail: henri@facilnet.es
www: www.fincasantamarta.es

Management: Marta Rodríguez-Gimeno and Henri Elink

Santa Marta is a fine example of an Extremadura *lagar* where the owner lived on the top floor and made oil in the basement. This one has been totally transformed by interior designer Marta Rodríguez-Gimeno and her husband Henri into a very special country inn. In the vaulted olive-pressing area there is now an enormous guest lounge and library; it is cool and elegant with *estera* matting, neo-*mudéjar* ceilings, interesting old furniture and subtle lighting. The rooms are a delight; some have antiques, some have hand-painted Portuguese furniture, no two are alike. Those in the 'other half', Finca Santa Teresa, may be rather more rustic with more locally-produced furniture but the effect is equally appealing. The whole house is a treasure trove of antiques, painting and good taste. Why so many South American bits and pieces? Henri was ambassador to Peru and it was sympathy for that Latin readiness to share that inspired him to open his home to guests. He and Marta do so with grace and charm. Thirty hectares of peace and fabulous birdlife. Bring binoculars.

Rooms: 13 with bath & wc.
Price: D/Tw 9500 Pts.
Breakfast: Included.
Meals: Lunch/Dinner 2900 Pts. Book ahead.
Closed: Never.

How to get there: From Trujillo C324 towards Guadalupe. After 14km Finca is on the right where you see eucalyptus trees with storks' nests (km89 post).

108

Casa Manadero

Calle Manadero 2
10867
Robledillo de Gata
Cáceres

Tel: 927 671118/233142
Fax: 927 671115

Management:
Caridad Hernández

What is so thrilling about Spain is the *space*. There are still vast, untamed parts of its interior. Few of us would have heard of Robledillo yet it lies at the heart of the Sierra de Gata and you can combine a visit to Salamanca and/or Portugal. The village architecture makes extensive use of the local dark slate; it is christened 'black architecture' by the locals but it is not in the least bit gloomy. Robledillo is one of the region's prettiest villages and was recently declared a 'protected nucleus' by the regional government. It is surrounded by forests of oaks, olive groves and vineyards; no less a man than Cervantes was fond of the local wines. In the restoration of this tall building wood and slate have been combined to create a really warm, welcoming hostelry. The tiny restaurant has heavy old beams, delicate lighting and excellent regional fare; "100% natural products" says Caridad who has pillaged the family recipe books for your benefit. Apartments vary in size and layout following the dictates of the original building; they all are centrally-heated, have views, fully-equipped kitchens, the same warm-and-rustic style of décor. This is another of our addresses which is actively helping to preserve regional differences; bravo!

Rooms: 5 studios and apartments sleeping up to 4.
Price: Studio Apt (for 2) 6420 Pts; 1 bed Apt (for 2) 8560 Pts; 2 bed Apt (for 4) 10700 Pts inc. VAT.
Breakfast: Included.
Meals: Lunch/Dinner on request 1500 Pts (M).
Closed: Never.

How to get there: From Salamanca N620 towards Portugal. In Ciudad Rodrigo C526 south over the pass of Puerto de los Perales. Approx. 8km from top of pass left via Villasbuenas de G./Cadalso/Descargamaría to Robledillo.

Map No: 10

La Posada de Amonaría

Calle de la Luz 7	**Tel:** 927 459446 or
10680	608 702070
Malpartida de Plasencia	**Fax:** 927 459446
Cáceres	

Management: Juan Tomé and Cruz Ibarra

The wide open spaces of Estremadura form one of Spain's most memorable landscapes; come if only to see the birdlife (great bustards, black vultures, long-tailed jays and red kites to mention but a few). Juan Tomé's feelings for the land and its people run deep; Armonaria was his grandmother. The house is tucked away at the top of Malpartida: its meticulously restored chocolate-and-coffee coloured frontage is easy to recognise. Its walls bear the gentle finish which only countless layers of lime-wash can give, whilst beams have been treated with beeswax and floors with linseed oil in a conscious effort to use only natural finishes. The dining room is staggered on different levels with a handsome slate floor and an enormous hearth; it gives onto the house's original *bodega* where wine was once pressed: the huge amphorae are still in place and you could have a glass of wine and a *tapa* before heading out for dinner in the village. Return to light, airy, antique-filled bedrooms which retain the original geometric floor tiles from the last century. Juan and his wife Cruz have endeavoured to recreate the spirit of the age when the house was built; perhaps it is affection for that era which explains their love of ballroom dancing: you can learn to tango or foxtrot with them. If you prefer stargazing (skies are often astonishingly clear), Juan also gives astronomy classes!

Rooms: 6 with bath & wc.
Price: D/Tw 8200 Pts; Ste 10200 Pts.
Breakfast: 550 Pts.
Meals: None available.
Closed: Occasionally in July. Please check.

How to get there: N630 south to Plasencia and then onto C511 to Malpartida de Plasencia. The Posada is at the top of the village, next to the church: follow signs for 'Ayuntamiento'.

110

Finca La Casería

10613
Navaconcejo
Cáceres

Tel: 927 173141
Fax: 927 173141

Management: David Pink & María Cruz Barona

This lovely old farmhouse has been the home of Señora Barona Hernández' family for some 200 years. A monastery stood here originally and we all know that few have as keen a nose for a good site as the religious orders. The granite building stands in cherry groves to one side of the lovely Jerte valley; be here at the end of March when blossom fills the valley or early summer when you can help to harvest the fruit! There are plums and figs and sheep and cows; between directing his guests to the extraordinary natural history or archaeological spots of the area David Pink works hard at his smallholding. This is much more home than hotel (there is an abundance of dogs). The huge sitting room has books and an open hearth. Of the six guestrooms, mostly furnished with old pieces, the *cuarto de arriba* has a screen and lovely wrought-iron bed. Dinner or lunch is a relaxed occasion with home-made puddings to complement regional dishes. Many come to walk but you can fish for tench or swim in the nearby reservoir... or relax.

Rooms: 4 with own bath & wc; 2 sharing shower/bath & wc + 1 cottage.
Price: D/Tw 6000-8000 Pts; D/Tw (sharing bath & wc) 6000-8000 Pts inc. VAT. Cottage 10000 Pts. *Minimum stay 2 nights.*
Breakfast: Included; cottage — self-catering.
Meals: Dinner 2000 Pts (M); book ahead.
Closed: August.

How to get there: From Madrid E90 to Navalmoral de la Mata; C511 to Plasencia; N110 towards Avila. At km378.5 post (about 27km from Plasencia), right at small sign for La Casería (3km before Navaconcejo).

Map No: 10

111

Finca El Carpintero

Ctra. N-110 km 360.5
10611
Tornavacas
Cáceres

Tel: 927 177089 or
608 328110
Fax: 927 177089

Management: Ana Zapatero and Javier González Navarro

The Jerté valley is best seen in springtime when the blossom of thousands and thousands of cherry trees turns the green sides of the valley a stunning hue of pink. Anna and Javier, an engaging young couple from Madrid, have turned these old farm buildings into a country B&B with a difference: a happy marriage of things rustic with turn-of-the-millenium creature comforts. Enter the building through a large terracotta tiled dining room, bar in one corner and 'Bigotines' the dog in another, then climb up to the enormous guest lounge of the photo: its most striking features are a wall of solid rock, huge granite hearth, high beamed ceiling and an enormous window that lets the light come streaming in. Here and in the bedrooms, too, are cut flowers, paintings and carefully matched prints. Ana's artistic flair is on show throughout the house and the hand-painted furniture, the bows on the sash windows, the drapes behind the beds are all her work. A first-class breakfast is included and you should give lunch or dinner a go: Ana and Javier's cuisine follows the seasons and they buy local produce whenever possible. Both speak excellent English and take real pleasure in their newly adopted profession.

Rooms: 4 with bath & wc.
Price: D/Tw 8000 Pts inc.VAT.
Breakfast: Included.
Meals: Lunch 1500-2000 Pts (C).
Closed: Never.

How to get there: From Madrid NVI then N110 to Ávila and then on towards Plasencia. Pass village of Tornavacas, house signposted on right after 1.5km.

Map No: 11

Antigua Casa del Heno

Finca Valdepimienta
10460
Losar de la Vera
Cáceres

Tel: 927 198077 or 689 879006
Fax: 927 198077
www: www.pglocal.com/cáceres(jarandilla)

Management: Graciela Rosso and Javier Tejero Vivo

The Casa del Heno stands superbly isolated on the southern side of the Gredos mountain range hidden away at the end of a the 4km track that follows the river out from Losar. The 150-year-old building has been sympathetically restored by its young owners; there is much exposed stone, beams and use of cork in the decoration. Solar panels provide a large part of the house's hot water. The eight guestrooms are just right; no television, good beds and views across the surrounding farm. Just 150 yards away is a crystalline river and beyond are the mountains begging to be walked. Horse-riding can be arranged, too. The whole of the valley is at its best in spring when the many thousands of cherry trees come into blossom but you'll need to book well ahead if wanting a room during this annual spectacle. And ornithologists can expect a feast: azure-winged magpies, kites, vultures and much more besides. The owners welcome their guests as friends; there is good home cooking and barbecued meat is a speciality.

Rooms: 8 with bath & wc.
Price: D/Tw 7300 Pts.
Breakfast: 500 Pts.
Meals: Lunch/Dinner 2500 Pts (M), 2500-3000 Pts (C).
Closed: Christmas & for a month after Epiphany.

How to get there: From Madrid N V to Navalmoral de la Mata. Right onto cc 904 towards Jarandilla to to Losar de la Vera. Here to 'piscina de Vadilla' then mountain track 3.5km to hotel.

Map No: 10

113

Hotel Rector

Rector Esperabé 10
Apartado 399
37008 Salamanca
Salamanca

Tel: 923 218482
Fax: 923 214008

Management: D. Eduardo Ferrán Riba

Just a two-minute walk from the cathedral and hard by the Roman bridge this *palacete* or town mansion is one of the smartest small hotels we have come across and it was a joy to discover it in a city of such interest and ineffable loveliness. Much love and lolly have been lavished here — and the family antiques, too —, to the delight of their guests. Wood is used to good effect throughout; there are sparkling parquet floors, stained-glass windows and old tapestries downstairs, inlaid bedside tables, writing desks and hand-crafted bedheads in mahogany and olive wood in the bedrooms. Wide corridors lead to large plush rooms which have all the fittings of a five-star hotel. You might not need the telephone in the bathroom or the fax points, but you will certainly appreciate the double glazing, air conditioning and deep armchairs. In bathrooms the same luxurious note is held — marble, double basins, thick towels. Most of the rooms are salmon-pink and blue and they all have framed prints on the walls. Leave your car in the hotel car park and go walking: perhaps into the wonderful Cas Lis, right next door, a museum dedicated to Spanish Art Deco.

Rooms: 14 with bath & wc.
Price: S 12500 Pts; D/Tw 17000 Pts;
Larger D/Tw 22000 Pts.
Breakfast: 1000 Pts.
Meals: None available.
Closed: Never.

How to get there: From Madrid, follow signs round Salamanca towards Zamora. Do not take 1st bridge, pass Roman bridge on right, take next bridge & turn right back along river. Hotel is on right after about 400m: next to Casa Lis museum.

"The stern landscapes of the tablelands are like sounding boards for the spirit. Here, though your voice often falls upon dry soil, or is whisked away by the bitter wind, ideas seem to echo and expand, visions form in the great distances, and Man, all alone in the emptiness, seems only the agent of some much greater Power . . . no wonder the Spaniards have built upon this plateau some of the grandest of all human artifacts".

JAN MORRIS - *Spain*

Central Spain –
The Meseta

Hostal El Milano Real

Calle Toleo s/n
05634
Hoyos del Espino
Ávila

Tel: 920 349108
Fax: 920 349156

Management: Francisco Sánchez and Teresa Dorn

If you insist on an historic building when sleeping out — Milano Real is not for you. But if you pass this small modern hotel by you miss a very special experience. With the Gredos range all about, the hotel feels rather like a Swiss chalet; this feeling is heightened by the carved wood of the balconies and the cosy atmosphere within. Up at the top, beneath the rafters, is a huge attic lounge and, down a floor, a second reading lounge. But the festivities really get under way in the dining room. The food brings people all the way from Madrid; Basque/French influenced, and with some fine regional dishes, the restaurant wins a mention in all the famous guide books, Michelin included. Francisco ('Paco') knows his wine; he has a selection of 135 of his favourites to choose from and alongside each wine lists year, *bodega*, D.O. — then gives each and every one his personal score out of ten! And when you wend your way to your room more treats are in store: decorated by Madrid's best, the fabrics, polished wooden floors, antique prints and views set the rooms solidly in the special bracket. Food and rooms are incredible value; worth a VERY long detour and the Gredos are another of Spain's better-kept secrets.

Rooms: 13 with bath & wc + 1 suite.
Price: S 7500 Pts; D/Tw 8500 Pts; Ste 11500 Pts.
Breakfast: 650-1400 Pts.
Meals: Lunch/Dinner 3500 Pts (M), approx. 4500 Pts (C). Restaurant closed on Tuesdays.
Closed: 10-30 November.

How to get there: From Avila N110 towards Bejar/Plasencia. After 6km take N502 left towards Arena de San Pedro and after 45km right on C500 to Hoyos del Espino: hotel to right.

115

Map No: 10

Hostal Don Diego

Calle Marqués de Canales y Chozas 5
05001
Ávila
Ávila

Tel: 920 255475/254549
Fax: 920 254549

Management: Miguel Angel Verguera

This sparkling little hostal, directly opposite the Parador and within the old city walls, is definitely a family affair. It is modest and unpretentious, offering you a clean room, a comfortable bed and a smile as you arrive. The smallish rooms are on three floors, each one named after one of the owner Miguel's children. His fourth child, Diego, gives the hostal its name. The bedrooms combine pine furniture with modern brass bedsteads; there are good bedcovers and plenty of blankets in winter. All the fittings are modern; half the rooms have baths, the others small shower rooms. Light sleepers would probably prefer a room at the back of the hostal. It is all unmistakably Spanish with more than a hint of kitsch. Although the hostal has no breakfast facilities the Parador opposite serves breakfast in a setting somewhat grander but less friendly than the hostal's. Or take a five-minute stroll up to one of the cafés in the Plaza to breakfast amid the hubbub of this lovely old town.

Rooms: 13 with shower or bath & wc.
Price: S 3000-3500 Pts; Tw 4800-5800 Pts; D 5000-6000 Pts.
Breakfast: None available; Parador open opposite.
Meals: None available.
Closed: Never.

How to get there: Entering Ávila by Puerta del Carmen, follow signs to Parador Nacional. Hostal is opposite Parador.

La Posada del Balneario

Camino del Balneario s/n
09145
Valdelateja
Burgos

Tel: 947 150220
Fax: 947 150271
E-mail: rusticae@edigital.es
www: www.openclick.com/rusticae

Management:
José Ramón Ríos Ramos

The original spa hotel at Valdelateja first opened its doors in 1872, when the well-heeled would ride up from Burgos or down from Santander to take the waters. But spas ceased to be fashionable; then came the war and, by the beginning of the decade, the site lay abandoned. But after the Dark Ages, the Renaissance! — total rehabilitation of the two original buildings has produced one of Spain's loveliest small hotels. The setting is wild and wonderful; look out to woods of holm and evergreen oak that cling to the sides of the canyon cut by the river Rudrón. The building is rather 'Swiss-chalet', with wooden balconies, galleries and ornately carved eaves; inside wood is again the primary element, whether in darkened beam or polished parquet floor. The lantern-ceiling of the lounge — the former ballroom — is a real beauty. No two guestrooms are the same; some have antique bedsteads of wrought-iron, other beds are of padded fabric; they have wonderful walnut floors and all have big bathrooms with full-length baths. The dining rooms looks out to the river, and the views are a wonderful accompaniment to the home-cooking. The staff are young, bright and friendly.

Rooms: 22 with bath & wc.
Price: D/Tw 9500-10500 Pts; Ste 16500 Pts inc. breakfast.
Breakfast: Included.
Meals: Lunch/Dinner 1850 Pts (M), 3000-4000 Pts (C).
Closed: 12 January-12 February.

How to get there: From Burgos N623 towards Santander. Through San Felices, and just before Valdelateja turn right to Balneario; signposted.

Mesón del Cid

Plaza Santa María 8
09003
Burgos
Burgos

Tel: 947 208715
Fax: 947 269460

Management: José Luis Alzaga

Few are the cathedrals to match that of Burgos and if you come to see this marvel of the Spanish Gothic stay at Mesón del Cid; from the rooms at the front you can almost reach out and touch the buttresses, pinnacles and grimacing gargoyles. The building once housed one of the first printing presses in Spain, established by an acolyte of Gutemberg more than 500 years ago, and the hotel takes its name from an illuminated manuscript of *Mío Cid* displayed at reception. This fine old townhouse is quite naturally considered THE place to stay in Burgos. We liked the bedrooms; they are carpeted (right for winter), many have old wrought-iron bedsteads, all have prints, tables, plants and decent bathrooms. The suites are grander still; one has period furnishings, bronze taps and even an old-fashioned 'phone. If we were invited to choose a room it would be No. 302. Good things await you in the timbered restaurant where the setting is perfect for trying the traditional thick stews and roast meats that are so typical of this part of Spain.

Rooms: 44 with bath & wc + 3 suites.
Price: D/Tw 16000 Pts; Ste 19500 Pts.
Breakfast: 1000 Pts.
Meals: Lunch/Dinner approx. 4000 Pts (M), 5000 Pts (C).
Closed: Never.

How to get there: In old town directly opposite main entrance to cathedral on Plaza de Santa María. Car park next door.

Map No: 4

118

Hotel Arlanza

Calle Mayor 11
09346
Covarrubias
Burgos

Tel: 947 406441
Fax: 947 406359
E-mail: arlanza@ctv.es
www: www.ctv.es/users/arlanza

Management: Mercedes de Miguel Briones

Covarrubias is a charming old town, well off the tourist-beaten track and a must if you love places where tradition still counts. The heart of the old town is a colonnaded square — the Arlanza is on one side of it. Mercedes and Juan José, two of the friendliest and most charming hoteliers you will meet anywhere, have created a hotel to match the charm and intimacy of the town. You enter under the colonnade through an arched doorway. Inside, there are lovely terracotta floors, ceramic tiles from Talavera on the walls, old chandeliers, original beams and lintels. Downstairs it is rather dark as little light enters through the small original windows. By contrast, the bedrooms that give onto the square (see photo) are lighter. All the rooms are reached by an impressive staircase; they are large, with tiled floors, old lamps and rustic furniture. There is good regional fare in the restaurant and maybe a chance to talk with the owners; they visit the U.K. every year, know its farthest corners and speak the language, too.

Rooms: 40 with bath & wc inc. 2 suites.
Price: S 5800 Pts; D/Tw 9650 Pts; Ste 10250 Pts inc. VAT.
Breakfast: 700 Pts.
Meals: Lunch/Dinner 2100 Pts (M), 3000 Pts (C).
Closed: 1 December-1 March.

How to get there: From Burgos N1 towards Madrid. In Lerma left on C110 towards Salas de los Infantes. Hotel in Covarrubias on Plaza Mayor.

Map No: 4

Hotel Tres Coronas de Silos

Plaza Mayor 6
09610
Santo Domingo de Silos
Burgos

Tel: 947 390047
Fax: 947 390065

Management:
Emeterio Martín García

Right on the main square of Santo Domingo, Tres Coronas used to be referred to simply as *la casa grande* by local folk. It is indeed a solid old building of elegant proportions and well suited to its latter-day role of hotel — it was once a chemist's. Once you have entered under the original coat of arms you see that much remains of its mid-18th-century origins. Throughout the building there are terracotta floors, heavy Castilian furniture and massive beams. Exposed stone alternates with plaster to give every bedroom an authentically 'country' feel. They are medium sized, have all the extras, but what we liked most were the tiled floors and the views onto the square. No 9 (beneath the coat of arms) has its own balcony; perhaps the place to practise your crowd-stopping speeches. The restaurant is very popular, especially at weekends; it won its colours many years back and continues to win praise for its roast meats from a wood-fired oven. Breakfast, however, is a rather paltry offering.

Rooms: 15 with bath & wc + 1 grander with balcony, bath & wc.
Price: S 6500-6800 Pts; D/Tw 10000-10500 Pts; Balcony room 10500-10900 Pts.
Breakfast: 975 Pts.
Meals: Lunch/Dinner 3000-3500 Pts (C).
Closed: Never.

How to get there: From Burgos N1 towards Madrid then N234 towards Soria. Right in Hacinas on BU903 to Santo Domingo de Silos. On right in centre of village.

Hotel Santo Domingo de Silos

Calle Santo Domingo 14   **Tel:** 947 390053
09610   **Fax:** 947 390052
Santo Domingo de Silos   **E-mail:** sdomingo@stnet.es
Burgos

Management: Eleutorio del Alamo Castrillo

The highlight of a stay in Santo Domingo de Silos is the Gregorian chant in the monastery chapel; you can hear it every day of the year and it is well worth a detour as you travel north or south. You may consider overnighting at this simple little family hotel. Its real *raison d'être* is its busy dining room; at weekends visitors come from far and near to eat roast lunch or dinner prepared by Eleuterio in a wood-fired oven. His portions of lamb, goat and pork are worthy of a medieval banquet — and the prices are almost medieval too. As far as the bedrooms go we'd recommend asking for one in the newly built extension (*"una habitación en la parte nueva"*). These are bigger than the old rooms and come with modern pine furniture and largish bathrooms. A friendly, unpretentious place where you come for the food, the value and the Gregorian chant. Sometimes used by tour groups in season.

Rooms: 35 with bath & wc.
Price: S 3500 Pts; D/Tw 4900-6000 Pts; 'Special' D/Tw 7500 Pts.
Breakfast: 425 Pts.
Meals: Lunch/Dinner 1200 Pts (M), approx. 3000 Pts (C).
Closed: Never.

How to get there: From Burgos N1 towards Madrid then N234 towards Soria.
Left in Hacinas on BU903 to Santo Domingo de Silos. On right as you go through village.

     Map No: 4

El Molino de Alcuneza

Carretera de Alboreca km 0.5
19264
Alcuneza
Guadalajara

Tel: 949 391501
Fax: 949 347004
E-mail: molinoal@teleline1

Management: Juan and Toñi Moreno

It's a family affair: El Molino de Alcuneza is handsome proof of just what can be achieved when love and energy are present in great measure. Little remained of the 400-year-old mill buildings when Juan and Toñi fell in love with this swathe of delicious greenery whose rushing millrace promised soothing respite from the baking summers of Spain's vast Meseta. Originally it was to be a weekend bolt-hole for the family but then the idea of a country hotel was mooted and Juan was hooked. Everything that could be saved from the old mill's installations was carefully restored. Every last detail of the rooms has been carefully mused upon: pine floors beneath darker beam above, rich fabrics, repro taps, trunks and cupboards that have long formed a part of the Moreno's collective memory, and, throughout the building, framed, pressed flowers by an aunt. Our favourite rooms are 3 or 4 (numbers too in pressed flowers!) but all are delightful. Guests each have a separate table; at dinner Toñi might serve up partridge with chick peas, trout baked in Albariño wine, duck à l'orange or cèpe mushrooms). Breakfast is a hearty affair and a picnic hamper can be arranged at lunch time. Arrive as an appreciated guest; leave as a friend of this delightful family.

Rooms: 11 with bath or shower & wc.
Price: S 8000 Pts; D/Tw 10000-12000 Pts.
Breakfast: 850 Pts.
Meals: Dinner 2900 Pts (M).
Closed: Sundays.

How to get there: From Sigüenza follow signs for Medinacelli. The Molino is well signposted just before you reach Alboreca on the righthand side.

Hotel Los Tilos

Extrarradio s/n
16870
Beteta
Cuenca

Tel: 969 318097/98
Fax: 969 318299

Management: Pedro Fernández Guillamon

Beteta is a small village 4,000 feet up in the spectacular limestone mountains that lie to the north of Cuenca, an area of lakes and gorges, a walker's dream. On the outskirts of the village, with long views across the valley, Los Tilos is a wonderful place to base oneself for exploring the area (one English walking company has done just that). The building is unexciting, a rather monolithic structure from the 70s. But the kind, caring manners of the owners dispel any doubts. In the enormous tiled dining room, screens help to dissipate a slightly stark feel as does the fireplace at one end. You eat well here; roasts are the speciality: particularly venison and lamb. There is locally farmed trout, too. The bedrooms have the same sober feel as the rest of the hotel but we rather liked them for that. They are large with wooden beds and writing desks, good cotton bedcovers and curtains, terracotta floors and views from their French windows. The peacefulness of the setting gives them an almost monastic air. Riding, walking and caving close by.

Rooms: 24 with bath & wc.
Price: Tw 6000 Pts; D 7000 Pts.
Breakfast: 500 Pts.
Meals: Lunch/Dinner 1700 Pts (M), 3000 Pts (C).
Closed: 24-25 December.

How to get there: From Madrid N111-E901 to Tarancón. Left on N400 towards Cuenca. 5km before Cuenca left on N320 towards Guadalajara. Just after Villar de Domingo right on CU904, then CU902 and CU202 to Beteta.

Posada de San José

Calle Julián Romero 4
16001
Cuenca
Cuenca

Tel: 969 211300
Fax: 969 230365
E-mail: psanjose@arrakis.es
www: www.arrakis.es/~psanjose

Management:
Antonio & Jennifer Cortinas

Cuenca is unique, a town that astonishes, delights and engraves itself on the memory. Sitting on the rim of the town's unforgettable gorge, the Posada de San José is an inn to match the town. A sculpted portal beckons you to enter but gives little away. For this is a labyrinthine house and only from inside do you realise that it is multi-levelled. Staircases lead up and down, twisting and turning... the perfect antidote to the mass-produced hotels that we so dislike. Every room is different, some small, some large, some with balconies, some without; most have bathrooms, a few share. Nearly all have old furniture, perhaps a canopied bed or a little terrace. We would all ask for one that looks out to the gorge but all of them, view or no view, are lovely and are witness to Antonio and Jennifer's decorative flair; they know that a vase of fresh flowers is a match for ANY number of satellite channels. In their welcoming little restaurant, with that heart-stopping view and a good meal to come, few could fail to feel content with their lot!

Rooms: 22 with bath or shower & wc.
Price: S 4100-4700 Pts; D/Tw 8200-9100 Pts; Tr 11100-14600 Pts.
Breakfast: 550 Pts.
Meals: Snacks (good tapas!) always available except Mondays.
Closed: Never.

How to get there: From Madrid N111-E901 to Tarancón. Left here on N400 to Cuenca. Follow signs to Casco Antiguo. Hostal is just 50m from main entrance to Cathedral. Best to park in Plaza Mayor by cathedral.

Hotel Leonor de Aquitania

San Pedro 60   **Tel:** 969 231000 or
16001   669 231000
Cuenca   **Fax:** 969 231004
Cuenca

Management: Francisco de Borja García

A grand 18th-century townhouse is now home to Cuenca's smartest small hotel. Its position could hardly be more magnificent — a perch right at the edge of the deep gorge, next to the church of San Pedro and a few hundred yards from the main square and cathedral. The well-known Spanish interior designer Gerardo Rueda has decorated the hotel, cleverly weaving innovation in and out of tradition. You see this immediately as you enter: first the heavy old wooden door, then a heavy modern glass door. In reception and bar, furniture that is unmistakably 90s goes well with terracotta floors and *estera* matting. In the dining room and bar, the lighting is subtle, diffuse and there are old tapestries and photographs — a lovely spot to dine. The rooms are equally enticing, with hand-painted tiles, wooden beds, matching fabrics on bedcovers and curtains and exposed beams (rafters on the top floor). Some have a terrace, many a balcony; the view has to be seen to be believed. And the suite is one of the most enchanting in Spain.

Rooms: 48 with bath & wc + 1 suite.
Price: S 8500 Pts; D/Tw 9500 Pts; Ste 15000 Pts.
Breakfast: 900 Pts.
Meals: Lunch/Dinner 2300 Pts. Closed Tuesdays.
Closed: Never.

How to get there: From Madrid N111-E901 to Tarancón. Left on N400 to Cuenca. Follow signs to Casco Antiguo. Cross Plaza Mayor: signposted (up Calle San Pedro. Hotel on right after 200m).

Casa Palacio Conde de Garcinaro

Calle Juan Carlos I, 19
16500
Huete
Cuenca

Tel: 969 372150 or
91 5323307
Fax: 91 5327378

Management: Conchi and Ramiro Fernández. Owner: Antonio Reneses Sanz

Antonio Reneses spent his childhood just along the street from this imposing baroque mansion house; you wonder if he dreamed then that one day he would give the building back its lost dignity by its complete restoration. He has been helped with this formidable challenge by his wife Encarna, an artist and antique restorer by profession; every last corner of the palace shows an eye for detail, a feel for what is right. This is every inch a noble Castilian residence: fine portal of dressed sandstone, coat of arms above, grilled windows and beyond an enormous studded door leading through to the colonnaded courtyard. Climb a wide walnut staircase to the first floor; off to one side the old chapel is now home to a vast lounge decked out in rich burgundy colours. If it feels too imposing there is a second less formal lounge. Bedrooms are vast, high-ceilinged and in wonderful pastel colours. Old prints, window seats, cushions, easy chairs and hand-painted furniture; it's all surprisingly sumptuous given Garcinaro's more than modest prices. Breakfast in the old kitchen on bright chequered table cloths then head off to discover the delights of this wild and untouristy part of Castille.

Rooms: 6 with bath & wc + 3 suites.
Price: D/Tw 7000-8000 Pts; Ste 10200 Pts.
Breakfast: 500 pts.
Meals: None available.
Closed: Never.

How to get there: From Madrid towards Valencia on the N3. Exit for Tarancón, follow signs for Cuenca/Carascosa, then CM310 to Huete. The palace is in village centre next to Santo Domingo church.

Palacio de la Serna

Calle Cervantes 18
13432
Ballasteros de Calatrava
Ciudad Real

Tel: 926 842208/842180
Fax: 926 842224

Management: Eugenio S. Bermejo

In the wide landscapes of Castilla-La Mancha the divide between vision and reality seems to blur — not just for hapless Quijotes lancing windmills. In a forgotten village of the province of Ciudad Real, this neo-classical palace may have you wondering if the sun hasn't got to you! Its unexpected opulence will remind you of a time when mining made many a fortune in the area. It was all abandoned to the Meseta, until designer Eugenio Bermejo saw in Serna a perfect outlet for his creative impulse. Two and a half years later nearly every corner of the Palace is embellished with his sculptures, paintings and eclectic taste in interior design. Each guestroom is different, all are huge fun, with colour schemes to match paintings — or sometimes vice versa. Post-modern to the core. There are red roses in the gardens, music is ever-present — from Nyman to Bach — as are intriguing *objets* at every turn. Dinners are by torchlight; you might expect a Knight of the Calatrava Order to wander in. Fun, whacky, and *very* different; well worth a detour as you drive north or south.

Rooms: 18 with bath & wc + 10 suites.
Price: D/Tw 15500 Pts; Ste 20000 Pts.
Breakfast: 2000 Pts.
Meals: Lunch/Dinner 3500 Pts (M).
Closed: 15-30 January.

How to get there: From Ciudad Real round town towards Puertollano then left on CR512 towards Aldea del Rey then right to Ballasteros de Calatrava. Palace to left, signposted.

Casa Labranza Cerromolino

La Alameda
13370
Calzada de Calatrava
Ciudad Real

Tel: 926 693087 or
689 406923
Fax: 926 879169

Management: Mercedes Barato

If, in your mind's eye, Spain is a land of crumbling castles, of open Meseta, of parched earth and of ochres and reds, then do come here. Cerromolino is a perfect place to get to grips with Cervante's Spain and that of the knight-monks of the Calatrava order. You arrive by way of a long sweep of track that leads you up to the cluster of farm buildings, huddled in the lee of the Sierra Morena. The farm house is from the beginning of the century, built by Aragonese shepherds who had abandoned 'transhumance' for a more sedentary existence. The lounge and dining room are low and welcoming and authentically 'country': framed cross-stitch, a collection of old irons, photos of grandparents and great-aunts, herbs and flowers hung to dry from the low beams, earthenware water pitchers, a marvellous old radio — and no T.V. Lots of the ingredients at mealtimes come from the farm and people come from miles away for the roast kid, venison and partridge; the gourmet menu is worth the extra. Bedrooms lead off a central, cobbled courtyard and have the same warm, family feel to them as the rest of the house: framed embroidery, antique beds and dressers, prints of El Quijote. (The owners have a second house in the village, La Encomienda. We liked it but would certainly prefer a room at Cerromolino).
Great country for cycling.

Rooms: 6 with bath or shower & wc.
Price: D/Tw 6500 Pts.
Breakfast: From 400 Pts.
Meals: Lunch/Dinner 1500 Pts (M) or 3200 Pts (gourmet M) incl. wine.
Closed: 24-25 December.

How to get there: From Madrid south on NIV. Exit for Santa Cruz de Mudela, then on to Calzada de Calatrava. Here towards Castillo de Calatrava then left to La Alameda. Here follow signs to Cerromolinos.

Map No: 19

128

Guts Muths

Calle Matanza s/n
Barrio de Abajo
24732 Santiago Millas
León

Tel: 987 691123
Fax: 987 691123

Management: Sjoerd Hers and Mari Paz Martínez

Santiago Millas and other villages in the area of La Maragatería drew their wealth from a virtual monopoly on the transport of merchandise by horse and cart throughout Spain. The coming of the railways put an end to all that. What remains of this past glory are some grand old village houses. Guts Muths is as fine an example as any. It is a big, solid house; you enter under an imposing arch to find yourself in a lovely flower and palm-filled courtyard. It is utterly peaceful. Hats off to owners Sjoerd and Mari Paz for the easy-going intimate atmosphere they have created. Part of this is decorative flair — simple but comfortable rooms where wood predominates; exposed stonework, dried and fresh flowers and a dining room with ceramic tiles, dark roof beams and an old bread oven: a proper backdrop for the honest regional dishes. Sjoerd is a no-nonsense sort: he loves to talk and will regale you with local history and folklore. Or he might take you out to explore the nearby gorges on foot, or mountain bike... or even attached to a climbing rope. Further rooms are on the way for summer '99.

Rooms: 8 with bath & wc.
Price: D/Tw 9000 Pts.
Breakfast: Included.
Meals: Lunch 2000-2500 Pts (M).
Closed: Never.

How to get there: From Astorga LE133 towards Destriana. After about 10km, left towards Santiago Millas, Barrio de Abajo — signposted.

Map No: 3

La Posada del Marqués

Plaza Mayor 4
24270
Carrizo de la Ribera
León

Tel: 987 357171
Fax: 987 358101
E-mail: marques@aletur.es
www: www.aletur.

Management: Carlos Velásquez-Duro

There are few places to stay in Spain quite as special as this old pilgrim's hospital, originally part of the Santa María monastery next door. Pass through the fine old portal and discover first a pebbled cloister and beyond a lovely mature garden with gurgling brook and big old trees. It reminded us slightly of an English rectory with its high walls and rambling roses. Carlos Velázquez (his family have owned the posada for generations) and his wife graciously greet their guests before showing them to the superb bedrooms. They are set round a gallery on the first floor and are all decorated with family heirlooms — lovely Portuguese (canopied) beds, original paintings, old lamps and dressers. One has a terrace over the cloisters; all are quite enchanting. The sitting and games rooms downstairs are similarly furnished. Heavy old wooden doors, carved chests and tables and comfy armchairs and sofa in front of the hearth. There is a snooker table. Although the posada only serves breakfast, meals can be organised at a restaurant close by. Kind and erudite hosts and the most beguiling of settings.

Rooms: 11 with bath & wc.
Price: D/Tw 9500 Pts inc. VAT.
Breakfast: Included.
Meals: Special prices at restaurant nearby.
Dinner 1600 Pts (M), 2700 Pts (C).
Closed: Christmas & New Year.

How to get there: From León N120 towards Astorga. After 18km, right on LE442 to Villanueva de Carrizo. Cross river into Carrizo de la Ribera and ask for Plaza Mayor.

La Posada Regia

Calle General Mola 9-11   **Tel:** 987 213173
24003   **Fax:** 987 213031
León
León

Management: Marcos Vidal Suárez

The stained-glass windows of Leon's gothic cathedral are reason enough to come to this lively provincial capital — and there is much more to do besides should you make the detour. By far the best place to stay here is the Posada Regia, plum in the centre of the old town and one of the brightest stars in the firmament of newly opened hotels in Spain. The building first saw the light in 1370 and it in turn had incorporated older elements: in the dining room you'll see parts of the old Roman wall. The warm ochre and beamed reception strikes a welcoming note as you arrive and the staff could not be more friendly. A fine old staircase leads up to the bedrooms which are some of the cosiest and most coquettish that you'll come across: soothing pastel shades, bright kilims, shining planked floors, old writing desks, brightly painted radiators, and really snazzy bathrooms which have all the extras like bath robes, embroidered towels, hairdryers etc. The hotel's restaurant, La Bodega Regia, which predates the hotel by 50 years and was founded by Marcos' grandfather, is one of Leon's most renowned.

Rooms: 20 with bath & wc.
Price: S 8500 Pts; D/Tw 12500 Pts.
Breakfast: Included.
Meals: 2000 Pts (M) or approx. 3500 Pts (C). Closed on Sundays.
Closed: Never.

How to get there: Hotel is in town centre approx. 150 m from the Cathedral. Best to park in Parking Ordoñez Segundo and then less than 100m to walk to hotel.

La Posada de los Vientos

Calle Encerradero 2   **Tel:** 91 8699195
28755   **Fax:** 91 8699195
La Acebeda
Madrid

Management: Jorge Mangrané

The small village of La Acebeda stands proudly 4,000 feet up on the flank of the Sierra del Norte. It is within easy driving distance of Madrid but is still an utterly peaceful rural spot, a perfect retreat for city dwellers in need of fresh mountain air and greenery. It would be hard to choose a favourite room here; throughout the house the emphasis is on the 'natural', the homespun, the handmade. There are old chests and beds, wood floors, bright Indian bedcovers, good cotton sheets. Each room is named after a different wind (*viento*) — whence the name of the inn. The dining and sitting rooms couldn't be better; here again the base elements are stone, antiques and beams. You have the choice of about half a dozen main courses at dinner — the focus is whatever is in season, local if possible, and much of it organic. Even if you choose just to break your journey do find time to walk out into the surrounding forest; you might meet local folk out collecting wild mushrooms, asparagus or blackberries. Note: only open Friday, Saturday nights and *dias festivos...*

Rooms: 9 with bath & wc.
Price: D/Tw 8000 Pts.
Breakfast: Included.
Meals: Lunch/Dinner 2500-3000 Pts (C).
Closed: Mon-Thur and Christmas & Twelfth Night.

How to get there: From Madrid N1 north; at km83 take exit to La Acebeda. In village first right to La Posada.

El Parador de la Puebla

Plaza de Carlos Ruiz 2
28190
Puebla de la Sierra
Madrid

Tel: 91 8697256 or
607 283023
Fax: 91 8697256

Management: Lola Herrero

Madrid may only be a couple of hour's drive yet it feels as if it were a million miles away. Puebla is a tiny village of fewer than 100 inhabitants high up in the Sierra that shelters Madrid's northern flank. Until recently there was nowhere to stay here; now, thanks to the efforts of a local co-operative venture and some of that Brussels money, there is a cosy little inn. Right on the main square of the village (though you might not recognise it as such), it stands on the spot where the priest's house once stood. It is very new but its stone walls, wooden porch and tiled roof allow it to sit harmoniously among the older village buildings. You enter through a lively little bar; above it are the dining and sitting rooms whose tiled floors and wooden ceilings are immediately appealing. The food is very good value, the emphasis always on what's local and in season. Try the *patatas resecas*; if you're lucky there will be freshly-picked mushrooms; "we enjoyed a vast plate of lamb chops" enthused a reader. The attic rooms are smallish, low-ceilinged and with skylight windows; at night the silence is all-enveloping, a joy to those aching from the din of Madrid. Lola is a vivacious and warm-hearted host: do make the journey.

Rooms: 5 with bath & wc.
Price: S 3500 Pts; D/Tw 7000 Pts inc. VAT.
Breakfast: Included.
Meals: Lunch/Dinner 1800 Pts (M), 3000 Pts (C).
Closed: Never.

How to get there: From Madrid N1 north. After Buitrago de Lozoya right on M127, through Gandullas to Pradena then M130 to Puebla de la Sierra.

Map No: 12

La Casa del Puente Colgante

Carretera a Uceda km 3   **Tel:** 91 8430595
28189   **Fax:** 91 8430595
Torremocha de Jarama   **www:** www.sierranorte.com/puentecolgante/
Madrid

Management: Silvia Leal

In this beautiful wooded spot on the banks of the Jarama river it's hard to believe that Madrid is less than an hour away. The name means 'the house of the suspension bridge': walk across to discover the waterfall, a river pool for bathing and to find a lovely grassy knoll from where you can observe the exceptional bird life — you should see kingfishers and herons if you're patient. The peace and beauty of the setting continue on into the house: you'll find no TV here but classical music, the sound of the river drifting up, even the song of the nightingale in the springtime. Silvia loves the spot dearly, knows its every tree and shrub and hopes that her guests leave with something of the tranquility of her home deep within them. The bedrooms are medium-sized with no fussy extras but are sparkling clean with the very best mattresses for comfort and eiderdowns for warmth. Silvia's lunches and dinners should be mentioned: organic fruit and veg, local cheeses, the best cuts of meat. Do try her delicious apple cake: its recollection works the same magic for me as madeleine cake did for Proust! You can easily bus it in and out of Madrid from here to avoid yet more driving (and expensive parking). *This is a non-smoking household.*

Rooms: 5 with bath or shower & wc.
Price: D 7500 Pts; Tw 5500-6500 Pts; Ste 7500 Pts.
Breakfast: Included.
Meals: Lunch/Dinner Mon-Fri 1700 Pts (M), Sat/Sun 3000-4000 Pts (C).
Closed: 23 – 25 December.

How to get there: From Madrid N1 towards Bugos and exit at km50 post for Torrelaguna. Here towards Patones de Arriba then right to Torremocha. Through village following signs 'farmacia/turismo rural', continue for 3km until you see 'casa rural' sign on left by 2 white columns.

Map No: 12   **134**

Hostal Andorra

Gran Vía 33, 7º
28013
Madrid
Madrid

Tel: 91 5323116/5316603
Fax: 91 5217931
E-mail: andorra@arrakis.es

Management: Angel Bertero

The Gran Vía is the broad avenue that cuts a path through the heart of the Spanish capital, a place where night or day the street is humming with life (high and low, depending which way you head). Why not stay here, up above it all, at the Hostal Andorra, run by the same family for more than 40 years? It is 100% Spanish, the furnishing nearly all modern but as you sit in its rounded dining room (see photo) or lie looking up at the high ceilings you still get some feel for how the building must have looked when completed in 1922. Rooms here are remarkably inexpensive considering the address and they have gadgets and trimmings that you might not expect to find in a hostal. Simply furnished and impeccably clean but with an occasionally dated look, about half have balconies that look out over the street; there are quiet (though smaller) interior rooms, too. Ceiling fans are a sensible alternative to noisy air conditioning. The Andorra is central, cheap, and adequate: step out onto the Gran Vía and get to grips with Madrid. Almost all the sights are within walking distance.

Rooms: 20 with bath & wc.
Price: S 4600 Pts; D/Tw 6500 Pts; Tr 8000 Pts inc. VAT.
Breakfast: 350 Pts
Meals: None available.
Closed: Never.

How to get there: On Gran Vía very close to 'Palacio de la Música' cinema. For the car: Parking Tudescos in Calle Tudescos.

La Residencia de El Viso.

Calle Nervión 8   **Tel:** 91 5640370
28002   **Fax:** 91 5641965
Madrid   **E-mail:** elviso@estanciases.es
Madrid

Management: Maria Colmenero Herrero

El Viso is one of Madrid's most chic areas, a quiet and leafy suburb but still surprisingly close to the centre. Until two years ago La Residencia was just one more of these smart private homes. Now, thanks to the enormous efforts of its young and engaging owner, María Colmenero, this interesting 30s-style edifice is a luxurious port of call if you want to escape the noise and fumes of the city centre. Beyond a cheery façade and swing-glass doors is a marbled reception area where you are greeted by piped music, friendly staff and probably Maria herself. The long glass French windows bring in the light (there's no high-rise in this area to rob you of the sun) and draw your gaze out to a walled garden-cum-patio where you eat when it's warm, perhaps under the shade of the magnolia. The rooms are elegant affairs: some have carpet, others parquet and all colours and fabrics have been well matched by Maria. All but two of the rooms look out across the garden and they all have the fittings of a luxury hotel: air-conditioning is a plus at the height of summer, sinks sparkle, floors shine, standards are high. In colder weather dine in the conservatory-style restaurant: good Spanish food and wines, and good value, too.

Rooms: 12 with bath & wc.
Price: S 9000 Pts; D/Tw 16000 Pts.
Breakfast: 750 Pts.
Meals: Lunch 2050 Pts (M) incl. wine; dinner 4000 Pts (C).
Closed: Never.

How to get there: From Puerta de Alcalá take Calle Serrano to Plaza de la Republica Argentina, straight across here and then first right into Nervión. Metro: Plaza Republica Argentina.

Hostal La Macarena

Cava de San Miguel s/n
28005
Madrid
Madrid

Tel: 91 3659221 or
       91 3666111
Fax: 91 3642757

Management:
Ricardo González Longres

If you're looking for somewhere cheap, cheerful, central and fun to stay when in Madrid then consider La Macarena. Calle Cuchillerios is just to the west of Madrid's beautiful Plaza Mayor with its plexus of narrow shopping streets leading off on all sides: some of the shops seem from another age. In spite of its elegant turn-of-the-century façade — just recently repainted in the wedding-cake cream and white of our photo — expect nothing too grand. The rooms are medium-sized with small bathrooms; some of the best we saw were 214 and 204 (both with balconies) and 303 gets the thumbs up because of its extra size. Décor is clean and simple: plastic moquette on the floor, perhaps a rather sugary print or two. The stucco mouldings and wrought-iron work at the windows remind you that this was once an aristocrat's home. Communal space is limited to just one small TV room, but you're in Madrid and there are a zillion things to do night or day. There's no breakfast room either but right below La Macarena is a lively bar where you can breakfast with the locals: watch them hit the anis and brandy first thing. Note: hostal reception is on the first floor.

Rooms: 25 with bath or shower & wc.
Price: D/Tw 6900 Pts; Tr 8900 Pts.
Breakfast: None available.
Meals: None available.
Closed: Never.

How to get there: Into centre of Madrid to Cibeles and on to Puerta del Sol. Park just past here in Parking Plaza Mayor. La Macarena is just off the Plaza M. on its west side.

Hotel Santo Domingo

Plaza de Santo Domingo 13	**Tel:** 91 5479800
28013	**Fax:** 91 5475995
Madrid	**E-mail:** sdomingo@stnet.es
Madrid	**www:** www.stnet.es/hotel santo domingo

Management: Antonio Muñez Tirado

Hotel Santo Domingo is larger than the other hotels in this book but we include it because, in spite of its size, it manages to retain an intimate and friendly atmosphere (many of the capital's chain hotels could heed the good example). It is right at the hub of old Madrid; close to the Opera, the Plaza Mayor and a stone's throw from the shops of the Gran Vía. Stepping in off the street it feels welcoming: reception and lounge are decorated in a warm, sandy tone; there are oil paintings and comfy sofas to flop into and a sparkling marble floor. And — take it in good faith — the décor in each of the 120 bedrooms is different. They contain all the extras you might expect given Santo Domingo's four-star status: mini-bars and T.V.s, bathrobes and stacks of toiletries, safety boxes, writing sets — hydro-massage baths in the 'superior' rooms. And the will to be as human as possible in the bedrooms holds true in the restaurant, too: even though you are in a large hotel there is "good home cooking" on the menu, in the words of Ana Hernández, the hotels ever-friendly manageress. Santo Domingo has long since won its laurels — but still aspires to be first past the post.

Rooms: 120 with bath & wc.
Price: Weekdays D/Tw 24625-27950 Pts; S 16925-21550 Pts. Weekends D/Tw 18950-1995 Pts; S 10475-14250 Pts.
Breakfast: 1450 Pts (buffet).
Meals: Lunch/Dinner weekdays 3950 Pts (M), weekends 2950 Pts (M).
Closed: Never.

How to get there: Head along Gran Vía away from Cibeles; pass Plaza de Callao then left into Calle San Bernardo to Plaza de Santo Domingo. Hotel on right. Pull up outside & porter will garage car.

Casa de las Campanas

34830
Salinas de Pisuerga
Palencia

Tel: 979 120118
Fax: 979 870450

Management: Isabel and Pedro Pablo López Duque

In a forgotten village in the little-known province of Palencia, Casa de las Campanas is one of a growing breed of rural hostelries which boldly dares to mix old and new, design and tradition. We think the mix has worked a treat here. Isabel and Pedro are sophisticated hosts yet receive guests with old-fashioned graciousness. The timbered dining room is well lit, with terracotta floors and — as throughout the house — carefully-chosen fabrics. Meals are generously priced; Isabel cooks well and in local tradition. An impressive modern spiral staircase winds up to the bedrooms. These, like the downstairs rooms, make good use of wood, traditional tiles and fabric. There are two sitting rooms on the upper floors; with sloping ceilings, good chairs and piles of books, they seemed just the spot to settle down to read up on Palencia's many Romanesque churches. The most intriguing feature of the house is its unusual shutters (*celosías* or 'jealousies'), inspired by an old design that allowed young maidens to observe their heart's desire yet remain unseen.

Rooms: 6 with bath & wc.
Price: D/Tw 5500 Pts inc. VAT.
Breakfast: 300 Pts.
Meals: Lunch/Dinner 1400 Pts.
Closed: Never.

How to get there: From Santander A67 towards Oviedo, then N611 south to Aguilar de Campoo. There towards Aguilar to Cervera de Pisuerga on P212. On right as you pass through village of Salinas de Pisuerga.

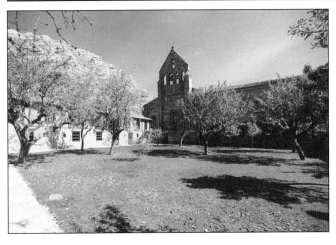

Posada de Santa Maria la Real

Avenida de Cervera s/n   **Tel:** 979 122000/122522
34800   **Fax:** 979 125680
Aguilar de Campoo
Palencia

Management: Elena Martín and Montserrat Becerrel

In a wing of the beautiful Cistercian monastery of Santa María la Real, eighteen guestrooms have recently been created by the local *escuela taller* - a scheme that teaches traditional skills to the young unemployed. While they have been utterly faithful to local building and restoration techniques, they have dared to let '90s design play a part too; the result is an exceptional hostelry. On arrival you are struck by its peacefulness — monks have always had an 'ear' for this, after all. A pebbled patio leads you up to the entrance; the façade of timbers, stone, wafer-bricking and eaves is beguiling. Once inside the building the marriage of old and new surprises and seduces. Every last corner has been carefully restored — and considered. There are pebbled and parquet floors, designer chairs and lamps snug beside hearth and beam. The design of the guestrooms follows the dictates of a tall building so they are small and 'mezzanine' and attractively decorated; we would willingly sacrifice space for charm and, let's not forget, we ARE in a monastery!

Rooms: 18 with bath & wc.
Price: S 5200-6400 Pts; D/Tw 7200-8400 Pts inc. VAT and breakfast.
Breakfast: Included — buffet.
Meals: Dinner 1500 Pts (M).
Closed: 23-25 December.

How to get there: From Santander A67 towards Oviedo, then N611 south to Aguilar de Campoo. Posada is on the left of the road that leads from Aguilar to Cervera de Pisuerga.

El Convento

Calle Convento s/n
34492
Santa María de Mave
Palencia

Tel: 979 123611/123095
Fax: 979 125492
E-mail: mave@eh-enterprises.com
www: www.eh-enterprises.com

Management: José Antonio Moral

You'll leave traffic, city, and pollution far behind when you come and stay at El Convento. The Moral family laboured long and hard to nurse this vine-clad 18th-century Benedictine monastery back to its former good health; thanks to their efforts it is now classified as a national monument! On weekdays the cloister, gardens and the old stone walls remain as conducive to meditation as in the days when the brothers were here; at weekends the place's popularity means there will be many more vistors. Some of the bedrooms (they are all named after other priories) are in what were once the monks' cells; they are medium-sized, simply furnished in dark-wooded *castellano* style and most give onto the cloister. The two suites have curtained four-poster beds and swish corner tubs. You dine in the former chapter house where, once again, heavy antique furniture, low beams and terracotta tiling feel in keeping with the building's past. Cuisine is traditional Castilian, thick chick-pea or bean soups and many lamb-based dishes. Roast from a wood-fired oven is the house speciality, as are freshly-picked strawberries when in season. Don't miss the chapel; it dates from 1208 and is considered one of the finest examples of Palencia's many Romanesque edifces.

Rooms: 23 with bath & wc + 2 suites.
Price: S 5500 Pts; D/Tw 7500 Pts; Ste 9500-11500 Pts.
Breakfast: 600 Pts.
Meals: Lunch/Dinner 1500 Pts (M), approx. 3500-4000 Pts (C).
Closed: Christmas Eve.

How to get there: From Aguilar de Campo south towards Palencia on N611. After 5km, in Olleros de Pisuerga, left at sign for Santa María de Mave.

Casón de la Pinilla

La Rinconada s/n
40592
Cerezo de Arriba
Segovia

Tel: 921 557201
Fax: 921 557209

Management: Juncal Chaves & Carmen de Frías

The few lucky *Madrileños* who are in on the secret flee the madness and pollution of the capital and drive over the mountains to be guests of Carmen Frías and Juncal Chaves. Both left successful careers to create a backdrop for their *tertulias* in the peaceful outskirts of Cereza de Arriba. They wanted it to be more than simply a good stopover for the skiers who head for the lifts at nearby Pinilla (snow normally from the end of December to March); they like to treat you as friends. Conversation before and after dinner is as important as silence at bedtime. The building is long and modern, with books, comfy chairs and a dining room of human proportions to provide timeless warmth. The guestrooms are large and simply furnished. But our memories are more of food. Expect only the best cuts of meat, fresh veg and home-made puddings. When dining on the terrace as the mountains turn purple you'll be glad you stopped an hour short of the metropolis as guests of these two charming ladies. Medieval villages and spectacular mountain gorges are close by. *Cookery courses also take place regularly — write or phone for details.*

Rooms: 9 with bath & wc.
Price: S 5800 Pts; D/Tw 9100 Pts.
Breakfast: 800 Pts.
Meals: Lunch/Dinner 1850 Pts (M), 2500 Pts (C).
Closed: Never.

How to get there: From Madrid N1 towards Burgos. Leave at exit 104 onto N110 towards Soria. After 1.5km, right

towards Cerezo de Arriba. Hotel on right shortly before entering village.

La Posada de Sigueruelo

Calle Badén 40
40590
Sigueruelo
Segovia

Tel: 921 508135
Fax: 921 508135
E-mail: siguerelo@c.alarcos

Management: Concha Alarcos Rodriges

Concha Alarcos left her former life as a social worker to open this tiny country inn. You approach her house down the old cobbled streets in the tiniest of hamlets; the outside of the building gives little away but inside her 120-year-old farmhouse is all homely comfort and warmth and there is Concha with the gentlest of welcomes. After a day's walking, enjoy the comfy chairs, dark beams and open fire in the sitting room. A delicious smell of wood pervades the house; when renovating they only used 100% natural oils to treat rafters, doors and lintels. There are dried flowers, antique trunks, old wooden harvesting tools and six attractive bedrooms. One of them has Art Deco beds; others have ones of wrought-iron. Concha has gradually gathered in the furnishings from the Madrid antique markets. The rooms have showers (a water-saving measure). Dinner is good regional cooking and there are vegetarian dishes if requested. Riding in the hills or canoeing (with the owner's son and equipment) in the unforgettable Duratón gorge can be arranged and there is free use of mountain bikes. Our readers have enthusiastically agreed that Siguerelo is a special place to stay .

Rooms: 6 with shower & wc.
Price: Half-board only: D/Tw 14000 Pts.
Breakfast: Included.
Meals: Lunch 1500-3000 Pts (M). Dinner included.
Closed: Never.

How to get there: From Madrid N1 towards Burgos. At km99 post, exit towards Santo Tomé del Puerto onto N110 towards Segovia. After 3km left to Sigueruelo. Ask for Posada in village.

Posada del Acebo

Calle de la Iglesia 7
40165
Prádena
Segovia

Tel: 921 507260
Fax: 921 507260
E-mail: posada.acebo@mx4.redestb.es
www: www.personal12.redestb.es/posada.ac

Management:
José Luis Martín Aranguez

Prádena sits snug in the lee of the Guadarrama sierra, the high chain of mountains that lie just to the north of Madrid. The scale of some of its older houses comes as a surprise: their stones are from an age when the villagers were granted royal privileges for the magnificence of their livestock whose meat and wool were famous throughout the land. Enter the house by way of the diminutive dining room-cum-lounge; the delicious smell of seasoned timber, a fire in the wood-stove, photos of shepherds and their flocks and heavy bench seating feel truly *gemütlich*. Young and brimming with pride, Ramón will show you upstairs by way of a fine old bannistered staircase — his great grandparents once lived here. The bedrooms are real gems; a lovely mix of the old (washstands, wrought iron bedsteads, lamps, prints) and the new (central heating, properly firm mattresses, double glazing to keep the fearsome Meseta winters at bay). There are mountain walks on your doorstep (route notes provided), the mighty Duraton river gorges to explore (on foot or by canoe), a feast of Romanesque churches and then dinner to look forward to back in that cosy dining room. We think both rooms and food are worth every last peseta. If you're missing them, don't be afraid to ask for eggs and bacon first thing!

Rooms: 8 with bath or shower & wc.
Price: S 5000 Pts; D/Tw 8000 Pts.
Breakfast: Included.
Meals: Light lunch 700 Pts; dinner 1500 Pts inc. wine (M).
Closed: Never.

How to get there: From Madrid take N1 towards Burgos. At km99 post exit towards Santo Tomé del Puerto and follow N110 towards Segovia. After 12km right into Prádena. House just off main square.

La Tejera de Fausto

Carretera la Salceda a Sepúlveda Km 7
40173
Requijada
Segovia

Tel: 921 127087 or
    619 240355
Fax: 91 5641520
E-mail: armero@nauta.es
www: www.arroba.es/tejera

Management: Jaime Armero

The two old stone buildings of the Tejera del Fausto stand gloriously alone more than a mile from the nearest village by the banks of the Cega river. It is no coincidence that the roofs are terracotta: tiles (*tejas*) used to be made here. Close by are the Guadarrama mountains, sentinels guarding Madrid and the Meseta; the setting is as Castilian as you could hope to find. The decoration is in perfect keeping; rooms have simple and attractive rustic furniture, central heating in winter, good bathrooms and neither telephone nor television to distract you from the views. There are books and local information in the lounge. The restaurant — a series of small rooms with blazing fires in the colder months — is pure Castile again; specialities are roast lamb, suckling pig and game dishes (often wild boar). Jaime is a gregarious and entertaining host; he loves communicating his knowledge of the area. Next door is a Romanesque chapel built with foundation stones from a Roman villa and you can walk out from your inn on the old transhumance routes that criss-cross the region.

Rooms: 7 with bath & wc + 1 suite.
Price: D/Tw 10000 Pts; Ste 16000 Pts inc. VAT.
Breakfast: 800 Pts.
Meals: Lunch/Dinner 3000-4000 Pts (C). Weekends only.
Closed: Never.

How to get there: From Segovia, N110 towards Soria to La Salceda. There, left towards Pedraza. Hotel on left after Torre Val de San Pedro.

El Zaguán

Plaza de España 16
40370
Turégano
Segovia

Tel: 921 501165/501156
Fax: 921 501156
E-mail: zaguan@ctv.es
www: www.ctv.es/users/zaguan

Management: Mario García

Turégano often gets forgotten as people flock by en route for nearby Pedraza. But this village is every bit as attractive. It has a wonderful porticoed main square and an enormous castle dominating the skyline: Ferdinand the Catholic rested here between Crusades to oust the Infidel. On the main square, El Zaguán is every inch the grand Castilian house: casement windows, dressed stone and its own stables, grain store and *bodega*. The warmest, quietest and cosiest of hostelries awaits you. Downstairs is the bar (lively at weekends) and dining room: pine beams, wafer-bricks and terracotta flooring, with beautifully laid tables and sensitive lighting. There's a wood-fired oven where roasts are prepared: beef and lamb as well as (the ubiquitous) suckling pig. Here, in a lovely upstairs sitting room and in the bedrooms, you could be stepping into the pages of an interior design magazine. Underfloor heating through the building is a real boon during the Castilian winter. The sitting room has comfy sofas, a wood-burner and a view out to the castle and you sleep in style and comfort: much care has been taken so that no two rooms are the same and they are some of the most handsome we've seen. A special small hotel with the hard-working and thoroughly likeable Mario at the reins.

Rooms: 12 with bath & wc + 3 suites.
Price: S 4200-6000 Pts; D/Tw 7000-10000 Pts; Ste 10500-15000 Pts.
Breakfast: 700 Pts.
Meals: Lunch/Dinner 1500 Pts (M), approx. 2750 Pts (C).
Closed: Never.

How to get there: From Segovia take N601 towards Valladolid. After 7km right for Turégano/Cantalejo. Hotel in main square of the village.

Hostal de Buen Amor

Eras 7
40170
Sotosalbos
Segovia

Tel: 921 403020
Fax: 921 403022

Management: Victor L. Soste and Dora P. Villamide

When Madrid folk tire of the capital they often head over the mountains to the green and fertile valleys of Segovia: tradition demands that a roast lunch or dinner should complete the excursion. Dora and Victor's restaurant has long been famous, while their delightful small hotel, yards away, recently opened its heavy old doors to their many friends. Their niece, a designer, took charge of nursing the hamlet's finest old house back to good health: her creation is warm and intimate, an almost perfect blend of comfort and authenticity. The house is memorably silent: when sipping your aperitif you'll hear just the grandfather clock or perhaps distant church bells; the blaze from the centrally suspended chimney is visible from all sides. Dora, a self-confessed antique shop addict, has waived a magic wand over the bedrooms: here you'll find old writing tables, cheery fabrics, superb mattresses and wooden beams. And those English engravings? Dora and Victor have both lived in England and speak English brilliantly. In this delicious hostelry of 'Good Loving' you are pampered in every way: under-floor heating to keep you warm when temperatures plummet in the wintertime and a breakfast that will send you contentedly on your way.

Rooms: 11 with bath & wc + 1 suite.
Price: Tw 8500 Pts; D 10500-12000 Pts; Ste 15000 Pts.
Breakfast: 500 Pts.
Meals: Lunch/Dinner (in restaurant next door) 3500-4000 Pts (C).
Closed: Never.

How to get there: From Madrid N6 towards La Coruña. After passing through tunnel, right towards Segovia. Here N110 towards Soria. Hamlet of Sotosalbos is on left after 18km.

Map No: 12

Hotel Los Linajes

Dr. Velasco 9   **Tel:** 921 460475
40003   **Fax:** 921 460479
Segovia
Segovia

Management: Miguel Borreguero Rubio

Just a stone's throw from Segovia's Plaza Mayor and wondrous cathedral, Los Linajes is cheek-to-jowl with the old city wall; the land drops away steeply here so the building is 'stepped' to give the maximum number of rooms with a view across the green valley of the river Eresma. Miguel Borreguero officiates in reception: this amiable gentleman is deeply committed to Los Linajes and not a year passes by when he isn't involved in some new project to improve the hotel. Parts of the building, true, feel a little dated but a thorough revamp is under way. The oldest part of the building is 17th century: its portal of dressed sandstone leads to the beamed reception area where there's heavy Castilian-style furniture and oil paintings. What makes the rooms special are their views across the river valley: the best have terraces too, where you can breakfast if the weather's right. You're only really aware this is a 50+ room hotel in the dining room and bar. The food is classically Castilian-Spanish; if you prefer a cosier venue for dinner there are plenty of restaurants very close. A huge plus is the hotel's large underground car park.

Rooms: 53 with bath & wc.
Price: S 7000-8250 Pts ; D/Tw 9900-11900 Pts; Tr 11900-14000 Pts.
Breakfast: 850 Pts.
Meals: Lunch/Dinner 2700 Pts.
Closed: Never.

How to get there: As you arrive in Segovia from Madrid follow signs for Zona Oriental/Acueducto. By the Roman aqueduct follow signs for El Alcázar and then signs for hotel.

Hotel Infanta Isabel

Calle Isabel La Católica 1   **Tel:** 921 461300
40001   **Fax:** 921 462217
Segovia
Segovia

Management: Dr. Enrique Cañada Cardo

Segovia's cathedral is one of the great sights of Castile, especially when glimpsed for the first time as you approach from Madrid. Where better to stay than on the main square beside the great Gothic masterpiece in a room reaching out to the pinnacles, flying buttresses and gargoyles? The hotel is a fine old 19th-century townhouse and the decoration is in keeping — carved mirrors, elegant armchairs, a lovely staircase leading up and up — with a liberal dash of more modern furnishing. Each room has a different (pastel) colour scheme; headboards are hand-painted; there are carefully chosen rugs on the parquet floors with curtains to match, chandeliers — all slightly wedding-cakey but very welcoming and fairly priced given the level of comfort. We enjoyed having a room giving onto the square; the double glazing means you get a good night's sleep to go with the view. In the morning you can wander down to a small breakfast room or treat yourself to breakfast in bed. Come to Segovia for the cathedral, the aqueduct and this charming hotel.

Rooms: 27 with bath & wc + 3 suites.
Price: S 7750 Pts; D/Tw 12100 Pts; Ste 13350 Pts.
Breakfast: 900 Pts (buffet).
Meals: None available.
Closed: Never.

How to get there: In Segovia, follow signs for Cathedral and Plaza Mayor. Hotel in main square.

149   **Map No:** 12

Hostal del Cardenal

Paseo de Recaredo 24
45004
Toledo
Toledo

Tel: 925 224900
Fax: 925 222991
E-mail: cardenal@macom.es
www: www.cardenal.macom.es

Management: Luis González

Bartolomé Cossio wrote of Toledo that "it is the city which offers the most complete and characteristic evidence of what was genuinely Spanish soil and civilisation". Quintessentially Spanish it is and it is tempting to stay at the Cardenal; like Cossio's city it seems to have absorbed the richest elements of Moorish and Christian Spain. It was built as a mansion house by the Archbishop of Toledo, Cardenal Lorenzana, in the 13th century. The gardens are unforgettable — fountains and ponds and geraniums and climbing plants set against the rich ochres of the brick. Within there are patios, screens, arches and columns. There are lounges with oil paintings and *mudéjar* brickwork. A peaceful mantle lies softly over it all; you hear the tock-tock of the grandfather clock. Wide *estera*-matted corridors and a domed staircase lead up to the rooms; they have latticed cupboards, tiled floors, sensitive lighting and heavy wooden furniture. You can choose between several small dining rooms to feast on roast lamb, suckling pig or stewed partridge. Vintage stuff.

Rooms: 25 with bath & wc + 2 suites.
Price: S 5650-7550 Pts; D/Tw 9150-12150 Pts; Ste 12000-16550 Pts.
Breakfast: 875 Pts.
Meals: Lunch/Dinner 2675 Pts(M), 4000-5000 Pts (C).
Closed: Never.

How to get there: From Madrid N401 to Toledo. As you arrive at old town walls and Puerta de la Bisagra turn right; hotel 25m on left beside ramparts.

Hostal Descalzos

Calle de los Descalzos 30
45002
Toledo
Toledo

Tel: 925 222888
Fax: 925 222888
E-mail: h-descalzos@jet.es
www: www.fedeto.es/h-descalzos

Management: Julio Luis García

Hostal Descalzos is certainly different from some of our grander hotels but having spent two happy nights here we feel that it, too, is 'special' enough to be included — providing you get that room with a view. For it sits high up by the old city wall, just yards from El Greco's house. There is nothing fancy; the fittings are modern and the combination of pine furniture and satiny curtains will win no prizes for (conventional) good taste. But the view from those special rooms — especially at night when the old bridge down below is illuminated — is what we will remember. When you book choose one of the doubles at the front (like 31, 32, 41 or 42). The singles we saw were very small. The family who run the hostal are quiet, unassuming folk. They serve you breakfast in a tiny downstairs room; there is a photo-menu with 13 different breakfasts(!) and a cheap but adequate lunch and dinner are available in the recently opened cafeteria/restaurant. At the foot of the hostal is a pretty walled garden with a fountain and flowers, a place to sit out and watch the sun set over the Meseta after a day exploring the city.

Rooms: 14 with bath & wc; 2 sharing bath & wc.
Price: S 2500-3700 Pts; D/Tw 5900-5600 Pts; D/Tw 'Special' with view 6000-6500 Pts.
Breakfast: 300 Pts.
Meals: Lunch/Dinner 1000 Pts (M).
Closed: Never.

How to get there: From Madrid N401 to Toledo, then follow signs to old town. At town walls (Puerta de la Bisagra) right; continue with wall on left until you see signs for Casa del Greco to left; hostal signposted off to right in front of Hotel Pintor El Greco.

151

Hotel Pintor El Greco

Calle Alamillos del Tránsito 13
45002
Toledo
Toledo

Tel: 925 214250
Fax: 925 215819
E-mail: elgreco@estanciases.es

Management: Mariano Sánchez Torregrosa

At the heart of Toledo's old Jewish quarter, just yards from the El Greco house and synagogue museum, this small hotel, which was once a bakery, has had much praise heaped upon it — and rightly so. Restoration was completed less than ten years ago and both façade and patio have been handsomely returned to their former glory. Although the main building is 17th-century, parts of the 'Pintor' were already standing when Toledo was the capital of the Moorish kingdom; there is even an escape tunnel, built when the Inquisition was at work. The interior is cool, quiet, plush; there is mainly modern furniture, lots of paintings and handicrafts by local artists, tiled floors and plants. The rooms are on three floors around the patio; some have balconies looking out to the front. There are armchairs, thick Zamora blankets and more paintings; the colours are warm and the beds have very good mattresses. At breakfast there is fresh fruit juice, cheese and cold sausage as well as fresh bread — alas, no longer baked in situ.

Rooms: 33 with bath & wc.
Price: S 10960 Pts; D/Tw 13700 Pts.
Breakfast: 800 Pts (buffet).
Meals: None available.
Closed: Never.

How to get there: From Madrid N401 to Toledo, then follow signs to old town. At town walls right; continue with wall on left until roundabout. Left here and along to end of tree-lined ave. Left through wall; along this street to Transito and hotel.

La Almazara

Carretera Toledo-Argés y Polan km 3.4 **Tel:** 925 223866
Apartado 6   **Fax:** 925 250562
45004 Toledo   **E-mail:** hotelalmazara@ribernet
Toledo   **www:** www.frontpage-98.com/hotelalmazara/home.htm

Management: Paulino Villamor

One of Toledo's most illustrious *Cardenals* had this delectable house built as a summer palace in the 16th century; high up on a hillside overlooking Toledo it catches the breezes that sweep in across the *Meseta*. He milled oil here: there are still huge vats of the stuff deep in the gunnels of the building. You arrive by way of a grand old portal and long drive to be greeted by Paulino: he is incredibly helpful and takes obvious pleasure in welcoming you and, later, in advising you on where best to eat in town. Downstairs is a large lounge with a fire in the hearth during the colder months but you may well prefer to linger in the vaulted dining room which looks out over the fruit orchards to the old town of Toledo. Take a closer look at those oil paintings; these were all painted by Paulino's 13-year-old daughter. I stayed in one of the nine rooms with views and sat enthralled on the terrace, contemplating the lights of the old town and lapping up the silence, almost uncanny so close to a city. Bedrooms score full marks for comfort and cleanliness, and the bathrooms have lovely repro taps and gallons of hot water. The large private car park outside is a real plus too: you could leave the car and wander down to the town, about a twenty-minute stroll. Brilliantly priced, so book ahead.

Rooms: 24 with bath or shower & wc.
Price: S 3700 Pts; D/Tw (with view) 6300 Pts; D/Tw 5500 Pts.
Breakfast: 500 Pts.
Meals: None available.
Closed: 10 December-1 March.

How to get there: Arriving from Madrid turn right in front of town wall towards Navahermosa. After crossing bridge, turn left: hotel on left after 2km (says 'Quinta de Mirabel' over entrance).

153

Casa Bermeja

Plaza del Piloncillo s/n
45572
Valdeverdeja
Toledo

Tel: 925 454586
Fax: 925 454595
E-mail: zabzab@arrakis.es

Management: Ana Hermida

Angela González happened upon this old house in a village that the twentieth century seemed to have passed by. She'd found the place where a long-nurtured dream could be realised: a house where her many friends could get together, far from the noise and pollution of Madrid, to share food, conversation — and fun. Luckily for us she later decided to share her home with paying guests too. Architect brother Luis took renovation in hand: Angela, an interior designer, took care of furnishings and fittings. Beyond the exuberant red and cream façade with its stately entrance is a truly coquettish home. The sun and red earth of Castille inspired the warm colours chosen for paint and fabric. Antiques mingle with 90s 'design'; there's a lofty lounge and dining room with beams above and terracotta beneath and magazines and books in several languages. The apartments look onto the inner patio; the rooms are in the main house: they are attractive, comfortable and blissfully quiet. A wild and undiscovered corner of the Meseta and an ornithological dreamland. When Angela is in Madrid the good-natured Ana is in charge.

Rooms: 7 with bath & wc + 7 Suite/studio apartments.
Price: D/Tw 11900-15200 Pts; Ste 16000-22000 Pts.
Breakfast: Included.
Meals: Lunch/Dinner 2400 Pts (M). Closed Mondays and Tuesdays.
Closed: Never.

How to get there: From Madrid NV/E90 towards Badajoz. Exit at km148 for Oropesa. From there to Puente del Arzobispo and here, right to Valdeverdeja. In main square, opposite 'Ayuntamiento', turn left to Casa Bermeja.

Map No: 18

154

"Spain is the only land for travel . . . the Alhambra is the most imaginative, the most delicate and fantastic creation that ever sprang up on a summer night in a fairy tale".

BENJAMIN DISRAELI

Andalusia

Number Ten

Calle Mar 10
04288
Bédar
Almería

Tel: 950 398025
Fax: 950 398025
E-mail: pamsam@compuserve.com

Management: Sheila and Peter Mills

Bédar stands at over a thousand feet, between the Cabrera and Filabres mountain ranges, with inspirational views east across the Med. This part of Almeria is blessed with year-round sunshine and abundant spring water; it is surprising to stumble on such exuberant vegetation so close to those dry gulches and gullies of 'spaghetti western' fame. Sheila and Peter know the land and its people, having restored a 400-year-old village house then thrown it open to all. Comfort was a first priority; marble floors and ceiling fans will keep you cool in summer, but when colder weather arrives the house is properly heated and a log fire will be burning in the large open-plan sitting room. Bedrooms are beamed, decorated with traditional wooden furniture and all have views over the rooftops towards coast and Sierra. Best of all is the rooftop terrace; have an aperitif here before joining Peter and Sheila for dinner. I spent a blissful night as guests of the Mills and can't wait to return.

Rooms: 2 with bath & wc.
Price: S 4000 Pts; D/Tw 5500-6500 Pts inc. VAT.
Breakfast: Included.
Meals: Dinner 2500(M). Book ahead. No meals on Sundays.
Closed: Never.

How to get there: From Alicante A7 south. Exit 525 for Los Gallardos. Onto N340 then right by cemetery following signs to Bédar. Under motorway; 4.6km from here you turn left; on up this road to Calle Mar and Number 10.

Finca Listonero

Cortijo Grande
04639
Turre
Almería

Tel: 950 479094
Fax: 950 479094

Management: Graeme Gibson and David Rice

Lovers of desert landscapes, their barrenness, aridity, sense of eternity and proportion will be richly rewarded at the Finca Listonero with its wraparound views of the Sierra Cabrera. For the sybaritic, this sensitively extended pink (original colour) farmhouse has all the luxuries. David and Graeme, cultured and gourmet Anglo-Australians, have lavished much affection on this conversion. This and their attention to guests make it very special. Bougainvillaea defies the dry sierra with every flower; the delightful dining and drawing rooms, the fern-filled atrium, the antiques and *objets* impose grandeur on the lowly origins. The guestrooms are all differently decorated and furnished. Breakfast is an easy-going occasion while dinner is definitely a serious matter with excellent regional and international dishes (ingredients from the garden) and good wines. Let yourself be pampered by the pool and guided towards the loveliest walks, villages or beaches in the area.

Rooms: 5 with bath or shower & wc.
Price: Tw 10000-14000 Pts.
Breakfast: Included.
Meals: Lunch: light meals; dinner 4500 Pts (M). Closed on Sundays
Closed: Never.

How to get there: From N340/E15 exit 520 towards Turre/Mojácar. 3km on, right through entrance to Cortijo Grande. Finca signposted on right after approx. 3.5km.

Mamabel's

Calle Embajadores 5
Mojácar Pueblo
04638 Mojácar
Almería

Tel: 950 472448
Fax: 950 472448

Management: Isabel and Juan Carlos Aznar

Artists long ago discovered the charms of this pretty white village near the beach yet it is still a real clifftop village: slightly touristy but it has kept its identity. So has Isabel Aznar ('Mamabel'), your hostess; she greets you with the loveliest of smiles and likes to treat her guests as she would her friends. Well-known and loved locally, she is proud of her village and the small guesthouse which she has gradually rebuilt and added to since first arriving in the mid-sixties. The rooms are prettily decorated with a rather feminine feel; number 1 is the grandest with its canopied bed, antique table and many knick-knacks; not a hint of 'hotel' here. But all the rooms are charming and of course we'd all love one of those with a terrace looking down to the glittering sea. There is a cosy little dining room where there are stacks of paintings by Mamabel's husband, hand-painted chairs and simple food with an unmistakably Mediterranean flavour. If you head out for dinner there's lots of choice in the village. A casual and homely place but be aware it's a steep climb to reach it from where you park your car.

Rooms: 8 with bath & wc + 1 'special' room (no 1).
Price: D/Tw 6500-8500 Pts; Ste 8000-10000 Pts.
Breakfast: 700 Pts or 1100 Pts (full English).
Meals: Dinner 1800 Pts (M).
Closed: Never.

How to get there: From N340/E15 exit 520 then towards Turre/Mojácar. Up into village of Mojácar and signposted to right.

Hostal Family

Calle La Lomilla s/n
04149
Agua Amarga
Almería

Tel: 950 138014
Fax: 950 138070

Management: Marcos, René and Michèle Maingnon Salmeron

Gentle-mannered Frenchman René Salmeron came to Agua Amarga on holiday and, like many of us who discover places as beautiful as this, he dreamed of coming to live and work here. And here he is, just behind one of southern Spain's most seductive beaches, running this simple whitewashed hostal and restaurant and making new friends. A bumpy track leads you to the building which has just acquired a second floor; rooms at the front have sea views. Downstairs and upstairs rooms are simply furnished with all-wooden furniture and thick, Alpujarran blankets as bedspreads. In the rather kitsch courtyard restaurant (covered in winter) you can expect to eat well; René's food is 'Mediterranean with a French touch' — try his paté as a starter. There are decent breakfasts with home-made jams, yoghurt and fruit — or pancakes if you prefer. Thank heavens that there are still places on the Costa like this little fishing village worth visiting. Stay a couple of nights and explore the nearby Cabo de Gata National Park.

Rooms: 9 with bath & wc.
Price: D/TW 7000-10000 Pts inc.
breakfast and VAT.
Breakfast: Included.
Meals: Dinner 2000 (M); lunch weekends only.
Closed: Never.

How to get there: From N344 exit 494 for Venta del Pobre/Carboneras. Continue towards Carboneras then right towards Agua Amarga. Signposted to right in village.

158

Map No: *27*

Mikasa

Calle Carboneras s/n
04149
Agua Amarga
Almería

Tel: 950 138073
Fax: 950 138219
E-mail: suite000@aranzadi.esps

Management: Manuel Lezcano de Orleans

A modern building, an interior designer (Lidia's dried flowers and rustic tiles have been in *Vogue* magazine) and much attention to detail. Mikasa is a luxurious mixture of the clean-cut and the plush. Manuel and Lidia are much travelled, cultivated, multi-lingual, enjoy all things cosmopolitan and know how to make guests feel cared for. Newspapers are provided according to nationality, beds are turned down every evening and adorned with a few chocolates, there are ceiling fans as well as air conditioning, contemporary paintings on the walls and high-quality insulation. Some of the carefully fitted bedrooms have king-size beds, some have terraces; they vary in size but all have excellent bathrooms. Breakfast is a huge spread that you can enjoy inside or out. The beach here is very secluded (and quiet except in August) and one can swim here at least 10, sometimes 12 months a year. But, if you prefer, Mikasa has two pools (one of them heated). It also has a gym, tennis court, Turkish bath and even a masseur who can be called in to get those muscles toned up.

Rooms: 15 with bath & wc + 5 suites.
Price: D 10000-15000 Pts; Tw 12000-14000 Pts; D (king-size bed) 16000-20000 Pts; Ste 15000-20000 Pts.
Breakfast: Included — buffet.
Meals: Lunch 1000-2000 Pts (M) (July-October); Dinner 2500-3500 Pts (M).
Closed: January 7-March 10.

How to get there: From N344 take exit 494 for Venta del Pobre/Carboneras. Continue towards Carboneras then right towards Agua Amarga. Signposted in village.

Posada de Palacio

Calle Caballeros 11
11540
Sanlúcar de Barrameda
Cádiz

Tel: 956 364840
Fax: 956 365060

Management: Renata Strobel
and Antonio Naverrete

A sleepy town at the mouth of the Guadalquivir, Sanlúcar has one great claim to fame — it is home to delectable pale dry Manzanilla. Among the *bodegas* and palaces of the old town this 18th-century mansion house is our favourite place to stay in this part of Spain. Every corner has a flavour of its own; the house has grown organically, decorated with things collected piecemeal by Renata and Antonio. You enter a slightly magical world as you take the grand old entrance into the courtyard. Some rooms have sitting rooms, others have terraces, many have beautiful period tiled floors (perhaps why the house was chosen as a film set for a period drama) and high ceilings; some of the bathrooms are vast. There are geraniums, fans and mementoes from South American travels; fern and jasmine-shaded corners in which to sit and read. Next to the small bar is a newly opened restaurant where the stables once stood. As you might expect, the fish is first-class and there lots of vegetables and salads, all fresh from the market. The house is infused with the easy good-nature of its owners who will help arrange boat tours of the nearby Doñana wetlands. Don't miss Sanlúcar and the Posada!

Rooms: 10 with shower or bath & wc + 3 suites.
Price: S 6000 Pts; D/Tw 8000 Pts; Ste 10000 Pts.
Breakfast: 800 Pts.
Meals: Lunch 1200 Pts (M); dinner approx. 2000 Pts (C).
Closed: January-February.

How to get there: From Sevilla, A4 motorway. Leave at Las Cabezas exit onto C441 to Sanlúcar (via Lebrija and Trebujena). In town, follow signs to Casco Antiguo then Palacio Municipal. Hostal is opposite Palacio.

160   Map No: 24

El Convento

Calle Maldonado 2   **Tel:** 956 702333
11630   **Fax:** 956 704128
Arcos de la Frontera
Cádiz

Management: María Moreno Moreno and José Antonio Roldán Caro

Arcos is spread like icing along the top of a craggy limestone outcrop. It was a great stronghold when Moors and Christians fought over the ever-shifting *frontera*. The Convento, a former cloister, is perched right at the edge of the cliff in the heart of the old town. Behind the plain white façade is a deliciously labyrinthine hotel whose rooms have views to die for. The best have terraces over the cliff where watching the sun set will make your heart soar. José Roldán Caros knows and loves his *patria chica* and he and his wife have filled their hotel with works by local artists. Decoration varies in the original part of the hotel and like, the paintings, is sometimes a little dated, while in the newly opened annex just across the way the fittings are much smarter and the views the same. The small dining room — with rather inappropriate plastic furniture — is in the old sacristy but on warm days you can eat in the patio. The Roldán Caros also own a restaurant in the covered colonnaded patio of a 16th-century palace just up the road (see photo) which serves some of the best food in the Province of Cadiz. This delightfully friendly and hard-working couple are reason enough for heading for El Convento.

Rooms: 11 with bath & wc.
Price: S 8000 Pts; D/Tw 10000 Pts.
Breakfast: 800 Pts.
Meals: Sister restaurant — Lunch/Dinner 3000 Pts (C).
Closed: Never.

How to get there: In Arcos, follow signs to Parador. Park in front of Santa María church; hotel is 100m behind Parador.

Map No: 25

161

Hotel Los Olivos del Convento

Paseo de Boliches 30 **Tel:** 956 700811
11630 **Fax:** 956 702018
Arcos de la Frontera
Cádiz

Management: Management: José Antonio Roldán Caro

Just off a street leading to the old quarter of Arcos, Los Olivos is an unmistakably Andalusian townhouse with arches, geraniums and palms, terracotta floors, white walls and a huge oak door into a cool wicker-furnished lounge. Beyond is the courtyard bringing in light and air. The bedrooms all give onto it and those at the front of the building have views across the gentle hills and olive groves down towards the Atlantic. If you're a light sleeper choose a room at the back; they are very quiet. They all have high ceilings and a pleasant mix of old and modern furniture. You can have breakfast in the patio until the hotter summer days chase you indoors to breathe conditioned air. The staff clearly enjoy working here and their eagerness to please is reflected in the hotel's participation in the scheme offering visitors free guided tours of Arcos (twice daily in season). The old town with its arches (*arcos*) and narrow winding streets is a short walk from Los Olivos whose owner also runs El Convento in another part of town.

Rooms: 19 with bath & wc.
Price: S 4000-5000 Pts; D/Tw 7000-9000 Pts.
Breakfast: 600 Pts.
Meals: Sister restaurant — Lunch/Dinner 2500 Pts (M), 3000-3500 Pts (C).
Closed: Never.

How to get there: In Arcos, follow signs for 'Conjunto Monumental'/Parador. As you climb up into town following one-way system, hotel is on left of road parallel to main street.

162 **Map No:** 25

Hacienda El Santiscal

Avenida El Santiscal 129 (Lago de Arcos)
11630
Arcos de la Frontera
Cádiz

Tel: 956 708313
Fax: 956 708268
E-mail: santiscal@estancias.es
www: www.guiaoro.com

Management: Paqui Gallardo

After many years of working with tourists Paqui and Rocío Gallardo, the dynamic managers of El Santiscal, had a very clear idea of what a small hotel should be. Much the sort of thing that we would look for, too. This grand old *cortijo* is a short drive from Arcos yet in a place of perfect quiet. The building has been sensitively converted from a forgotten family home into an elegant but simple hotel. The building is Andalusian to the core: an austere whitewashed façade, a grand portal and then the blissful peace and cool of the inner sanctum of the central courtyard. Each of the rooms leads off from the patio (and nearly all have views out across the estate too) and all have a slightly different feel, but scrupulous attention to detail is a leitmotiv running through them all: matching fabrics, lovely old beds, terracotta floors and good bathrooms. The suite was really special, we thought, and probably worth the extra if you are feeling flush. Either dine in on classical Andalusian dishes or head up to wonderful old Arcos where there are loads of interesting *tapas* bars and a couple of good restaurants.

Rooms: 11 with bath & wc + 1 suite.
Price: Tw 10000-16000 Pts; Ste 16000-20000 Pts.
Breakfast: Included.
Meals: Lunch/Dinner 3000 Pts (M).
Closed: Never.

How to get there: From Arcos C334 towards El Bosque. 1km after crossing bridge turn left into Urbanización Dominio El Santiscal and follow signs (carefully) to El Santiscal.

Map No: 25

163

Cortijo Barranco

Apartado de Correos 169
11630
Arcos de la Frontera
Cádiz

Tel: 956 231402
Fax: 956 231402

Management: María José Gil Amián

Barranco gives as authentic an insight into Andalusian country life as you could hope for. Leave the main road, drive up through the olive groves and you feel you are leaving the 'real' world behind. The feeling gets stronger when you arrive at this magnificently, isolated place. It is a classic *cortijo* — private living quarters and (former) stables giving onto the inner sanctum. The guestrooms and the apartment are perfect; terracotta floors, old wrought-iron bedsteads, lovely heavy linen curtains and hand-crocheted and knitted bedspreads. The big bathrooms have the same tiles and generous baths. The whole place is uncannily quiet: pin back your ears to hear the owls hoot or the birds hymn the dawn. The sitting room is enormous with space for a billiard table; most memorable of all is the dining room with a gallery, a lofty beamed ceiling and a handsome open hearth. The food is good solid Andalusian fare served with panache. *The above address is for correspondence and is not that of the farm.*

Rooms: 8 with bath & wc + 1 apartment.
Price: D/Tw 8000-9000 Pts. Apt 15000-17000 Pts inc VAT.
Breakfast: 500 Pts.
Meals: Lunch/Dinner 2500-3000 Pts (M). Book ahead.
Closed: 15 December-15 January.

How to get there: From Arcos de la Frontera C344 towards El Bosque. After 5.7km, at end of long straight section, left at sign onto track for 2km to farm.

Map No: 25

Hacienda Buena Suerte

Apartado 60
11650
Villamartín
Cádiz

Tel: 956 231286
Fax: 956 231275
E-mail: jcdysli@aol.com
www: www.steinwand.com/westernriding/jcdysli.htm

Management: Magda and Jean-Claude Dysli

What a grand arrival! As you pass under the great portal and up the drive you feel the marriage of Andalusia's past — the great estates or *latifundia* — and its present — Judas trees, bougainvillaea, palm trees, whitewash and terracotta tiles. All this in the loveliest of settings — the gently rolling olive groves and wheat fields of the foothills of the Grazalema mountains. But the real star here is the horse. Groups of riders come to learn with owners Jean-Claude and Magda Dysli. They are rarely out of the saddle, either teaching in the riding school or trekking in the hills with their guests. Non-riders are also very welcome and there are lovely walks from the farm. The rooms, most of them in the converted granary, are large and simply furnished, decorated — naturally — with prints of horses and riders and animal skins on the floors. You may find sweets on pillows or a candle in the corner. Meals, taken round the huge dining table, are 'international' — everything from goulash to bouillabaisse to couscous, all with organic ingredients.

Rooms: 11 with bath & wc.
Price: S 7500 Pts; D/Tw 15000 Pts.
Breakfast: Included.
Meals: Lunch 2000 Pts (M); dinner 3000 Pts (M).
Closed: July-August.

How to get there: From Ronda, C339 towards Sevilla. At junction with N342, left towards Jerez. 7km before Villamartín, left at sign for El Bosque & Ubrique. Buena Suerte is about 1.5km along on the left.

Map No: 25

Hostal Casa de las Piedras

Calle las Piedras 32
11610
Grazalema
Cádiz

Tel: 956 132014/132323
Fax: 956 132014/132238

Management:
Rafael and Katy Lirio Sánchez

Grazalema is one of the most dazzling of Andalusia's mountain villages, clinging to grey and ochre cliffs and dominated by craggy peaks that are home to eagles and mountain goats. A special place with a special *hostal*, half of which is in a grand 300-year-old house (witness to the days when a thriving weaving industry made many a Grazalema fortune) where rooms vary in size, are full of family antiques and loaded with charm. The new half, built and decorated in traditional style, has 16 simple and attractive rooms with their own bathrooms and central heating (temperatures can drop sharply during winter nights). Some have views across the terracotta roofs to the mountains beyond. Rafael, Jacinto and Katy are enthusiastic young hosts and serve much-appreciated local dishes in their lively restaurant. Don't miss the wild thistle or asparagus omelettes (in the right season), roast partridge or quail, or trout baked with a slice of mountain ham. This is a base for walkers with a healthy appetite and breakfast is appropriately hearty. An unassuming and charming place with owners who understand the art of good, old-fashioned inn-keeping.

Rooms: 16 with bath or shower & wc; 16 sharing.
Price: S (sharing bath & wc) 1500 Pts; S 3600 Pts ; D/Tw (sharing bath & wc) 3000 Pts; D/Tw 4900 Pts inc. VAT.
Breakfast: 225 Pts.
Meals: Lunch/Dinner 1100 Pts (M), 2000 Pts (C).
Closed: Never.

How to get there: From Ronda, C339 towards Sevilla. After about 14km left to Grazalema. Enter main square & turn directly right up street beside Unicaja. Hotel is 100m up on right.

Hostal El Anón

Calle Consuelo 34-40
11330
Jimena de la Frontera
Cádiz

Tel: 956 640113/640416
Fax: 956 641110
E-mail: elanon@mx3.redestb.es
www: www.andalucia.com

Management: Suzana Odell

Five village houses and stables have been joined to make an organic whole of changing levels, interconnecting patios and intimate terraces. It is a delicious little piece of authentic Spain. Suzana is warm and relaxed and welcoming. She has lived in Jimena for years and knows the people and country like her own. She will disentangle the rich web of local history for you while organising horse-riding or advising on painting, bird-watching and flora-spotting expeditions. The countryside has treasures galore for nature-lovers. See it from the little rooftop swimming pool where the eye travels over the roofs of Jimena and across to Gibraltar. Dine off spare ribs or *tapas* among geraniums on the terrace. Enjoy the cool peace of the arched main courtyard and the exotic banana and custard-fruit trees, rejoice in the rich furnishings collected over the years (wall-hangings, paintings, imaginative sculptural bits and pieces) and the heavy beams and low ceilings of the old buildings. Come and soak up quantities of Spanishness in a congenial, cosmopolitan, atmosphere.

Rooms: 11 with bath & wc + 1 suite.
Price: S 3800 Pts; D/Tw 7000 Pts; Ste 8000 Pts inc. VAT.
Breakfast: Included.
Meals: Lunch/Dinner 3000 Pts (C). Bar snacks also available. Restaurant & bar closed on Wednesdays.
Closed: 16 June-July 16.

How to get there: From Málaga N340 towards Algeciras. At roundabout in Pueblo Nuevo de Guadiaro right for San Martín del Tesorillo and on to Jimena; in village centre left by taxi rank and 2nd right.

Map No: 25

Posada La Casa Grande

Calle Fuentenueva 42
11330
Jimena de la Frontera
Cádiz

Tel: 956 640578
Fax: 956 640491
E-mail: tcag@mx4.redestb.es

Management: Tom Andrésen

Jimena is one of the most spectacular of the white villages: a cluster of whitewashed houses fan out around a limestone crag topped by a Moorish castle. The two Toms (father and son) have lived in the village for many years. The restoration of this grand old village house has taken them eight years. Hats off to them for creating a hostelry that feels much more home than hotel. There's an easy, informal atmosphere at La Casa Grande: you may well be greeted by loud pop music. Pass through a flagged courtyard with an exuberant honeysuckle to find an enormous guest lounge (see small photo) and, up another level, the reading room with hundreds of books. The base elements are those you expect in the south: wafer bricking, tiled floors, potted palms, open hearths, heavy old beams. We liked the bedrooms: clean and comfortable and little matter that they share bathrooms. Breakfast is the only meal served but with a lively bar next door which serves the best *tapas* in the village (Tom would say "in Spain"!) you're off to a flying start and there are plenty of restaurants in the village. The mighty Atlantic is close by and the walking round here is fantastic: don't miss the climb up to the castle for an unbelievable sunset.

Rooms: 7 sharing 3 baths & wcs.
Price: S 4000 Pts; D/Tw 5000 Pts.
Breakfast: approx. 500 Pts.
Meals: None available.
Closed: Never.

How to get there: From Málaga N340 towards Cádiz. Right via San Martín del Tesorillo towards Ronda. In Jimena follow main street all way through village; last (sharp) right down to Casa Grande on right.

Rancho Los lobos

11339
Estación de Jimena de la Frontera
Cádiz

Tel: 956 640429
Fax: 956 641180
E-mail: loslobos@teleline.es

Management: Wolf and Esther Zissler

It's all about the great outdoors at Los Lobos, an old farmstead that hugs the side of a valley just outside the beautiful white village of Jimena de la Fontera (all of these *'de la frontera'* villages once marked the boundary between Christian and Moorish Spain). Wolf and Esther have lived here since the early eighties and have gradually converted a series of outbuildings to house their guests and their horses: riding is their first love. Head out through old oak forests on your beautifully groomed steed, stop to swim (with your horse) in river pools or if you're not horsey choose between mountain-biking, hiking, tennis, swimming and Russian bowling. Your hosts have created a perfect balance: the atmosphere is easy-going yet everything is very well organised. Eat in the old farm kitchen or across the courtyard in a larger dining room with blazing fire in the colder months. Breakfasts are bountiful affairs, picnics can be prepared and in the evening (perhaps after a sauna and then an aperitif in the cosy stable bar) dinner is a combination of Swiss and traditional Spanish cuisine. We really liked the bedrooms with their bright rugs and wall hangings and clean, uncluttered feel.

Rooms: 8 with bath or shower & wc + 1 apartment.
Price: D/Tw 8000 Pts; Apt (for 2) 12000 Pts.
Breakfast: Included.
Meals: Light lunches 550 Pts; dinner 2000 Pts (M).
Closed: Never.

How to get there: Arriving in Jimena left at Bar Cuenca then right past Guardia Civil building. Cross bridge and follow track until farm on right. (Phone and Wolf will fax you a map.)

Map No: 25

169

Casa Convento La Almoraima

Carretera Algeciras-Ronda   **Tel:** 956 693002
11350   **Fax:** 956 693214
Castellar de la Frontera
Cádiz

Management: Isabel Oroco

Just inland from the Mediterranean, within reach of the big Atlantic breakers, La Almoraima is one of Spain's more remarkable 'historic' hotels. The convent (cum hunting lodge!), built nearly 400 years ago, has been expropriated twice during its troubled history: once from the religious order, more recently from maverick financier Ruiz Mateos. It remains one of the largest *latifundia* in Europe. At the end of the main drive that winds up through the forest you are greeted by palm trees, a colonnaded façade, a Florentine tower and a belfry where storks return year after year to nest — a bewitching sight. The balustraded façade gives way to an inner patio; there are areas of shade beneath the citrus trees with tables for sitting out; it's an irresistible spot. The bedrooms are simply furnished and some have fireplaces for the colder months. They give onto the patio or onto the gardens. A rather colonial air is added by the billiards room, grand piano and tapestries. You can play tennis or explore the huge estate on horseback, foot or by jeep, or just listen to the silence.

Rooms: 17 with bath & wc.
Price: S 8000 Pts; D/Tw 13000 Pts.
Breakfast: 750 Pts.
Meals: Lunch/Dinner 3000 Pts (M), 4000 Pts (C).
Closed: Never.

How to get there: From Algeciras, N340 north then C3331 towards Jimena de la Frontera. Hotel is signposted on the left near the turning to Castellar.

Hotel Casa Señorial La Solana

Carretera Cádiz-Málaga
N340 km 116.5 North Side
11360
San Roque
Cádiz

Tel: 956 780236
Fax: 956 780236

Management: José Antonio Ceballos Calahoro

An unmistakably Spanish house, La Solana was built for a noble family in the 18th century. It stands grandly in 14 hectares of lush gardens and parkland; brilliant southern blooms climb the façade. The beautifully glazed door beckons you in. A decade ago, the present owner, an artist and sculptor, restored it with great sensitivity and the overhanging eaves outside, and the covered patio inside, give it a colonial air. The interior is finely furnished with 16th-and 17th-century antiques from Spain's *alta época*, a profusion of carved wood, rich rugs, velvets and brocades, crystal chandeliers and heavy wardrobes. The very comfortable bedrooms are furnished with a mixture of old and less old pieces and the bathrooms are thoroughly modern. The bright 'white villages' of the Grazalema Sierra and the lesser-known beaches of the Atlantic coast are magnificent in their rhythm and colour. After a day delighting in these hidden treasures of Andalusia it is an extra joy to return to the secluded comfort of your country mansion.

Rooms: 18 with bath & wc + 6 suites.
Price: S 8000 Pts; D/Tw 10000 Pts; Ste 12000 Pts inc. VAT.
Breakfast: 750 Pts.
Meals: None available.
Closed: Never.

How to get there: From Málaga take N340 towards Algeciras. Leave road at km116.5 and follow signs to hotel for 0.8km. (Or coming from Cádiz leave at exit 117, then U-turn).

Monte de la Torre

Apartado 66
11370
Los Barrios
Cádiz

Tel: 956 660000
Fax: 956 634863
E-mail: mdlt@mercuryin.es
www: www.andalucia.com.es

Management:
Sue and Quentin Agnew-Larios

Quentin Agnew's family has farmed this estate for generations. It is puzzling to come across this utterly Edwardian building in the very south of Spain; it was built by the British when they were pushing the railway through the mountains to Ronda. This commingling of northern architecture and southern vegetation and climate is every bit as seductive as it is unexpected. The house stands alone on a hill, surrounded by palm trees, with views across the Gibraltar hinterland towards Morocco. The drawing room is panelled, the dining room elegant; there are masses of books, family portraits, a grandfather clock and dogs... this is a home, not a hotel. The bedrooms (reached by a grand staircase) are high-ceilinged, decorated with family heirlooms and have period bathrooms — a festival of tubs and taps. Each is different, all are lovely. The apartments are in the former servants' quarters; lucky servants if they could stay here now! Sue and Quentin are gracious hosts and it is wonderful to meet them and share the beauty of their home and estate. A very special place.

Rooms: 3 twins with bath or shower + 2 apartments in house.
Price: Tw 16000 Pts; Tw (adj bathroom) 14000 Pts; Apt for 4/5 64000-115000 Pts weekly inc. VAT.
Breakfast: Included.
Meals: None available.
Closed: 15 December-15 January.

How to get there: From Málaga N340 towards Algeciras. 8km after San Roque right on C440 towards Jerez; take first exit for Los Barrios and in town at roundabout with fountains turn left and continue 3km; at stone marker right into main drive. 1km to house.

100% Fun

Carretera Cádiz — Málaga Km 76
11380
Tarifa
Cádiz

Tel: 956 680013/680330
Fax: 956 680013
E-mail: 100x100@tnet
www: www.tarifanet/100fun

Management: Ula Walters and Barry Pussell

With such a name you expect something out of the ordinary — and this young, distinctly wacky hotel caught our imagination. The busy N340 lies between it and that oh-so-desirable surf but, in the exuberant greenery of the garden with thatched roofs overhead, we felt we were in deepest Mexico... or an Amazonian lodge... or was it Polynesia? Amazing to have transformed a bog-standard roadside hostel into something quite as spicy as this. The decoration is like the nearby Hurricane's, only simpler with a pleasing combination of floor tiles, warm ochres and fans to beat the sizzling summers. The rooms have a fresh if rather spartan feel, comfortable beds and terraces over the garden. There are gurgling fountains, a swimming pool and an airy restaurant serving spicy Tex-Mex dishes as well as some interesting vegetarian alternatives. It also has the best-equipped surf shop on the Tarifa coast, selling the owner's hand-crafted windsurfing boards. Especially good value out of (surf) season, this is a young, fun hotel!

Rooms: 16 with bath & wc.
Price: S 5900-7900 Pts; D/Tw 7900-9900 Pts; Q 11900-14900 Pts inc. VAT.
Breakfast: Included.
Meals: Lunch/Dinner 1900 Pts (M), 2500 Pts (C).
Closed: 1 November-28 February.

How to get there: From Cádiz N340 towards Algeciras. At beginning of Tarifa Beach, hotel flagged on left, next to La Enseñada (10km north of Tarifa) close to km76 post.

Hurricane Hotel

Carretera de Málaga a Cádiz km78
11380
Tarifa
Cádiz

Tel: 956 684919
Fax: 956 684508

Management: James Whaley

You could be on a film set as you look through the Hurricane's high arches to the palm trees, the glinting ocean and beyond to the Rif rising on the African shore. But despite the echoes of Al Andalus, this place is anchored in the 1990s surf culture — here are the best waves in Europe and a definite whiff of California (fully-equipped gym, two pools, windsurfing school, horses and mountain bikes). The debt to the East is clear in the guestrooms. They are uncluttered, decorated with geometric designs and whirling fans, here a keyhole arch over the bath, there an oriental couch with cotton bolsters. Some reminded us of palace hotels in Rajasthan. Sea-facing rooms are preferable: the busy N340 might disturb Arabian-night dreams on the other side. The food unashamedly mixes America, Spain and the East too. Ingredients are fresh (fish of the day, home-made pasta, herbs from the garden), there are Louisiana prawns with basmati rice, spicy chicken with Peruvian sauce and good vegetarian dishes. The quality, the views, the furnishings make it worth the price and it would be wonderful to ride out from the Hurricane along the beach and up into the mountains, perhaps with James as your guide.

Rooms: 35 with bath & wc.
Price: S 6000-12100 Pts; D 8000-16500 Pts; Ste 14500-29500 Pts.
Breakfast: Included.
Meals: Lunch/Dinner 1500 Pts (M), 3500 Pts (C).
Closed: Never.

How to get there: From Cádiz, N340 south. Hurricane is 7km before Tarifa on the right.

Hotel Restaurante Antonio

Bahia de la Plata
Atlanterra km 1
11393 Zahara de los Atunes
Cádiz

Tel: 956 439141/439346
Fax: 956 439135

Management: Antonio Mota

A short drive from the workaday little fishing village of Zahara de los Atunes, and with a garden that leads straight out to one of the best beaches on the Atlantic coast, Antonio Mota's hotel is in a very special position. Few foreigners seem to be in the know, but this family-run hotel is deservedly popular with the Spanish. It is an utterly southern hotel: repro prints of some rather sugary subjects (swans etc) and other rather grisly ones (bull-fighting). Rooms and restaurant are light, clean and functional; expect the fish to be memorable and prices more than reasonable. It is unusual to come across so hearty a breakfast in Spain: eggs, fruit, cheeses and hams. Some rooms give onto an inner patio with fountain, palms and geraniums; pretty enough, but we'd prefer a room with a small terrace looking out over the palm-filled gardens to the sea. Some rooms have a lounge-cum-second bedroom, ideal for families. And there are horses for hire — try and stay at least two nights and ride (or walk) along the beach to Bolonia, where there are Roman ruins and more good restaurants. Old faithfuls return time and again.

Rooms: 25 with bath & wc + 5 suites.
Price: S 5000-8500 Pts; D/Tw 8500-12000 Pts; Ste 11000-15000 Pts inc. VAT.
Breakfast: 800 Pts.
Meals: Lunch/Dinner 2000 Pts (M), 3500-4500 Pts (C).
Closed: Never.

How to get there: From Algeciras E5/N340 to Cádiz. 25km after Tarifa take left turning to Barbate and Zahara on left after 10km. Hotel signposted in village.

Map No: 25

La Fuente del Madroño

Fuente del Madroño 6
11159
Los Caños de Meca
Cádiz

Tel: 956 437067 or 649 780834
Fax: 956 437067
E-mail: karen@jet.es
www: www.jet.es/karen

Management: Karen Abrahams

La Fuente del Madroño is imbued with the creative spirit and natural optimism of Karen Abrahams. She worked in the music business in the UK before seeing in this group of old farm buildings an outlet for her energies and her desire to create something new and interesting. Her accommodation, set back from the Atlantic, has grown organically over the years and so you choose between several different types of living space. 'Casa Karen 1 & 2' are more independent while rooms and apartments in the 'Casa del Monte' and 'Casa del Medio' are better if you want to be more sociable. The decoration takes its inspiration from the local surroundings; local here means Andalusian and Moroccan — the high mountains of the Magreb are visible on clear days from the garden. The place seems to attract people with a creative impulse and people often book in for longer stays over the winter, however, Karen values her short-stay guests just as highly. She'll advise on walks and rides out in the Natural Park just behind Caños and will tell you where to eat the best fish. If the self-catering seems daunting a friend can come and cook for you (veggie, organic) and a massage with aromatic oils is always available.

Rooms: 4 hses + 1 studio + 1 trad. style thatched house.
Price: D/Tw 4500 Pts; Studio (for 2) 6400-9600 Pts; 1 bed house 7200-10800; 2 bed houses 10200-15600 Pts; thatched house 7200-10800 Pts.
Breakfast: Self-catering.
Meals: Self-catering.
Closed: Never.

How to get there: From Málaga towards Cádiz on N340. Just past Vejer de la Frontera at km35 turn left and at first roundabout right towards Los Caños de Meca. Here pass turn for Faro Trafalgar and after approx. 500m turn left onto track at sign 'apartments and bungalows'. Signposted.

176

Hotel Los Abetos del Maestre Escuela

Calle Santo Domingo Km 2.8   **Tel:** 957 282132/282105
14012   **Fax:** 957 282175
Córdoba
Córdoba

Management: Rafael Jurado Diáz

Los Abetos (a type of yew) is in a quiet residential area to the north of the city, just at the foot of the Sierra Morena and a ten-minute drive from the centre. The 200-year-old colonial-style hotel stands among lovely palm trees; these and the hotel's pink and white façade give it a most beguiling look. There is a peaceful pebbled courtyard with wicker chairs for sitting out and other equally attractive spots beneath the palms. The restaurant and lounge have much less of a period feel. The hotel was very considerably renovated in 1992, perhaps for the business folk who often come to stay or to dine; this too explains why the dining room is so cavernous — banquets are often held here. The guestrooms have all the finery you need. We certainly preferred those with views across the estate towards Córdoba; they have Provençal furniture and modern tiled floors. In spite of the muzak and a definite 'hotelly' feel, this is a good place if you want to be just out of town.

Rooms: 34 with bath & wc + 2 suites.
Price: S 6900-8900 Pts; D/Tw 9500-11500 Pts; Ste 11500-13500 Pts.
Breakfast: 700 Pts.
Meals: Lunch/Dinner 2000 Pts (M), 3000 Pts (C).
Closed: Never.

How to get there: From centre of Córdoba, Avenida del Brillante northwards. As you arrive in more residential area, right onto Avenida San José de Calasanz (formerly called Santo Domingo if asking way!). Continue to hotel.

Map No: 25   **177**

Los Omeyas
Calle Encarnación 17
14003
Córdoba
Córdoba

Tel: 957 492267/492199
Fax: 957 491659

Management:
Juan de la Rubia Villalba

This, one of the latest small hotels to open in Córdoba, is a real gem. Juan de la Rubia Villalba's many years of experience in hostelry were put to good use when he came to build and decorate Los Omeyas. The position is a delight, just a few yards to the east of the great Mezquita in a narrow street of the old Jewish quarter (a plexus of mystic alleys beyond the souvenir shops). The building is in harmony with much older neighbours; the whitewashed façade with its wrought-iron balconies and wooden shutters is classic Cordoban architecture. And so too within, where a small patio gives access to rooms on two levels. The design may seem a bit theatrical — the mezquita-style arches in reception, the marble staircase — but then we are in the larger-than-life south and the whole hotel is as clean as the newest pin. Everything is brand new from curtains to mattresses to bedcovers. Marble floors throughout the building and whitewashed walls are the perfect foil for the summer heat and there's air conditioning, too. Kind and helpful staff and a reliable little inn. "The best of all our stays" wrote some readers. And good coffee at breakfast.

Rooms: 38 with bath & wc.
Price: S 4300-5000 Pts; D/Tw 7500-8500 Pts.
Breakfast: 500 Pts.
Meals: None available.
Closed: Never.

How to get there: Entering Córdoba follow signs for centre then Mezquita. In a street just off north-east corner of the Mezquita. Nearest parking by Alcázar de los Reyes Católicos.

Hotel Zuhayra

Calle Mirador 10
14870
Zuheros
Córdoba

Tel: 957 694693
Fax: 957 694702

Management: Juan Carlos Ábalos Guerrero

The rather monolithic structure of the hotel might have you wondering: it's the building at the centre of the photo above. But do come and stay and so discover the beauty of this small village which lies at the heart of the virtually unknown Natural Park of Subbetica: 3,000 hectares of wilderness. Zuheros is quintessentially Andalusian: its houses hug the hillside beneath the old castle. Up above are the greys and ochres of the mountains while below are mile after mile of silver-green olive groves. Two gentle-mannered brothers and their wives manage the hotel and they are exceptionally kind hosts. Zuhayra's downstairs café-cum-bar is vast but climb up to the first floor to find a cosier dining room where local specialities include partridge, *clavillina* (a thick stew served with a fried egg on top) and delicious *remojón* (a potato, onion and pepper salad with oranges). Wonderful bread, too, from the local bakers. Bedrooms are functional rather than memorable: modern pine furniture, hot-air heating and really comfy beds (no wonder walkers like it so much here) and bathrooms are surprisingly plush. Ask for a second floor room to get the best views. Footpaths galore radiate out from Zuheros; there are cave paintings at 'The Cave of the Bats' just outside the village. Córdoba is an hour's drive and you're light years away from the Costa.

Rooms: 18 with bath & wc.
Price: D/Tw 6000-7000 Pts.
Breakfast: Included.
Meals: Lunch/Dinner 1500 Pts (M), 2500 Pts (C).
Closed: Never.

How to get there: From Málaga towards Cordoba on N331and just past Lucena right to Cabra. On towards Dona Mencia then right towards Luque/Zuheros. Here through village to Castillo — same street 200m down hill.

Palacio de Santa Inés

Cuesta de Santa Inés 9
Barrio del Albayzín
18010
Granada
Granada

Tel: 958 222362
Fax: 958 222465

Management:
Nicolás Garrido Berastegui

Just yards from the Plaza Nueva, tucked away to the side of a quiet and leafy square at the heart of the Albaicin (the hill rising opposite the Alhambra was recently declared a World Heritage Site by UNESCO), is this 16th-century palace. The building came to be known as 'The House of the Eternal Father' after the frescoes that surround the inner patio; perhaps the creation of a pupil of Raphael. Above them, two storeys of wooden galleries lead to bedrooms or suites. These are the delight of owner Nicolás Garrido. His love of antiques, modern art and interior design has been given free rein; his creation is elegant, southern and unique. Hang expense and book one of the suites with small terraces looking straight out to the Alhambra; ask for 'Morayma' or 'Mirador de Daraxa' or the 'Alhambra' suite which has a wonderful 16th century *Mudejar* panelled ceiling. But come also to meet the delightful manageress, Mari-Luz; her warmth makes a stay at Inés a double treat. She serves you breakfast in a cosy breakfast room. There is also a large lounge with a *mudéjar* ceiling, a quiet retreat for musing over the wonders of the Alhambra.

Rooms: 7 with bath & wc + 6 suites.
Price: S 1000 Pts; D/Tw 13750-16500 Pts; Ste 19800-22000 Pts.
Breakfast: 800 Pts.
Meals: None available.
Closed: Never.

How to get there: Into centre to Plaza Nueva; then Carrera del Darro and, by FIRST BRIDGE, best to leave car, walk to hotel just up to left; someone from hotel can show you where to park. Or easier: any central public car park then taxi to hotel.

180

Map No: 26

Hotel Reina Cristina
Tablas 4
18002
Granada
Granada

Tel: 958 253211
Fax: 958 255728
E-mail: clientes@hotelreinacristina.com
www: www.hotelreinacristina.com

Management:
Federico Jiménez González

The Reina Cristina is a grand 19th-century townhouse, close to the cathedral and the lovely pedestrianised 'Bib-Rambla' square. Legend has it that Lorca spent his last night here, hidden by his friend Rosales who was living in this house. The hotel sits comfortably astride time past and time present, quite able to please the most demanding of modern travellers. The very dapper rooms are set round an elegant lobby (it has a neo-*mudéjar* ceiling, a fountain, aspidistras and marble columns), all of it utterly in sympathy with tradition and climate. The downstairs dining room is lovely for dinner: the original Art Deco fittings and a series of photos are from the period when Lorca was around. Make sure you eat at least once at the Cristina; the owner is very proud of the cuisine, which is a mix of local dishes and those "we create ourselves". There are also excellent *tapas* in the café as well as home-made cakes... all mouth-watering. A favourite Granada address.

Rooms: 43 with bath & wc.
Price: S 8700 Pts; D/Tw 13500 Pts.
Breakfast: 900 Pts.
Meals: Lunch/Dinner 2000 Pts (M), 5000 Pts (C).
Closed: Never.

How to get there: From A92 exit 131 onto Mendez Nuñez then right onto Camino de Ronda. Just before bus station right into C/Emperatriz Eugenia then C/Gran Capitán. Right into Carril del Picón, left at end into Calle Tablas.

Map No: 26

181

Hostal Suecia

Calle Molinos (Huerta de los Angeles) 8   **Tel:** 958 225044/227781
18009   **Fax:** 958 225044
Granada
Granada

Management: Mari-Carmen Cerdan Mejías

Hostal Suecia is tucked away at the end of a quiet little street at the very foot of the Alhambra hill. It seems hard to believe that you're in the city and just a few hundred yards from one of Europe's architectural wonders. The Suecia is most seductive too, every inch a southern house with terracotta roof tiles, arched windows and an old sharon-fruit tree (that of the photo) in the front. But don't get the idea that the Suecia pretends to anything: within it feels like a family home. There is a pretty sitting room downstairs, a tiny breakfast room up above and bedrooms which vary in size and comfort, like those of your own house. The beds are comfortable, the rooms are spotless. Come for the most peaceful spot in town, the rooftop terrace (no better place to read *Tales from the Alhambra*) and leisurely breakfasts. Or relax in the nearby 'Campo del Príncipe' where you can sit in a café and think of the generations who have fleeted across this lively square.

Rooms: 7 with bath or shower & wc; 4 sharing.
Price: S 3000-5000 Pts; D/Tw 6000 Pts; D/Tw (sharing bath & wc) 4000 Pts.
Breakfast: 450 Pts.
Meals: None available.
Closed: Never.

How to get there: Entering Granada follow signs for Alhambra. Near Alhambra Palace hotel (by Alhambra) turn down Antequerela Baja which becomes Cuesta del Caidero. At bottom turn right into C/Molinos. After 30m right under arch to Suecia. If you get lost pay taxi to guide you!

Hotel Carmen de Santa Inés

Placeta Porras 7
C/ San Juan de los Reyes,15
18010 Granada
Granada

Tel: 958 226380/224511
Fax: 958 224404

Management: Nicolás Garrido Berastegui

Nicolás Garrido's second Albaicín hotel is another gem and it is right at the heart of one of the city's most beautiful quarters. We defy you to find a more deliciously intimate hotel! Push aside the heavy old studded door to emerge into the small flagged patio. Here to greet you are a tinkling fountain, potted aspidistra and deeply comfortable sofas. Marble columns still support the original three hundred year old beams and off to one end, beyond another fine old door is a small formal garden, the most romantic spot imaginable: there are roses, a lemon tree, a vine, gold fish and a view up to the Alhambra. Climb up a marble staircase, pass the tiny chapel and know that you'll love your room — even if it might be a little small. Or opt for a suite: El Mirador is the very loveliest, with its own private terrace, but I liked all the rooms and their pot-pourri of antique and modern art, fine fabrics and lovely tiles. Breakfast in the honeycomb-tiled dining room where there are just three tables, then wander the Albaicín's labyrinthine streets by way of other 'Carmens': this is the name given by the people of Granada to these fine old houses with a walled garden. A favourite: our congratulations to Nicolás!

Rooms: 5 with bath & wc + 4 suites.
Price: S 10000 Pts; D 12500-16500 Pts; Tw 16500-19800 Pts; Ste 19800-26000 Pts.
Breakfast: 800 Pts.
Meals: None available.
Closed: Never.

How to get there: Go to sister hotel, El Palacio de Santa Inés (see our description), staff will park car & accompany you to hotel. Easier still, park in Parking San Agustín and then take a taxi.

Map No: 26

183

Hotel La Fragua
Calle San Antonio 4
18417
Trevélez
Granada

Tel: 958 858626/858573
Fax: 958 858614

Management:
Antonio Espinosa González

Just to the south of the towering peak of Mulhacén (at 3,481 metres the highest in the Sierra Nevada), Trevélez is one of the prettiest villages of the Alpujarra. You climb steeply up to the heart of the village; La Fragua is shared between two old village houses next to the town hall. In one building there is the friendly little bar and above it a real eagle's nest of a pine-clad dining room with a panoramic view across the flat rooftops. A wonderful place to sit and gaze between courses. The food is just like the place — simple and authentic. The locally cured ham is utterly delicious and whatever you do leave some space for one of the home-made puddings. Just a few yards along the narrow street is the second house where you find your room; no fussy extras here, just terracotta floors, timbered ceilings and comfy beds. Up above is a roof terrace with tables and the same heavenly view. Your host, Antonio, knows walkers and their ways and will gladly help you plan your hikes. Visit the Alpujarra before it gets too well known!!

Rooms: 14 with bath & wc.
Price: S 3000 Pts; D/Tw 4800 Pts.
Breakfast: 350 Pts.
Meals: Lunch/Dinner 1500-2000 Pts (M/C).
Closed: 10 January-10 February.

How to get there: From Granada N323 towards Motril; C333 through Lanjarón; just before Orgiva take road to Trevélez.
Up into village asking for 'barrio medio'; park in or near to Plaza Las Pulgas. La Fragua is next to Town Hall (Ayuntamiento).

Las Terrazas

Plaza del Sol 7
18412
Bubión
Granada

Tel: 958 763252/763034
Fax: 958 763034

Management:
Francisco Puga Salguero

You are high up in the Alpujarra, so high that on a clear day you can see down to the coast, across the Mediterranean and all the way to Africa. Las Terrazas, as the name implies, stands on a terraced hillside on the southern edge of Bubión. You enter by a quiet bar; this is the only place in Spain apart from monasteries and churches where we have ever seen a 'Silence Please' sign on the wall. Breakfast is taken here. Unusually, it includes cheeses and cold sausage. No other meals are served but there are many places to eat in the village. The rooms are just fine; nothing fancy but with their terracotta floors, locally-woven blankets and framed photographs they have simple charm. Even if they are smallish those with their own terrace are remarkably inexpensive. (There are also self-catering apartments at Las Terrazas.) Your hosts are the kindest of folk; they have 13 mountain bikes and happily help you plan your sorties on two wheels — or two feet.

Rooms: 17 with bath or shower & wc.
Price: S 2500 Pts; D/Tw 3740 Pts.
Breakfast: 250 Pts.
Meals: None available.
Closed: Never.

How to get there: From Granada N323 towards Motril; C333 through Lanjarón; just before Orgiva take road to Pampaneira and then left to Bubión. In village on left.

Villa Turística de Bubión

Barrio Alto s/n
18412
Bubión
Granada

Tel: 958 763112/763111
Fax: 958 763136

Management: Victor M. Fernández Garcés

A magic mountain hides under the Sierra Nevada. It protects soaring southern hills and plunging gorges where streams run through lines of leafy poplars to water the fertile fields and refresh the impeccably white villages that cling to the slopes. You too can belong to the Alpujarra for a spell, be dazzled by the contrasted 'Alpine' snow and Mediterranean sun, discover the myriads of wild flowers and perhaps some of the indigenous wild animals. Simply take a house in this village and live here. The village is a perfect replica of Alpujarran architecture, using the proper materials and colours with the right shapes, volumes and distribution. The houses are neat, functional, fully equipped; each has a terrace or garden with well established plants and those heart-lifting views. Mottled light plays on the public spaces with their cool sitting areas and luxuriant plants; even the restaurant gets it just right. Odd to have a specially created village in this book but it will work its magic on you too.

Rooms: 43 apartments with lounge, bath & wc.
Price: Apt (for 2-3) 12000 Pts; Apt (for 4-5; 1 bathroom) 18000 Pts; Apt (for 4-6; 2 bathrooms) 20000 Pts.
Breakfast: 925 Pts.
Meals: Lunch/Dinner 2500 Pts (M) 3500 Pts (C).
Closed: Never.

How to get there: From Granada N323 towards Motril; C333 through Lanjarón; just before Orgiva take road to Pampaneira. Just after left to Bubión. In village to top of village; signposted.

186

Sierra y Mar

Calle Albaycín 16
18416
Ferreirola
Granada

Tel: 958 766171
Fax: 958 857367

Management: Inge Norgaard and Giuseppe Heiss

Take the blue door for paradise; enter a sunny/shady, flowery/leafy walled garden, a magic world apart. Mention breakfast; you will eat a minor feast under the spreading mulberry tree. This is a gorgeous place run by two northerners (Italian and Danish) who know and love their adopted country. They are relaxed, intelligent and 'green'. They have converted and extended an old Alpujarran house with utter respect for its origins; they like things simple, the emphasis being on the natural treasures that surround them, not on modern gadgets or plastic paraphernalia. The house is furnished with old rural pieces, lovely materials for curtains and bedcovers, all in good simple taste. Fear not, there are modern bathrooms and central heating. José (Giuseppe) and Inge run Spanish courses and organise walking tours. They delight in having guests. Rejoicing each day in the exceptional gift to man that is the Alpujarra, they want to share all this with you. You can cook your own meals here or explore the nearby villages for restaurants.

Rooms: 9 with own bath & wc.
Price: S 4000 Pts; D/Tw 7000 Pts inc. VAT. *Minimum stay 2 nights.*
Breakfast: Included.
Meals: None available; kitchen for guests.
Closed: Occasionally in winter: check!

How to get there: From Granada N323, towards Motril, then C333 through Lanjarón. Just before Orgiva take road to Pampaneira. Just before Pitres turn right towards Mecina; through village to Ferreirola.

Alquería de Morayma

A348 Cádiar-Torvizcón
18440
Cádiar
Granada

Tel: 958 343221/343303
Fax: 958 343221

Management: Mariano Cruz Fajardo

Mariano Cruz is deeply committed to the Alpujarra and its people: he hopes that those who stay at La Morayma will leave with a deeper understanding of the traditions of these high mountain villages. Such was the care with which this small complex was built that it won first prize last year for the 'Best New Tourism Initiative in Andalusia' (if you'll forgive our rather awkward translation!) and the Spanish daily *El País* lists it among its top small hotels. Amid olive groves and vineyards both the main farmstead and the individual houses (one in the old chapel) have been built in the local vernacular. This goes well with the decorative bits: old brass bedsteads, bright Alpujarra bed covers, marble-topped dressers, grilled windows, old paintings. Each room is different and the houses have been built on different levels to create the asymmetry of a local village. The cuisine, too, is a celebration of things local: olive oil and tomato, fennel, wild capers, goats cheese, thick stews and *migas* (semolina flour cakes to accompany tomatoes and peppers or fish). There is wonderful walking, the chance to see olives being milled during the winter and you could even join in with sausage-making! One night would seem too little here.

Rooms: 8 with bath & wc + 5 houses.
Price: D/Tw 6000-7000 Pts; House (for 2) 8300 Pts; House (for 4) 10000-11000 Pts.
Breakfast: 400 Pts.
Meals: Lunch/Dinner 1500 Pts (M), approx. 2500 Pts (C).
Closed: Never.

How to get there: From Granada N323 south towards Motril then A348 via Lanjarón, Órgiva and Torvizcón. 2km before Cádiar, signposted to left.

Map No: 26

Refugio de Nevada

Carretera de Mairena s/n
18493
Laroles
Granada

Tel: 958 760320/760338
Fax: 958 760304
E-mail: alpujarr@ctv.es
www: www.ctv.es/alpujarr

Management: Victor M.Fernández Garcés

More proof: small IS beautiful. The Refugio de Nevada opened just two years ago but it already has a growing number of old faithfuls. The building makes extensive use, inside and out, of local slate — entirely in keeping with traditional Alpujarran architecture — and it sits well among the older village houses of Laroles. The lounge and bar area is a perfectly cosy spot and the restaurant even more so: here there are just half a dozen tables, crocheted lace curtains, cut flowers, rush-seated chairs and old prints of Granada. The bedrooms have the same quiet intimacy about them: beams and terracotta, chimneys in the studios (open plan with a lounge area), feather duvets, and simple wooden tables and chairs. They aren't enormous but it all works perfectly. They are light, too: the hotel faces the south so the maximum sunlight is captured. Rooms and food are very reasonably priced: the set menu particularly so. Try the roast goat with garlic and perhaps some wild asparagus as a starter. This is a hotel of very human dimensions, the staff are young and friendly, and the Alpujarras are waiting to be walked: book a studio in winter and hunker down by a blazing fire.

Rooms: 5 with bath & wc + 7 studios.
Price: D/Tw 6800 Pts.
Breakfast: 650 Pts.
Meals: Lunch/Dinner 1800 Pts.
Closed: Never.

How to get there: From Granada A92 to Guadix, then right towards El Puerto de La Ragua and continue to Laroles. Signposted to right as you reach village.

El Rincón de Yegen

Camino de Gerald Brennan
18460
Yegen
Granada

Tel: 958 851270/ 851276
Fax: 958 851270/851068

Management: Agustín and
Mari-Carmen Rodríguez

Yegen is the village where Gerald Brennan — one of the century's best writers on Spain — came to live: required reading before, during or after your stay here must be his *South from Granada*. Getting here is much easier than in Brennan's day and the twentieth century *has* caught up with the villages of La Alpujarra but there's still beauty in great measure to be found here. The hotel is just three years old but is happy among its older neighbours thanks to the architects scrupulously sticking to the dictates of local tradition: thus local slate, beam and bamboo are used in abundance throughout the building. Agustín is a trained cook who delights in reworking local dishes in a more "modern" (read "slightly lighter") way. We'll vouch for his onion and goats cheese tart: it makes a heavenly starter. Bedrooms are away to the back of the restaurant and built high to catch the views from the hotel's 3,500-foot perch: you are treated to lots of space, brand new pine furniture, bright bedspreads, shining floor tiles and it's all as spick and span as can be. Underfloor heating is a marvellous solution to the cold winters of this area and if you're into self-catering the apartments have all you need and more. El Rincón is close to the GR7 long distance path which takes you from here on towards Trevélez.

Rooms: 4 with bath & wc + 3 houses.
Price: D/Tw 5000 Pts; House (for 4) 8600 Pts or 48000 Pts weekly.
Breakfast: 500 Pts.
Meals: Lunch/Dinner 1100 Pts (M), 2500-3000 Pts (C).
Closed: Out of season on Tuesdays for rooms.

How to get there: From Málaga N340 towards Almería. Exit for La Rábita/Albuñol. Here on to Cádiar, then on via Mecina Bombarón to Yégen. Signposted on left as you go through the village.

190

Hotel Rural El Montañero

Carretera Orgiva-Pitres s/n	**Tel:** 958 787528 or 629 115238
18410	**Fax:** 958 787528
Carataunas	**E-mail:** hrural@clientes.unicaja.es
Granada	**www:** www.bd-andalucia.es/esp l/ma 10056.html

Management: Enrique Jimena and Marian Gibert Astelarra

Enrique and Marian are young and charged with enthusiasm for their small, mountain hotel high up in the wonderful Alpujarra. The building may look unexciting from the outside but this young couple have stamped their personality on it and if you want an active holiday, do stay here. On offer are guided walks, horse-riding, canoeing, scuba-diving (just three-quarters of an hour gets you down to the Med and Enrique is a qualified teacher) plus mountain biking for the really energetic and moped hire for the less so. The bedrooms all open onto a central lounge: they are simply furnished with bright bedspreads of local weave and with small bathrooms; the best have views over the valley so check when you book if they're available. The restaurant-cum-bar is a cosy spot and looks out across a long rectangular pool running the length of the building. Guests are often non-Spaniards who come for the mix of traditional Andalusian fare and good vegetarian food. (Alternative therapies can be arranged: ask for more info.) But we'll leave the last word to two readers who both recommended the place to us: "Friendly owners, good food and all very reasonably priced" said one; "we'll definitely be back" promised another.

Rooms: 8 with bath or shower & wc.
Price: S 3500-4000 Pts; D/Tw 5800-6500 Pts; Ste 6900-7900 Pts.
Breakfast: 600 Pts.
Meals: Lunch/Dinner 1700 Pts (M), approx. 2500 Pts (C).
Closed: Never.

How to get there: From Granada towards Motril then left on A348 via Lanjarón & just before Orgiva left towards Carataunas. Hotel on right just before village.

Palacete de Cazulas

18698   **Tel:** 958 644036
Otivar   **Fax:** 958 644048
Granada   **E-mail:** info@cazulas.com.
                         www: www.info@hotelcazulas.com.

Management: Brenda Watkins and Richard Russell-Cowan

The oldest deeds of Cazulas date back to 1492 and are in Arabic! The main building came later but its debt to 'Alhambra' style, to things Moorish, is manifest. Wafer brick, terracotta, fountain, clipped hedge and palm combine exquisitely in this utterly southern, seductive summer palace. And to think that the Costa is so close! Hidden away at the end of a subtropical valley, the setting could not be more peaceful. It is like being in a time warp; the shepherd passing with his flock is the only traffic you'll see here. Rooms are plush, the furnishing antique; there are sparkling new bathrooms, four-posters, views out across the estate. There is a columned and vaulted lounge with books, an honesty bar and a grand, panelled dining room decorated with old pieces. Dinner is a labour of love for Brenda and is served with great panache by Richard. And Cazulla is much more: there is a private chapel, hidden corners of the garden where you could book down, a spring-fed swimming pool and a heavenly walk along the valley floor to a towering gorge where rock-pools are fed by crystalline water. Granada is close and you'll soon warm to your genial hosts: we, at least, will never forget our stay here.

Rooms: 9 with bath & wc.
Price: D/Tw 14000-16000 Pts; Larger D 18000 Pts; Ste 22000 Pts.
Breakfast: Included.
Meals: Lunch (summer only) from 2000 Pts; dinner 3750 Pts (M). Book ahead.
Closed: Never.

How to get there: From Almuñecar follow old road towards Granada via Jete to Otívar. Continue on for 5km then left at sign 'central Cazulas'. Continue for 1.5km until you see the twin-towered house.

Finca Buen Vino

Los Marines
21293
Aracena
Huelva

Tel: 959 124034
Fax: 959 501029
E-mail: buenvino@facilnet.es

Management: Sam and Jeannie Chesterton

After running shooting lodges in the Scottish Highlands, Sam and Jeannie knew that to settle happily in Spain they would need to find a place of wild natural beauty — whence this divinely isolated spot amid the thick oak and chestnut woods of the Aracena mountains. It is hard to believe that the Finca Buen Vino was only built 12 years ago. Indeed, many of the building materials are old; we especially liked the panelled dining room, the arched doors and the very fine wooden staircase leading to the guestrooms. The Chestertons' sense of hospitality is Scottish and after one night there we had made new friends. It is supremely elegant, Jeannie is a *Cordon Bleu* cook and the candlelit dinner with quail and *Cerdo Ibérico* (Iberian pork with woodland *setas*) was unforgettable (starlit on the terrace in summer). The guestrooms are all different: the Pink room has a bathtub with a view, the Yellow room a sitting-cum-dressing room, the Bird room its own hearth. There's also an independent cottage that can be rented — no better place to pen that novel. Sam will take you out walking, Jeannie will reveal the secrets of her culinary magic and a stay with them is a pleasure that you will never forget.

Rooms: 4 with bath & wc + 1 cottage.
Price: D/Tw 26000-30000 Pts (half-board). Cottage: ring/fax for details.
Breakfast: Included.
Meals: Lunch (in summer, only on request) 2500 Pts (M). Dinner included.
Closed: August, Christmas & New Year.

How to get there: From Seville N630 north for 37km then N433 towards Portugal/Aracena. Los Marines is 6km west of Aracena; Finca Buen Vino is 1.5km west of Los Marines off to the right at km95 post.

Map No: 17

193

Hospedería Fuentenueva

Paseo Arca del Agua s/n
23440
Baeza
Jaén

Tel: 953 743100/243200
Fax: 953 743200

Management: Victor Rodríguez

The Fuentenueva, behind a rather forbidding façade, was once a womens' prison. Under the aegis of the town council it is now an open, airy, friendly hotel run by a co-operative of five delightfully enthusiastic and professional young people. Inside, the arches and vistas, the marble floors, the tinkling fountain and the neo-Moorish cupola create impressions of space and gentle cool. Exhibitions of works by local artists and craftsmen are held in the salons. The bedrooms are mostly large and light with modern, locally built, furniture and fittings, bright bedcovers and plush bathrooms. On summer evenings drink in the outside bar in the shadow of the old prison tower then dine in the patio on local fish specialities. When all the windows are opened in the morning, the characteristic scent of high-quality olive oil will drift in and envelop you. Visit unsung Baeza, revel in her exuberant Renaissance palaces and richly endowed churches and don't miss the cathedral's silver monstrance (hidden behind St Peter...).

Rooms: 12 with bath & wc.
Price: S 5700-6000 Pts; D/Tw 8800-9100 Pts.
Breakfast: Included.
Meals: Lunch/Dinner approx. 2000 Pts (M), 3000 Pts (C).
Closed: Never.

How to get there: From Granada N323 to just before Jaén and then N321 to Baeza.
On far side of Baeza on left as you leave in direction of Úbeda.

Map No: 19

Palacio de la Rambla

Plaza del Marques 1
23400
Úbeda
Jaén

Tel: 953 750196
Fax: 953 750267

Management: Elena Meneses de Orozco

The old towns of Úbeda and nearby Baeza are often missed as travellers hurry between Madrid and the Costa. They are two of the brightest jewels in the crown of Spanish Renaissance architecture. At the heart of old Úbeda, exquisite Palacio de la Rambla dates from this period and has never left the Orozco family; bless the day the family decided to share it all with you and me! A frisson of excitement passes through you as you go through the ornate Corinthian columned portal into the main patio; colonnaded on two levels, ivy-covered and with delicately carved lozenges and heraldry, its opulence takes you by surprise. Lounge, dining room and bedroom are a match for their setting; there are antique beds, chests, lamps, claw-footed bath tubs, oil paintings of religious themes and — as you might expect — the family portraits. Native terracotta is softened by *estera* matting. Anita the maid is here to fuss over you, and in the morning, serves a full Andalusian breakfast: eggs, toast with olive oil, fresh orange juice — have it in your room if you like. A home with a tradition of regal welcoming; King Alfonso XIII stayed here when he was in town.

Rooms: 8 with bath & wc + 1 suite.
Price: S 10000 Pts; D/Tw 14000 Pts; Ste 16000 Pts.
Breakfast: Included.
Meals: None available.
Closed: 15 July-15 August.

How to get there: From Madrid south on NVI. At km292 take N322 to Úbeda. There, follow 'Centro Ciudad' until Palace in front of you between c/Caja and c/Rastro opposite cafetería 'La Paloma'.

Map No: 24

195

Cortijo El Horcajo

Apartado de Correos 149
29400
Ronda
Málaga

Tel: 95 2184080
Fax: 95 2184080
E-mail: gcdl@apdo.com
www: www.serraniaronda.org

Management: David Barrera

The old farmstead of El Horcajo lies at the northern boundary of the Grazalema Natural Park; you reach it via a long track which snakes down to the bottom of a hidden valley. This is every inch the classic Andalusian *coritjo*; outbuildings are wrapped around a sheltered inner courtyard — designed not only for aesthetic appeal but also as a means of escaping the heat of the Andalusian summer. The farm's owner (David manages it for him) teaches in the Regional Tourism School and has brought professional clout to bear when rehabilitating his family home to hostelry. Thus whilst things local are to the fore in cobble, beam, tile and ceramics he wanted to be sure that his splendidly isolated hotel was in touch with the outside world; there is an Internet connection in every room! The large lounge, dining room and reception area is in the old cattle byre; original vaulting was preserved and new windows opened to bring light into a rather dark space. The trad-Andalusian cooking is tasty and honestly priced. You should like your room; the ones around the courtyard have terraces and the flavour throughout is local-yet-comfortable. The walking in this area is superb, Ronda is very close or you could just chill out back at the ranch. (A further 10 rooms are on the way).

Rooms: 14 with bath & wc.
Price: D/Tw 9000 Pts; D/Tw (with terrace) 10000 Pts; D/Tw (larger) 11000 Pts.
Breakfast: Included.
Meals: Lunch/Dinner approx. 1700 Pts (C).
Closed: Never.

How to get there: From Ronda take A376 towards Sevilla. After approx. 15km left towards Grazalema. Don't take next left turn for Grazalema, continue towards Zahara and at km95.5 post turn left and down track to the farm.

196   **Map No:** 25

El Tejar

Calle Nacimiento 38
29430
Montecorto
Málaga

Tel: 95 2184053
Fax: 95 2184053
E-mail: eltejar@mercuryin.es

Management: Emma Baverstock and Guy Hunter-Watts

El Tejar is tucked away in a pine forest at the very top of the village of Montecorto; it looks out to a panorama of mountain, hill and cork forest. The village is a charming, workaday sort of place with exceptionally friendly locals and those sell-everything shops of your childhood. Emma and Guy have lived in Spain for many years; she managed some of the area's best restaurants, he has written books on walking (and hotels!) in the area. The house, retains the flavour of its peasant origins; open hearth, whitewashed beams and terracotta tiles (made here — El Tejar means 'the tile factory'). Bright textiles and rugs collected on travels in Asia, Africa and South America create a feeling of warmth — as do wood-burners in the cooler months. There are books, a large collection of music and a sitting room with high French windows opening onto a terrace by *al fresco* meals. Bedrooms share the view; more books, photos and bright bedspreads feel similarly cosy. The suite has an eagle's nest of a lounge reached by a steep wooden staircase. Dinner is a relaxed occasion; expect the best of things local and included wines are good. Stay a second night and walk with Guy along forgotten drover's paths up to Grazalema. Intimate, fun and friendly this is our favourite place to stay in Spain... but then it would be!

Rooms: 2 with bath & wc + 1 suite.
Price: D/Tw 9000 Pts; Ste 10000 Pts.
Breakfast: 500 Pts.
Meals: Dinner 3000 Pts (M).
Closed: Never.

How to get there: From Málaga towards Cádiz on N340, then A376 to Ronda. Continue round Ronda on A376 towards Seville. After 20km right into Montecorto. El Tejar is at top of village via track through pines. Ask for 'la casa del inglés'!

Map No: 25

197

Hotel Polo

Mariano Soubirón 8
29400
Ronda
Málaga

Tel: 95 2872447/48
Fax: 95 2872449
E-mail: jpuya@clientes.unicaja.es

Management: Rafael, Javier, Marta and Blanca Puya García de Leaniz

One of Ronda's oldest hotels, the Polo just recently celebrated its twenty-fifth birthday. It remains the pride and joy of the Puya family and a favoured stopover in this remarkable town. A sober, almost austere façade is softened with simple mouldings; some of the tall stone-framed windows have authentic *cierros* (the *mudéjar*-inspired observation window enclosed in decorative wrought-iron work). The aristocratic elegance is echoed inside where the marble hall, columns, antiques and deep sofas promise cool comfort and attentive service. Brothers Javier and Rafael and sister Blanca have taken over the family business; they are warm, generous and welcoming — another touch of class. Bedrooms are large and light with a blue-and-white theme and on the top floor some have views across the rooftops to the mountains beyond. One of the best even has a bathroom with a view. The decoration is classically Spanish with wrought-iron bedheads, Mallorca weave curtains; carpeted throughout, mattresses are brand new and double-glazing cuts out the noise from the surrounding street life. In the lively and animated centre of Ronda, with a congenial bar and excellent restaurant under the caring and expert eye of sister Marta, this is real Andalusian hospitality.

Rooms: 30 with bath & wc + 3 suites.
Price: D/Tw 6750-9500 Pts.
Breakfast: 525 Pts.
Meals: Lunch/Dinner 1250 Pts (M), 2500 Pts (C).
Closed: Never.

How to get there: In centre of Ronda, very near Plaza del Socorro (best place to park is underground car park; only 1000 Pts daily for hotel guests).

Map No: 25

Alavera de los Baños

Apartado de Correos 97   **Tel:** 95 2879143
29400   **Fax:** 95 2879143
Ronda
Málaga

Management: Inmaculada Villanueva Ayala and Christian Reichardt

This is the latest small hotel to open in wonderful old Ronda and is at the heart of *el barrio de las Curtidurias* or the Tanners' Quarter: they established workshops here because of the abundant supply of water. *A-la-vera de* means 'by the side of' — your hotel is right next to what was the first *hammam* (or public baths) of the Moorish citadel: a visit is a must. Christian and Inma are young, brimming with enthusiasm for their (second) hotel and restaurant and the kindest hosts imaginable. Their brief to architect-friend Pedro Enrique was to create a building entirely in keeping with the Hispano-Moorish elements of its surroundings: thus terracotta tiles, wafer bricks, keyhole arches without and in the bedrooms a deliberately oriental feel: kilims, mosquito nets, colour washes of ochres, blue and yellow. The shower rooms are small but it all works wonderfully. The dining room is evocative of the desert with its sandy tones; its eight metre height is cut across by an arched central walkway leading to the rooms at either end. You eat well: lamb is the speciality (a change from the ubiquitous pork) and there is tasty veggie fare too, nearly all of it organically grown. Home-made puds provide the proper finish. There are a reading room and small lounge beyond the restaurant and the possibility of Spanish classes with Inma.

Rooms: 10 with shower & wc.
Price: S 6500 Pts; D/Tw 7500 Pts; D/Tw (with terrace) 8000 Pts inc. breakfast.
Breakfast: Included.
Meals: Lunch/Dinner 2500 Pts (M).
Closed: Never.

How to get there: In Ronda, directly opposite the Parador, take Calle Villanueva. Right at end and down hill to Fuente de los Ocho Caños. Here left and first right to Arab Baths; hotel next door. Park here.

Map No: 25

La Fuente de la Higuera

Partido de los Frontones
29400
Ronda
Málaga

Tel: 95 2114355 or
   610 847731
Fax: 95 2114356

Management: Christina and Pom Piek

Pom and Tina have travel in the blood; he sailed the oceans, she worked for an airline company. But then the magic of the Ronda mountains put them under its spell and they saw in this old mill a new dream; of a luxurious retreat for friends (and soon-to-be-friends) from the city, where good food, music, wine and company could ease away urban worries. Tina is the 'spark' — an enormously vivacious and likeable woman, it was she who travelled the Far East in search of the furnishings and fabrics which add razzmatazz to the enormous rooms and suites. Pom, too, seems born to the role of host; a raconteur by nature he has a dry humour born — perhaps — of many years in the UK. The conversion from mill to hotel has been accomplished with great style by the best local craftsmen; good plastering and beautiful planked floors give the place a manicured and stylish look and make a nice change from the usual beam and terracotta. And beds, lamps, chairs and tables bought out East (Tina's design) add a rich, exotic feel. The focus of the house is poolwards; beyond groves of olives and the changing colours of the Ronda mountains are a perfect backdrop for your sun-downer. At dinner feast on locally inspired cuisine and benefit from Pom's love of good wine.

Rooms: 3 with bath & wc + 5 Suites.
Price: Tw 14500 Pts; Ste (for 2) 16500-19500 Pts; Ste (for 4) 29000 Pts; Apt 18000 Pts.
Breakfast: Included.
Meals: On request. 2500 Pts (M).
Closed: Never.

How to get there: From Málaga N340 towards Cádiz then A376 to Ronda. Bypass Ronda on A376 towards Sevilla. Shortly after turning to Benaoján (don't take this!) turn right at sign for hotel. Pass under bridge then left at first fork, over bridge, left after approx. 200 yards then first track on right. Signposted.

200   **Map No:** 25

Molino del Santo

Bda. Estación s/n
29370
Benaoján
Málaga

Tel: 95 2167151
Fax: 95 2167327
E-mail: molino@logiccontrol.es
www: www.andalucia.com/molino

Management: Pauline Elkin and Andy Chapell

Pauline and Andy moved south in search of a better life. They restored a century-old mill in a spectacular area of the Grazalema National Park and are now thoroughly part of local life. Water rushes past flower filled terraces, under willows and fig trees, into the pool (heated for the cooler months). Rooms and restaurant all wear local garb — terracotta tiles, beams and rustic chairs. Some rooms have private terraces. Fresh flowers are ever present and the Molino's reputation for good Spanish food is made; most hotel guests are British but the Spanish flock in at weekends to enjoy local hams and sausages, rabbit and fresh fish as well as imaginative vegetarian cooking. Staff and owners are generous with advice on walks or bike rides straight from the hotel or will direct you to the sleepy little station for trains to Ronda or in the other direction past some of the loveliest 'white villages' of Andalusia. Fly to Gibraltar and then come by train! The Molino is deservedly one of the Sierra's most popular small hotels, with a clear will to make things better and better with each passing year — book ahead to guarantee a room. *Note: Superior rooms all have terraces!*

Rooms: 13 with bath or shower & wc + 1 suite.
Price: D/Tw 'Standard' 10400-14000 Pts; D/Tw 'Superior' 11950-14450; Ste 14200-16900 Pts inc. VAT and breakfast.
Breakfast: Included.
Meals: Lunch/Dinner 3000-3500 Pts (C).
Closed: 14 November-mid-February.

How to get there: From Ronda, C339/A473 towards Seville; just after km118 post, left towards Benaoján. After 10km, having crossed railway and river bridges, left to station and follow signs.

Map No: 25

201

Hotel Posada del Canónigo

Calle Mesones 24   **Tel:** 95 2160185
29420   **Fax:** 95 2160185
El Burgo
Málaga

Management: María Reyes

Your arrival in the mountain village of El Burgo will be memorable: it is a splash of brilliant white amid the ochres and greys of the surrounding limestone massif. Little visited, it will give you as essential a taste of Andalusian mountain life as can be found anywhere. This grand old village house is another good reason for coming. It is very much a family affair; 13(!) brothers and sisters helped restore and decorate the house. Bedrooms are simply furnished in local style with tiled floors, old bedsteads and lots of family things: prints, paintings and dried flowers have been lovingly arranged by María Reyes. It is all spotless and the owners are visibly proud of every last corner of this inn. There is a small dining room leading to a little patio where you breakfast in the morning sun and a newly opened *bodega*-style restaurant where only local dishes are on offer. Both sitting rooms have open hearths and exposed stonework and the whole place is uncannily quiet by Andalusian standards. Stay two nights to walk or let the owners take you riding in the virtually unknown National Park of the Sierra de la Nieves above Ronda.

Rooms: 12 with bath & wc + 1 suite.
Price: D/Tw 6000-7000 Pts; Ste 7500-8000 Pts.
Breakfast: 500 Pts.
Meals: Lunch/Dinner 1500 Pts(M).
Closed: Never.

How to get there: From Torremolinos to Cártama then continue to Calea, Alozaina, Yunquera and El Burgo. Turn right into village and ask — hotel is next to church of San Agustín.

La Posada del Torcal

Carretera La Hoya-La Higuera
29230
Villanueva de la Concepción
Málaga

Tel: 95 2031177/2111983
Fax: 95 2031006
E-mail: laposada@mercuryin.es
www: www.andalucia.com/posada-torcal

Management: Jan Rautavuori and Karen Ducker

Jan and Karen lived and worked on the nearby Costa until, one happy day, they ventured up into the magnificent Torcal National Park and saw the light! The fruit of their conversion from Costa to Sierra is a most fetching small hotel. The posada's base elements — tile, beam and woodwork — are true to local tradition; inside and out it feels first and foremost *Andaluz*. Each guest bedroom is dedicated to a different Spanish artist; oils are copies of the originals painted by Karen's brother Greg. Trimmings come from further afield — most remarkable are the king-size beds, some brass, some Gothic, some four-poster; they were shipped out from England. No expense nor care has been spared for your comfort; we liked the open-plan rooms which allow you to sip your welcoming bottle of *cava* from a corner tub yet not miss a second of the amazing views beyond. Underfloor heating warms in winter; Casablanca-style fans cool in summer. Most dishes on the posada's menu are local/Spanish but there are more familiar sounding ones, too. We were impressed by the friendliness and efficiency of the staff; there's good walking close by and a sauna to look forward to at the end of the day.

Rooms: 8 with bath & wc.
Price: S 12000 Pts; D/Tw 18000 Pts.
Breakfast: 1200 Pts.
Meals: Lunch/Dinner 4500 Pts (M).
Closed: 1 November-31 January.

How to get there: From Málaga N331 towards Antequera; take exit 148 for Casabermeja/Colmenar. In Casabermeja right (signed Almogía) then at next junction left to Villanueva de la C. At top of village, left at junction; after 1.5km right for La Joya/La Higuera. 3km to Hotel; on left.

Map No: 25

203

Casa de Elrond

Barrio Seco s/n
29230
Villanueva de la Concepción
Málaga

Tel: 95 2754091 or
689 939840
Fax: 95 2754091
E-mail: elrond@mercuryin.es
www: www.mercuryin.es

Management: Mike and Una Cooper

This is a favourite stopover in Andalusia and the reason why I'm such a fan is that Mike and Una are such genuinely <u>nice</u> people. I and a friend were there while on a walking holiday and Una made such a fuss of us that we were loath to leave! This mostly modern house is set back from a quiet road, surrounded by a carefully tended garden and has an amazing view down towards the Mediterranean. Don't miss sundown when range after range of mountains take on every imaginable hue of blue and purple. There are just three bedrooms leading off a small guest lounge: Mike, immensely practical, has just added a wood-burner. The rooms have modern pine furniture and duvets; one of them is large enough to sleep a family of three or four. It's a perfect place for walkers: return after a day in the remarkable Torcal Park to one of Una's vegetarian suppers: you eat out, of course, in the warmer months and in the kitchen-diner the rest of the year. Dinner includes a house red but you're welcome to bring your own if you prefer. Excellent value: do give it a go.

Rooms: 3 with shower & wc.
Price: D/Tw 5000 inc. breakfast.
Breakfast: Included.
Meals: Dinner 1200 Pts inc. a half-litre of wine.
Closed: Never.

How to get there: From Málaga N340 towards Antequera and Granada. At km241 post take N331 to Casabermeja and on to Villanueva de la C. Here turn left at junction and Casa de Elrond on right after 3km.

Map No: 26

Villa Turistica de la Axarquia

Carril del Cortijo Blanco s/n   **Tel:** 95 2536222
29710   **Fax:** 95 2536222
Periana   **E-mail:** vtaxarquia@arrakis.es
Málaga

Management: José Antonio Garcia

La Axarquia is another of the little known parts of the Costa hinterland: it's just beginning to make waves among those happy to trade beach for mountain. Head for Periana then follow a winding track up to this newborn holiday village which is taking root down among the much older olive groves surrounding it. It's all about the great outdoors here; horse-riding, volley ball, tennis, mountain-biking and canoeing — as well as swimming and walking — are all on tap. The hotel's architects have tried to create a villagey feel; houses are staggered along the different streets, colours vary, paths zigzag between the different levels. The interior décor is 'rustic-comfortable' and nearly all the rooms have views. The restaurant (open to non-residents) was busy the day we visited; breakfast here is buffet whilst at lunch and dinner emphasis is on local dishes: kid and rabbit are recommended by your chef. After dinner there are sometimes guitar concerts during the busier months. Out of season, relax with a good book or two and let the long, long vistas work their magic. It's good to see a hotel in this part of the world with an organic vegetable garden and proper facilities for the handicapped.

Rooms: 14 with bath or shower & wc + 6 studio flats + 20 houses.
Price: D/Tw 7500-8750 Pts; House (with 1 bedroom) 13500-16000 Pts; House (with 2 bedrooms) 17250-20250 Pts. All prices inc. VAT & breakfast.
Breakfast: Included — buffet.
Meals: Lunch/Dinner 1875 Pts (M); 3000 Pts (C).
Closed: Never.

How to get there: From N340 to Torre del Mar and here exit for Vélez Málaga. Bypass village, on towards Alhama, then left at signs to Periana; from here La Villa Turistica is signposted.

Hotel Paraíso del Mar

Calle Prolongación de Carabeo 22
29780
Nerja
Málaga

Tel: 95 2521621
Fax: 95 2522309
E-mail: info@hispanica-colint.es

Management: Enrique Caro Bernal

Nerja is one of the better known resort towns of the Costa del Sol, hardly an auspicious beginning when searching for that 'special' hotel; but the Paraíso is just that. In a quiet corner of the town and well away from the main drag of bars and restaurants, it stands at the edge of a cliff looking out to sea. It has been thoroughly revamped thanks to the unflagging efforts of the hotel's most charming young manager. The main house was built some 40 years ago by an English doctor; the other part is more recent. There are mature terraced gardens dropping down towards the beach; jasmine, palms and bougainvillaea give it all an utterly southern air. Many guestrooms have a view and some their own terrace. They are large with mostly modern furniture and all the trimmings; some have jacuzzi baths, all have bathrobes and good towels. Beneath the hotel are a sauna and a hot-tub, dug out of solid rock. It is all run on solar energy and it could be just the place to recharge your batteries and still survive on the 'Costa'. And there are six new suites just being finished as we go to press!

Rooms: 12 with bath & wc.
Price: S 6500-10000 Pts; D 7500-1200 Pts; D (with sea view) 10000-14500 Pts; D/Tw (with jacuzzi) 9500-13500 Pts; Ste 14000-19000 Pts.
Breakfast: Included.
Meals: None available.
Closed: Never.

How to get there: From Málaga N340 towards Motril. Arriving in Nerja follow signs to Parador; the Paraíso del Mar is next door.

Map No: 26

Molino de Santillán

Ctra. de Macharaviaya km 3
29730
Rincón de Victoria
Málaga

Tel: 95 2115780/2115781
Fax: 95 2115782

Management: Carlo Marchini

Carlo Marchini, tired of the cut and thrust of business in Madrid, has moved to the softer climes of Andalusia, bought an old farmhouse and, after years of careful restoration and planting he is — literally and metaphorically — beginning to harvest the fruits of all his efforts. The building is inspired by the hacienda style architecture of the New World: an arched patio opens at its southern end to catch the light and the view down to the sea. One of its wings is given over in its entirety to the restaurant where many ingredients come straight from the farm gardens. There's an interesting menu: especially popular with guests are aubergines stuffed with hake or loin of pork in honey and apple sauce; there's a good *paella*, too, if you ask Carlos in advance. Both the arched terraced area looking seawards and the ochre-coloured dining room are attractive backdrops for your feast. Rooms feel properly Andalusian. Stencilling and interesting colours add zest and there are Casablanca fans to keep the temperatures down and netting on windows to keep the mosquitoes at bay. Both Carlos and his daughter Adriana speak excellent English and are a winning combination.

Rooms: 9 with bath & wc.
Price: S 10900 Pts; D/Tw 13900 Pts.
Breakfast: 1300 Pts (buffet).
Meals: Lunch/Dinner 3000 Pts (M), 4500 Pts (C).
Closed: 15 January-18 February.

How to get there: From Málaga towards Motril on N340. Turn off for Macharaviaya and turn right at signs to right before you reach village. 1km of track to hotel.

Map No: 26

La Fonda
Calle Santo Domingo 7
29639
Benalmádena Pueblo
Málaga

Tel: 95 2568273
Fax: 95 2568273

Management:
José Antonio García

There *are* places on the Costa that have retained their identity and dignity through all those years of unbridled development. One of them is whitewashed, geranium-clad Benalmádena Pueblo; don't confuse it with Benalmádena Playa, which is best avoided. In a quiet street just off the pretty main square, La Fonda is a perfect place for a first or last night in Spain — it is just a quarter of an hour from the airport. The Fonda was the creation of architect Cesar Manrique; he is known for his lifelong battle to show that old and new buildings CAN look well together, providing the latter respect local custom. And this building is a hymn to the south; there are cool patios shaded by palms, potted aspidistras, geometric tiles, fountains, pebbled floors, all set off by glimpses of the glittering sea. Rooms are large, light, airy and marble-floored. Downstairs are wicker chairs and a shaded terrace. La Fonda's restaurant doubles as a Cookery School; treat yourself to a southern gourmet meal at half of the cost elsewhere. Or wander along to the square and watch the night in with a plate of olives, a glass of *fino* and the gaiety of Andalusian street-life.

Rooms: 27 with bath & wc + 7 in adjacent building.
Price: S 5300-8600; D/Tw 7600-12000 Pts inc. VAT.
Breakfast: Included.
Meals: Lunch/Dinner 3500 Pts (M), 4500 Pts (C).
Closed: Never.

How to get there: From Málaga take N340 towards Algeciras. Exit 223 for Benalmádena/Arroyo de la MIel. Follow signs to Benalmádena Pueblo; signposted in village.

Casa Aloha

Playa El Chaparral
CN.340 km.203
29648 Mijas Costa
Málaga

Tel: 95 2494540
Fax: 95 2494540

Management: Trisha and Ray Goddard

Caught between the devil and the deep blue sea? Well, perhaps, because Casa Aloha has the busy N340 coastal road to one side and the sparkling Mediterranean on the other. But the focus at Casa Aloha is certainly seawards, both from poolside and your restaurant table. The Goddards have many loyal (mostly British) fans who would stay nowhere else. Décor is certainly 'Costa-fancy' with a lacquered dining room suite, stuccoed ceilings (see photo), thick-pile carpets and an abundance of marble; the villa was owned by a wealthy middle-eastern gentleman. Ray (he played first division football) and Trisha (she "once had a farm in Africa") are a great partnership; he busies over the barbecue whilst she is front-of-house with guests. If you like your steaks big, eat here — and when it comes to *paella* Trisha says it's "hunt the rice!". The Beach room takes first prize with the swash of the waves just yards away; watch them from the *chaise longue* before slipping into your corner tub (yes, the taps *are* gold-plated!). Although you hear the rumble of traffic from the side bedrooms, a new bypass will soon take the gas-guzzlers away from Casa Aloha. Expect a generous welcome from your hosts.

Rooms: 5 with bath & wc.
Price: D/Tw 8050-9200 Pts inc. breakfast.
Breakfast: Included; cooked breakfasts on request.
Meals: Lunch 1500 Pts (M); dinner 4600 Pts (M).
Closed: Never.

How to get there: From Málaga N340 towards Cádiz/Algeciras. Just past km202 post exit for Cala de Mijas. Follow signs for Fuengirola/Málaga back onto motorway. Keep hard to right and take first slip road off to right. Casa Aloha on right.

Map No: 26

209

Santa Fe

Carretera de Monda Km3
Apartado 147
29100 Coín
Málaga

Tel: 95 2452916
Fax: 95 2453843
E-mail: santafe@v.net.es

Management: Warden and Arjan van de Vrande

Two young, enthusiastic and multi-lingual Dutch brothers have begun to make a name for themselves since taking over at Santa Fe. Warden and Arjan's old farmhouse sits among the citrus groves of the Guadalhorce valley, to one side of the road from Marbella up to Coín. The transformation from farm to small guest house has been scrupulously faithful to local tradition; bedrooms have pretty ceramic basins, rustic furniture and terracotta floors (tiles fired with the dog-paw print bring good luck!). Ochre walls feel properly ethnic; kilims add colour. Guests are Spanish and Costa-cosmopolitan. A Belgian chef waves his wand in the kitchen and devotees will drive miles for their feast: flambéed langoustines in brandy, sirloin of pork with a cream, raisin, sherry and pine kernel sauce and Dutch apple pie to follow. There is an attractive dining room of friendly proportions — log-fired in the winter — but most of the time you dine out beneath the old olive tree. Occasional, and imaginative, attractions include barbecues and live jazz. A casual, relaxed atmosphere but plenty of attention to the details too.

Rooms: 3 with bath & wc + 2 with basins sharing bathroom.
Price: D/Tw (sharing bath & wc) 7500 Pts; D/Tw 8500 Pts inc. VAT.
Breakfast: Included.
Meals: Lunch/Dinner 1600 Pts (M), 2500 Pts (C).
Closed: Last 2 weeks in November, last week in January & first week in February.

How to get there: From Málaga, N340 towards Cádiz. About 1km after airport, right to Coín. In Coín take Marbella road. After 3km Santa Fe is on right (signposted).

El Castillo de Monda
29110
Monda
Málaga

Tel: 95 2457142
Fax: 95 2457336
E-mail: monda@spa.es
www: www.costadelsol.spa.es/hotel/mc

Management: John Norris and Bruce Freestone

Caesar and Pompey fought it out in Spain at Munda and ever since historians have argued (remember the beginning of Mérimée's *Carmen*?) as to where the place really was: many would have the battlefield in the plain beneath the village of Monda. It's been an important strategic site over the centuries: your hotel has parts of 8th-century Moorish fortifications wrapped into its fabric. And what a position! High up above the village, reached by a series of steep switch-backs, the matchless panorama takes in the Sierra Nevada, the Torcal Park and the Ronda mountains. The hotel owes much to the Moorish tradition: there are fountains, wafer-bricked arches, ceramic tiles and extensive use of *muqarna*, the delicate stucco bas-relief which is the delight of the Alhambra Palace in Granada. But there are some rather English touches as well: prints along corridors and a collection of tankards in a smaller dining room suggest a certain nostalgia for Blighty. The main dining room evokes a medieval banqueting hall with its arches and flags. The classical Andalusian mix spills over to bedrooms too: four-posters and Moorish arches, terracotta and snazzy fabrics, and marbled and heated bathroom floors. Luxurious and fun.

Rooms: 24 with bath & wc + 2 suites.
Price: S 12500 Pts; D/Tw 15000 Pts; D/Tw 'Deluxe' 25000 Pts; D/Tw 'Deluxe' (with terrace) 28000 Pts; Ste (for 4) 70000 Pts. *20% supplement at Easter and Christmas.*
Breakfast: 750 Pts or 1500 Pts (full Engl.).
Meals: Lunch/Dinner 3000 Pts (M), 5000-6000 Pts (C).
Closed: Never.

How to get there: From Málaga N340 towqards Cádiz/Algeciras. Shortly before Marbella (don't turn off N340!) right towards Ojen/Coín. After 16km right into Monda and follow signs.

Map No: 25

211

Breakers Lodge Hostal

Avenida Las Mimosas 189
Linda Vista Baja
29678 San Pedro de Alcantara
Málaga

Tel: 95 2784780
Fax: 95 2784780

Management: Sharon and Mark Knight

Although no longer the little fishing village of yore, San Pedro is one of the Costa villages that has managed to retain its Spanishness. This modern villa is tucked away in one of its residential areas on a quiet road that leads straight down to the beach. Mark and Sharon have been in Southern Spain for many years and, though widely travelled, would live nowhere else. You'll be greeted with a smile here; they are sociable, talkative types, but know that your privacy is precious. An electronic gate pulls shut behind you, reminding you that things have moved on since Laurie Lee arrived, fiddle in hand. The style of the place is very 'Marbella': a bit ritzy with Doric columns, white cane furniture, a corner bar, padded headboards in the bedrooms. Some of the rooms give onto the pool at the back of the house; there is also a terrace area for sitting out with tea, or a beer. Give Sharon advance warning and her maid will come in and prepare you a *paella*. If not, walk into San Pedro and ask for Fernando's fish restaurant. You'll bless us for sending you there...

Rooms: 6 with bath & wc.
Price: D/Tw 10000-14000 Pts.
Breakfast: Included.
Meals: None available.
Closed: Never.

How to get there: From Málaga N340 towards Algecíras. Through San Pedro de Alcántara, under arch across road and exit shortly after for Benahavis. Back towards Málaga, under arch again and turn immediately right. House on right after approx. 200m.

Map No: 25

Casa Tanga Tanga

Apartado 349
29680
Estepona
Málaga

Tel: 95 2886590
Fax: 95 2886590

Management: Glenn & Caro Wallace-Davis

This is a fun place to stay — Glenn ran a safari lodge for 10 years in Kenya and *tanga tanga* means to enjoy oneself in Swahili. Guests become members of a lively family; join them and other visitors at the 'Dog & Duck' (sic) poolhouse for the daily cocktail or weekly barbecue; improve your tennis (Glenn is a qualified tennis coach); laze in the guests' sitting/music room in its own *casita*, or on the veranda beside the pool. Although life is mostly lived out of doors, the old house is large, rambling and welcoming with its durries, bookshelves and generous dining table. Caro has a designer's touch and loves cooking, both Spanish and other food. She grows her own Mediterranean vegetables and makes her own marmalade. The lovely bedrooms are big and filled with light from the windows that gaze over the hills. There are bits of old furniture, soft materials and cool tiles as well as attractive well-fitted bathrooms. Glenn and Caro organise local visits, 10-day Moroccan trips and willingly help with requests for bird-watching, golf or bikes.

Rooms: 6 doubles (one with adjacent single room) with shower or bath & wc (one not en suite).
Price: D/Tw 15000 Pts.
Breakfast: Included.
Meals: Dinner 4000 Pts (M).
Closed: 1 November-1 March.

How to get there: From San Pedro de Alcántara N340 towards Estepona. After 4.5km right to Cancelada. Through village following signs to Clínica Dr Oliver. Follow unsurfaced road for 1km to Tanga Tanga on the right. (Details on booking.)

Banu Rabbah

Calle Sierra Bermeja s/n
29490
Benarrabá
Málaga

Tel: 95 2150288/2150144
Fax: 95 2150208

Management: Jesús García

Benarrabá is named after the Berber tribesman who first settled here with his family: the Banu Rabbah of the hotel's name. The hotel, built on the initiative of the local council, is in the capable hands of a group of six young people from the village. What makes this place special is its exhilarating position: almost 2,000 feet up with a magnificent panoramic sweep of mountain, white village and wooded hillsides. The building has a rather cumbersome design but wins points for its bedrooms: their best feature is the generous terraces. The hand-painted wooden beds, writing desks and the bright bedspreads add a merry note and their French windows bring in the light and the view. The restaurant, open to non-residents, makes a feature of local produce: try the *saltavallao*, a sort of hot gazpacho and perhaps one of the local almond cakes for desert. After dinner do take a stroll through the village: unlike in nearby Gaucín you are unlikely to meet other foreigners. And if you're feeling more energetic hike down to the Genal (route notes provided by the hotel) where you can swim in the warmer months. Local legend has it that the Moors built a secret tunnel between here and Gaucín.

Rooms: 12 with bath & wc.
Price: Tw 7000- 8000 Pts.
Breakfast: 450 Pts.
Meals: Lunch/dinner 1450 Pts inc. wine.
Closed: Never.

How to get there: From Málaga N340 towards Cádiz. Then take A377 via Manilva to Gaucín. Here towards Ronda on A369 and after 4.5km right to Benarrabá. Signposted.

Map No: 25

Hotel Casablanca

Calle Teodoro de Molina 12   **Tel:** 95 2151019
29480   **Fax:** 95 2151019
Gaucín
Málaga

Management: Susan and Michael Dring

Gaucín is one of Andalusia's most spectacular mountain villages. Its labyrinthine, whitewashed streets huddle against a hillside beneath a Moorish castle; eagles wheel overhead, the views are glorious. But the town lacked anywhere decent to stay until Mike and Sue — they once ran another of the delectable places included in this guide! — came across this grand old village house and set about creating the hotel of their dreams. You too will soon fall under its spell; pass through the enormous wooden doors to emerge into the bar. Beyond is a walled garden where palms, magnolia and jacaranda lend colour and shade — a fountain murmurs beside the pool. Terraces on different levels look out across terracotta rooftops to the castle and all the way to the distant Rif mountains of Morocco; the sunsets from here are amazing! Most rooms have their own private terrace; there are parquet or terracotta floors, good beds, and bright colours jazz up the bathrooms. Dine in at least once; the food is spicy and cosmopolitan, following the dictates of what's in season. And the included breakfast is properly generous.

Rooms: 6 with bath & wc.
Price: S 7000 Pts; D/Tw 10000-15000 Pts.
Breakfast: Included.
Meals: Light lunches approx. 1500 Pts; dinner 3000 Pts (closed on Mondays).
Closed: 1 November-1 March.

How to get there: From Málaga N340 towards Algeciras. After Estepona right on MA539 via Manilva to Gaucín (don't take Casares turn!). Here into centre and to street of San Sebastián church; follow one way system right towards Ronda; hotel on left.

La Almuña

Apartado 20
29480
Gaucín
Málaga

Tel: 95 2151200
Fax: 95 2151343
www: www.andalucia.com/gaucin/almuna

Management: Diana Paget

The old farmstead of La Almuña sits high up on a mountainside beside ancient footpaths used in former days by smugglers and *bandaleros,* later, officers and their mounts would pass by en route from Gibraltar to Ronda. Views from the house's terrace are dreamlike; the eye reaches across the last foothills of the Sierra, white hilltop villages, all the way down to the coast and on to Africa. Diana's is a warm, relaxed home; she greets you with a smile and always the offer of tea or something stronger. Her cooking is legendary in the area; expect to be dining in company. Much of her food has come from the estate and what doesn't is carefully chosen locally; you may be treated to smoked salmon, lamb, partridge or quail. Veg are fresh, herbs straight from the garden and wine always *à volonté.* Diana and her mother busy to and fro from kitchen to table; four Staffordshire bull terriers look on. The drawing room (see photo) is utterly homely; bedrooms are a happy marriage of 'English-country' and 'Spanish rustic'. Come to La Almuña to walk, talk and dine in the most congenial of company. And there are four horses just waiting to be saddled for exploring this beautiful area.

Rooms: 4 with bath & wc.
Price: S 7000 Pts; D/Tw 14000 Pts.
Breakfast: Included.
Meals: Dinner 3500 Pts (M); lunch by prior arrangment.
Closed: Never.

How to get there: From Gaucín take C341 towards Algeciras. At km 44.8 turn left onto estate's private drive (white and ochre post at entrance); La Almuña 2nd house to right behind cypress trees.

Map No: 25

Las Navezuelas

A-432 km 43.5
Apartado 14
41370 Cazalla de la Sierra
Sevilla

Tel: 95 4884764
Fax: 95 4884764

Management: Luca Cicorella and Mariló Tena Martín

A place of peace and great natural beauty, Las Navezuelas is a 16th-century olive mill on a farm set in 136 hectares of green meadows, oak forest and olive groves. Water streams down from the Sierra, often along Moorish-built channels. Boar and deer roam the Aracena range to the north and pretty Cazalla is two miles away. The house is pure Andalusia with beams and tiles while the garden is a southern feast too with its palms and orange trees. The rooms are fresh, light and simple with old bits of furniture and nothing fussy to distract you from the pleasure of simply being here. There are two sitting rooms and a welcoming restaurant with log fires in winter. The menu includes delicious local dishes made almost exclusively with ingredients from the farm — from veg to chicken, lamb and ham. And there's home-made jam for breakfast. The friendly young owners will go out of their way to help and give advice on expeditions on foot, horse or bicycle and where best to watch birds; the whole area is an ornithologist's dream. Many of our readers have written to say how much they like it!

Rooms: 4 with shower & wc + 2 suites + 2 studios for 2.
Price: D/Tw 7500-8500 Pts; Ste 9000-9800 Pts; Studio 10500-11500 inc. VAT.
Breakfast: Included.
Meals: Lunch/Dinner 2000 Pts (M).
Closed: 7 January-20 February.

How to get there: From Sevilla A431 to Cantillana. Here take A432 towards El Pedroso/Cazalla. At km43.5 post right at sign for Las Navezuelas.

Map No: 18

217

Hotel Restaurante Posada del Moro

Paseo del Moro s/n
41370
Cazalla de la Sierra
Sevilla

Tel: 95 4884858
Fax: 95 4884858

Management: Julia and Lucía Piñero Marrón

Cazalla is a summer refuge for Sevillians gasping for clean cool air. The well-advised stay with Julia and Lucía Piñeiro Marrón, the charming and gregarious sisters who have devoted themselves to this hotel with much warmth and unflagging enthusiasm for the past decade. If it looks rather like a wedding cake, maybe it's because staying here *is* something of an occasion, especially for lovers of good food. The restaurant is decorated in 1920s style; it has a name for its roast game — try the rabbit or hare — or the mountain-cured ham, it's out of this world. In the summer months you may be treated to a poolside barbecue or perhaps a flamenco evening. The bedrooms all look out over the garden at the back. They are smart, comfortable and very southern with lots of marble and original paintings, many of them by Julia. It is all delectably Andalusian with an amusing hint of kitsch. Base yourselves here and explore the narrow streets of Cazalla and the lovely mountains just beyond. Rooms and food are both good value and these two sisters clearly enjoy their hotel as much as their guests.

Rooms: 15 with bath or shower & wc.
Price: S 5000 Pts; D/Tw 8000 Pts; Tr 10000 Pts inc. VAT.
Breakfast: 500 Pts.
Meals: Lunch/Dinner 2500 Pts (M), 5000 Pts (C).
Closed: Never.

How to get there: From Sevilla N630 towards Mérida. Shortly after Santiponce, right onto C431 to Alcalá del Río, then via Cantillana/Pedroso on C433 to Cazalla. At roundabout entering Cazalla, right at sign for hotel — 200m on left.

Map No: 18

La Cartuja de Cazalla

Ctra Cazalla — Constantina A455 km 55.2 **Tel:** 95 4884516
41370   **Fax:** 95 4883515
Cazalla de la Sierra
Sevilla

Management: Carmen Ladrón de Guevara Bracho

An exceptional place, an exceptional owner. The 15th-century monastery lay empty for 150 years until Carmen Ladrón, visiting in the 1970s, knew she had found her mission. She founded a Centre for Contemporary Culture with an art gallery (paintings by resident artist Amaya Espinoza). The rooms are decorated with works by artist guests; painters, sculptors or musicians can sometimes give their art in exchange for their stay. The guestrooms (they finance the centre) are in the old monastery gatehouse. It has been daringly restored with light streaming in through a huge skylight. It marries 90s designer chic with a sense of the past; Carmen calls it a building for the 21st century! The bedrooms have modern furniture and bathrooms and no telephones or TVs to spoil the peace; some of them have views of the chapel. Dine with Carmen in her home next door (local dishes often made with home-grown ingredients) but give most importance to the *tertulia* afterwards, a forum for sharing knowledge and ideas. Uncannily peaceful, we still savour memories of a wander through the monastery's grounds in the early morning light with only birdsong reaching our soothed ears.

Rooms: 8 with bath or shower & wc + 4 suites.
Price: S 9000 Pts; D/Tw 12000-15000; Ste 18000 inc. VAT.
Breakfast: Included.
Meals: Lunch/Dinner 3000 Pts (M).
Closed: Christmas.

How to get there: From Sevilla C431 to Cantillana then A432 to El Pedroso & Cazalla. There, right onto A455 towards Constantina. La Cartuja is at km2.5 post.

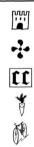

Casa Montehuéznar

Avenida de la Estación 15
41360
El Pedroso
Sevilla

Tel: 95 4889000/4889015
Fax: 95 4889304
E-mail: hueznar@arrakis.es
www: www.arrakis.es/~hueznar

Management: Pablo García Rios

This could be a perfect place to stay if you want to combine walks in the Sierra Morena with day trips to Seville; from El Pedroso you can take a train to the city mid-morning and then back early in the evening — and it is a lovely ride. This grand town house was built at the end of the last century, when mineral extraction briefly brought wealth and fame to the area. Last year two young brothers joined a growing number of hoteliers who believe that small can be just as beautiful. It is all utterly *Andaluz*: a sober façade with the original wrought-iron balconies and window grilles; a weighty door leads through to the central patio, where ferns, aspidistra, geraniums, palm tree and fountain make it the spot to breakfast or dine when the weather is right. The original tiled and bannistered staircase leads to the rooms; they have attractively carved wooden furniture and each is named after one of Andalusia's provinces — Seville being the biggest. Food is regional/family with deer, boar and rabbit the specialities; Riojas and Ribera del Duero are the right accompaniment. Kind staff and very kind prices too.

Rooms: 8 with bath & wc.
Price: S 4000 Pts; D/Tw 7500 Pts.
Breakfast: 500 Pts.
Meals: Lunch/Dinner 1950 Pts (M), approx. 2500-3000 Pts (C).
Closed: Never.

How to get there: Arriving in Seville from Madrid take SE30 ringroad towards Mérida. Exit off this ring road at signs for C433 La Rinconada. Follow C443 towards Cazalla to Pedroso, where hotel is opposite the railway station.

Hotel Cortijo Aguila Real

Carretera Guillena-Burguillos, Km 4   **Tel:** 95 5785006
41210   **Fax:** 95 5784330
Guillena
Sevilla

Management: Isabel Martínez

If you are seeking a taste of refined aristocratic Andalusia... this could be for you. Aguila Real is every inch the classic *cortijo* and just a dozen miles from the narcotic charms of Sevilla (you can just see the Giralda tower from the gardens). Passing under the main gate you enter the huge inner courtyard where there is bougainvillaea in profusion; the old dovecote and a water trough remind you that this was once a working farm. The public rooms are an exercise in controlled elegance, decorated in pastel colours with heavy old tables, paintings and lots of books — and beautiful barrel-vaulted ceilings. Silver cutlery and classical music in the dining room seem perfectly in keeping with the food, which is fairly *haute cuisine*. Most vegetables are home-grown, portions are generous, the wine list extensive. The rooms are plush with hand-painted furniture, huge double beds and attractive bathrooms; some have their own terrace. But what makes it unforgettable is the palm-filled garden, carefully lit at night — an irresistibly romantic spot.

Rooms: 12 with bath & wc + 3 suites.
Price: D/Tw 15000-18000 Pts; Ste 20000-25000 Pts.
Breakfast: 1500 Pts (buffet).
Meals: Lunch/Dinner 3500 Pts.
Closed: Never.

How to get there: From Sevilla N630 towards Mérida. After approx 9km right on SE180 to Guillena. Through village and at first traffic-lights right on SE181 towards Burguillos: hotel signposted after 4km on right.

Map No: 24   **221**

Cortijo Torre de la Reina

Paseo de la Alameda s/n
41209
Torre de la Reina (Guillena)
Sevilla

Tel: 95 5780136
Fax: 95 5780122
E-mail: torredelareina@sarenet.es

Management: José María Medina

We were instantly won over by the silence of the *cortijo*; we have enticing memories of a wander through its gardens at night with the courtyard, gardens and old watchtower all delicately lit. Originally this was a medieval house-fortress. Later it was converted into a true Renaissance hacienda and it was recently declared a national monument. The gardens are a southern feast of huge palm trees, bougainvillaea and scented jasmine. The house is just as peaceful and elegant inside. In what used to be the granary is a vast guest lounge with antique furniture, lovely *estera* matting, chess sets and plenty of books. Yellow, ochre and white combine to give warmth to this light airy building and in winter a log fire burns in the great old hearth. This is a hotel that courts both travellers and business people; your bedroom comes equipped with mini-bar, satellite television and super-plush bathrooms. But it still feels homely thanks to the warm earthy colours, old prints, bright rugs and fireplaces (in the suites). An elegant and utterly southern hostelry and only a shake away from beautiful Seville.

Rooms: 12 with bath & wc + 6 suites.
Price: D/Tw 15000-19000 Pts; Ste 19000-24000 Pts.
Breakfast: 1200 Pts.
Meals: Lunch/Dinner 3200 Pts (M).
Closed: Never.

How to get there: From Sevilla N630 towards Mérida. After Itálica ruins, right towards Córdoba/La Algaba. At roundabout in La Alcaba, road towards Alcalá del Río. After about 1.5km left to Torre de la Reina. On left as you enter village: white and yellow gate.

El Esparragal

Carretera de Mérida Km 795   **Tel:** 95 5782702
41860   **Fax:** 95 5782783
Gerena
Sevilla

Management: The Oriol Ybarra Family

Monks of the order of San Jerónimo built a monastery here in the 15th century in a setting of isolated, rare beauty; later, a *cortijo* was carefully grafted on to the religious edifice when Disestablishment sent the Brothers packing. At the end of the nineteenth century came extensive reform and embellishment; thus was created one of the most beguiling buildings of southern Spain. The main façade will raise a sigh with its ceramic tiled tower, Roman arched windows and bougainvillaea; its left flank takes in the 17th-century chapel. Beyond it are two main patios (one of them the original cloister) and the guest rooms and suites; you will travel far to find any that quite match them. Approach them past fountains and arches; Spain's best-known designers have created a southern miracle in salons, dining room and guest suites; the whole hotel is a 'Who's Who' of fabric, tile, and furniture 'names'. Rooms fit for a king and for you; we can only *begin* to describe the oil paintings, the *mudéjar* doors, the gilt mirrors, the tapestries and the elegance that permeates every corner. Ride out into Esparragal's 3,000 hectares on Andalusian thoroughbreds, dine in on game or estate-raised beef; treat yourself to an Arabian night that you'll never forget.

Rooms: 18 with bath & wc.
Price: D/Tw 16000-21000 Pts.
Breakfast: Included.
Meals: Lunch/Dinner 3000 Pts (M).
Closed: 15 July-15 August.

How to get there: From Seville N630 north towards Mérida. After 21km left towards Gerena (having earlier passed another turn for Gerena). Signposted on left after 1.5 km.

Map No: 24   **223**

El Triguero
Calle Nardos 26
41410
Carmona
Sevilla

Tel: 955 953626 or
91 4116974
Fax: 91 6611742

Management: Teresa Mencos

El Triguero is cradled by low hills looking out across the rich farmlands of Sevilla's hinterland: fields of wheat and sunflowers are interspersed with pastureland where beef cattle and fighting bulls are reared. Although you are very close to beautiful Carmona (why do so many miss this unforgettable town?) and Sevilla too, the setting could hardly be more bucolic. As you enter the grand reception hall and are shown up to your room by the cheery housekeeper, a veil of silence seems to wrap around you. I stayed in the amazing tower room of the photo: the views from here are, of course, the best and I loved its warm colours and collection of old prints and was happy with a small shower room. The other bedrooms are larger and are graced with the family antiques: old writing desks, carved figurines of the Saints, probably cut flowers, maybe a brightly painted rush-seated chair. It feels just like a grand family home, not a mite studied but with a simple elegance just the same. Both meals and rooms are brilliant value and the dining room, looking out across a citrus grove to the pool, is heavenly: just birdsong to accompany you at breakfast. Visits to the stud-farm next door can be arranged.

Rooms: 9 with bath or shower & wc.
Price: S 5000 Pts; D/Tw 7000 Pts inc. breakfast.
Breakfast: Included.
Meals: Lunch/Dinner 2000 Pts (M).
Closed: Never.

How to get there: From Sevilla towards Cordoba on NIV then right to Carmona. Here take N392 for El Viso del Alcor (signs too for LIDL). Hotel entrance is on left at km29 post. Signposted

Hotel Simón

Calle García de Vinuesa 19
41001
Sevilla
Sevilla

Tel: 95 4226660/4226615
Fax: 95 4562241
E-mail: hotel-simon@jet.es
www: www.sol.comysimon@estanciases.es

Management:
Francisco Aguayo

A stone's throw from the Cathedral in a quiet street leading down towards the Guadalquivir river, the Simón is a friendly, unpretentious little hotel that is ideal for those travelling on a tighter budget. The gentle-mannered owner, Francisco ('Frank') Aguayo García enjoys receiving English guests and practising his (excellent) English. The hotel is utterly Sevillian; you pass through the main portal, then a second wrought-iron door and on into a cool inner patio. There are tables and chairs here to sit amid aspidistras and ferns, the perfect escape from the throbbing heat. The dining room has mirrors and ceramic-tiled walls, period tables and chandeliers to remind you that this was once a bourgeois residence. The guestrooms are set around the patio and reached by a marble staircase. They are clean, bright, simply decorated, come in varying sizes and have that blissful summer luxury — air conditioning. There are plenty of restaurants and bars nearby and advice from the young, friendly staff on where to find the best *tapas*. A hotel with an obvious will to improve with each passing year.

Rooms: 25 with bath & wc + 4 suites.
Price: S 6000-7500 Pts; D/Tw 9000-11500 Pts; Ste 12500-15000 Pts.
Breakfast: 500 Pts.
Meals: None available.
Closed: Never.

How to get there: From Plaza Nueva in centre of Seville take Avenida de la Constitución (if closed to traffic tell police you are going to hotel) then right onto Calle Vinuesa (one way).

Map No: 25

225

Casa Nº 7

Calle Virgenes 7
41004
Sevilla
Sevilla

Tel: 95 4221581 or
607 323665
Fax: 95 421527

Management: Gonzalo del
Río y Gonzalez-Gordon

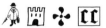

The idea of a hotel with the feel of a private home is a rare thing in Spain, but this exceptionally kind aristocrat from Jerez has a great fondness for Britain and the British. It was perhaps memories of England's country houses which inspired the conversion of his Seville home to a hostelry. It was no rush job; he preferred to spend "an extra year or two" so that every last inch should evoke the mood of privileged intimacy which is utterly in keeping with Sevilla's Moorish architecture. Bedrooms are regal affairs; fabrics, furniture, lighting and bathrooms are all top-notch and the photos of famous forebears, books (*Who's Who*!) and magazines help create the mood of home from home. Three first floor reception rooms give into the patio-bedroom. The cool and elegant drawing room is a perfect spot for a pre-dinner glass of *fino*; it will be from the family's Jerez *bodega*, of course. In a quiet dining room there are scrambled eggs for breakfast served by a white-gloved butler. You are in a quiet Santa Cruz street (you can see the Giralda from the roof terrace), Gonzalo knows all the best places to eat and drink and nearby is a great flamenco bar. A further two rooms are in the pipeline.

Rooms: 4 with bath & wc.
Price: D/Tw 22000 Pts.
Breakfast: Included (full English).
Meals: None available.
Closed: Never.

How to get there: At heart of Santa Cruz quarter. Park in Aparcamento 'Cana y Cueto' at junction of Calle Cano y Cueto and Menendez Pelayo (next to the Jardines de Murillo). Tell attendant you are staying at Casa Nº 7. From here 5 minutes walk to hotel (or take taxi).

225A

Map No: 25

Hostería del Laurel

Plaza de los Venerables 5
41004
Sevilla
Sevilla

Tel: 95 4220295/4210759
Fax: 95 4210450

Management:
David Márquez López

The Laurel stands in an attractively authentic setting at the heart of Santa Cruz (the old Jewish quarter); you knew there must be a friendly small hotel somewhere in the delicious anarchy of this labyrinthine quarter but it just wasn't there until the Marquez family converted the space above their restaurant to create 21 guestrooms. The *bodega* has been here forever — it is mentioned in Zorilla's *Don Juan Tenorio*. You enter by way of a classic Sevillian bar with its hams and beautiful old tiles. Its reputation with the locals is clearly well-established if a head count is anything to go by! We agree with the hotel's young owner, David Marquez, who describes the home cooking here as simply *buenísima*. If you're in carnivorous mood try the oxtail — *rabo de toro* — if not, the *merluza* (hake) *Doña Inés*. The setting alone would make it memorable. The bedrooms are on two floors, those up above are rather quieter and refreshingly simple (well-equipped nonetheless), spotlessly clean and worth every peseta. They are all named after one of Zorilla's characters. Best to garage the car and then taxi to the hotel if you´re carrying heavy suitcases.

Rooms: 21 with bath or shower & wc.
Price: S 5000-9000 Pts; D/Tw 7500-12500 Pts; Tr 9000-15000 Pts.
Breakfast: 650 Pts.
Meals: Lunch/Dinner 2200 Pts (M), 4500 Pts (C).
Closed: Never.

How to get there: On foot: From the Giralda, take Calle Mateos Gago. Take first right at bar Las Columnas and ask for Plaza de los Venerables. Nearest parking next to Hotel Alfonso XIII.

Map No: 25

226

Hacienda de San Rafael

Apartado 28
Carretera Nacional IV (km 594)
41730 Las Cabezas de San Juan
Sevilla

Tel: 95 5872193
Fax: 95 5872201

Management: Kuky and Tim Reid

As southern Spanish as can be. Handsome San Rafael lies contentedly amid the gently undulating farmlands of Seville's hinterland. Half a mile or so of olive-lined drive leads to its cheery main façade, doors and windows picked out against the white with a simple band of ochre paint. Olives were once milled here; Kuky remembers it all from her childhood. She could scarcely have imagined that one day she and an English gentleman husband would be be at the reins! Guestrooms give onto a cobbled central patio, the inner sanctuary of any true *cortijo*; the glorious bougainvillaea is just three years old! Each room has a shady, veranda with cane furniture for sitting out — you can dine here should you prefer. They also have a mezzanine sitting area beneath high ceilings, 'Casablanca' fans and open-plan bathrooms beyond an open arch and antique dresser. There are two lounges where oriental furnishings and prints collected on trips to the East go well with more local pieces. But the tranquility of the place and the vastness of the views from the house are what we most remember. We liked Tim and Kuky's enthusiasm for their home and new role as hosts.

Rooms: 11 with bath & wc.
Price: D/Tw 28000 inc. breakfast.
Breakfast: Included.
Meals: Picnic 3000 Pts; Dinner 7000 Pts.
Closed: 16 November-14 March.

How to get there: Leave Seville following signs for Cádiz. BEFORE you get to motorway branch off onto the NIV. Just past km594 post and over brow of hill (keep well to right here!) right into main entrance to farm.

227

Map No: 25

The Balearics

Les Terrasses

Ctra de Santa Eulària km 10
Apartado 1235
07800 Ibiza
Ibiza

Tel: 971 332643
Fax: 971 338978

Management: Françoise Pialoux

Françoise Pialoux has crafted, planted and furnished a remarkable vision in this hidden corner of Ibiza. She is an immensely likeable, vivacious woman and her character seems to infuse every last corner of Les Terrasses. The farm stands alone on a knoll in the island's centre surrounded by terraces of fruit trees and exotic plants. In the sitting room there are deep sofas, lace curtains, books and a piano; hammocks await you in the shade outside and two secluded pools, one of them heated, are hidden away behind stands of bamboo. The bedrooms are on different levels, some in the main house and others in the converted outbuildings. No two are alike and nearly all the well-known design mags have run articles on them; the rich colours, hand-embroidered bedspreads, bamboo-shaded terraces, open hearths, candelabras, wooden and terracotta floors are a photographer's dream. Choose where and when you'd like to breakfast — by one of the two pools, in the house or in your room. Stay for dinner, too: fish is usually a strong feature. But do book well in advance to be sure of a room; there is no better place to unwind.

Rooms: 7 with bath & wc + 1 suite.
Price: S 15000-16500 Pts; D/Tw 17000-20000 Pts;
Ste 23000-28000 Pts.
Breakfast: 1000 Pts.
Meals: Lunch 2500 Pts; dinner 3900 Pts (M). Closed
Wednesday nights.
Closed: 15 November-20 January.

How to get there: From Ibiza towards Santa Eulària.
After 9km on right hand side you will see a rock painted
cobalt blue. Right here, on up the track and Les
Terrasses is on your left.

El Palacio

Calle de la Conquista 2
07800
Ibiza
Ibiza

Tel: 971 301478
Fax: 971 391581
E-mail: etienne@ctv.es
www: www.elpalacio.com

Management: Corinne Etienne

Five Swiss friends stumbled on this thousand year-old Palace, bought it on a whim and the rest, as they say, is just film history. Because every corner of El Palacio is dedicated to the Seventh Art, if you have more than a passing interest in cinema this is your hotel. Prized artefacts include Casablanca's Oscar, James Dean's only film awards, Norma Jean's handbag, the sledge from Citizen Kane, signed portraits of all the stars and much, much more. And you're at the heart of Ibiza's old town with an enticing walled garden where palm and fig, banana and vine add an almost tropical veneer. A marble foyer with photos and memorabilia leads you towards a lounge with books and all the great films on video. Each bedroom pays homage to a different artist (see below) with posters, photos, cuttings and a potted biography. Marilyn's two suites reign supreme at the top, Garbo's room is 'retro', James Dean has a brilliant view and is... well, cool. The price of your room includes free entry to two of the town's best discos. *Note: when hotel is closed reservations via: Marlise Etienne, Büro Cortesi Biel, Burggasse 14, CH-2502 Biel/Bienne, Switzerland. Tel: 41-32 3293929 Fax: 41-32 3293938*

Rooms: 2 doubles + 5 suites.
Price: D (Bogart) 25000-28000 Pts; D (Disney) 27000-31000 Pts; Ste (Chaplin, Dean, Garbo, Monroe West) 33000-37000 Pts; Ste (Monroe Pink) 41000-47000 Pts.
Breakfast: Included.
Meals: None available.
Closed: November-pre-Easter week.

How to get there: In Ibiza town follow signs for Dalt Vila/Centro Histórico. Enter old walled town and continue climbing up towards Castle. El Palacio is to right about half way up (with clapper-board sign).

Can Curreu

Ctra. San Carlos km 12
07850
Santa Eulària
Ibiza

Tel: 971 335280
Fax: 971 335280
E-mail: curreu@ibiza-hotels.com
www: www.ibiza-hotels.com/CAN-CURREU

Management: Vicente Marí

Can Curreu is up with the *crème de la crème* of the Balearic's small country hotels, a place where every last detail, finish, brushstroke, and corner has been crafted with the patience and care of a Zen monk. No monolith, this; the idea was to recreate the feel of an Ibizan village, so each room stands apart from its neighbours, terraces are multi-levelled, paths twist and turn. All the rooms have private terraces. The décor in the bedrooms is local, fresh, and designed for deep comfort. There are handsome olive-planked ceilings, curtained-off bathrooms (the loo is separate) and a whole host of little details like a daily change of sheets and the possibility of having breakfast served on your terrace. The disciplined may like to use the gymnasium and the pool and afterwards flop in the sauna or on the sun terrace. Horse-riding and cycling can be arranged and so, too, can sailing trips with Vicente to little-known *calas* off the southern coast. Well worth the expense. The restaurant is getting a name for itself too.

Rooms: 6 with bath & wc + 5 suites.
Price: Tw 25000-30000 Pts; Ste 35000-40000 Pts.
Breakfast: Included — buffet.
Meals: Dinner approx. 4000 Pts (C).
Closed: Never.

How to get there: From Ibiza to Santa Eulària. Here towards San Carlos. 1km before San Carlos (at km12 post) turn left at signs for Can Curreu.

230

Ca's Pla

Venda de Rubio 59
Apartado de Correos 777
07800 Ibiza
Ibiza

Tel: 971 334587 /334603
Fax: 971 334604

Management: Massimo and Natalia Fenaroli

Although you're only a few miles from the sea Ca's Pla feels deeply rural, hidden away among pine forest and groves of carob and olive. We spent two happy nights here and it evoked strong memories of a South American hacienda with its low terracotta tiled buildings, colour-washed walls, wooden porches, and wicker furniture. This 17th century farmhouse has seen many a change since Italians Massimo and Natalia came to holiday at the beginning of the seventies; later came the idea of sharing it with guests and they seem born to it — polyglot, sophisticated and as relaxed as you'd like to feel yourself when on holiday. They've worked wonders in Ca's Pla's gardens; camellia, elephant grass, palm and agave add exotic spice between house, pool and bedrooms. What bedrooms! — they reminded us of a special box of chocolates: bright wrapping, rich insides, for a special occasion. There are ribboned and cushioned beds, ceiling fans, rugged floors, hand-embroidered sheets and gauzed windows to catch the breeze and keep out the mosquitoes. There are any number of enchanting spots in which to read or daydream. Breakfast heartily, then let Massimo advise on where to visit, walk or swim.

Rooms: 16 with bath & wc + 4 suites.
Price: Tw 14000-18000 Pts; Tw 'Superior' 16000-20000 Pts; Ste 18000-28000 Pts.
Breakfast: 1300 Pts (buffet).
Meals: Occasionally available, prices vary. Please ask.
Closed: Mid November-end March.

How to get there: From Ibiza towards Santa Eulària, then left to Sant Miquel de Balansat. Here carry on towards Port de Sant Miquel de B., and at km14 post turn left (just before tight bend to right). Up hill to house on left.

Sa Posada d'Aumallia

Camino Son Prohens 1027   **Tel:** 971 582657
07200   **Fax:** 971 721221
Felanitx
Mallorca

Management: The Martí Gomila family

Just to the side of a narrow lane that cuts a secret way through Mallorca's garrigue (with its cypress trees and vines so reminiscent of parts of Provence) Sa Posada d'Aumalia has established a name for good old-fashioned hostelry in a not so old-fashioned building. Entertaining comes naturally to the Martí Gomilla family; all are musicians and five times a week during the season one of the brothers gives a piano recital — and once a month one of the island's better-known musicians performs. Cane furniture beneath wooden-raftered porches give the place a rather colonial air even though Aumalia is just 20 years old. Aspidistra, rubber plants, bananas and errant peacock reinforce the 'hacienda' feel; sun-loungers around the pool and modern globe lampshades add an assertive modern touch. Your bedroom is a large, airy affair with its own terrace and garden furniture. There will be a basket of fruit, a welcoming bottle of Cava and loads of extras in the bathroom. A cool, scented breeze cutting down from the nearby peak of San Salvador helped make the meal that we shared with Maria Antonia a double treat; food is refined, local, fairly priced and prepared with love by both mother and daughter. There are lots of good bottles on the wine list, too.

Rooms: 14 with bath & wc.
Price: S 13500-16500 Pts; D/Tw 18000-22000 Pts.
Breakfast: Included — buffet.
Meals: Lunch/Dinner 1500-1600 Pts (M) exc. wine. Book ahead.
Closed: December & January.

How to get there: From Airport on motorway to Llucmajor then on to Campos then to Felanitx. Here first follow signs for Manacor, and at roundabout on outskirts towards Son Prohens. Aumallia signposted after 5km.

Hotel San Lorenzo

San Lorenzo 14
07012
Palma de Mallorca
Mallorca

Tel: 971 728200
Fax: 971 711901
E-mail: sanlorenzo@fehm.es
www: www.fehm.es/pmi/sanlorenzo

Management: Rudolf Schmid

Dominating the waterfront, Palma's gigantic Cathedral is the most tangible reminder of an age when the town was a major hub on the Mediterranean trading routes. The many grand mansion houses of the old town — rebuilt after a great fire in the Miiddle Ages — also bear witness to that era. Among them don't miss diminutive San Lorenzo, standing cheek-by-jowl with the buttresses of the Santa Cruz church in a pretty street of pastel façades. An imposing portal, wrought-iron grille and then a wide sweep of staircase usher you up and into a hotel that is as intimate and caring as they come. Each of the plush bedrooms differs from the next; No.6 has its own terrace, No.2 a mezzanine with a view of the Cathedral, No. 5 leads directly out to the central patio. Most of the inner courtyard is given over to the pool which is surrounded by wicker chairs, tables and loungers. Fan palms, a potted geranium, and the basking cat, Chiquito, help create the mood of an inner sanctum. San Lorenzo's lounge-cum-diner-cum-bar reflects an eclectic taste: original hexagonal tiles, a genuine Art Deco bar from Paris and a collection of modern art spills out along the narrow corridors that lead to bedrooms. And the details are all there; Mallorcan weave for fabrics, an ingenious hoist to winch your cases up to your room and staff who help without intruding.

Rooms: 4 with bath & wc + 2 suites.
Price: D 16000 Pts; D 'Special' 20000-23000 Pts; Ste 31000 Pts.
Breakfast: 1000 Pts; Special 1400 Pts.
Meals: None available.
Closed: Never.

How to get there: From Airport to centre. Then from Paseo Marítimo right into Avenida Argentina. Right at first traffic lights, cross river and turn immed. right. Down Paseo Mallorca to Porta Santa Catalina square. Park around here; hotel behind church.

Map No: 22

233

Son Penyaflor

Camino del Castillo
07340
Alaró
Mallorca

Tel: 971 510071 / 879443
Fax: 971 510607

Management: Mateo Gamundi Rosselló

The sleepy little town of Alaró (do find time to linger in its delightful main square) hugs a terraced hillside at the eastern flank of the Tramuntana mountains. From here a narrow lane cuts steeply up past almonds, carob, fig and vine towards craggy limestone outcrops — and a hilltop castle. But first you happen upon the beautiful sand coloured farm buildings of Son Penyaflor. The estate (*posesio*) dates back to the Reconquest when King Jaime divided up the island between 14 of his loyal knights. Pool and terrace, shaded by an old ficus, vine and lemon tree and looking out to the thickly wooded hillsides, are a relief for sore eyes; ears will delight in multi-layered birdsong. Inside (the owners live next door) are two lounges, one with open hearth, both with masses of comfy sofa space. Beams and hearth, trunks and board games, and a large collection of Mateo's paintings give the place a *family* feel. Most of the furniture in the bedrooms is antique, ceilings are low, and the windows (sometimes skylights) are netted to keep mosquitoes at bay. Catalina will show you Penyaflor's centuries-old olive mill, help plan your walks or recommend *cellers* for wine tastings. At dinner the food and wine are the best the island has to offer. A fabulous (re)treat and a perfect base for walks.

Rooms: 8 with bath & wc.
Price: S 8000 Pts; Tw 16000 Pts.
Breakfast: Included: Continental.
Meals: Dinner 3000 Pts inc. wine (M).
Closed: Never.

How to get there: From Palma take motorway towards Inca. Exit for Alaró. Here take road towards Orient, and after approx. 400m turn left at sign for Castell d'Alaró. From this turning it is exactly 1.2 km to the house, to left of road.

Es Castell

Finca Es Castell
Binibona
07314 Caimari-Selva
Mallorca

Tel: 971 875154
Fax: 971 875154
E-mail: castell@mallorcaonline.com

Management: Mía Amer Fuster

Secreted away among 300 acres of pine and olive, a shake away from sleepy Caimari, you'd never guess that Es Castell lay abandoned and ramshackle just 10 years ago. Mia Amer's architect-father knew that these old stones deserved better; they had, after all, been in the family since the 11th century! After much sympathetic restoration (not renovation) it first became a weekend retreat for the Amer clan and now, praise the heavens, its doors are open to all. Cross an aspidistra-filled cobbled patio then enter by way of the heavy, old oak doors to a grand vestibule that now doubles as salon. This, in turn, connects with a more intimate room where books, old photos, oils, and claret-coloured chairs and sofas promise solid comfort. The south facing dining room is a happy, light-filled space with gaily painted dining chairs, fresh Mallorca weave curtains and neatly laid tables. It spills over into the old kitchen, a wonderful cubby-hole where a fire is lit in the colder months. No two bedrooms are alike but the common thread — in fabric, furnishing and the overall 'feel' — *is* Mallorca. Ask Mía to show you the old olive press and advise on forays out from the farm, ideally on foot. A place of great tranquility.

Rooms: 7 with bath & wc.
Price: D/Tw 20000 Pts. *Reductions in low season.*
Breakfast: Included — buffet.
Meals: Dinner 3500 Pts (M).
Closed: Never.

How to get there: From Palma towards Andratx on m'way. Exit for Inca. Here towards Alcudia, & at 2nd r'bout left towards Selva-Lluc, then to Caimari. Here right at Banca March. Left at church, then right by next church towards Binibona. Here Es Castell is signposted at bottom of 'square' as you arrive in hamlet.

Es Figueral

Ctra. Palma-Santanyí km 42
Apartado de Correos 33
07360 Campos
Mallorca

Tel: 971 181023
Fax: 971 181023

Management: Miguel Suñer and María Moranta

The mingling of working farm and hostelry works well at Es Figueral; a seductive ochre farmstead clad with honeysuckle and bougainvillaea. You'll like Miguel and María — easy, spontaneous people; "We're all one big family here," enthuses Miguel. Life in the warmer months is lived mostly round the pool and at tables laid out in the shade of the olive, palm and fig trees. When days and nights get cooler the lounge-cum-breakfast room is a congenial spot — a collection of antique plates, a grandfather clock, hand-crocheted curtains and for colder months a brazier beneath each of the guest tables. Breakfast is home-made: breads and jams, freshly squeezed orange juice, milk from the farm next door and María's own cold meats and sausages. Dinner, too: chicken, goat, rabbit, turkey and goose, all farm-raised, and an extraordinary array of fruit straight from El Figueral's groves. The bedrooms (suites really) were built in the old cattle byre and hay barn, and the latest one in the old milling tower. They're large, each one quite independent from the next, and generously furnished. Miguel likes to show both children and grown-ups round his 12 hectares of well-worked land.

Rooms: 4 with bath & wc + 3 suites.
Price: D/Tw 16000 Pts; Ste 17500-19000 Pts.
Breakfast: Included — buffet.
Meals: Dinner 3000 Pts exc. wine.
Closed: January.

How to get there: From Palma towards Santyaní. Pass Campos then turn left just before km42 post and follow signs to Es Figueral.

Son Galileu

Ctra. Vieja de Cala Plí km 6
07620
LLucmajor
Mallorca

Tel: 971 721508
Fax: 971 717317
E-mail: fincas@baleares.com

Management: Francisca Tomás Tomás

This is an old, old farmhouse — about 400 years old, Francisca reckons. Your arrival here is magical: down along the narrow lane and then off onto a stone-walled track that cuts through stands of twisted fig and gnarled olive to lead up to the sombre, much-weathered façade of Son Galileu. A home rather than a hotel, Galileu is an idyllic retreat for those seeking utter peace and those who can forgo jacuzzi and satellite TV for a week; a perfect place for a family or a group of friends to congregate. Push back the door and a sense of family history emerges: here are old trunks and dressers, grandfather clock, hand-embroidered bedspreads, an antique cot filled with books. The downstairs lounge is cool and high ceilinged with metre-thick walls softened by countless layers of whitewash; upstairs is a second little sitting room. A well equipped kitchen leads to a private terrace, an enchanting spot surrounded by prickly pears with a table in the shade of a lemon and a medlar. No house 'rules' here — you can cook, but ask Francisca and she will make your breakfast and, occasionally, a wholesome dinner. If you're a couple the house will be yours alone.

Rooms: 1 house with 2 bathrooms & wc for up to 6 people.
Price: House: (for 2) 15000 Pts; (for 3 or 4) 18000 Pts; (for 5 or 6) 25000 Pts.
Breakfast: 1200 pts.
Meals: Dinner approx. 2500 Pts (M). Book ahead.
Closed: Never.

How to get there: From Palma to Llucmajor. Pass roundabout and turn right (just before palm trees coming up on your left) at sign 'Camí de Cala Plí'. Son Galileu is on the right after 6km.

Map No: 22

Sa Campaneta

Calle Can Campos 4   **Tel:** 971 180392
07190
Esporles
Mallorca

Management: Jaime Pou

Sa Campaneta rejoices in as glorious a setting as you'll find anywhere on Mallorca; from Esporles climb up to the very top of the pass, and along three exhilarating kilometres of track, then catch sight of the farmhouse on top of a terraced ridge. Walkers and lovers of high places will love it here; you can see forever from this dizzy perch (the reason why both Roman and Moor were here before you). To either side of a high, Roman-arched gateway two enormous *almeces* (nettle trees) stand sentinel and spread shade over terrace where peacock and hen basked the day we visited. Beyond lies a cool courtyard leading to the working olive mill, the private chapel and a stone staircase which winds up to the guest apartment and rooms. The Pous greet you with an unaffected simplicity: don't expect hotel reception formalities. There's no pretence to grandeur here; rooms have been decorated piecemeal with whatever was to hand but we liked the apartment's cosy dining room and a little sitting room along the corridor shared by the doubles — reserve a seat for sunset. Water comes straight from the well, the wind and the sun heat your water and light your way to bed, and wild mountain goats roam the crags. Unique. *Note: address above is for correspondence and not that of house.*

Rooms: 2 with bath & wc + 1 family apartment.
Price: Tw 12000 Pts; Apt (2 bedrooms-1 bathroom) 6000 Pts p.p.
Breakfast: Included.
Meals: Dinner 1500 Pts inc. wine.
Closed: Never.

How to get there: From Palma to Puigpunyent. Here towards Esporles and after 3.4km (check km as you leave Puigpunyent) just after top of pass turn left by a stone shed onto track. Follow for 3km to house.

C'an Coll
Camino de C'an Coll no. 1
07100
Soller
Mallorca

Tel: 971 633244
Fax: 971 631905
E-mail: Julia@BITEL.es

Management: Emma
Rodríguez and Antonio Flores

Soller has a catchy, informal charm with its narrow streets, old merchants' mansions and people-watching possibilities from the café tables in Plaça Constitució. High above the town, with a glorious panoramic view out across 'citrus valley' and up to the moody massif of Puig Mayor, this little guesthouse is among our favourites. With Nature's best all about you, life is spent mostly outdoors; fan palms and lemon trees shade the wicker chairs of the first terrace; fig, olive, oleander, gladioli and geranium colour the way down to a pool-with-a-view. In cooler weather, or if you tire of the sun, retire to C'an Coll's cool interior where contemporary art, music at most times, cut flowers, candelabra and huge dining table still paint a lovely picture in our mind's eye. Bedrooms and suites have hand-painted furniture and friezes, local fabrics, large spaces and treasured antiques. Breakfast is the time to meet Emma and Antonio. Heed their advice and take the train from Soller to Palma and back, or hike over the mountains to Deía. Then complete a memorable day with a candlelit dinner.

Rooms: 9 with bath & wc.
Price: S 17000 Pts; D/Tw 21000 Pts; Ste 30000 Pts.
Breakfast: 1500 Pts.
Meals: Light lunches available. Dinner 4000 Pts exc. wine (M).
Closed: Never.

How to get there: From Palma towards Soller. Through tunnel (toll). After approx. 2km (staying on main road with Soller to your right), opposite first petrol station, left into Camino Can Coll. House on right as you go up hill.

Map No: 22

Ets Albellons

Calle Binibona s/n
07314
Caimari
Mallorca

Tel: 971 825069
Fax: 971 825143
E-mail: albellons.rese@jet.es

Management: The Vicens family

What an amazing approach! Drive through the sleepy back lanes of Alaró to the tiny hamlet of Binibona, on past mind-boggling feats of ancient terracing, twisting and turning all the way up to a spur dominating a vast swathe of Mallorca's centre. Ets Albellons may feel as if it's always been here but Juan and Vicente totally rebuilt the old farm house — taking four long years to get things just right. This is now a home of comfort, elegance, seclusion and style from which you can gaze out across 30 acres of olive, pine and carob. Visitors' books, we all know, only get handed to those who sing songs of praise, but this spot comes close to meriting its description as a 'little piece of paradise'. Bedrooms and suites are pampered and preened: hand-crocheted bedspreads, high ceilings, big spaces, cut flowers, grand Mallorcan wooden beds, terraces and swish bathrooms. You could send a fax, blow-dry your hair, zap on the air-con or soak in your whirlpool bath. You should enjoy your food too: local cheeses and sausage, bread from the village and Mama's time-tested recipes for dinner with most vegetables farm-grown. Try and take the time to accompany Juan on one of his half-day rambles out to Lluc through this extraordinary countryside.

Rooms: 9 with bath & wc + 3 suites.
Price: S 15500-16800 Pts; D 21000-23500 Pts; D 'Deluxe' 27800-30500 Pts; Ste 28400-31600 Pts; Ste (with terrace) 29600-33000 Pts.
Breakfast: Included — buffet.
Meals: Dinner 3300 Pts exc. wine (M).
Closed: Never.

How to get there: From Palma towards Andratx. Exit for Inca. Here towards Alcudia, and at 2nd r'bout left via Selva-Lluc to Caimar. Turn right at Banca March, left at church, right by next church to Binibona. Signposted.

Map No: 22

Mofarès

Avenida Calvía-Capdellá s/n
Apartado de Correos 17
07184 Calvía
Mallorca

Tel: 971 670242
Fax: 971 670071

Management: Antonio Rotger

'Mofarès' comes from the Arabic; there was an estate here at the time of the Reconquest in 1229. All these years later it remains a working farm; the house and cluster of outbuildings stand amid neatly tended groves of olive and carob, beyond which a flock contentedly ruminated the day we passed by. Life looks inwards to a beautiful cobbled central patio (*clastra*) where potted exotic plants offset the dazzling lime-washed walls. Antonio has brilliantly succeeded in creating comfort in an historical setting; he'll eagerly show you the old olive mill, the bakery and his collection of agricultural instruments in the old stables. In the lounge are old photos of the farm and a wood-burning stove but better still is the dining room in the old kitchen with vaulted ceiling, original ceramic tiles and space to pull up a chair beside the hearth. At breakfast and dinner Antonio has a simple rule-of-thumb: you have whatever you like! Profit from his love of wine and choose a special bottle from his *bodega*, complete with carefully compiled maps of Spain's different wine regions. Bedrooms (more like suites) vary in size and shape; all are pleasant, with elegant repro Mallorcan beds, *yengo* weave curtains and bedspreads and most creature comforts.

Rooms: 6 with bath & wc.
Price:S 18000 Pts; D/Tw 22000 Pts inc. breakfast.
Breakfast: Included.
Meals: Dinner occasionally on request from 3000 Pts exc. wine (M).
Closed: January & February.

How to get there: From Palma towards Andratx. Exit for Palma Nova. From here to Calvía. There take road towards Capdellá. Mofarès is on the right just 700m after leaving Calvía.

Sa Pletassa

Camino Viejo S'Horta
Cala Marçal No. 362
07669 S'Horta
Mallorca

Tel: 971 837069
Fax: 971 837320

Management: Bernardo Amengual

This old farmstead — hard by one of the island's loveliest beaches — lay forgotten amid groves of almond, fig, citrus and carob. Bernardo discovered it some ten years ago and for the next five restored, embellished, planted and irrigated and so created the luxurious retreat of his mind's eye. The earthy colours of the main façade's stonework are a perfect backdrop to the deep mauve of a riotous bougainvillaea. The glass frontage of Pletassa's sparkling lounge-diner-bar beckons in the myriad changes of the Mediterranean light and looks out to a palm-fringed pool. In one corner there's a huge wrap-around sofa and an extraordinary fireplace of polished pink stucco. Bedrooms have a clean, uncluttered agenda — bright kilims marry well with modern floor tiles and attractive vaulted ceilings. They are large (40 square metres), some have traditionally turned Mallorcan beds, most of them private terraces and four of them twin arches between bedroom and lounge. And pleasures for the palate too; fresh veg from the garden, Bernardo's own wine (Merlot) and unashamed predilection for the island's traditional dishes. Lamb is especially good. Your hosts are young, friendly and know of some fabulous beaches close by. Visitors — mostly German — return year after year so book early.

Rooms: 10 suites + 1 house for up to 6.
Price: S 12000 Pts; D/Tw Ste 18900 Pts.
Breakfast: Included — buffet.
Meals: Snacks at lunchtime; Dinner 2700 Pts (M).
Closed: Last 2 weeks of January.

How to get there: From Palma to Felanitx. From here to Port Colon and there follow signs to Cala Marsal. By hotel Cala Marsal turn right and follow road for 1.5km. Sa Pletassa is on the left.

Map No: 22

Es Passarell

2a. Vuelta No. 117
07200
Felanitx
Mallorca

Tel: 971 183091/557133
Fax: 971 183091
www: www.todoesp.es/es-passarell

Management: Lola Suberviola Alberdi

Far from the madding crowds of the beach resorts Es Passarell is right up with the avant-garde of Mallorca's small country hotels, testimony to the boundless energy of María Dolores ('Lola') who saw in these old stones a vision of better things to come. Outbuildings were reconverted, gardens were planted: you now approach this isolated farm through a swathe of colour where palm and vine, honeysuckle and geranium, almond, fig and citrus jostle for position. And so to the rooms: no two are alike and size and configuration follow the dictates of the old farm buildings. Choose between house, apartment, suite or double room, between self-catering and catered-for. It's all been converted and decorated with a designer's touch; the mix of antique furnishing and modern art feels good and you can understand why some of Europe's most prestigious magazines have featured the place. There are bright rugs, dried flowers, unusual angles, intimate terraces for *al fresco* thinking and a delicious whiff of the linseed used to treat beam and tile. Breakfast is buffet and big; four types of bread, mountain-cured ham, fresh fruit salads, cereals and eggs. Twice weekly there are 'gourmet' dinners; Monday's is meat based whilst on Friday salmon is the main theme.

Rooms: 9 with bath & wc incl. apartments + suites + small house.
Price: D 8000-12000 Pts; Ste 14000-16000 Pts; Apt (for 3) 12000-15000 Pts; Small House (for 3-4) 16000-24000 Pts; Apt (for 4) 16000-24000 Pts.
Breakfast: Included.
Meals: Twice weekly Gourmet dinners 6500 Pts (M).
Closed: Never.

How to get there: From Llucmajor to Porreres. Here continue towards Felanitx. Between km2 and km3, at sharp bend in the road, turn right and follow road for approx. 2.5km. House to right, signposted.

Map No: 22

243

Son Xotano

Ctra Pina-Sencelles km 1.5
07220
Pina
Mallorca

Tel: 971 872500
Fax: 971 872501

Management: Cristina Ramonell Arbona

Eight generations of Ramonells have farmed the fertile lands of Son Xotano that lie deep in Mallorca's little-known central region. One of King Jaime's knights so loved it that he traded in his Deía estate to come here! Philoxera put paid to once extensive vineyards; Spanish thoroughbreds are now raised among groves of almond and carob. Your first sight is of Xotano's cherry coloured frontage half hidden behind an amazing stand of oleander. In the house the lounge's *estera* matting, family portraits, gilt mirrors and potted aspidistra are a perfect backdrop for occasional *soirées musicales* when guests feast then dance the bolero. But, grand balls excepted, this is a blissfully quiet place and birdsong and the occasional distant horse's whinny are about all you'll hear. Each bedroom is named after one of Mallorca's different winds. They are guardians of fine Mallorca-weave fabrics, rugs and family heirlooms (grandfather's trunk to boot); Cristina's father is an interior designer. You dine in the old *bodega* with a high vaulted ceiling, enormous oak vat and inglenook. Choose between two set meals but check to see if lamb *a las finas hierbas* is on the menu. After your meal retire to the cosiest of lounges in the old kitchen with a glass of Xotano's own carob liqueur.

Rooms: 8 with bath & wc + 8 suites.
Price: D/Tw 19000-24000 Pts; D/Tw (with terrace) 22000-28000 Pts; Ste 23000-28000 Pts; Ste (with terrace) 27000-31000 Pts.
Breakfast: Included — buffet.
Meals: Snacks at lunchtime; dinner 3750 Pts exc. wine (M).
Closed: Never.

How to get there: From Airport towards Palma then follow signs for Santany on motorway. Exit for Manacor, on towards Manacor to Algaida turn towards Pina. Here towards Sencelles. Signposted on left after 1.5km.

La Reserva Rotana

Apartado de Correos 69
07500
Manacor
Mallorca

Tel: 971 845685
Fax: 971 555258
www: www.todoesp.es/la-rotana

Management: María Rodríguez Bécares

A world away from the crowded beaches and package hotels of the coast La Reserva Rotana sits contentedly amid 200 hectares of almond, carob, olive and indigenous oak. This was one of the island's original *posesiós* — the huge estates granted to Christian knights when Mallorca was snatched back from the Moors. Three kilometres of track give way to clipped lawns, palm, cactus, and old oleander; the main buildings radiate mellowness and warmth from their undressed *marés* stone. The rooms are to hostelry what Steinway is to the piano: as grand as grand can be. Most are vast, many have private gardens, all are decorated with antique pieces, *estera* matting and lush fabrics. Bathrooms are worthy of a Bond film, (Venetian stucco, hand-crafted tiles), floors are heated from below, beds are two metres across. The hotel's restaurant is up in Mallorca's top ten (Mediterranean cuisine 'with a hint of France') and is in a converted granary with gurgling fountain and a view across a putting green? Rotana is the island's only hotel to boast a 9-hole golf course exclusively for guests (unlimited use included in the room price). Non-golfers will love it too; cycle to the estate's inner reserve and birdwatch, play tennis, take a sauna... or just luxuriate.

Rooms: 10 with bath & wc, 10 junior suites + 1 suite.
Price: S 32000 Pts; Tw 34650 Pts; Junior Ste 39375 Pts; Ste 55650 Pts.
Breakfast: Included — buffet.
Meals: Lunch/Dinner 5500 Pts (M), 6000 Pts (C) exc. wine.
Closed: January.

How to get there: From Palma C715 to Manacor. As you bypass town on main road turn left at Repsol garage (to do so you must turn right and cross lights). Follow signs for 3km.

Map No: 22

245

Hotel del Almirante (Collingwood House)

Ctra. de Villacarlos
07720
Es Castell
Menorca

Tel: 971362700
Fax: 971362704
E-mail: hotel.almirante@menorca.net
www: www.menorca.net/~almirant

Management: Francisco Pons Montanari

A Georgian-style mansion house with the glittering deep water harbour of Mahon on one side and palm fronds and an enormous ficus on t'other... an attractive if curious sight. This was the residence of an English gentleman, Nelson's second-in-command at Trafalgar, Lord Collingwood. Engaging, relaxed and caring, Francisco Pons is a real gent too; he opened the house to guests in 1964 and has been at the helm ever since. Nearly all guests are British; many come first through the tour operators then return later under their own steam. The best rooms have antiques and period bathrooms and are in the main house. Collingwood's was No.7 because from here he could keep vigil over the fleet. Others are in a hacienda-style outbuilding that horseshoes round the pool — less memorable but good value. In the public rooms maritime paintings (even a Titian), potted aspidistra, a grandfather clock, faded art nouveau painted panels, a piano and a stuffed grey heron all strive rather consciously to create an atmosphere of home-away-from-home. The dining room looks out across the harbour, lovely with the morning light, but the coffee was disappointing; perhaps we should have ordered tea! Francisco gives a weekly lecture on Collingwood and his home, and on Fridays there's a dinner-dance!

Rooms: 40 with bath & wc.
Price: S 4050-6425 Pts; D/Tw 5800-10650 Pts.
Breakfast: Included — buffet.
Meals: Lunch/ Dinner 1350 Pts (C) exc. wine.
Closed: 1 November-30 April.

How to get there: From Airport towards Mahón (Mão). Follow signs to Es Castell (Villacarlos) and at 6th roundabout right. Hotel is on left after 300m.

246   **Map No:** 22

Son Triay Nou

San Jorge 13
07702
Mão
Menorca

Tel: 971 155078
Fax: 971 360446

Management: Son Triay Nou SRM

It is puzzling to come across the salmon coloured frontage of Son Triay Nou hidden away on Menorca; it seems more in keeping with the woods of Fontainebleau or deepest Gloucestershire. But when Son Triay Nou was born at the end of the 18th century northern European design was all the rage. Gracious, easy-mannered María Socorro Moysí will tell you more of the place's history, perhaps in the conservatory over a cup of tea, before showing you to your room. Everything here makes you feel that you are in a family home, a rare thing in Spain; the cat Misha basks in the sunlight, the daughter's oil paintings grace the walls, and meals are taken round a large table. We loved the dining room with its collection of old plates and extraordinary rounded inglenook, the only one of its kind on the island. Bedrooms, too, are just right: more oils, antique beds with brand-new mattresses, a rocking chair here and a hand-painted mirror there. They look out over an ordered garden of oleander, palm and caper; off to one side is a tennis court, pool, and the *casita*, a heavenly place to hunker down for a week or more. There's the huge estate to explore, mushrooming in season, home-made sausages at breakfast and beaches close by. The owners can organise car hire for guests.

Rooms: 4 with bath & wc + 1 house.
Price: D/Tw 13000 Pts; House *la casita* 16000 Pts.
Breakfast: Included.
Meals: Lunch/Dinner approx. 1500 Pts exc. wine. Book well ahead.
Closed: November-Easter.

How to get there: From Mahón towards Ciudadela. Just past Ferrerías left towards Santa Galdana. After 2.5km (shortly after passing a plant nursery) turn right along a track to house: recognisable because of colour.

Map No: 22

PORTUGAL

"Sometimes a nation catches fire, and like a shooting star flames for a few generations across the dark sky of history. Then exhausted, it sinks again into the dreaming sleep of centuries... The people that once made the world's destiny had in the end to resign themselves to it."

JOHN TRAIN - *Wohl (Portugal)*

"I awoke wrapped in a vast sweet silence. Along the river, where the slow and muddy water flowed past the rocks without breaking, a boat was descending slowly, with sail filled, and laden with barrels. On the far side, more terraces, pale green with olive trees, climbed to other crags, all bleached and exposed, drunk on the fine abundance of blue."

EÇA DE QUEIRO

Northern Portugal

Quinta da Graça

Vilarelho
4910
Caminha
Minho

Tel: (0)58 921157 or (0)2 6090751
Fax: (0)58 921157

Management: Maria Helena Pacheco de Amorim

The pretty little town of Caminha hugs the southern bank of the Minho where it meets the mighty Atlantic; the town's fortifications speak of an age when this was an important frontier post between Portugal and Spain. Close by are some of the country's loveliest beaches and, cradled on a hillside of the Coura Valley with heavenly views down to the sea, is the Quinta da Graça. This elegantly-mannered farmhouse dates back to the 17th century; ivy, flowered borders and a statue of the Virgin grace the main façade. We loved the guestrooms and apartments (in what were the servants' quarters); most have period furnishing — some of it locally crafted, some of it more exotic Indo-Portuguese ware — and one bedroom has a complete set of Victorian furniture. The old hand-painted tiles in the bathrooms (some come with baths, others with shower) are works of art in themselves. You breakfast at a heavy chestnut table in the charming old rustic kitchen. After your meal wander through Graca's peaceful garden, take a pool-side seat overlooking river and valley, or settle down in the library with one of the hundreds of old tomes. Apartments have their own kitchenette and are more simply furnished. There are restaurants for all budgets close by.

Rooms: 7 with bath & wc + 1 suite + 3 apartments.
Price: D/Tw 12500-14000 Esc; Ste 17500-20000 Esc; Apt 14000 Esc.
Breakfast: Included.
Meals: On request 4000 Esc. Not available from 1 July-15 Sept.
Closed: Easter & Christmas.

How to get there: From Porto IC1 to Viana do Castelo then towards Valença to Caminha. There to centre, right to main square with fountain. Then 2nd left up hill towards fortress. House just after sign 'Miradouro' close to block of flats.

Casa de Rodas

Lugar de Rodas
4950
Monção
Minho

Tel: (0)51 652105

Management: Maria Luísa Távora

Casa de Rodas is certainly a site for (city) sore eyes; à long sweep of lawn bordering the main drive then in the distance the low, clean-cut manor house with its chapel grafted on to one flank. This impressive home has been in the same family for more than four hundred years but don't expect your hosts to be pretentious about their aristocratic lineage; Maria Luisa's casual manner and her genuine friendliness when she greets you are a lovely appetiser for the experience of being here. There are a number of reception rooms on the ground floor, each quite different to the next; they have m arvellous wooden ceilings, stucco and panelling, *trompe l'oiel* marble, painted friezes and flourishes. The overall effect is festive and fun. There are family antiques, portraits and photos; masses of books and comfy sofas to read them in, a grandfather clock, piano and games table. The bedrooms are just as memorable, each one is different, most vast and with their own dressing rooms. The newer rooms are beautiful too and have bigger bathrooms and their own balconies but less of a feel for the past. Our inspector purred "one of the most beautiful houses I've visited... a knockout place".

Rooms: 10 with bath or shower & wc.
Price: S 10000-11600 Esc; D/Tw 12500-14000 Esc.
Breakfast: Included.
Meals: None available.
Closed: Never.

How to get there: From Valenca, just after turn to Moncao, turn right at Turismo de Habitacão sign. Gateway to Casa de Rodas after 200m.

Map No: 1

249

Casa Santa Filomena

Estrada de Cabanas
Afife
4900
Viana do Castelo
Minho
Management: José Street Kendall

Tel: (0)58 981619 or (0)2 6174161/2
Fax: (0)2 6175936
E-mail: soc.com.smiths@mail.telepac.pt

A grand entrance gate beckons you in to the Casa Santa Filomena, a solid, stone-walled building that dates back to the twenties. It is hidden away in a quiet corner of an already quiet village; your rest is assured. When we visited in early spring the old wisteria was a riot of tumbling lilac and mauve, as pretty a welcome as you could wish for. A high wall runs round the property; it girdles a small vineyard where *Vinho Verde* grapes are grown. Elsewhere the profusion of flowers is heady proof of the microclimate that this part of the Minho enjoys; it seems as if anything will grow here. Rooms are rather functional, but perfectly clean and comfortable. If staying here, have dinner in; much of your meal will have been grown in Filomena's garden and this is the occasion to try the estate's wine. If there's anything that you'd especially like to eat — just tell José. A delightful, secluded spot — and very good value.

Rooms: 4 with bath & wc + 1 suite.
Price: D/Tw 8000-9000 Esc; Ste 10000 Esc.
Breakfast: Included.
Meals: Lunch/Dinner on request 2500-3500 Esc (M).
Closed: Never.

How to get there: From Valença towards Viana/Porto on N13. Pass sign for Afife beach; 800m on, opp. bus stop turn right cross railway then straight on at crossroads; house on left after 700m.

250

Casa de Pomarchão

Arcozelo
4990
Ponte de Lima
Minho

Tel: (0)58 741742 or
    0931 204615
Fax: (0)58 742742

Management: Frederico Villar

This would be a wonderful place to head for if you are planning a longer stay in Portugal. Casa de Pomarchão dates all the way back to the fifteenth century but owes its present look to an extensive rebuild of 1775 when a baroque chapel and veranda were added. The manor is at the centre of a 60-hectare estate of vineyards and thick forest of Mediterranean pines. Your choice is between an apartment in the wonderful main building (every inch the aristocrat's residence) or your own solidly built house. Some are classical in style (Milho or Celeiro), others have been given a more rustic feel (Toca or Pomarchão). What is so refreshing is their utter comfort; no corners have been cut to ensure that your feel *chez toi*. The houses all have hearths, top-quality sofas, warm curtains, paintings, good beds and really well-equipped kitchens. French windows take you out to your own garden or terrace and the whole of the estate is yours for the walking. You can swim in the huge old water tank, visit nearby Ponte de Lima and the beach is just a short drive away. Frederico's wife greets you with a smile; she's a friendly lady and speaks excellent English. You'll be loathe to pack your suitcase and to say goodbye to (we quote our inspector) "the biggest, softest dog I have ever seen".

Rooms: 10 self-catering apartments and houses with bath or shower & wc.
Price: D/Tw 12000 Esc for 2. Prices for larger apartments/houses on request.
Breakfast: Included.
Meals: None available.
Closed: 10-30 December.

How to get there: 2km outside Ponte de Lima on road to Valenca N201. Signposted.

Casa da Várzea

Beiral   **Tel:** (0)58 948603
4990
Ponte do Lima
Minho

Management: Inácio Barreto Caldas Costa

You'll spot Casa da Várzea from way off as you wind your way up from the valley below. It would be hard not to fall in love with the beauty of the place, cradled among terraced vineyards. Like so many of the grand old homes of Portugal it lay abandoned for many years. But Inácio Caldas da Costa, whose feelings ran deep for the house where he was born, took courage and after his retirement set about the restoration of the family seat. Várzea now has six big, light and charmingly decorated rooms. Family antiques are here for you to enjoy; you may find yourself sleeping in grandmother's or great-uncle's bed. One room has a lovely old chest, typical of the Minho region, with a secret drawer for hiding away those gold sovereigns. Prints and framed embroidery, polished wooden floors and rugs are endearingly domestic. And in the public rooms wood-clad floors and ceilings lend warmth to grandeur. At breakfast there are long views from the airy dining room, not to mention home-made jams and fruit from the farm. There's a library, a pool with-a-view and the old wooden 'drying house' which now houses a second lounge-cum-playroom. And there is a special room set aside for tastings of the local *Vinho Verde*!

Rooms: 6 with bath & wc.
Price: S 10000-11600 Esc; D/Tw 12500-14000 Esc.
Breakfast: Included.
Meals: Dinner on request 2500 Esc (M).
Closed: Never.

How to get there: From Porto-Valença dual carriageway exit for Ponte da Barca. Continue for 6km to S. Martinho Gandra. Here right to Beiral. 100m past church turn left at stone cross. Along this lane to house.

252   **Map No:** 9

Quinta de Vermil

Ardegão
S.Julião do Freixo
4990 Ponte de Lima
Minho

Tel: (0)58 761595
Fax: (0)58 761801

Management: Maria Helena Torres Fernandes Westebbe

Quinta de Vermil is cradled by the pine and eucalyptus forests of the Minho, just an hour's drive from Porto and twelve miles from the Atlantic coast. This is a home whose fabric seems to have absorbed the friendliness and generosity of your hosts; it is a light, gracious building decorated with much flair. Your first visual treat is the Quinta's garden, terraced down the hillside with well tended paths and hedges breaking up lawns and patio areas. Here are enchanting shady spots, the murmur of fountains and an interesting collection of trees and plants. It leads on to the vineyards whence the grapes for Vermil's excellent *Vinho Verde*. The building was designed to bring this wonderful outdoors indoors. The dining room has large windows on two sides and its huge gilt mirror increases the luminosity. Breakfast here is big and buffet: three kinds of bread, fruit compote, eggs, cheese and more. Dinners are rather less local in conception (Minho cooking can be rather porkocentric) apart from on Thursdays when sardines are charcoal-grilled on the barbecue. Bedrooms and apartments combine modern comforts with period furniture and have wonderful mattresses, good linen, big windows and handsome rugs.

Rooms: 8 with bath or shower & wc + 4 apartments.
Price: S 11600 Esc; D 14000 Esc; Apt (for 2) 14000 Esc; Apt (for 4) 22400 Esc.
Breakfast: Included (or 1000 Esc if in Apt).
Meals: Dinner 3200 Esc.
Closed: Never.

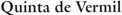

How to get there: From Porto A3 south and exit Vila Verde. After toll booths right towards Braga and after 1.5km right for Freixo/Viana do C. 1km after Freixol left for Ardegão. Quinta on left.

Casa de Dentro "Capitaõ — Mor"

Vila-Ruivães
C.180
4850 Vieira do Minho
Minho

Tel: (0)53 658117
Fax: (0)53 658117

Management: Ilda de Jesus Trufa de Miranda Fernandes

This was once the home of none other than Capitão-Mor de Ruivães who put the French to rout during the Peninsular War (the 'War of Independence' to the Portuguese). It sits proudly on one side of the valley which divides the Cabeira and Gerês mountain ranges in the tiniest of hamlets amid the terraced vineyards and deep greenery of the Minho. Both hosts and home exude warmth and welcome. Ilda, a retired school teacher, relishes in sharing her intimate knowledge of this corner of the Minho — she has special maps ready for your walks and sight-seeing and will tell you about the region's fascinating mythology. We loved the lounge with its low beams, granite hearth, old copper still and wall cabinets displaying the family china — just the place for settling down with a good book. The guest rooms are as unassuming as the rest of Ilda's home: they vary in size but all have antique beds and wardrobes, parquet floors, rugs and pretty bedside lamps. Central heating is a boon in the colder months: you will be comfortable here in any season. Breakfast is as generous as Ilda herself: yoghurts, home-made jams, fruit juice and very special cake, Ilda's *bola de carne solar* (visit to discover the secret!). There is a tennis court, pool-with-a-view and the wonderful Gerês Park right on your doorstep.

Rooms: 5 with bath & wc.
Price: D/Tw 10000 Esc.
Breakfast: Included.
Meals: None available.
Closed: Never.

How to get there: From Braga take EN103 for 42km to Ruivães. House is in centre of village to right of church.

Map No: 9

Casa São Vicente

Lugar de Portas
Geraz do Minho
4830 Póvoa de Lanhoso
Minho

Tel: (0)53 632466
Fax: (0)53 632466

Management: Teresa V. Ferreira

Another wonderful address for those who love the grape; the Minho's delightful young petillant *'Vinho Verde'* is produced here and you can visit and buy from the bedega (did you know that verde refers to age not colour? You may be surprised to learn that red wine accounts for more than half of the *Vinho Verde* production). Teresa and her husband will share much more wine-talk should you stay with them at this old bougainvillaea-clad farmhouse. This is a relaxed sort of place; solidly comfortable and not a bit ostentatious. An enormous drawing room feels more like a conservatory with high windows opening on two sides; family photos, a wood burner and plenty of sofa space. The dining room is off to one end; at breakfast expect cut flowers, a big spread and a chance to admire the large collection of porcelain figurines and jugs. In milder weather you will eat out under the orange trees with a view of the vineyards. And your sleep should be deep; bedrooms are manicured, mannered, large, light and surprisingly inexpensive. 'Cor de Rosa' has its own veranda, 'Amerelo' would be perfect for a famiy, 'Azul' is rather smaller but pretty just the same. Ask to be shown the unusual paintings in the Quinta's chapel (1623) and find time to visit the diminutive castle of nearby Povoa de Lanhoso. There are good restaurants there, too.

Rooms: 5 with bath or shower & wc.
Price: D 12000 Esc.
Breakfast: Included.
Meals: None available.
Closed: Never.

How to get there: From Porto take the A3, exit to Braga and here towards Chaves through Bom Jesus to Arcas. Towards Amares then after 1.5km turn left for Gerás/Ferreiros/Covelas. Signposted.

Casa dos Lagos

Bom Jesus
4710
Braga
Minho

Tel: (0)53 676738
Fax: (0)53 676738

Management:
Andrelina Pinto Barbosa

A warm, dignified welcome awaits you at Casa dos Lagos. The house was built by a viscount at the end of the eighteenth century on a thickly wooded hillside which it shares with the Bom Jesus sanctuary; don't miss the extraordinary baroque staircase which zigzags up to the chapel on top of the hill but do visit on a weekday to avoid the crowds of pilgrims. Both the devout and not so devout are welcome at Andrelina's home which is a lesson in quiet, measured elegance. Light floods in through the French windows of the lounge/dining room; at one end there is a drop-leaf table beneath a fine chandelier (there will be cake for breakfast), and at the other is a velvet sofa drawn up to a large fireplace where you may sip a pre-dinner glass of port served from a cut-glass decanter. The terrace gives onto a garden where stands of camellias break up the order of carefully-clipped box hedges and ornamental fountains; the views from here are breathtaking. Just one bedroom is in the main house. It is large, elegantly corniced and has a fine antique bedroom set: marble-topped dresser, cavernous wardrobe and ornately carved bed. Other rooms and the apartments are more modern and these, too, are large and well equipped. There are dozens of churches to be visited in Braga and good places to eat too; the family-run Inácio has excellent regional cooking.

Rooms: 6 with bath & wc + 4 apartments.
Price: D/Tw 12500-14000 Esc; Apt (for 2) 12500-14000 Esc; Apt (for 4) 19500-22400 Esc; Apt (for 6) 26000-28800 Esc.
Breakfast: Included.
Meals: None available.
Closed: Never.

How to get there: From Braga take EN103 to Bom Jesus. Here, turn right at signs.

Castelo de Bom Jesus

Bom Jesus
4710
Braga
Minho

Tel: (0)53 676566
Fax: (0)53 677691

Management: Dr. Manuel de Castro Meirelles

Castelo do Bom Jesus looks down over the city of Braga and all the way to the Atlantic coast. Enter beneath the grand portal sculpted with the family coat-of-arms; the blue-blooded Meirelles, part of the House of Bragança, have lived here since an ancestor built this grandest of homes in the 18th century. Foundations rest on those of a much older medieval fortress. Abandon yourself to an oasis of green and calm; palm fronds sway in the breeze, peacocks roam the gardens. The outside of the building was reformed in the Italian, Romantic style; the present generation of the Meirelles restored and renovated the interiors. Rooms are as sumptuous as you'd expect; the presidential suite is the grandest, with *trompe l'oeil* frescoes, period furniture and jacuzzi. (Suites have air-conditioning). You breakfast at a huge dining table in a light, graceful room beneath the family portraits; dress for dinner in the oval, chandeliered dining room with its beautiful wrap-around fresco of fabulous gardens. In the lounge are grand piano and harp; a second salon is given over to the billiard table. And the gardens! — wind your way past exotic plants and trees via a grotto and on up to the belvedere. The estate has its own vineyards.

Rooms: 11 with bath & wc + 2 suites.
Price: D/Tw 15000-20000 Esc; Ste 35000 Esc.
Breakfast: Included.
Meals: Lunch/Dinner 4000 Esc (M).
Closed: Never.

How to get there: From Porto A3-IP then N14 to Braga. Here follow signs for Bom Jesus to top of the hill; right through gate just before Sanctuary car park.

Map No: 9

Quinta de Cima de Eiriz

Calvos
4810
Guimarães
Minho

Tel: (0)53 541750
Fax: (0)53 420559

Management: Dr. João Gomes Alves

On a south-facing slope of the beautiful Penha mountain, this old Minho quinta has been completely restored. In the beamed and terracotta tiled lounge, the old grape press has been transformed into an unusual raised bar. Marvel at the size of the granite lintels, flagstones and building blocks of the entrance hall. The post box red of the doors and windows lends a lighter note. Bedrooms are in the old stable blocks, are 'mod-conned' with central heating and phone and have sparkling marbled and tiled bathrooms. Most memorable are their views over the well-trimmed lawns and across the valley. Breakfast is a big meal; expect fresh orange juice, yoghurts, several types of bread and cake and Maria Adelaide's jams. Afterwards you could walk straight out to explore the Penha National Park; in the warmer months plunge into the pool on your return, and the balconied terrace is just the spot for a sun-downer; the views are long and rural. Just 10km away is Guimarães with narrow streets, castle and superb municipal museum, while closer still is the Santa Marinha da Costa Monastery, the best preserved medieval building of the region. Good value in a lovely area.

Rooms: 4 with bath & wc.
Price: D/Tw 9500 Esc.
Breakfast: Included.
Meals: None available.
Closed: Never.

How to get there: From Braga N01 to Guimarães. There take road towards Fafe/Felgueiras. After 4km right towards Felgueiras. After another 4km right at sign Penha/Lapinha (don't take first turn Penha/Calvos!). After 3km left at a stone cross; signposted.

Casa do Campo

Molares
4890
Celorico de Basto
Minho

Tel: (0)55 361231
Fax: (0)55 361231

Management: Maria Armanda Meireles

Casa do Campo is every inch the classic *solar* or country manor. An enormous, ornately sculpted portal and turreted outer wall protect the paved inner courtyard. The prize-winning gardens are a hymn to the camellia — the oldest one in the country is meant to be here and, thanks to careful topiary, they take on fabulous forms. The Meireles family has been here for centuries farming the surrounding estate and its vines. The art of receiving guests comes naturally to gracious Maria Armanda. Her guest bedrooms are in a renovated wing and are of the sort that we love; no two are the same, they are decorated in classical style and have polished wooden floors, elegantly stuccoed ceilings, cut flowers, magazines and a feeling of space. Breakfast in the classically elegant dining room; or there is a smaller, less formal alternative. Settle into the lounge with its old harpsichord or into the dream of a library with one of the many tomes on the gardens of Portugal — Casa do Campo features in them all, of course. The manor's splendid Renaissance chapel still has a weekly Mass.

Rooms: 7 with bath & wc + 1 suite.
Price: Tw 11600 Esc; D 14000 Esc; Ste approx. 16000 Esc.
Breakfast: Included.
Meals: Lunch/Dinner on request approx. 4500 Esc (M).
Closed: Never.

How to get there: From Braga N101 to Guimarães then N206 towards Fafe and Celorico de Basto/Mondim. At Gandarela right onto N304 to Fermil; here right onto N210 towards Celorico. House signposted after 1.5km.

Casa de Sezim

Santo Amaro
4800
Guimarães
Minho

Tel: (0)53 523000/523196
Fax: (0)53 523196
E-mail: sezim@mail.telepac.pt
www: www.sezim.pt

Management: António Pinto de Mesquita

The owners must be fond of Casa de Sezim — it has been in the family for more than 700 years. The first grapes were trod here in 1390! Today the estate's *Vinho Verde* is of prize-winning quality. The elegant portal in Sezim's rich ochre façade (the present building is mostly 18th-century) strikes a properly welcoming note and this grand old house — it bears the patina of long use — will utterly seduce you with its understated elegance. You enter via an enormous, sober lounge with heavy old oak beams, granite floor and walls. The family coat-of-arms graces the hearth and blue-blooded forebears look down from their gilt frames — if only one could invite them down for a game of billiards. The fun really begins upstairs in the bedrooms. Some have four-poster beds, others have tapestried headboards, perhaps a writing desk; all have some antique pieces and rich patterns on wallpaper, bedspreads and curtains. But the gaily decorated panelling is their joy. We'd probably sacrifice space and go for a tower room with a view. Most memorable are Sezim's panoramic paintings that date from the early 19th century with exotic scenes from the Old and the New Worlds.

Rooms: 9 with bath & wc + 1 suite.
Price: S 13000-14600 Esc; D/Tw 16500-18500 Esc; Ste 18500 Esc inc. VAT.
Breakfast: Included.
Meals: Lunch/Dinner on request 4000 Esc.
Closed: Never.

How to get there: From Porto A3 towards Braga, then A7 to Gumarães. Then N105 towards Santo Tirso. Right in Covas (after passing petrol station and Ford garage); house 2.2km from here directly opp. 'Tecidos ASA'.

Quinta das Camélias

Lugar de Vilar-Lemenhe
4775
Vila Nova de Famalicão
Minho

Tel: (0)52 961676
Fax: (0)52 963998
E-mail: aqueiros@pobox.com
www: www.portugal_insite.pt/cima.asp

Management: Rosa de Fátima F.M. Queiros

As you would expect from the name, the gardens of this noble 19th-century villa are awash with glorious camellias; this plant is to the Minho garden what the rose is to the English. The Quinta's young owners, Antonio and Rosa, left no stone unturned when converting and decorating their home. Silver-grey granite is the building's base element while well-fashioned wood in parquet, panel and beam adds the finishing touch. There are wonderful old tiles, too. The public rooms are elegant yet not contrived; a bright durry in the lounge/reading room, cheerful colours in the old kitchen, lots of windows bringing in the light and taking your gaze out to the lovely surroundings. There is a large panelled dining room but when the weather's right you may breakfast out under the camellias. Bedrooms are a match for the rest of the house: we might choose the yellow room with its gorgeous hand-painted tiles or perhaps the pretty twin-bedded green room. All of them have attractive furniture, fabrics and colours. A fountain murmurs outside and in the vibrant gardens you'll find a pool, tennis court and shady spots for whiling away an afternoon in the Minho. The house is within a 15-mile drive of "everything important" — Porto, Braga, Guimarães, Barcelos and the sea.

Rooms: 4 with bath & wc.
Price: D/Tw 13000 Esc.
Breakfast: Included.
Meals: None available.
Closed: Never.

How to get there: From Vila Nova de Famalicão take N201 towards Braga. After 500m left for Mouquim and on to Lemenhe then follow signs.

Quinta de Santa Comba

Crujães-Várzea
4750
Barcelos
Minho

Tel: (0)53 832101/831440
Fax: (0)53 832101

Management: Jorge Enrique Carvalho de Campos

This exquisite Quinta was built by Jorge Enrique's ancestors but then passed into the hands of another aristocratic Minho family: in 1975 he bought it back in a state of near abandon and since then has been at the reins of the 14 hectares of surrounding vineyards. In 1986 Jorge began welcoming guests to his ancestral seat. Enter the estate beneath a grand Baroque portal; then take the long flight of stairs which leads to the double-doored entrance: a grand arrival. The Carvalho family live in the rooms on this floor: the guest bedrooms and apartments are in converted outbuildings. Here there are thick walls of granite, terracotta floors and smallish windows which keep the summer heat at bay but make the rooms a little dark if you're here in winter. No meals apart from breakfast are served but there are two good restaurants within walking distance — or take any apartment and transform the wonderful *materia prima* of the Barcelos market. Then there is the Quinta to explore: you can help yourself to cherries, figs and walnuts when they're in season. Jorge will proudly show you his visitors' book; many folk are on their second or third visit and they enthuse about being made to feel a part of the family at Santa Comba.

Rooms: 7 with bath or shower + 3 apartments.
Price: D/Tw or Apt 10500 Esc.
Breakfast: Included.
Meals: None available.
Closed: Never.

How to get there: From Barcelos towards Vila Nova de Familiacão. Signosted to left after 5km.

Quinta do Convento da Franqueira

Carvalhal CC 301 **Tel:** (0)53 831606/831853
Franquiera **Fax:** (0)53 832231
4750 Barcelos
Minho

Management: Piers and Kate Gallie

This gorgeous 16th-century monastery hides away among pine trees, cork oaks, eucalyptus and cypress — rich in history. The cloister is thought to have been built with stones taken from the ruins of the nearby castle of Faria; the Brothers came here for the splendid isolation and the abundant spring waters which now feed a swimming-pool. The buildings have been gradually restored to their former grace by the Gallie family; a labour of love and respect for 'how things were'. Rooms and suite are lovely indeed, of generous proportions, and furnished with fine antiques. There's a a four-poster in one room, old prints, pretty bedside lamps and tables and stuccoed ceilings. Colours are soothing and bathrooms have traditional hand-painted tiles. The house produces its own *Vinho Verde* from the six hectares of vineyards that lap right up to Franqueira's walls; Piers Gallie enjoys showing his guests round the winery and talking of wine. Children would be more interested in the swings, gardens and the rocking horse in the play room. There is a huge tiled terrace overlooking lush and colourful gardens. Try to coincide with the wonderful Thursday market in nearby Barcelos.

Rooms: 4 with bath & wc + 1 suite.
Price: D/Tw 15000 Esc; Ste (for 2) 15000 Esc, (for 3) 19000 Esc.
Breakfast: Included.
Meals: Occasionally available, approx. 4500 Esc (M).
Closed: End October-end April.

How to get there: From Braga N103 to Barcelos; at end of N103 right round ring road. Pass Renault garage then 2nd right towards Povoa de Varzim. Under bridge then left to Franqueira. Through village; take middle road of three up hill into woods to blue bar. Here right, pass church and left through gates.

Map No: 9

263

Casa da Torre de Nossa Senhora das Neves

Lugar das Neves
Barroselas-Vila de Punhe
4900 Viana do Castelo
Minho

Tel: (0)58 771300
Fax: (0)2 6178854

Management: Maria João M.de Brito e Cunha

This Minho manor house was built more than three hundred years ago, extensively remodelled in the 19th century and completely restored just a decade ago. A rampant virginia creeper has all but covered the building and when we visited in November, its myriad autumnal colours were a spectacular sight. Fernanda, the cheery housekeeper, is normally here to greet you; you may not meet Maria João whose work as an interior decorator often takes her away from home. And this does indeed remain a home; on entering the building you are swaddled in a wholesome, relaxed atmosphere. In a well-proportioned and nicely lit lounge there are family photos, ancestral portraits and elegant armchairs; the dining room is similarly 'family' with its one large table, silver candelabras and china plate collection. French windows lead out on to the terrace where you might have your pre-dinner drinks and nibbles (there is a second dining room with rattan furniture for poolside breakfasts in the summer). Bedrooms are, of course, Maria João's creation; we would choose the wonderful Quarto da Torre which has its own private staircase or the suite with two single four-posters and direct access to the walled garden. A road passes quite close to the house so light sleepers should ask for a room on the other side of the building.

Rooms: 5 with bath & wc + 1 suite.
Price: D 14000 Esc; Tw 14000 Esc; Ste 14000 Esc + 5000 Esc for extra bed.
Breakfast: Included.
Meals: Dinner 4000 Esc (C).
Closed: November-March.

How to get there: From Viana do Castelo turn off at Barroselas. After the sign to the right of the church, turn left.

Casa do Ameal

Rua do Ameal
4900-204
Viana do Castelo
Minho

Tel: (0)58 822403

Management: Maria Elisa de Magalhães Faria Araújo

Although it has now has been absorbed into the urban fabric of Viana, once you pass into the entrance courtyard of Casa do Ameal, with its box hedges and gurgling fountain, you can leave the outside world behind. The Casa do Ameal was bought in 1669 by the de Faria Araújo family whose very numerous descendants still watch over the place; there are fourteen siblings in the present generation and five of the sisters still live at the house (most of the others arrive at the weekend!). These lovable elderly ladies welcome you with tea and a tour of the house; they will proudly show off the collection of handicrafts and the family costume 'museum' with such delights as their grandparents' christening robes. Accommodation is in two guestrooms and seven apartments, some sleeping two, others four; most have their own kitchenette. The rooms are furnished in simple 'rustic' style that goes well with the exposed stone walls. The sisters speak English, French and Spanish and will gladly help you plan your excursions to Viana do Castelo, just two kilometres away.

Rooms: 2 doubles + 7 apartments (for 2 or 4 persons)
Price: S 11600 Esc; D 14000 Esc; Apt (for 2) 14000 Esc, (for 4) 22400 Esc.
Breakfast: Included.
Meals: On request + self-catering.
Closed: Never.

How to get there: From Porto take the N13/IC1 towards Viana do Castelo. Just before Viana enter village Meadela, pass main square, church and drive on until big supermaket 'Modelo'. Turn left as if to go to supermarket, but pass their parking, drive up the hill and turn left at gates to the house.

Map No: 9

265

Casa do Monte

Lugar do Barreiro
Abade de Neiva
4750 Barcelos
Minho

Tel: (0)53 811519 or (0)936 776125
Fax: (0)53 813341

Management: José Sousa Coutinho

The house stands proud on a hillside in a tiny hamlet looking out across the green valley of Barcelos. The main drive cuts an arc upwards past carefully clipped hedges of box, enormous camellias, a statue and a ceramic plaque; it praises God for blessing the Minho with places as heavenly as this. Come if only to see these pampered gardens. The house is a well-mannered building which you might well imagine to be older than its 60 years; light granite lintels, bright sky-blue window frames and *azulejos* lend the façade a merry air. And the gaiety is mirrored inside the house; bright primary colours decorate panelling, skirting, chairs and tables in the unforgettable dining room. In the bedrooms the same idea adds cheer to radiators and window seats, beds and wardrobes. We marginally preferred those on the first floor but those giving out onto the lower terrace are special too — and all of the rooms have views across the valley. In among the carefully clipped hedges are a pool and tennis court but your attention will first be caught by the profusion of shrubs, trees and flowers; this is one of the loveliest gardens of northern Portugal. Try to catch the Thursday market in Barcelos.

Rooms: 7 with bath & wc + 2 suites.
Price: S 8400 Esc; D/Tw 10600 Esc; Ste 10600 Esc.
Breakfast: Included.
Meals: None available.
Closed: Never.

How to get there: From Barcelos take road to Viana do Castelo. After 4km you arrive in hamlet of Abade de Neiva; Casa do Monte on right.

Map No: 9

Quinta da Mata

Estrada de Valpaços
5400
Chaves
Trás-os-Montes

Tel: (0)76 340030
Fax: (0)76 340038

Management: Filinto Moura Morais

Filinto found this 17th-century Trás-os-Monte house in ruins and completely restored it, retaining nearly all of the building's original features. He is endearingly enthusiastic about his home and this region's people and their gastronomy. For breakfast try miniature pasties, home-made bread, local Chaves ham and perhaps some smoked sausage. For dinner he may suggest kid or a delicious *cocido* (thick stew) or some of the excellent local sausages, and will certainly encourage you to try the wine from Valpaços. Quinta da Mata's guest rooms are as special as your host. The fine craftsmanship of the wooden floors and ceilings perfectly sets off the walls of dressed stone; Arraiolos rugs, crocheted bedcovers, repro beds and cut flowers lend warmth to large spaces. You might choose the Presidential suite (Mario Soares stayed) which has an office/library, or the Imperial which is more private and has a whirlpool bath. There are two tennis courts (coaching can be arranged), a sauna, free use of bikes and walks out through the thickly wooded slopes of the Brunheiro mountains. "Filinto is charm itself" wrote our inspector who has marvellous memories of afternoon tea with him and a table groaning under cheese, jam, doughnuts and cake.

Rooms: 6 with bath or shower & wc.
Price: S 9000-11500 Esc; D/Tw 10000-13500 Esc.
Breakfast: Included.
Meals: Dinner 2000-3000 Esc (C).
Closed: Never.

How to get there: Just outside Chaves take road to Valpacos, go through Nantes and the Quinta is well signposted.

Map No: 10

267

Quinta do Real

Matosinhos
5400
Chaves
Trás-os-Montes

Tel: (0)76 966253
Fax: (0)76 966253

Management: Ramiro Guerra

You will travel far to find as elegant a building or as romantic a rural setting as will be yours at Quinta do Real. The main façade of this deeply appealing edifice is a real gem, a masterpiece of understated elegance. Long and low it looks much gentler, somehow more integrated into its surroundings, than some Portuguese manor house; perhaps it is the feminine touch for it was built in 1697 for the Vice Countess of Rio Maior. You pass through the entrance portal which is topped by a granite cross to enter a cobbled courtyard; the weeping willow, and perhaps corn or pumpkins drying in the sun offer an unassuming welcome. We would go for a room in the main house with views across the valley, probably the 'master bedroom', but they all (except the attic room) are large, spotlessly clean and prettily decorated with good-looking antique pieces. The other rooms are in outbuildings which give onto the patio; these are more basic but have more privacy, if you need it. Back in the house is a cosy lounge with a wood-burning stove and another much larger one with a minstrels' gallery. The dining room is an appealing space, too; it has a chandelier, single table and a 'tall boy' brimming with old china and glass. Your hosts are the charming Dona Celeste and her son Ramiro; he recently left a city career to dedicate himself to running the house.

Rooms: 10 with bath or shower & wc.
Price: D/Tw 10000-10500 Esc.
Breakfast: Included.
Meals: Dinner on request 3500 Esc. Restaurant closed on Sundays.
Closed: Never.

How to get there: From Vidago towards Loivos, then right for Quinta do Real. Through forest to village of Matosinhos: through village then follow signs to Quinta.

Solar das Arcas

Arcas
5340
Macedo de Cavaleiro
Trás-os-Montes

Tel: (0)78 401135
Fax: (0)78 401233

Management: Maria Francisca Pessanha

In this forgotten corner of Portugal this lovely mansion, or *solar*, has graced the centre of the village of Arcas for over 300 years. The owners are direct descendants of Manuel Pessanha of Genoa, who came to Portugal to teach the Portuguese the art of navigation. The house lies at the midst of an extensive estate of fruit orchards and olive groves. The building is of lovely proportions; graciously carved mouldings surround windows and doors while the family coat of arms above the portal reminds you that this is a noble house — as does the imposing private chapel. "Cosy privacy" is how the brochure (correctly) describes rooms and apartments. They have antique beds — the four-poster in one of them really caught our eye — and the apartments come with kitchenette and small lounge; one of them has its own bread oven. Food? Forgive us for quoting Arcas' brochure again: "You will feel that you belong to a real Portuguese family when you sit on a footstool savouring a glass of wine and nibbling at a piece of a smoked delicacy before the fireplace where iron vessels boil and the revolving plate grills simple, but first-rate meals".

Rooms: 8 apartments.
Price: Apt (for 2) 10000 Esc; Apt (for 4) 20000 Esc. Add 5% VAT 20% more in July/August.
Breakfast: Included.
Meals: Lunch/Dinner on request 4000 Esc.
Closed: Never.

How to get there: From IP4 exit for Macedo de Cavaleiros. Here right onto N15 towards Zoio and after 1.7km left via Ferreira to Arcas. House in village centre.

Estalagem do Caçador

Largo Manuel Pinto de
Azevedo
5340
Macedo de Cavaleiros
Trás-os-Montes

Tel: (0)78 426356/54
Fax: (0)78 426381

Management: Maria Antonia
Pinto de Azevedo

"Are you tired of big town's rush and longing for mountain's fresh air?" (sic) enquires the Estalagem's brochure. Well, perhaps you are and, providing you're not vehemently anti-hunting you should enjoy staying at this handsome hotel. Even our normally vegetarian inspector forgot the meat issue and awarded it a near-perfect score! This was once the town hall of Macedo: it burnt down and the present owner's great-grandfather turned the building into a hotel nearly 40 years ago. His collection of prints and Toby jugs from around the world are still on display. But his first love was the pursuit of game: from your deeply comfortable velour or leather armchair in both bar and lounge you look up to antlers, shotguns and prints of horse and hounds; there are stuffed birds and leopard skins and photographs of huntsmen and their trophies. The bedrooms also have the leitmotiv of the Hunt: prints and paintings of birds, pheasants, buffalo, rabbits together with *toile de Jouy* and some interesting antique pieces. Maria gives a genuinely warm welcome at this unusual hotel; it was she who crocheted the rabbits on your bedroom curtains. There is an excellent restaurant — locals come for the trout and ribs of wild boar. The journey takes you through varied, dramatic and unforgettable scenery — an integral part of the experience.

Rooms: 25 with bath or shower & wc.
Price: S 10000 – 12000 Esc; D/Tw 13000 – 16000 Esc.
Breakfast: Included.
Meals: Lunch/Dinner 3000 Esc (C).
Closed: 24-25 December.

How to get there: Turn off the Porto to Braganca road at Macedo do Cavaleiro, turn left in the centre of the town.

Casa das Cardosas

Rua Central
Folhadela
5000 Vila Real
Trás-os-Montes

Tel: (0)59 331487 or 0936 2929750
Fax: (0)59 331487

Management: Maria Teresa Cardosa Barata Lima

What views! Although you are just a mile from Vila Real this grand Trás-os-Montes manor enjoys as bucolic a setting as you could hope to find; the hills roll out before you, sprinkled with white villages and farmsteads. The Cardosa family has been here for more than two and a half centuries and made wine here until phylloxera struck and they were forced to diversify. Find time to let the gracious and warm-natured Maria Teresa tell you a little of the area's history. Her three bedrooms are quiet, elegantly decorated and have not a hint of hotel. There are rugs, shining parquet and one bedroom has a wonderful *Bilros* bed (an extraordinary lathe-turned affair), the green room a chandelier and pretty fabrics, and the smallest room has direct access to the terrace. The lounge and dining room have parquet floors and period tables and chairs; cut flowers and family mementoes, displayed in glass wall cabinets, heighten the mood of unaffected intimacy. Breakfast at Cardosas is a generous meal with various breads, home-made jams, juices and eggs; at dinner you may be treated to roast beef or hake from the wood-fired oven. Make sure you have time to explore the deep gorges (or peaks) of the Alvão Natural Park and don't miss the fabulous Solar de Mateus.

Rooms: 3 with bath or shower & wc.
Price: D/Tw 9000-10000 Esc.
Breakfast: Included.
Meals: Lunch/Dinner on request 2500 Esc (M).
Closed: Never.

How to get there: In Vila Real go to University and here, to left of main entrance, house is signposted.

Map No: 10

271

Casa Agricola da Levada

Avenida de Ier Maio 70
Timpeira
5000
Vila Real
Trás-os-Montes

Tel: (0)59 322190
Fax: (0)59 346955

Management:
Albano Paganini da Costa Lobo

When built in 1922 Casa Agricola de Levada stood alone, but the expansion of Vila Real has brought new neighbours and roads. Nevertheless it has kept its charm and there are long walks out from the house, quiet spots galore in the grounds and fishing in the river Corgo that cuts across the estate. House and chapel were designed by the Portuguese architect Raul Lino; this graceful architectural style was the Portuguese answer to the French Art Deco. It is most attractive: granite offset by white rendering and burgundy windows and doors. There are four stone-walled guestrooms whose comfortable beds and utter quiet guarantee a deep sleep. Young, friendly and gracious Inês and Albano always find time to share conversation – in the evening over a glass of wine or with a coffee at breakfast. And food is special at Levada; home-made breads and jams at breakfast (in the garden in summer) and dinners lovingly prepared by the farm's 72 year-old cook who has been at Levada for as long as anyone can remember. Nearly everything is home-grown, produced or baked. Try the estate-reared boar. There is a good house red or finer wines if you prefer. At nearby Casa Mateus there are regular concerts during the summer months. Albano is actively involved and will tell you what´s on.

Rooms: 4 with bath & wc.
Price: D/Tw 10000-12000 Esc.
Breakfast: Included.
Meals: On request 3500 Esc (M)
Closed: Never.

How to get there: From Porto IP4 towards Bragança. Exit for Vila Real Norte then follow signs for centre and then towards Sabrosa. At junction (Palacio of Mateus to right) turn left, through Murça, over railway then river and house to right.

Map No: 10

Casa do Marechal

Avenida do Boavista 2652   **Tel:** (0)2 6104702/03/04/05
4100   **Fax:** (0)2 6103241
Porto
Douro

Management: João Paulo Baganha

Elegant, cream and white, utterly-deco Casa do Marechal was built in 1940 and would sit as happily on the front in Miami as it does here in one of Porto's smarter residential areas. It looks like a wedding cake, with a rich layer of cream stucco running round at second floor level. Inside, things are just as flamboyant; the present owners have transformed an already grand house into a refined and luxurious guesthouse. There are just five bedrooms, decked out in pink, blue, green, beige and yellow. They are good-sized and carefully manicured; beds are five-star, each has a small writing table and all the usual modern extras, even hydro-massage tubs with sparkling tiles all round. There is an orange-coloured lounge with a balcony, a roof terrace and a garden with shady corners. At breakfast you can expect all the normal fare plus fresh fruit and even porridge if you're missing it. The restaurant serves dinners on weekdays; everything's bought fresh at the local market. The owners describe the food as "a new gastronomic interpretation of French and Portuguese traditional cuisine". (You may need the gym, sauna and Turkish bath in the basement!).

Rooms: 5 with bath & wc.
Price: D/Tw 22000-25000 Esc.
Breakfast: Included.
Meals: Lunch/Dinner 5000 Esc (C).
Restaurant closed at weekends.
Closed: August & Christmas.

How to get there: Arriving on motorway from Lisbon after toll booths towards Arrabida, then Boa Vista and then Foz/Castelo do Queijo. Hotel on right after 3km. The hotel has its own parking.

Residencial Castelo Santa Catarina

Rua Santa Catarina 1347
4000-457
Porto
Douro

Tel: (0)2 5095599
Fax: (0)2 5506613

Management:
Joaquim Teixeira Brás

This eye-catching building was built high up above Porto during the period which the Portuguese call the "Gothic Revival". Even if the corner turrets and window arches don't remind you of Notre Dame, you can't fail to be intrigued by this tile-clad edifice, which stands like a folly, surrounded by swaying palms, in an otherwise rather conservative suburb of the city. The interior décor is as extravagant as the building's exterior. You are regaled by gilt and stucco, chandeliers and mirrors, cherubs and lozenges, Tiffany lamps and roses, repro beds and cavernous wardrobes. It is showy, over the top, faded in parts, rather garish in others and incredible fun. Your choice of carpet colour? Turquoise, lime green or perhaps a navy paisley print. There is the odd patch of peeling paint, the bathroom tiles are often out of step with the rooms but the whiff of the past is a part of the charm of the place. The owner's affable son João is normally about in reception and with fluent English can answer all your questions about this whimsical building. Try and book the Tower suite; it's worth the extra for the views. An enormously entertaining city hotel.

Rooms: 21 with bath or shower & wc + 3 suites.
Price: S 6500 Esc; D/Tw 9000 Esc; Ste 10000 Esc.
Breakfast: Included.
Meals: None available.
Closed: Never.

How to get there: At the top of Rua Sta Catarina, just below Plaza Marques Pombal, follow signs and ask directions!

Quinta da Granja

Rua Manuel Francisco de Araujo 444   **Tel:** (0)2 9710147 or 0931 9248311
Aguas Santas-Maia
4445 Ermesinde
Douro

Management: António Nunes da Ponte

Porto may be just a few minutes drive away but Quinta da Granja's setting is utterly rural. This genteel *solar* dates from the 18th century, though parts of the estate predate the house. The beautiful gardens, with their ancient stands of camellias, azaleas and carefully trimmed box, were planted out some four hundred years ago! Both house and gardens have been sensitively restored by António Nunes da Ponte. Things are on a grand scale here, like the lounge which is more than a hundred feet long; it still feels most welcoming with its terracotta floor, rugs, period furnishing and family portraits in oil and photo. At one end it leads through into the solar's own Baroque chapel — nowadays only used for family weddings and other special occasions. The bedrooms are in the main building, the apartment in what was once the Priest's house. Here the mood is of simple elegance; there are handsome *Dona Mária* beds, carpeted floors and period bedside tables. Stay a couple of days here and find a favourite spot in the oasis of calm that is the garden; come late winter or early spring to see the camellias at their very best.

Rooms: 3 with bath & wc + 2 apartments.
Price: S 14500 Esc; D/Tw/Apt (for 2) 18500 Esc.
Breakfast: Included.
Meals: None available.
Closed: 1 November-30 April.

How to get there: From Porto towards Braga/Vila Real on ring road, then A4 towards Vila Real. Take first exit for Ermesinde/Rio Tinto, then left towards Alto da Maia. After 500m over bridge then immediately left and first right. Signposted.

Map No: 9

275

Casa de Pascoaes

São João de Gatão   **Tel:** (0)55 422595/423953
4600
Amarante
Douro

Management: Maria Amélia Teixeira de Vasconcellos

Leave Amarante and follow a beautiful oak-lined lane alongside the wall of the estate, turn in beneath a magnificent main gate to a shady, cobbled courtyard — and there to greet you is the gracious double sweep of Pascoae's main house. Maria Amélia greets you and will lead you through the labyrinthine interior to an enormous terrace on the far side of the building; she will tell of how the retreating French army put the building to the torch (in the chapel the bayonetted paintings remain) and of her husband's forebear, the poet Teixera, who would meet here with leading intellectuals of the day, Unamuno included. One imagines the garden and neo-classical fountain may have inspired them all. The house is decorated with an interesting melange of traditional and contemporary elements; most striking are the abstract paintings and the work of Maria Amélia's husband which add life and colour to the vast, granite-hearthed lounge/dining room. Choose one of just three guest bedrooms on the house's lower floor which all have period wooden beds, framed prints and dark wood on floor and ceiling: we most liked the one with a tiny terrace looking over the gardens. Simple suppers can be prepared, you can prepare your picnics if you prefer or take that heavenly lane back to Amarante where you have a good choice of eateries.

Rooms: 3 with bath & wc.
Price: D/Tw 14000 – 16000 Esc.
Breakfast: Included.
Meals: Lunch 3300 Esc (M).
Closed: Never.

How to get there: From Amarante take N210 towards Celorico de Basto. Turn right down a lane which borders the property wall.

Casa de Aboadela

Aboadela
4600
Amarante
Douro

Tel: (0)55 441141 or
(0)2 9513055

Management:
Jose Silva Rebelo and family

You'll long remember arriving at this old granite farm house; once you turn off the main road you twist and turn along the narrowest of lanes which leads you to this delightfully sleepy hamlet and to this old Douro farmhouse. There is many a treat in the rambling gardens: an old granite maize store, a bubbling spring, gourds and pumpkins drying in the sun. Old millstones evoke the building's infancy. There are roses and oranges and vines and, in among them, secluded places for contemplation; it would be a perfect place to paint. Bedrooms and suite are in the main house, simply attired with the family furniture and lacking nothing; and just to one side in a converted outbuilding is the 'stone little house' (sic) which would be just right for a longer stay. The guest lounge/dining room is similarly unpretentious: granite-walled with a tiled floor and potted plants. A French window gives onto a small balcony and lets in the morning light and the view. There are lovely rambles straight out from the house and the São Gonçalo monastery in Amarante is just a short drive away. This is good base from which to explore the Douro, Minho and little-known Trás-Os-Montes areas.

Rooms: 3 with bath & wc + 1 suite + 1 house.
Price: D/Tw 7000 Esc; Ste 10000 Esc; Hse 9000 Esc.
Breakfast: Included.
Meals: None available.
Closed: Never.

How to get there: From Amarante towards Vila Real on IP4. 9km after passing Amarante, left to Aboadela and follow signs for 'turismo rural', then 'tr' to the house.

Casa d'Além

Oliveira
5040
Mesão Frio
Douro

Tel: (0)54 321991
Fax: (0)54 321991

Management:
Paulo Dias Pinheiro

The cheerful façade of Casa d'Além looks out across the terraced vineyards of the Douro valley and reflects the optimism that was in the air in the early '20s. It also suggests a rather diminutive residence but behind its frontage the house widens out and becomes a surprisingly large and airy residence. The public rooms are the most refined: the Rennie Macintosh print on easy chairs, sofas and drapes is perfectly balanced by the delicate wrought-iron work of the balconies. Shining parquet, piano and card table create an atmosphere of old Portugal. Next door is a panelled dining room and, still more remarkable, a long painted corridor, a 'marbled sunburst', which leads to your bedroom. It will be a feast of period pieces: there are rugs and marble-topped dressers, generous old tubs and wash stands... the perfect place to film a Twenties drama. There are heavenly views from some rooms (e.g. *el quarto do Avó, el quarto azul*). Paulo and his wife speak excellent English and their marvellous housekeeper Maria will take care of you. Be sure not to miss dinner; perhaps a roast from their bread oven, home-made ice-cream and a chilled glass of the local wine.

Rooms: 4 with bath or shower & wc.
Price: D/Tw 11300 Esc.
Breakfast: Included.
Meals: Dinner 3100 Esc (M).
Closed: Never.

How to get there: From Porto IP4 towards Vila Real, then N101 towards Mesão Frio. Here N108 towards Peso da Regua to Granjao. Under railway bridge then left to Oliveira and follow signs to Casa d'Alem.

Map No: 9

Casa das Torres de Oliveira

Oliveira **Tel:** (0)54 336743 or (0)1 8406486
Vila Real **Fax:** (0)54 336195 or (0)1 8463319
5040 Mesão Frio
Douro

Management: Isidora Reguela Benito Sousa Girão

Arriving in Oliveira, you won't miss this magnificent twin-towered building sitting proudly up on a terraced hillside off to one side of the village. This is a classic *'solar'* or manor house but, if things at first glance appear on a very grand scale, fear not; this is a comfortable, welcoming place. The estate's vineyards lap right up to the house on all four sides, and the grapes go for port as well as white and red *'Sedinhas'*, named after the present owner's 7th removed grandfather who built the house. Cross a cobbled patio with a fountain to reach the main entrance; from here there are long vistas out across the valley (and swimming-pool) and down to the river Duoro, serpentine in the far distance. To one side of a high entrance hall, Oliveira's lounge is generous with space and light; it has a rugged parquet floor and sashed-back curtains to let in the glorious setting. Cushioned sofas, old china, a piano and a Madonna and Child speak 'vieux Portugal'. From the high-ceilinged dining room you look out the bodega where vats of the estate's wine is stored. You can visit and sample the wine; a bottle will be yours at dinner providing you can tear yourself away from your bedroom. It will come with a beautiful bed and dresser, rugs and lamps and a shining wooden floor; the tower room is a great favourite and well worth the splurge. And Régua, 'capital of Port', is an easy drive.

Rooms: 4 with bath or shower & wc.
Price: S 13000-13800 Esc; D 16500-17500 Esc; Ste 16500-17500 Esc.
Breakfast: Included.
Meals: Lunch/Dinner 3200 Esc (M).
Closed: November-March.

How to get there: From Porto IP4 towardsVila Real to Amarante. Here take N101 towards Mesão Frio, then N108 towards Régua. In village of Granjão turn left to Oliviera (just before bridge and signs Qtas du Douro). After 3km second left to Oliviera: house on right.

Map No: 9

279

Quinta de la Rosa

5085
Pinhão
Douro

Tel: (0)54 72254 (UK 01296 748989)
Fax: (0)54 72346 (UK 01296 747212)
E-mail: sophia@quintadelarosa.com
www: www.quintadelarosa.com

Management: Sophia Bergqvist

If you have an interest in Port, then do stay as guests of the Bergqvists at Quinta de la Rosa. The family have been in the trade for nearly two centuries and the estate matures its wines 'in house' and sells direct to private customers. What better incentive to come? But first a hard choice is yours between a room or your very own Douro farmhouse. Three new bedrooms share a terrace high above the Douro whilst those in the main house are lower and nearer to the river. All are special; some have brightly-painted Alentejo furniture, others are more antique-inspired. 'Dona Clara' has its own little lounge and a view of Pinhão. Of the two houses, each with its own pool, we loved Lamelas which is hidden away at the very top of the estate and approached through a forest of pine and chestnut. It is splendidly decorated and equipped with space enough for a large family or group of friends. 'Amerala', further down the hill, has similar standards of decor. If you're not into self-catering breakfast in the light, sunny dining room with more of that view, you will be in the able hands of housekeeper Filomena. What to do? First priority must be a tour of the cellars and a port tasting followed, perhaps, by a cruise on the river and, if you're here in September, a chance to join in with the grape harvest. Tell your friends and several years hence they'll be drining what you picked! (Our large photo is of 'Amarela'.)

Rooms: 3 + 2 self-catering houses.
Price: D/Tw 11000 Esc; 15000 Esc.
Breakfast: Included.
Meals: None available.
Closed: Never.

How to get there: From Regna cross bridge, driving up river. Just before Pinhão, Quinta de la Rosa visible on the other side, drive through village and back along to La Quinta.

"The village of Sintra is... the most delightful in Europe: it contains beauties of every description natural and artificial. Places and gardens rising in the midst of roads, cataracts and precipices; convents on stupendous heights - a distant view of the sea and the Ragus... It unites in itself the wildness of the Western Highlands of Scotland with the verdure of the south of France."

LORD BYRON

Central Portugal

Quinta da Comenda

3660
São Pedro do Sul
Beira

Tel: (0)32 711101 or (0)2 6183491
Fax: (0)32 711101 or (0)2 6183491

Management: Maria Laura Rocha

This lovely group of buildings most "sweetly recommends itself unto the senses": the local Beira granite of manor and outbuildings is softened by a rampant camellia which lends swathes of colour when in flower. Lovers of good organic wine may have heard of Quinta da Comenda; it exports its prize-winning whites and rosés all over the world. What you probably won't have heard is that the first King of Portugal, Dom Afonso Enriques, did battle nearby, broke a leg and was forced to stay at his uncle's place, the Quinta da Comenda. It later passed into the hands of the Order of Malta; hence the cross above the main entrance. Guest rooms match expectations after such an impressive arrival: polished parquet floors, elegant antique beds and pretty tiles in the bathroom (Maria's own design). Lounge and dining room double up in a huge *salão* which leads to the old wine cellar, and you are treated to a real feast at the breakfast table. Little details such as the fruit basket and bottled water in your room show how much the Rocha family care. Wander down to the river and a Roman bridge, through the vineyards and orchards, stock up on wine and find time for conversation with your charming and cultured hosts. On most Saturdays in summer there are wedding parties; the ivy-clad chapel is to one end of the courtyard.

Rooms: 6 with bath or shower & wc + 1 apartment for 4.
Price: S 8800-11600 Esc; D/Tw 10700-14000 Esc; Apt (for 4) 22400 Esc.
Breakfast: Included.
Meals: None available.
Closed: Never.

How to get there: From Viseu IP5 towards S Pedro do Sul on N16. A few km before S Pedro follow 'Agro Turismo' sign; Quinta on left, well signposted.

Casa de Rebordinho

Rebordinho	**Tel:** (0)32 461258
3500	**Fax:** (0)32 461258
Viseu	
Beira	

Management: Álvaro Calheiros Ponces

If you like wine then you will have heard of the Dão. You might not know of the region's great natural beauty or of the walking in the Estrela and Caramula mountains and you will probably not have heard mention of Casa de Rebordinho. This is an unassuming building from the outside; but behind its long, rather plain frontage, a marvellously intimate, warm and relaxing home awaits you as a guest of the Calheiros family. It's 18 years now since they welcomed their first guest but they still do so with obvious pleasure; your gracious host Alvaro likes to greet his visitors with the words "now my house is your house". Meet him in Rebordinho's wonderful lounge-cum-dining room; in spite of its vast measurements it is a highly appealing space thanks to the warm colours (pinks and burgundies) and the way space is cleverly divided; granite walls are softened by arches and sensitive lighting. There are family photos, books, cut flowers, a family tree, rugs and old oil paintings that are properly lit. Windows to three sides bring in the light. In your rooms it feels as if the duster has just passed over the shining terracotta floors and period furnishings. Rugs and central heating guarantee your comfort when cold; but when it is warm, open the shutters wide and look out over the surrounding estate. Nothing showy or in excess: in a word, perfect.

Rooms: 4 with bath & wc.
Price: D/Tw 15000 Esc.
Breakfast: Included.
Meals: None available.
Closed: Never.

How to get there: From Viseu towards Nelas/Seia. After approx. 5km turn right to Rebordinho then fork left. In village centre signposted on right.

Casa da Quinta de São Lourenço

São Lourenço do Bairro
3780
Anadia
Beira

Tel: (0)31 528168
Fax: (0)31 528594

Management: Lígia Mexia Leitão

This lovely 19th-century manor house stands quietly at the edge of a tiny hamlet surrounded by vineyards, olives, palms and pines. A carefully swept dragon-tooth inner courtyard, then a flight of stairs, lead you to the main entrance where you are greeted by the radiant smile of housekeeper Maria. She will usher you up to your room and will be at your beck and call throughout your stay. Once within, you soon become aware of owner Lígia's passion for interior decoration. Every corner of the house has been carefully considered; there are exuberant arrangements of dried flowers and fruit, carefully matched fabrics, hand-painted tiles. Flounces, canopies, sashed curtains and bows give it an unmistakably feminine feel with pinks, greens and creams. Each room is different from the next, not a bit hotelly. We'd choose one on the first floor looking out across the vineyards — but all are splendid. Downstairs, lounge and dining room are as spruce as the rest of the house. At dinner — on the terrace in summer — the slant is distinctly regional, with suckling pig the speciality; the estate's Bairrada wine is the obvious first choice to accompany it. The right choice if you are a lover of tranquil and intimate places.

Rooms: 6 with bath & wc + 1 apartment.
Price: D/Tw 14000 Esc; Ste 14000 Esc.
Breakfast: Included.
Meals: Not available.
Closed: Never.

How to get there: From Lisbon, A1 towards Porto. Exit for Mealhade. Then follow N1 towards Porto. Pass Anadia, then left towards Vagos/Mogofores. After 1km, left again towards Mira. Through Mogoflores and after 3km, left at sign for house; careful not to miss it.

Map No: 9

Quinta do Rio Dão

Quinta do Rio
3440
Santa Comba Dão
Beira

Tel: (0)32 880240 or in Holland: 00 31 35 6917203
Fax: (0)32 880249 or in Holland: 00 31 35 6930371
E-mail: quintadoriodao@mail.telepac.pt

Management: Pieter Gruppelaar and Juliette Spierings

The setting is a dream, with the house almost hidden in a stand of old oaks right on the bank of the river Dão at the very point where it opens out to form a small lagoon. Pieter and Juliette came across the farmhouse when it stood in ruins and have sensitively restored it and the neighbouring buildings in traditional Beira style. They offer you the choice of a room, an apartment or a whole house: the common threads are a beautiful use of wood, big verandas and captivating prospects down towards the river. Pieter and Juliette have masterfully married traditional Portugal with a clean, uncluttered (and Dutch) approach to space: there is nothing too showy to detract from the sheer pleasure of being here. In summer life is spent mostly outdoors; breakfast on the veranda to birdsong and dine on traditional Beira dishes at night with the lights of nearby Santa Comba Dão reflected in the water. Rooms and food are marvellous value; there are kayaks, canoes and a windsurfer for guests to use and your hosts are intelligent, easy and friendly. Our inspector loved her stay here: "in a word, idyllic". This is just the place for a really energising holiday and children would love it too. Do stay for several days.

Rooms: 6 with bath & wc + 1 house
sleeping up to 6.
Price: D/Tw 11000 Esc; house (for 2)
from 12500-20000 Esc.
Breakfast: Included.
Meals: Lunch just snacks; dinner 2500 Esc
(M).
Closed: Never.

How to get there: From Lisbon towards
Porto on A1 then IP3 (not IP5!) to Viseu. After 40km right on IC12 for
Carregal/Mangualde, then after 1km right for Tabua and immed. turn for
S.Miguel; follow signs.

Quinta da Geía

Aldeia das Dez
3400
Oliveira do Hospital
Beira

Tel: (0)38 670010
Fax: (0)38 670019
www: www.quintadageia.lda

Management: Fir Tiebout

Aldeia das Dez lies in the foothills of the Serra da Estrella, an old hamlet to which the twentieth century seems only to have given a passing glance. This solid, granite-built house appears to be part of the hamlet yet is still surrounded (we quote the archives) "with so much land that it cannot be ploughed with an ox in one day". From the outside you'd never guess that the house is several hundred years old: Dutch Frans and Fir have completely renovated the place. Life at Quinta da Geía centres on the lively bar and restaurant. It has stained wooden tables and chairs, bright table cloths, paintings by local artists and is well frequented by the local folk who obviously approve of the cooking; Frans describes it as "trad Portuguese with a difference", the difference being an Italian/French slant in the preparation of sauces and veg. Once a week bread is baked in the original brick oven. Bedrooms are large, light and funtional; they have pine floors (from recycled East German railway carriages!), interesting angles and are beautifully crafted and finished. A suite or apartment would be perfect for families. Your hosts are well integrated into their adopted community and have mapped out the best walks in the area; follow ancient (Roman) pathways through forests of oak and chestnut, perhaps with Max the dog.

Rooms: 14 with bath & wc + suites and apartments.
Price: D/Tw 7700-9500 Esc; D/Tw 'Superior' 10500-13500 Esc; Ste 12400-15800 Esc; Apt (for 4) 11000-15500 Esc; Apt (for 6) 13600-18200 Esc.
Breakfast: Included in price of rooms, not apartments.
Meals: Lunch/Dinner 2500 Esc.
Closed: Never.

How to get there: From Coimbra take N17 towards Guarda. About 10km before Oliveira do Hospital, at Vendas de Galizes, right at sign for 'Hotel Rural'. Follow signs on for 14km.

Map No: 9

Casa da Azenha Velha

Caceira de Cima   **Tel:** (0)33 425041 or
3080   0931 6407493
Figueira da Foz   **Fax:** (0)33 429704
Beira

Management: Maria de Lourdes Nogueira

This cream-coloured house (it's been repainted since the photo) was once a flour mill (*azenha*) and has been carefully renovated; the decorative flourishes above doors and windows suggest a rather genteel history. Maria de Lourdes and her two dogs, a friendly boxer and a husky, emerge to greet you. Bedrooms and the apartment are separate from the main house; surprisingly luxurious for their price, they've been decorated with great attention to detail and colour-coordination; even tiles match the fabrics, and bathrooms have enormous sunken baths. You breakfast in the kitchen of the main house; rail-sleepers support the roof-bricks, an original and attractive feature. Here too is a snug living-room with leather sofas, a hearth and lots of knick-knacks. There's a large lounge in the old stable block with an honesty bar — jot down what you've had in a little notebook. Azenha is well geared towards family visits: there are plenty of board games, snooker table, pool, tennis court and six horses to be ridden. You're close to the busy little port of Figueira da Foz with restaurants and bars galore or just north is Buarcos, much quieter and with a long sandy beach.

Rooms: 5 with bath & wc + 1 apartment for 4.
Price: D/Tw 12800 Esc; Apt 19800 Esc.
Breakfast: Included.
Meals: Snacks normally available.
Closed: Never.

How to get there: From Coimbra N111 towards Figueira da Foz. Shortly before arriving there turn off towards Caceira and then immediately left following signs 'Turismo rural'. After approx. 2km right and after 500m right again. House on left.

Map No: 9   **286**

Quinta das Lagrimas

Santa Clara
Apart. 5053
3041-901 Coimbra
Beira

Tel: (0)39 441615
Fax: (0)39 441695
E-mail: hotelagrimas@mail.telepac.pt
www: www.supernet.pt/hotelagrimas

Management: Jose Miguel Júdice & João Nuno Ferreira

Quinta das Lagrimas has a place among the most remarkable hostelries in Portugal, perhaps in Europe. The Palace is almost three hundred years old but was rebuilt after a fire a century ago. Wellington stayed here as a guest of his aide-de-camp and was captivated by the place and the legend which gives the hotel its name. It tells that the tears (*lagrimas*) of the Quinta's name were those shed by Dona Inês when put to the dagger by the knights of King Alfonso. He was enraged by his son's affair with an illegitimate (if noble) woman who was Galician to boot. Come to see ten acres of the most gorgeous gardens to which species have been brought from all over the world; two giant sequoias were a gift from the Iron Duke himself (hence *Wellingtonia*). The elegance of the double sweep of staircase leading up to the main front is mirrored within. The dining room is stuccoed, panelled and chandeliered; dignitaries are international but the the food is Portuguese and accompanied by fine wines from Lagrima's extensive cellars. Bedrooms are fit for kings (a number have stayed here); they are elegant and deeply luxurious with rich fabrics, vast beds and marbled bathrooms. The 'normal' rooms are anything but normal; the suites to write home about.

Rooms: 35 with bath & wc + 4 suites.
Price: D/Tw 22000-28000 Esc; Ste 60000-70000 Esc.
Breakfast: Included.
Meals: Lunch/Dinner approx. 5000 Esc (C).
Closed: Never.

How to get there: Just outside Coimbra, behind Portugal dos Pequenitos, take EN1 as if going to Lisbon, and turn off to the right at the hotel sign.

Map No: 9

Casa Pombal

Rua dos Flores 18
3300
Coimbra
Beira

Tel: (0)39 835175
Fax: (0)39 821548

Management: Else Denninghoff Stelling

Coimbra is a town to explore slowly; once capital of the (young) nation it is most famous for its VERY old University; try to visit in term time when the students add so much life and colour to the town. At the heart of Coimbra, in a narrow street on a hill close to the famous seat of learning, Casa Pombal is a delectable place; friendly, utterly unpretentious, it will stir feelings of nostalgia for your student years and have you wondering about mature student grants. Four of the rooms have breathtaking views over the old city roofscape and down to the Mondego river. They are 'basic' but very clean and comfortable, just three have their own bathrooms. But sacrifice the en-suite for the much sweeter pleasures of those views and the relaxed atmosphere created by the friendly Dutch owners. Single folk would especially like this place where you're bound to meet up with fellow travellers. Breakfast comes with eggs, cereals, fresh juices and home-made jams and there are good (vegetarian if ordered) dinners served in the cosiest of dining rooms. *Pombal* is the Portuguese for 'dovecote' and this old town house certainly got us cooing.

Rooms: 3 with bath & wc; 7 sharing bathrooms & wcs.
Price: Tw 6200-7900 Esc; D/Tw (sharing bath & wc) 4800-6800 Esc.
Breakfast: Included.
Meals: Dinner on request 2900 Esc (M).
Closed: January-March.

How to get there: In Coimbra follow signs 'Universidad' via Avenida Sá da Bandeira then towards Praça da Republica; last right just before the Praça (don't go as far as the University), right again on Rua Padre António Vieira. Park as close to end of street as possible. If lost ask for Rua da Matematica.

Villa Isaura

Troviscais Cimeiros
3270
Pedrógão Grande
Beira

Tel: (0)36 45246 or 0931 856297

Management: António Henriques & Fernanda de Jesus Neves Barata

Fernanda is deeply attached to this old Beira house; it was built by her grandmother who had a weaving workshop on the ground floor and her mother, Isaura, lived here too. Things here aren't on the grand scale you'll find in some of the *casas nobres* in this book but we enjoyed the unaffected informality of the place. There's a small lounge where breakfast (waffles, cheese, delicious home-made pear jam, herb teas...) is served; it has an old planked ceiling and an extraordinary, eclectic collection of naïve pottery and posters from the time of the Republic. Old musical instruments, collections of cow and goat bells, of masks, and of pestles and mortars give the place a quirky museum atmosphere; António and Fernanda happily show you round before taking you to your room. The bedrooms are as unpretentious as the rest of the house and charmingly simple with Fernanda's patchwork quilts adding zest to the old brass bedsteads. Forgive the rather basic bathrooms and enjoy instead the pretty balconies of two of the rooms and the views out across the courtyard to orchards and open countryside. You are close to to the Cabril reservoir; Fernanda insists this is one of Portugal's most beautiful places. A small shop selling local crafts and agricultural products is due to open soon at Villa Isaura.

Rooms: 6 with bath or shower & wc + 1 suite.
Price: D/Tw 8000-10000 Esc; Ste 12000-15000 Esc.
Breakfast: Included.
Meals: None available.
Closed: Never.

How to get there: Exit from IC8 (between Portalegre and Castelo Branco) at km88 for Troviscais Cimeiros. Then follow signs for Pedrógão Grande/Turismo Rural.

Solar do Ervedal

Rua Dr Francisco Brandão 12
3400
Ervedal da Beira
Beira

Tel: (0)38 644283
Fax: (0)38 641133
E-mail: solardoervedal@mail.telepac.pt

Management: Maria Helena de Albuquerque

Even though the architectural styles have come and gone this noble residence has never once left the hands of the descendants of Diogo Braz Pinto. High walls surround the estate on all sides; you enter through elegant wrought-iron gates and once within it seems hard to imagine you are actually in the village of Ervedal. A cobbled courtyard awash with pots and pots of geraniums leads to the house; behind it are acres of organically farmed orchards and a stand of two hundred-year-old oaks. Guest rooms are in the south wing, the oldest part of the manor. The lounge has an unusual octagonal ceiling, original gothic door arches of local granite and two burgundy-coloured sofas pulled up to the hearth. Good to see a chessboard on display whilst the TV stays hidden away in a specially designed cupboard. The dining room is just as delectable and you simply must dine in at Ervedal: roast duck with rice is a speciality, desserts are homemade and wines are local. Bedrooms have the same quite elegance; furniture is grand, antique and set off by parquet floors, stuccoed ceilings and window seats. The present Viscountess Maria Helena is a kind, gracious hostess and you will be reluctant to leave her — and her delectable home.

Rooms: 5 with bath or shower & wc + 1 suite.
Price: S 14000 Esc; D/Tw 16000 Esc; Ste 22000 Esc.
Breakfast: Included.
Meals: Lunch/Dinner on request 3500 Esc (M) (exc drinks).
Closed: Never.

How to get there: Just before the town centre of Oliveira do Hospital (off N17 Coimbra — Guarda), turn right just after VW garage — signposted Ervedal da Beira. 16km to village. Solar is signposted from village centre.

Map No: 9

290

Estalagem Casa D'Azurara

Rua Nova 78
3530
Mangualde
Beira

Tel: (0)32 612010
Fax: (0)32 622575

Management:
Sofia da Costa Cabral

In a quiet corner of a sleepy town Casa D'Azurara is a pefect place to unwind and let yourself be pampered. This manor house was built by the Counts of Mangualde in the 17th century, added to at the end of the 19th century and renovated to create a small, luxurious hotel. There are two guest lounges downstairs; one has an enormous old granite hearth, the other high French windows with draped and flounced curtains. There are framed etchings, potted palms, books, cut flowers and a good choice of fabric on chairs and sofas. Carpeted corridors (a lift if you need it) lead to the rooms, where furnishing is either antique or repro; rich fabrics are used for bedspreads and curtains. Our first choice would be suite-like 206; it has a sloping ceiling, *Dona Mária* beds and double French windows. Breakfast here is more interesting than some and includes a choice of breads, cheeses and cold meats whilst the dinner menu has a strong regional bias; there are interesting fish dishes and among the specialities is the duck — *pato Conde Melo*. Don't miss the gardens; magnolia, hortensias and camellia are all of amazing size. The staff are friendly and caring and can organise wine tastings at nearby *bodegas*. A place that successfully welcomes both business people and travellers.

Rooms: 14 with bath & wc + 1 suite.
Price: S 17000-19500 Esc; D/Tw 18500-21000 Esc; Ste 25000 Esc.
Breakfast: Included.
Meals: Lunch 3500 Esc(M); dinner 4000 Esc (M).
Closed: Never.

How to get there: From Porto IP5 towards Guarda. Exit for Mangualde; Estalagem in town centre, signposted. Careful not to confuse with 2nd modern Estalagem as you enter town.

Casas do Toural

Rua Direita 74
6290
Gouveia
Beira

Tel: (0)38 42132 or 0936 323893
Fax: (0)1 3821390

Management: Maria José Tinoco Beja Osório

This imposing building is at the very heart of Gouveia; you won't miss its attractive salmon façade when you arrive. You would never guess that behind it is a large estate of terraced orchards and pastures stretching all the way up to the Serra da Estrela. The house was built when Gouveia was the centre of a thriving wool trade. It is every inch the aristocratic residence; panelled and antiqued, the main house is normally the preserve of the Osório famiy but you may be invited in for tea and cakes by vivacious Maria José; when we visited, although in a rush to leave, she still found time to cook us pancakes! Her guests stay in the house's outbuildings which have been converted into self-catering houses and apartments, each facing out onto the terraced garden. The style is simple, modern and comfortable and you will have terrace space for sitting out, either a kitchen or kitchenette and a wood-burner in your lounge. Pine is used to good effect, bathrooms are small but pristine and the occasional antique bed softens less traditional elements (like the aluminium windows). Paths into the wonderful Serra da Estrela's begin, literally, at your door; this would be a good base for a walking holiday. Or just hang loose at the manor; pool, tennis, snooker and the bar are yours for the using.

Rooms: 7 self-catering houses .
Price: House (for 2) 10000-14000 Esc;
House (for 4) 17500-24000 Esc; House
(for 6) 27500-32000 Esc. *Minimum stay
2 nights.*
Breakfast: Included.
Meals: None available.
Closed: Never.

How to get there: From Porto A1
towards Lisboa, then IP5 via Viseu to Mangualde. Here take N232 to Gouveia. In town centre the house is behind Tourist Office car park.

Quinta da Ponte

Faia
6300
Guarda
Beira

Tel: (0)71 926126
Fax: (0)71 926126

Management: M. Joaquina Aragão de Sousa Alvim

Just a short drive from Guarda, at the edge of the Serra da Estrêla and beside an old Roman bridge that crosses the river Mondego, this elegant 17th-century manor house is as seductive as they come. The main façade is what first holds the eye; at one end is the Quinta's private chapel and next to it a granite portal leads through to the inner courtyard. In the main house is one of two guest lounges; it has an extraordinary stucco ceiling, family portraits and an abundance of dried flower displays. Next door is an elegant billiards room looking out over the park, it has *estera* matting and a fine wooden ceiling. The dining room is in what was once the stable block; the granite feeding troughs have been kept as a feature but you will eat your (generous) breakfast from a china plate! Choose between a room in the old house or a modern apartment looking across the pool to the park beyond. Rooms are light (French windows on two sides), decorated in greens and pinks, tiled throughout and each has a lounge with hearth; furniture is a mix of old and new. There is a second, larger guest lounge in a modern building next to the apartments. To top it all there is a beautiful garden, and walks along the river.

Rooms: 2 with bath & wc + 5 apartments.
Price: Tw 15000 Esc; Apt (for 2) 17000 Esc.
Breakfast: Included.
Meals: None available.
Closed: Never.

How to get there: Leave the IP5 at exit 26 for EN16/Porto da Carne. House signposted to right; follow this road down to river and house (signposted 'turismo rural').

293

Casa das Tílias

São Romão
6270
Seia
Beira

Tel: (0)38 390055
Fax: (0)38 390123
E-mail: lufilipe@mail.telepac.pt
www: www.tilias.com

Management: José Figueiredo Lopes

This is an ideal place if you want to combine the rigours of mountain walks (you are at the heart of the Natural Park of Serra da Estrêla) with the indulgence of staying in an extremely elegant, manicured home. When you first see the sumptuous decoration of the reception rooms at Tilias it is hard to believe that José found the house a near ruin and needed two long years of inspired restoration work to return things to the way they were. Although you are in a small town (a most attractive one, too) the high wall which surrounds the gardens creates a mood of peaceful privacy. The house's most remarkable feature is the corniced and painted 'empire' ceiling of the first-floor lounge; at its centre is a glorious bas-relief stucco of Santa Rainha Isabel of Coimbra. She gazes down on an elegant room where shining parquet, card table, a period dresser and old prints evoke the Portugal of yesteryear. The dining room is also a grand affair with chandelier, family china, silver service and an elegant table decoration at breakfast (when you can try the local cheese and honey). The bar has a much more rustic, relaxed mien with exposed granite masonry and wood burner; try the local *'aguardente'* of a cold night. Wood panelled corridors take you to the guest bedrooms which are large, airy, prettily decorated and look out to the garden.

Rooms: 6 with bath or shower & wc + 1 suite.
Price: D/Tw 12000 Esc; Ste 13500 Esc.
Breakfast: Included.
Meals: Only for groups.
Closed: 16-30 September.

How to get there: From Porto A1 towards Lisbon, then IP5 to Viseu. Into centre then to Seia via Nelas. Here in town centre follow sign for São Romão for 2km. Signposted.

Map No: 10

294

Quinta do Albergue do Bonjardim

Nesperal
Cernache do Bonjardim
6100 Sertã
Beira

Tel: (0)74 809647
Fax: (0)74 809647

Management: Hubertus Johannes Lenders

Eden-esque countryside laps ups to this elegant country house, approached along the narrowest of country lanes flanked by vineyards and groves of orange, olive and almond. If you enjoy wine you should book at least a night at Bonjardim; the Lenders have a well-stocked cellar and there is a cosy bar for tastings of the estate's wine; you could follow it with a glass of their own *coñac*. The four guest bedrooms are just right: big, light rooms with pine floors, high ceilings, antique beds and dressers, and carefully chosen fabrics and colours. Two of them are in the main house and reached via a fine old granite staircase. The other two are in an outbuilding and, if booked together, can be joined to make one huge apartment for six; these have a south-facing veranda and there is a wood-burning stove and the same light and uncluttered feel of the main house. You can swim all year round here; the pool is indoors and there is a sauna and Turkish bath. There are also horses to ride, canoeing nearby and good walks galore; but find time to visit the winery with Hubertus — he will gladly reveal his oenological secrets and is a convivial host.

Rooms: 4 with bath & wc.
Price: D/Tw 12500-14000 Esc.
Breakfast: Included.
Meals: None available.
Closed: December & January.

How to get there: From Coimbra, IC8 towards Castelo Branco and exit to Sertã. There take N238 towards Tomar. At sign marking beg. of village of Cernache do Bonjardim, left at sign 'Nesperal-turismo rural'. Follow signs (1.4km).

295

Map No: 16

Casa do Outeiro

Largo Carvalho do Outeiro 4
2440-128
Batalha
Estremadura

Tel: (0)44 765806
Fax: (0)44 765806

Management: José Victor Pereira Madeira

The colossal Abbey of Batalha was built in thanks for Dom João's victory over the Castilian army in 1385; the independence of Portugal had been secured. From the outside it feels something of a Gothic white elephant, but the innards are of exceptional beauty. Do stay at Outeiro if you come to visit even if at first appearance it is a rather unexciting edifice. This small modern guesthouse is right in the centre of Batalha, its hillside perch ensuring that some bedrooms have a view across the town's rooftops to the great Abbey. José and Odete are the best of hosts; both manage to combine careers in the town with attending to their guests. Their bedrooms are roomy and functional; all have modern pine furniture but their private terraces and size lifts them into the 'special' league. And the extensive use of wood for floors and ceilings helps to add warmth to a modern building. Most of the area to the rear of the building is given over to the swimming-pool. Your ever-helpful owners will advise you where to dine out and, in the morning, treat you to a generous breakfast that includes five or six home-made jams. Excellent value.

Rooms: 8 with bath & wc + 1 suite.
Price: D/Tw 8000-10000 Esc; Ste 9000-12000 Esc.
Breakfast: Included.
Meals: None available.
Closed: Never.

How to get there: On arriving in Batalha follow signs for centre. Casa do Outeiro is well signposted.

Map No: 16

296

Casa de S. Tiago do Castelo

Largo de S. Tiago   **Tel:** (0)62 959587
2510   **Fax:** (0)62 959587
Obidos
Estremadura

Management: Carlos Lopes

Don't miss Obidos. This prettiest of villages, cradled by its very old (14th-century) wall, is a beguiling maze of narrow cobbled streets softened by blue and ochre pastel washes and exuberant stands of bourgainvillea and jasmine. There are cameo views at every turn. The 'house of St James' has been in the family for more than a century, though it was just recently that Carlos decided to throw it open to guests. A cheery French housekeeper welcomes you in; you'd never, from the outside, guess the extent of this old house. Decoration has been meticulously studied and carefully crafted. The bedrooms' most memorable features are massively thick walls (some windows are large enough for *conversadeiros* — gossiping seats!) and dark wood ceilings. There are wrought-iron bedsteads, matching prints for curtains and bedspreads, swanky bathrooms and details that you'd only expect of a larger hotel, like logo-ed writing paper and envelopes. On one level is a small lounge with open hearth; down below is a bar (try a glass of the local cherry liqueur *ginjinha*), a billiard room and, in the lee of the castle battlements, the most peaceful of patios for sitting out. Carlos enjoys exchanging anecdotes with his guests.

Rooms: 7 with bath & wc.
Price: D/Tw 16000 Esc.
Breakfast: Included.
Meals: On request. Prices vary.
Closed: Never.

How to get there: On arrival in Obidos enter town through main gate. Continue to end of this street and house on right, just below castle.

Quinta de Santa Catarina

Rua Visconde da Palma d'Almeida
2530
Lourinhã
Estremadura

Tel: (0)61 422313
Fax: (0)61 414875

Management: Tereza Maria Palma de Alemeida Braga

If style, elegance, comfort and service are all high on your list of hotel essentials then Quinta de Santa Catarina is probably your type of place. It was built in the 16th century, subsequently rebuilt in the 18th and embellished by various illustrious forebears of the Almeida Braga family: they even managed to escape collectivisation at the time of the Revolution. The expanding suburbs of Lourinhã have brought new neighbours but the building still looks out across wooded grounds where the tallest of palm trees (you'll find them on the family coat of arms too) increase the sensation of coming across a genuine oasis. You may be met by a uniformed maid who will lead you to your room via elegant reception rooms where ancestral portraits, gilded mirrors and chandeliers, brilliant polished tables and dressers, candelabras and cut flowers would all provide a wonderful backdrop for the grandest of weddings. That frisson of expectation is rewarded when the door of your room is pushed open and you are greeted by polished antique beds dressers and occasional tables, more cut flowers, deep-pile carpets and captivating views out to the palm trees. Teresa teaches English and has a gift for making you feel immediately relaxed in these grand surroundings. Her charming elderly father will tell you more of the history of Santa Catarina, should you speak French.

Rooms: 5 with bath or shower & wc.
Price: S 11300-13800 Esc; D/Tw 13500-16400 Esc.
Breakfast: Included.
Meals: None, but snacks can be served by the pool.
Closed: 24-25 December.

How to get there: From Lisbon take A8 North towards Oporto then exit to Torres Vedras; from here to Lourinhã. Into centre and follow 'Turismo de Habitacão' signs (close to Restaurante D. Sebastião).

Quinta da Barbara

Av. da Nossa Senhora da Esperança 303/305
2710
Fontanelas-Sintra
Estremadura

Tel: (0)1 9282678
Fax: (0)1 9282597

Management: Maria Briscot

It is rather different from most places you´ll find in this book but Quinta da Barbara could be just the place if you want to stay in one spot for a longer period; the minimum stay here is three nights. The salmon-coloured houses are set among pine trees in a corner of the Sintra National Park, as peaceful and secluded a spot as you could hope to find. Each house, built to give the maximum privacy, has its own diner/open-plan kitchen/lounge with open fire place and three-piece suite. Each has a private terrace with attractive dragon-toothed cobbles and a barbecue. The kitchens are equipped with everything you may (or may not) need for self-catering; there is even a dishwasher. Maid service can be arranged if you like, but towels and linen are regularly changed. You share the large swimming pool (chlorine-free) with other guests, as well as a clay tennis court. A marvellous spot: the sea is just a kilometre away, Sintra a short drive, Azenhas do Mar a shake away and Lisbon a comfortable day-trip. Barbara could be a near perfect base for a longer stay.

Rooms: 5 houses.
Price: House (for 2) 9300-18800 Esc;
House (for 4) 13900 -27000 Esc; House
(for 6) 17700-34300 Esc. All inc. VAT.
Breakfast: None — self-catering.
Meals: None available.
Closed: 1 November-28 February.

How to get there: Lisbon to Sintra on
IC19. There take N247 towards Colares.
Here right to Praia da Maças. On through village to north and 1km after Azenhas do Mar Quinta signposted on right, before you reach Fontanelas.

Map No: 16

Casa Miradouro

Rua Sotto Mayor 55
2710
Sintra-Vila
Estremadura

Tel: (0)1 9235900
Fax: (0)1 9241836
www: www.portugalvirtual.pt/casa.miradouro

Management: Frederico Kneubühl

The gaily striped walls of Casa Miradouro make it an easy place to spot as you wind down from Sintra. The present owner left a successful career in Switzerland to launch himself into its restoration. This is a light, elegant and airy home with views on all sides. Pass through a palm-graced porch and a handsome bannistered staircase leads you up to the bedrooms. Here antique beds and wardrobes rest on sisal floor matting; ceilings are high and have the original stucco mouldings. It all feels fresh and uncluttered — helped by the SIZE of the rooms — the two in the attic included. Views are to the sea or to the hills. The guest lounge has a similar unfussy feel; here the sisal matting balances less ethnic flounced curtains. There is an honesty bar with several different ports (etc) — and a hearth for sitting round in the colder months. Further downstairs is a modern breakfast room, simply decorated with four round tables and giving onto a large terrace. Classical music accompanies breakfast: cereals, cheeses, juices, yoghurts, whatever fruit happens to be in season and both savoury and sweet breads. Frederico is a gentle-mannered, attentive and truly charming host, his home as well-manicured as any we came across in Portugal.

Rooms: 6 with bath & wc.
Price: S use of D/Tw 11500-16800 Esc;
D/Tw 14500-19800 Esc.
Breakfast: Included.
Meals: None available.
Closed: 30 December-12 February.

How to get there: From Lisbon IC19 to Sintra. Here, follow signs for 'turismo'. At square by palace, right (in front of Hotel Central) and continue to Tivoli Hotel. There, down hill for 400m. House on left.

Pensão Residencial Sintra

Quinta Visconde de Tojal
Travessa dos Avelares 12
2710 Sintra (S.Pedro)
Estremadura

Tel: (0)1 9230738
Fax: (0)1 9230738

Management: Susana Rosner Fragosa

Although it is rather 'basic' we loved the air of faded grandeur enveloping this family-run guesthouse. It was built on a thickly-wooded hillside as a Viscount's summer retreat in the days when fashionable Sintra was a hill station to local and international gentry — and became a guest house just after the war. An original bannistered staircase winds up to the first- and second-floor bedrooms. These are enormous with high ceilings, wooden floors and endearingly dated furniture and fittings; it all has a distinctly out-of-time feel about it. Ask for one of the two rooms with mountain views. Downstairs is an enormous dining room-cum-bar where snacks are normally available. But we'd all prefer to sit out on the terrace (with tea and cakes in the afternoon) with its beguiling views up to the fairy-tale Moorish Castle. And the garden is a delight: dripping with greenery, and with some old, old trees, a swimming pool and a small play area for children. Multilingual Susanna is a young, bright and caring hostess. The village centre with its numerous restaurants is a short stroll away or, for the more energetic, paths lead steeply up for some fine walks.

Rooms: 10 with bath & wc.
Price: D/Tw 8000-15000 Esc .
Breakfast: Included.
Meals: Snacks only — available all day.
Closed: Never.

How to get there: From Lisbon IC19 towards Cascais. Exit for Sintra then follow signs for 'S. Pedro'. Continue straight on through town;through town, hotel is signposted on left as you leave Sintra.

301

Map No: 16

Casa da Pérgola

Avenida Valbom 13
2750-508
Cascais
Estremadura

Tel: (0)1 4840040
Fax: (0)1 4834791

Management: Patricia Gonçalves

Cascais remains a fishing village, although holidaymakers and a growing number of Lisbon commuters have added a veneer of sophistication. Duck into the narrow, cobbled side-streets to find the old town and those cameo views for the camera. Casa da Pérgola remembers the days before the changes; the optimism of the belle époque is reflected in this grand villa's colourful façade with its red window surrounds, its purple tiles and a cloak of white, orange and mauve bougainvillea. Not a building that you'd miss as you wander by. Once inside, things take on a rather more subdued note: pastel colours, marble and antiques. In the upstairs lounge there are old paintings, pillars, elegant occasional tables and a grandfather clock whose gentle tock-tocking (paradoxically) makes it all feel slightly out-of-time; there is a faint whiff of a British seaside hotel. Bedrooms are all named after flowers, apart from one known as 'Angels'. Those at the front are larger; some have balconies, some period beds, nearly all have fancy stucco cornicing and all a comfy chair. Throughout there are old prints (some of the Saints) and the overall feel is more home than hotel. Particularly good value in the low season.

Rooms: 11 with bath & wc.
Price: D/Tw 13000 Esc; D/Tw with balcony 15000 Esc.
Breakfast: Included.
Meals: On request 1500-2000 Esc (M).
Closed: 1 December-1 March.

How to get there: From Lisbon A5 towards Cascais/Estoril. Exit for Abuxarda. Go to bottom of hill, turn right then straight over at roundabout. Pérgola in first street to left.

As Janelas Verdes

Rua das Janelas Verdes 47
1200
Lisbon
Estremadura

Tel: (0)1 3968143
Fax: (0)1 3968144

Management:
The Fernandes family

Tucked away in the old city just yards from the Museum of Ancient Art, this old aristocratic town house (the writer Eça de Queirós lived here) is a perfect place to lay your head when in Lisbon. From the moment you are greeted by the ever-smiling Palmira you feel like an honoured guest at As Janelas. Off to one side of reception is the lounge, graced by marble-topped tables (you breakfast here in winter), a handsome fireplace, piano and comfy chairs. Good weather means you can breakfast on the patio (or have a candlelit aperitif); enormous ficus and bougainvillea run riot, a fountain gurgles and wrought-iron tables stand on dragon-tooth cobbling. A grand old spiral staircase leads you to the rooms. Six of them have views down to the river (book early if you want one); they are furnished with repro beds, flounced curtains and delicate pastel colours. Dressing gowns, towels, even the bag for the spare loo roll, are embroidered with the JV logo. And instead of a 'do not disturb' sign you're provided with a hand-embroidered little pillow that says 'shhh!'. A delectable small hotel, as intimate a retreat as you could hope to find in the capital city.

Rooms: 17 with bath & wc.
Price: D/Tw 'Standard' 21800-27600 Esc;
D/Tw 'Superior' 27800-35200 Esc.
Breakfast: Included.
Meals: None available.
Closed: Never.

How to get there: E90 motorway across River Tejo then exit for Alcantara. Straight on at roundabout. Follow tram route for approx. 500m. Hotel close to Museo de Arte Antiga on right.

303   Map No: 16

Hotel Britânia

Rua Rodrigues Sampaio 17
1100
Lisbon
Estremadura

Tel: (0)1 3155016
Fax: (0)1 3155021

Management: The Cardosae Fernandes family

This gem of a hotel, just one street back from Av. da Liberdade, was designed by Cassiano Branco — it is a true museum-piece of '40s architecture and now ranks among Lisbon's classified buildings. The fun begins in the reception area which is flanked by twin ranks of marble columns; port-hole-windowed doors lead through to the bar, just the place for a gin sling. During recent renovation, paint was stripped away here to reveal what appears to be a sea-monster from Camoes 'Lusiades' (or there again, it may be Neptune); and there's more to be discovered. A stunning wood and chrome staircase leads to the bedrooms (there's a lift too); these are generous, with their own private entrance halls; beds, stools, chairs and writing table are all 'period', even if the fabrics look more modern and rather in the Laura Ashley vein. Bathrooms are also original, with huge sinks, tubs and marble walls. There's all the gadgetry that you'd expect of a 3-star hotel (you may manage to bath without recourse to your tub-side phone). And if beds are period, mattresses are new. Only breakfast is served at the Britânia; it's an enormous buffet, would probably keep you going all day and can be served in your room.

Rooms: 30 with bath & wc.
Price: D/Tw 'Standard' 19500-23500 Esc; D/Tw 'Superior' 22400-27300 Esc.
Breakfast: Included.
Meals: None available.
Closed: Never.

How to get there: Follow signs to centre and Pr. Marquês de Pombal then towards Praça dos Restauradores. Left just before Metro 'Avenida'. Rodrigues Sampaio 2 streets east of Av. de Liberdade.

Map No: 16

Residencial Florescente

Rua das Portas de Santo Antão 99
1150
Lisbon
Estremadura

Tel: (0)1 3425062/3426609
Fax: (0)1 3427733

Management: Jacinta Antunes

Another of the bright and cheerful family-run pensions that we are happy to include alongside some rather grander neighbours. Over many years, Florescente has built up a reputation as a friendly, clean and fun stopover right at the heart of Pombaline Lisbon. You are brilliantly central, yet spared the rumble of traffic; Santo Antão is a pedestrianised thoroughfare and a great place to sit out in a café or restaurant and watch the world go by. You dip in off the street into the small tiled reception area; a small fountain gurgles in the corner and the young staff are immediately attentive. The original bannistered and tiled staircase, more than a century old, leads up and up... and up. Narrowish corridors lead along to the bedrooms which are mostly medium-sized and simply decorated with a very southern choice of print on the walls. There are high-ceilings with stucco mouldings — a reminder of a more illustrious past. We loved the rather smaller attic rooms with their stand-up balconies, well worth the haul up to the fifth and top floor. No meals are on offer here, but just step outside and choose your café, restaurant or fruit shop. Ask for an air-conditioned room in the summer.

Rooms: 37 with bath & wc; 20 sharing + 8 suites.
Price: D/Tw 8000-9000 Esc; D/Tw (sharing bath & wc) 5000-6000 Esc; Ste 12000-14000 Esc.
Breakfast: None available.
Meals: None available.
Closed: Never.

How to get there: Arriving in Lisbon, follow signs into centre; down Avenida da Liberdade and park near Rossio in Restauradores car park. Residencial in pedestrian street parallel to Liberdade, approx 100m to north of Rossio. Metro: Restauradores.

Map No: 16

Residencial Alegria

Praça da Alegria 12
1250-004
Lisbon
Estremadura

Tel: (0)1 3220670
Fax: (0)1 3478070
E-mail: pensao.alegria@mail.telepac.pt

Management: Felix Santos

This family-run guest house could hardly be in a better position, just yards away from the multifarious street-life of the Avenida de Liberdade yet in a quiet palm-graced square which seems to belie its inner-city status. At first glance the building looks a bit tatty but a complete face-lift is due before the millennium is out and once you get inside you should approve of your room: "bright, cheerful, clean and basic" is how our inspector described her favourite Lisbon digs. For the moment there is not much in the way of public space apart from a small sitting area with rattan furniture next to the reception. But Alegria's very likeable owner, Felix Santos, plans to create a guest lounge very soon: it will be nothing large or too pretentious, he insists. Try to book our favourite room, number 114, which has just been redecorated in a happy mix of blues and yellows (see photo), and the double-glazing is good news for light sleepers. Some rooms share bathrooms and a few are a shade drab with rather tired-looking bathrooms. But the corridors have been cleverly decorated in cheerful yellow and this and the shining parquet floors give the place a friendly atmosphere. An inexpensive and central address, ideal for tighter budgets.

Rooms: 40 with bath or shower & wc + 1suite.
Price: D/Tw with shower 3500- 4500 Esc; D/Tw with bath 4500-5500 Esc; Ste 5000-6000 Esc.
Breakfast: None available.
Meals: None available.
Closed: Never.

How to get there: Turn off Avenida da Liberdade into Praca de Alegria. Residencial is between the police station and the bombeiros, behind Hotel Sofitel. Nearest metro: Avenida.

Hotel Veneza

Avenida da Liberdade 189
1250-141
Lisbon
Estremadura

Tel: (0)1 3522618 / 3526700
Fax: (0)1 3526678

Management:
Manuel Tomás Nunes

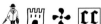

A wealthy Lisbon lawyer built this appealing edifice just over a century ago; the city he most loved after his native Lisbon was that of the Doges and thus the depiction of gondolas and the Rialto bridge which greet you when you pass beneath Veneza's arched entrance. This slightly whimsical decor continues as you climb up the stairway past a striking multi-coloured mural of Lisbon houses stepped up a little hillside. It is a festive entrée to what ranks among the friendliest and most reliable of the capital's small hotels. The reception and bar are in a much more modern style and in both rooms there is a curiously eclectic melange of classical and modern art; the breakfast room is a quieter, darker, rather more serious place. Take the lift or the fine sweep of stairs to your room; large Chinese vases in the corridors strike an oriental note while bedrooms are different again. They are large, carpeted and comfortable, have smart rattan furniture and are decorated in pinky-beige with green fabric on bedspread and curtain. All the extras are on tap; images via satellite, booze from the minibar, service via your phone, air conditioning via the zapper. You are plumb in the centre of this vibrant city, half way along its main thoroughfare. And good news for motorists — the Veneza has its own car park immediately behind the hotel.

Rooms: 38 with bath & wc.
Price: S 18000 Esc; D/Tw 20400 Esc.
Breakfast: Included.
Meals: None available.
Closed: Never.

How to get there: After entering Lisbon, turn onto the Avenida de Liberdale — just above the Tivoli Hotel.

Quinta de Santo Amaro

Aldeia da Piedade   **Tel:** (0)1 2189230
2925   **Fax:** (0)1 2189390
Azeitão
Estremadura

Management: Maria da Pureza de O'Neill de Mello

Looking out to the Arrábida mountains this genteel quinta was where the de Mello family would pass the summer months; first would come the harvesting of the grapes and then the winemaking. Maria had the fondest memories of it all from her childhood and she later decided to make it her first home and bring new life by opening her doors to paying guests. We loved the bedrooms and apartments because of their deliciously homely feel and each one is very different from the next. There are planked floors and ceilings, wrought-iron bedsteads, oil paintings and hearths, window seats and old tiles, period bathrooms and pianos. When you arrive in winter it is to a log fire and, throughout the year, to a bottle of wine. The larger apartment would be a wonderful base for several nights; Lisbon is an easy drive, as are the beaches of the Setúbal peninsula. But what makes it all so very special is Maria herself, a lady with boundless enthusiasm and energy; meet her at breakfast (a feast of home-made breads, jams, cheeses, ham and freshly squeezed orange juice from Amaro's groves) and heed her advice on where to eat and what to visit. *Grand Cru* Portugal… unforgettable.

Rooms: 5 with bath & wc + 2 apartments.
Price: D/Tw (for two) 14500 Esc; Apt (sleeps 6) approx. 21000 Esc weekly.
Breakfast: Included.
Meals: None available.
Closed: Never.

How to get there: From Lisbon, motorway towards Setúbal; exit for Vila Nova de Azeitão. Here towards Sesimbra and, after 3.5km, pass garish blue and white gate on left; take next turn on left, 'Estrada dos Arcos', and S. Amaro at end.

Map No: 16   **308**

Quinta da Alcaidaria — Mór

2490   **Tel:** (0)49 42231
Ourém   **Fax:** (0)49 42231
Ribatejo

Management: The Vasconcelos family

This lovely wisteria-clad manor has been the family seat for more than 300 years and is every inch the grand country house: stately cedar-lined main drive, box-hedged gardens and its own private chapel. The main house is a cool, gracious building; light streams in to the high-ceilinged rooms while marble floors, arches and delicate plasterwork remind you that you are in the South. Don't miss the chance to dine (remarkably inexpensively) around the enormous *pau santo* dining table. The chandeliers and the collection of old china may inspire you to dress for dinner. Guest apartments are in a converted outbuilding; doubles are in the main house and most pukka they are too. There are old dressers, *Dona María* beds, comfortable chairs, perhaps a grand old tub with clawed feet; all rooms have beautiful moulded pine ceilings and big bathrooms and are generously tiled and marbled. Each room is different from the next; all are first-class. Add to this the natural kindness of your English-speaking hosts (they often invite guests to join them for a glass of port) and you begin to get the measure of this altogether most charming guest house.

Rooms: 6 with bath & wc + 2 suites.
Price: D/Tw 18000-23000; Ste 18000-23000 Esc.
Breakfast: Included.
Meals: Light snacks and dinner on request 3000 Esc (M).
Closed: Never.

How to get there: From Ourém take Tomar road. After just 2km turn left at fork towards Seica and then IMMEDIATELY turn left into cedar-lined avenue leading to house.

           Map No: 16

Casa da Avó Genoveva

Rua 25 de Abril 16
Curvaceiras
2300 Tomar
Ribatejo

Tel: (0)49 982219
Fax: (0)49 982235

Management: José and Manuela Gomes da Costa

This is close to beautiful Tomar, but what first impresses you on arrival at Avó Genoveva is the serenity of the place. The huge old palm trees and pots of geraniums gracing the dragon-tooth courtyard, the soft-salmon and white of the buildings give it a truly southern charm. José or Manuela usher you through to public rooms which are plush but homely; in the lounge there are family photos, wood-burner, piano and card table while in the dining room there are antique dressers and a collection of old crockery. Not a bit hotelly. You're spoiled for choice when deciding where to hunker down: in the music room feel free to put on a record (classical and *fado* in abundance), the snooker room doubles as a library and there is a small bar, well stocked with Portuguese wines. And what bedrooms! Dark pine ceilings, family antiques, old paintings; doubles are up an old stone staircase in the main house, while the apartments are across the way in the old granary. A respectable distance from the house are tennis court, swings and pool — and there are bikes, too. Your hosts are kindly, educated people who delight in sharing their wonderful home.

Rooms: 6 with bath & wc + 2 apartments.
Price: D 12000 Esc; Apt (1 bedroom) 14000; Apt (2 bedroom) 22000 Esc.
Breakfast: Included.
Meals: None available.
Closed: Never.

How to get there: From Tomar take road towards Lisbon. After approx. 9km in Guerreira turn right to Curvaceiras. After 4km house signposted on left.

Map No: 16

310

Pensão Residencial União

Rua Serpa Pinto 94
2300 Tomar
Ribatejo

Tel: (0)49 323161
Fax: (0)49 321299

Management:
Joaquim Farinha Rodrigues

Plumb on the main artery through the old town this family-run pension has a long track record; it was the town's very first hotel and just recently celebrated its 100th birthday. The Gala dinners (see the scrapbook in reception) may no longer take place but the União remains the right choice in Tomar. A pretty tiled entrance beckons you in and up to the first floor reception and bar. Rooms are reached along corridors that twist and turn; easy to see why it took the painters six months to get round when last redecorating. The dining room is where you are most in touch with the history of the building; tables and chairs are distinctly forties whilst the door mouldings have an Art Deco air. High windows give onto the inner patio, a quiet spot to sit out when its warm enough. União's rooms are very simple and you'll forgive the rather kitsch prints and random mix of styles; they are roomy with high ceilings, have very comfy beds and there is plenty of hot water. 102 and 103 were the best that we saw, with their old Italian lamps. No meals are served apart from breakfast so head out into the backstreets of this lovely old town where there are restaurants galore. Book ahead in summer.

Rooms: 28 with bath & wc.
Price: S 4500 Esc; D/Tw 7000 Esc; Tr 8000 Esc.
Breakfast: Included.
Meals: None available.
Closed: Never.

How to get there: On right hand side of main street of 'centro histórico'.

Casa do Patriarca

Rua Patriarca D.José 134
Atalaia
2260 Vila Nova da Barquinha
Ribatejo

Tel: (0)49 710581
Fax: (0)49 710581
E-mail: mop59265@mail.telepac.pt

Management: Manuel d'Oliveira

This five hundred year old house (it was built at the same time as the adjoining church) has been the home of the d'Oliveira family for five generations. The building has seen many changes and you might not guess that it is so old. You may be greeted by Manuel's son, his daughter or his wife; two boxers, friendly canines both, will certainly want to say hello. The lounge has French windows which lead out to the walled garden; an enormous date palm towers above the pomegranate, medlar, orange and fig trees. It is a long, low room — comfortable rather than grand — and a cool retreat in the summer months. Just off it is a small kitchen for guests, a thoughtful touch for families not wanting to eat out. At breakfast you can have the full English variant; in winter your juice will be made fresh from Manuel's oranges. Bedrooms are great fun, each decorated to a different theme. 'Quinta' has the great-great-grandfather's bed, 'Oriente' lamps and cushions from India, 'Almirante' a naval theme and 'Sana Sana' evokes Mozambique where your hosts spent their honeymoon. Do visit Atalaia's church (it has a wonderful renaissance portal) and ask Manuel about the underground passageways which may link the town's church with Almoural.

Rooms: 6 with bath or shower & wc.
Price: D/Tw 10000-15000 Esc.
Breakfast: Included.
Meals: None available.
Closed: Never.

How to get there: From Motorway exit 1 for Torres Novas, then IP6, then IC3 for Tomar. After 1500m signposted for Atalaia and house.

Map No: 16

312

Quinta da Cortiçada

Outeiro da Cortiçada
2040
Rio Maior
Ribatejo

Tel: (0)43 470000
Fax: (0)43 470009

Management: Teresa Nobre

Few settings are as utterly peaceful as that of Quinta da Cortiçada; this soft-salmon-coloured building, reached by a long poplar-lined avenue, sits in the greenest of valleys. As we arrived a heron rose from the lake and flapped slowly away, the sweetest of welcomes — so too was the gentle smile of the housekeeper who was waiting at the main entrance. Inside the building the silence feels almost monastic — birdsong instead of vespers. You have the choice of two lounges; one has a games table, high French windows on two sides and is dignified by the family *oratorio* (altarpiece). The other leads to a covered veranda with wicker tables and chairs. Where Cortiçada feels most homely is in the dining room where, if you dine in, you´ll rub shoulders with your fellow guests round the old oval table. Along the marble-paved corridor the rooms have old *Dona Mária* beds, antique dressers, thick rugs on the pine floors — and all of it is utterly pristine. Bathrooms are 4-star plush, while sensitive lighting and carefully chosen fabrics help to make it all extra special. And, like that heron, you're welcome to fish in the lake.

Rooms: 6 with bath & wc + 2 suites.
Price: S 12000-16000 Esc; D/Tw 14000-18000 Esc; Ste 17000-21000 Esc.
Breakfast: Included.
Meals: Lunch/Dinner on request 3800 Esc (M).
Closed: Christmas Day.

How to get there: From Rio Maior follow signs towards Outeiro/Correias. Through Arruda dos Pisões and on to Outeiro; Quinta on left.

Quinta do Vale de Lobos

Azoia de Baixo   **Tel:** (0)43 429264
2000   **Fax:** (0)43 429313
Santarém   **E-mail:** valedelobos@mail.telepac.pt
Ribatejo   **www:** www.valedelobos.com

Management: Veronica and Joaquim Santos Lima

Such is the veiled privacy of this old manor house that the Portuguese saying "to go to the Vale de Lobos" came to mean to go back to nature or to get far from the madding crowd. Nowadays you may just hear traffic in the distance but staying here remains a deeply restful experience. Veronica and Joaquim share their home with three children, their housekeeper Cidalia and their guests; this much-travelled, polyglot couple receive you with great charm and their home is the sort in which most of us would love to live. Nothing superfluous or showy; elegant simplicity is the key note. The sitting room is light and cheery with striped curtains, deep sofas and an attractive wood and terracotta floor. There are books and magazines galore, mostly about things equestrian — you are in the Ribatejo, after all. We liked the bedrooms where the ornately turned *Bilros* beds, high ceilings, balconies and pretty bathrooms mirror the mood of the public rooms. The apartments are a treat, too; rather more modern in style, they also have cleverly hidden kitchenettes and would be perfect for a longer stay.

Rooms: 4 with bath & wc + 2 apartments.
Price: D/Tw 15000 Esc; Apt (for 2) 18000 Esc.
Breakfast: Included.
Meals: Lunch 2000 Esc (by pool in summer!)
Closed: 23-31 December.

How to get there: From Santarém north on N3 towards Torres Novas. Through Portela das Padeiras, then just past turning for Azoia de Baixo cross a small bridge. Road turns left and climbs. As it bends right you turn left into Quinta´s drive.

Quinta da Ferraria

Ribeira de S. João   **Tel:** (0)43 95001
2040   **Fax:** (0)43 95696
Rio Maior
Ribatejo

Management: Teresa Nobre

Quinta da Ferraria stands amid vineyards and olive groves; a channel cut from the nearby river powered the mill and ran a turbine powerful enough to light up the whole farm in the days before electricity arrived in Rio Maior. Recently the farm was totally renovated to create a handsome, small country hotel; although this has been set up for both business and pleasure, the exceptionally green and peaceful setting and the abundance of WATER make it special enough to please both types of guest. Guestrooms have pine floors and ceilings, soft *alcobaça* fabrics and head-to-toe tiling in bathrooms. Pine is also the main feature of the sitting room; sisal matting, rugs and an open hearth add warmth to a very large space. The dining room, by contrast, felt rather soulless due to its wedding-banquet dimensions. But this is a good stopover, especially for a family; there are riding stables, plenty of sheep and a farm museum. Next to the dining room you can still see the original olive-milling machinery. And, as the brochure points out, here are "blue-distanced horizons and clear, sparkling air to invigorate, stimulate and enhance life and living"!

Rooms: 12 with bath & wc, 1 suite + 2 apartments.
Price: S 11000-13000 Esc; D/Tw 12800-15500 Esc; Ste 14000-18000 Esc, all inc. breakfast. Apt 19000-23000 Esc excl. breakfast.
Breakfast: Included.
Meals: Lunch/Dinner on request 3800 Esc (M).
Closed: 24-25 December.

How to get there: From Rio Maior N114 towards Santarem. The Quinta is signposted on right 8km from Rio Maior.

315   **Map No:** 16

Quinta das Covas

Cachoeiras
2600
Vila Franca de Xira
Ribatejo

Tel: (0)63 283031/ 33031 or
00 49 171 8230796
Fax: (0)63 283031
www: www.rent-a-holiday.com

Management:
Susana Murschenhofer

This handsome manor house lies at the edge of the little village of Cachoeiras surrounded by vineyards, orchards and fabulous gardens. A Brazilian once owned the place and planted the garden with palms, aracaurias, medlars and some 20 different varieties of orange tree. Susana and Andreas fell in love with the place and somehow renovated, then decorated it all in just six months. No effort, or expense, was spared in creating an elegant, comfortable, luxurious and (occasionally) glitzy home. The most remarkable of the somewhat festive bedrooms is the *habitação do anjo*; it has an extraordinary gold and blue Rococo bedroom set with a guardian angel carved into the headboard to hover over you as you sleep. 'Portugal' has a palatial bathroom with claw-footed tub; another abandons tradition and has a wooden and steel bed supported on granite blocks: it's a copy of the one in the Museum of Modern Art in New York. Our favourite was the one with its own private vine-festooned terrace. Best of all is the beautiful dining room with its original tiles and panelling: it leads to the terrace with a vine-covered pergola, a heavenly spot for breakfast or for your afternoon tea which is included in the price of your room. A bar and restaurant are planned in the Quinta's *bodega*.

Rooms: 5 with bath or shower & wc + 4 sharing.
Price: D/Tw 12000 — 20000 Esc, sharing 10000-12000 Esc.
Breakfast: Included.
Meals: Lunch/Dinner 1000-5000 Esc.
Closed: Never.

How to get there: From Lisbon A1 towards Porto then exit for Vila Franca. Then towards Cochoeiras following signs for Montegordo. Here first right to Quinta.

*"the prevailing impression is one
of remoteness – little towns and
villages, church de-jewelled and
castle-crowned, on hills so far from
one another, with vast sweeps of
brown soil and green cork-wood
rolling between . . ."*

ANN BRIDGE AND SUSAN LOWNDES
- The Selective Traveller

Southern Portugal

Quinta da Bela Vista

7320-014
Póvoa e Meadas
Alentejo

Tel: (0)45 968125
Fax: (0)45 968132

Management:
Maria Teresa Monteiro Santos

The gently undulating hills planted with cork and olive, the long vistas and sense of space of this part of Portugal seem to make a visit here more than just a holiday; the place seems to get to you on a deeper level. Quinta da Bela Vista is at the edge of a tiny Alentejo village; a group of head-scarfed women sat embroidering the day we visited and were a gentle introduction to arriving at Dona Maria's home. Her family have been here since the twenties and an uncle built the nearby dam. This is a family home — and a lovely one to boot. Masses of books, magazines, photos, piano and card-table create a mood of intimacy while vast reception rooms, chandeliers and a busy maid evoke one of privilege. Of the bedrooms we best liked 'Rosa' (no numbers here, insists Maria), which is decorated in a white-on-pink print of flying ducks and has a veranda with a view and a period bathroom (weren't sinks so much nicer before?). All bedrooms are large, have wooden floors and are really quiet; most have views out to nearby Castelo de Vide. Staying here would be like staying with a favourite Aunt and you wouldn't dream of going out for dinner, you'd miss time-tested family recipes (much of the meat is from the farm) and the Quinta's own wine

and *aguardente* (grape liqueur). A good place for a family stay; kids would enjoy the huge games room (it has snooker, ping-pong and table football) and exploring the farm.

Rooms: 5 with bath or shower & wc + 1 hse.
Price: D/Tw 14000 Esc; House (for 4) 23000 Esc; House (for 6) 29000 Esc.
Breakfast: Included.
Meals: Lunch/Dinner 3000 Esc (M).
Closed: Never.

How to get there: From Lisbon on N46 before Castelo de Vide take signposted turnoff for Povoa e Meadas. Follow 'Turismo Rural' signs towards Povoa then the signs for Quinta da Bela Vista.

Map No: 17 **317**

Herdade da Sanguinheira

Longomel
7400
Ponte de Sôr
Alentejo

Tel: (0)931 269401
Fax: (0)42 26697

Management: Anette and Nuno Vaz Pinto

This lovely old *monte* (Alentejan farmstead) is hidden away in an undiscovered corner of the lovely northern Alentejo among stands of cork oak, mimosa, eucalyptus and pine. Four kilometres of (smooth) dirt track separate the farm from tarmac and traffic; you round a final bend and are greeted by a long, low building with the distinctive chimney stacks of the region, ochre edgings to doors and windows — and a front garden brimming with oleander, wisteria, palm and bougainvillea. Guests put up in their own houses; three of them sleep four, one of them six; all have their own kitchen and sitting rooms with open hearths. Furnishing is 'smart rustic' — so too is the dining room where meals are served should you prefer to let someone else do the cooking. And there's loads to do here: lessons and treks (up to a week!) on Lusitanian thoroughbreds at the equestrian centre, there are mountain bikes and even a ski-boat for hire and any number of lovely walks out into the forest. Add to this a games room, reading room and play room — and Sanguinheira becomes an obvious choice for a full and active family holiday.

Rooms: 3 houses with 2 twins + 1 house with 3 twins.
Price: House (for 4) 22000 Esc; House (for 6) 33000 Esc. *Minimium stay 2 nights.*
Breakfast: Included (self-service).
Meals: Self-catering or Lunch/Dinner 3000 Esc (M). Children under 12, 2000 Esc (M).
Closed: Never.

How to get there: From Ponte do Sôr take road towards Gavião. After approx 6km, pass by sign to Longomel. Pass sign at entrance to village of Escusa. 50m on, left onto track (past maguey cacti) and follow for just over 4km to farm.

Albergaria El Rei Don Miguel

Rua Bartolomeu Alvares da Santa 45 **Tel:** (0)45 919191/90
7320   **Fax:** (0)45 91592
Castelo de Vide
Alentejo

Management: Maria Vitoria Ribeiro Chamiço Heitor

Castelo de Vide is one of the Alentejo's most memorable hilltop villages; within the town walls built by Dom Afonso in the thirteenth century the old Jewish quarter (you can visit the synagogue) climbs anarchically up towards the castle. Just to one side of the lower town's main square this fine old town house has just recently been refurbished to create a small B&B. A granite staircase leads to the first floor and the living quarters. Perhaps the house's most salient feature is its polished wooden flooring in guest and public rooms. The many antiques in lounge and corridors give away Dona Maria Ribeiro's passion for period furniture. We particularly liked the quiet drawing room with its many old pieces and open hearth (there is always a fire in the colder months). Bedrooms are rather more modern; all of their wooden beds, writing and bedside tables are brand new — as are curtains and bedspreads in matching (local) fabric. Special wall insulation and double glazing guarantee a warm, peaceful night and the whole of the house is as clean as can be. Marvellous value at any time of the year and there's a cheerful little restaurant just yards away.

Rooms: 7 with bath & wc.
Price: Tw 8000-12000 Esc.
Breakfast: Included.
Meals: None available.
Closed: Never.

How to get there: From Portalege towards Marvão on E802, then left on E246 to Castelo de Vide. At main square of town, turn left onto main street (known as 'carreira de cima'); hotel on left.

Casa do Parque

Avenida da Aramenha 37
7320
Castelo de Vide
Alentejo

Tel: (0)45 901250
Fax: (0)45 901228

Management: Victor Guimarães

In a beautiful backwater of the Alentejo, surrounded by stands of chestnut and acacia, the hilltop village of Castelo de Vide is girt around with its 13th-century town wall. Steep cobblestone alleys run up the hill through the old Jewish *call* to the Castle; make sure to visit the spring whose waters are said to cure everything from diabetes to dermatitis. The nerve centre of the lower town is the leafy Praça Dom Pedro V and tucked away at one end of it you'll find the gaily canopied Casa do Parque. The family are proud of the *hospitalidade portuguesa* to which guests are treated; the feeling of homeliness spills over into the prettily-furnished guestrooms. They are surprisingly well furnished (even though bathrooms are smallish) considering the price, and are spotlessly clean; they have attractive wooden furniture and the mattresses lead you gently into the arms of Morpheus. In the colder months, hot-air heating warms the room in minutes (we joyfully discovered one cold December night). Don't miss dinner and a chance to try the *migas alentejanas*, or one of the roast dishes; the dining room is a large, functional affair where you'll probably be the only foreigner among many local enthusiasts. The owners have a private pool, a kilometre away, in which their guests can swim.

Rooms: 25 with bath & wc + 1 suite
Price: D/Tw 6500-8500 Esc; Ste 11000 Esc.
Breakfast: Included.
Meals: Lunch/Dinner 1980 Esc (M), approx. 4500 Esc (C).
Closed: Never.

How to get there: From Portalege towards Marvão on E802, then left on E246 to Castelo de Vide. Here into centre then right along the top of the park; hotel at end on left.

Monte dos Pensamentos

Estrada da Estação do Ameixial
7100
Estremoz
Alentejo

Tel: (0)68 333166
Fax: (0)68 332409

Management: Cristóvão Bach Andresen Leitão

The young, blue-blooded owners of Monte dos Pensamentos, Cristóvão and Teresa, are giving new life to this country house that looks up to the old town walls of Estremoz. The house has been owned by Cristóvão's family for nearly 200 years and successive generations have added to and embellished it. The towers and arches added by one forebear give it a distinctly oriental air. The style inside is more traditional: vaulted ceilings, a mix of terracotta and parquet floors, loads of family antiques and a huge collection of old hand-painted plates that spills out along the corridor. We liked the bedrooms. They are decorated with old dressers and beds, some have screens, some original fireplaces; parquet floors add cosiness as do comfy chairs, books, magazines and dried flowers. The owners, relaxed and utterly charming, have a young family but still find time to offer guests lunch or dinner — just discuss the sort of food you'd like with Teresa the morning before. Riding can be arranged with an English neighbour and nearby Estremoz is not to be missed.

Rooms: 4 with bath & wc.
Price: D/Tw 13000 Esc.
Breakfast: Included.
Meals: Lunch/Dinner 3000 Esc (M).
Closed: Never

How to get there: From Estremoz take Lisbon road. After 2km at sign for 'turismo rural' turn right and house is 200m along on right.

Casa de Borba

Rua da Cruz 5
7150-125
Borba
Alentejo

Tel: (0)68 894528
Fax: (0)68 841448

Management: Maria José Tavares Lobo de Vasconcelos

This gem of a house was built by Madame's forebears at the end of the 17th century; the surrounding estate is given over to olives, vineyards and livestock. The building earns a mention in the *inventario artistico de Portugal*; once you pass through the main entrance, an extraordinary neo-classical staircase leads you to the first floor living quarters. And what bedrooms await you here! They have high, delicately moulded ceilings, parquet floors softened by Arraiolos rugs, and are crammed with the family antiques. The 'Bishop's room' (where the Archbishop of Évora stayed) has an 18th-century canopied bed; 'Grandmother's room' has an unusual lift-up sink; there are baths with feet, old prints, and long curtains in front of the windows looking over a delectable garden. The lounge and breakfast room are similarly elegant; breakfast arrives via the 'dumb waiter'. Your hosts are quiet, refined folk and they skimp on nothing to help you; at night, hot water is delivered to your room together with cake and a selection of teas. During the day choose between the long covered gallery, a corner of the garden, or the billiards room.

Rooms: 5 with bath & wc.
Price: D/Tw 14700 Esc.
Breakfast: Included.
Meals: None available.
Closed: 20-28 December.

How to get there: From Estremoz N4 to Borba. Casa da Borba in town centre close to Correios.

Map No: 17

Quinta da Talha

Estrada do Freixo
7170
Redondo
Alentejo

Tel: (0)66 999468
Fax: (0)1 3433090

Management: Manuel António Mantero Moraes

This is an archetypal Alentejo farmhouse; long, low, broad-chimneyed, with windows and doors highlighted with broad bands of blue. You are just a mile or so from Redondo and the vines which surround the house go to make the gorgeous red wine of the same name. With luck you may meet Senhor Manuel (he is sometimes away in Lisbon); this genteel and friendly gent will regale you with the history of family and farm and has a fondness for England born of his wife's Anglo-Saxon lineage. See the photos of his 11 grandchildren in the Quinta's lounge; it is elegant, full of treasured family antiques but not at all intimidating. There are comfy blue and white striped sofas, Queen Anne chairs, a photo of the last Queen of Portugal and a framed Papal dispensation allowing Mass to be celebrated at the house next door. The dining room is just as quietly elegant. Rooms and apartments are just across the way in the farm's converted outbuildings. They are more rustic in feel and finish than the main building, but nice just the same. They have unusual paper cut *betinhos* above the beds from the Redondo Convent, old metal bedsteads, wood-burners and snazzy striped prints on bedspread and curtains. There is good walking, flattish terrain for biking and the old water tank for swimming.

Rooms: 3 with bath & wc + 1 apartment.
Price: Tw 11000 Esc; Ste 22000 Esc.
Breakfast: Included.
Meals: None available.
Closed: 23-26 April, 21-23 September & 23-26 December.

How to get there: From Évora take 254 to Redondo then 524 to Freixo. After 2.5km Quinta signposted to right.

Map No: 17

323

Hotel Convento de São Paulo

Aldeia da Serra
7170-118
Redondo
Alentejo

Tel: (0)66 989160/989100
Fax: (0)66 999104
E-mail:
hotelconvspaulo@mail.telepac.pt

Management:
João Oliveira Martins

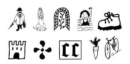

Superlatives do the setting no justice, so go and see. Monks of the Paulist Order came here at the end of the 14th century and for 500 years (until Pombal embarked on Disestablishment) embellished and beautified their place of work and worship. A mantle of quiet wraps the building; as you pass through the enormous old door your voice instinctively drops. Visit if only to see the hand-painted tiles that decorate chapel, corridors and gardens; the largest collection in Europe. A red carpet softens the roller-coaster terracotta floor and sweeps you along to the rooms. Each one occupies two of the former cells, their uncluttered feel entirely in keeping with São Paulo's past. But there are some lovely 'pieces', many of them heirlooms of the Leotte family (owners for the last 150 years). In bathrooms there are brass taps and white marble while public rooms, too, live up to expectations. The dining room feels cosy, the lounge has gracefully vaulted ceilings and well-dressed sofas; eclectic modern art lends a more frivolous note. Outside is a beautiful tiled patio depicting the four seasons and there are any number of walks out through the thickly wooded slopes of this 600-hectare estate. The spirit soars.

Rooms: 17 with bath & wc.
Price: Tw 20000-33000 Esc; 22500-40000 Esc.
Breakfast: Included.
Meals: Lunch/Dinner approx. 5000 Esc.
Closed: Never.

How to get there: From Lisbon towards Madrid on motorway. Exit for Estremoz and here towards Redondo. There towards Villa Viçosa road then follow signs to Aldeia da Serra. Monastery 2km beyond village: signposted.

324

Map No: 17

Albergaria Solar de Monfalim

Largo da Misericórdia No. 1
7000 Évora
Alentejo

Tel: (0)66 750000
Fax: (0)66 742367

Management:
Ana Ramalho Serrabulho

Monfalim is Évora's oldest hostelry and received its first paying guest in 1892. The building's history goes back further; built in the mid-16th century by a young courtier, it was to change hands many times. It is at the heart of beautiful old Évora on a cobbled square where huge jacaranda trees soften the urban contours; the façade is a treat with its elegant first floor arcade built up atop what were once the stables. Pass beneath the coat of arms, climb the heavy granite staircase and emerge to meet the smartly uniformed reception staff — all to the strains of piped muzak. But fear not, this is a truly friendly hostelry and you are made to feel a valued guest at all times. Maybe give a miss the lounge-cum-TV room and ensconce yourself instead in a delightfully *gemütlich* little bar where a wood-burner keeps the cold at bay in winter and old photos tell tales of the Alentejo's rural life. The dining room is large, light and leads out to the first floor arcaded terrace where you can linger over your (buffet) breakfast when the weather permits. And what perfect rooms! They are high-ceilinged with old wrought iron and brass bedsteads, lovely cotton sheets and bedspreads; old lamps, tiled floors and Arraiolos rugs together add up to our type of bedroom idyll. Best time to visit? It has to be May or June when those Jacaranda trees bring forth their glorious purple.

Rooms: 25 with bath or shower & wc + 1 suite.
Price: D/Tw 11500-14000 Esc; Ste 13000-16000 Esc.
Breakfast: Included.
Meals: None available.
Closed: Never.

How to get there: On arrival in Évora exit off from ring road up Rua de Machede via Portas de Moura into Rua Miguel Bombarda and turn right into Largo da Misericòrdia.

Map No: 17

Quinta da Espada

Apartado 68
Estrada de Arraiolos Km 4
7002-501 Évora
Alentejo

Tel: (0)66 734549/93130
Fax: (0)66 735264

Management: Isabel de Mello Cabral

Quinta da Espada ('of the sword'; the one hidden here by no less a man than Geraldo Geraldes, he who snatched Évora back from the Moors), surrounded by groves of olives and cork oaks and with views down to Évora, is a low, whitewashed, mimosa-graced building with ochre window surrounds and a perfectly authentic atmosphere. Guestrooms vary in size and colour scheme, with hand-painted Alentejo furniture everywhere; terracotta tiles, *estera* matting and dark beams creating further rustic warmth. Little touches, like towels with a hand-embroidered 'Quinta da Espada' motif, add a touch of gentility to it all. Slate, used in place of tiles, is an unusual and atttractive alternative to tiles in the bathrooms. The Green room occupies what was once the (small) family chapel. We particularly liked the smaller lounge where you breakfast and dine in front of the hearth during the colder months. You may well be tempted by the Alentejo cooking on offer, but if not you can make use of a well-equipped guest kitchen. Do stay two nights and walk into Évora along tracks that lead out from the Quinta, or ramble out and explore the 20-hectare estate.

Rooms: 6 with bath & wc + 1 suite.
Price: Tw 12500 Esc; Ste 16000 Esc.
Breakfast: Included.
Meals: Lunch/Dinner on request 3750 Esc (M).
Closed: Never.

How to get there: From Évora take the road towards Arraiolos and after 4km Quinta is signposted to right.

Quinta da Nora

Estrada dos Canaviais
7000
Évora
Alentejo

Tel: (0)66 732868
Fax: (0)66 733781

Management: Manuel Fialho

Although it is just 30 years old, once inside you might well imagine that Quinta da Nora is much older; many recycled materials were used during its construction, such as the hand-painted tiles that came from a Lisbon palace. On the (winter's) day that we passed, the welcome blaze in the hearth made us want to snuggle down and read up on nearby Évora. We liked the rooms; they are medium/large and have the gay hand-painted furniture of the Alentejo — from tables to wardrobe, to chairs, to candelabras, to mirrors. Parquet floors and dark roof beams add further cosiness. Breakfast is a sociable affair taken round the huge oak dining table; "almost a lunch" is how the owners described it. The house is surrounded by seven hectares of vineyards and you should sample the *tinto*; it is good. The Quinta's young owners are most charming and will happily help you plan your sorties, both gastronomic and cultural. Honest prices, particularly so with the irresistible Évora so close to you.

Rooms: 6 with bath & wc.
Price: D 8000-10000 Esc.
Breakfast: Included.
Meals: None available.
Closed: 15 December-15 January.

How to get there: From Lisbon to Évora. There, around ring road, under aqueduct, and left at roundabout towards Estremoz. After 100m, left towards Igrejinha. After approx. 400m right towards Bairro do Bacelo. Da Nora signposted on right.

Map No: 17

327

Pensão Policarpo

Rua da Freiria de Baixo 16
7000
Évora
Alentejo

Tel: (0)66 702424
Fax: (0)66 702424
www: www.localnet.pt/residencial Policarp

Management:
Michèle Policarpo

This grand town mansion was built by the Counts of Lousã in the 16th century, only to be lost to the State during the purges of Pombal. It was abandoned, but then rescued some 60 years ago by the Policarpo family. They carefully set about restoration and created the most intimate of guesthouses and all these years on still have buckets of enthusiasm for their work. The breakfast room is a delight; it has a high, vaulted ceiling and the three enormous windows capture the morning sunlight. *Fado* at breakfast takes your meal into another dimension; outside is a terrace where you can eat *al fresco* on warmer days. There is a cosy sitting room (in what once was the kitchen) with hand-painted tiles and a part of the old town wall has been swallowed up within the house as Évora grew outwards. Bedrooms are reached via the original granite staircase. Some have vaulted ceilings, many have pretty hand-painted Alentejo furniture and a number have antique bits and bobs. Our favourite was 101, with its original tiles and inspirational view. A private car park is a big plus in a town of narrow streets and zealous traffic wardens. Note that the entrance to the car park is in Rua Conde da Serra.

Rooms: 12 with bath or shower & wc; 8 sharing bath & wc.
Price: D/Tw bath & wc 7500-9500 Esc; D/Tw shower & wc 7000-8000 Esc; D/Tw (sharing bath & wc) 7000 Esc.
Breakfast: Included.
Meals: None available.
Closed: Never.

How to get there: Arriving in Évora from Lisbon, follow ring road round city until you see signs for Policarpo (close to University). Hotel has free car park under archway.

328   **Map No:** 17

Monte da Serralheira

Estrada de Bairro de Almeirim
7000
Évora
Alentejo

Tel: (0)66 741286/743957
Fax: (0)66 741286

Management: George and Lucia van der Feltz

George and Lucia discovered the wide, open space of the Alentejo more than twenty years ago and here they are now, farming the land just outside Évora and well integrated into the local community. And they are as enthralled by this wonderful land as they were in their pioneering days. The generosity of your hosts is reflected in the dimensions and fitting out of guest apartments that occupy what once were the workers' quarters. They have their own terraces, four of them have wood-burning stoves and all are high-ceilinged. They have all you need if self-catering. This could be the place for a longer (family) stay; leave guide books behind and instead let yourself be guided by Lucia or her recommendations; she is a professional guide and has a number of well-documented 'circuits' out from Serralheira. And if birds are your thing, stay here; George is an expert. You'll hear nightingales if here of a Spring night. This isolated 200-year-old farmhouse, with exuberant bougainvillea and wisteria, whitewashed walls offset by blue trimmings and splendidly isolated setting is a most 'special' place and perfect for a longer holiday in Portugal.

Rooms: 1, 2 and 3 bed apartments sleeping 2-6 with bath & wc.
Price: Apt (for 2) 7500-8500 Esc; Apt (for 4) 14000-15000 Esc.
Breakfast: 750 Esc (if not self-catering).
Meals: None available.
Closed: Never.

How to get there: From Lisbon to Évora. There right onto ring road. Right at roundabout next to Opel garage towards Almeirim (sul). Follow this road to very end to the farm.

Map No: 17

329

Monte Saraz

Horta dos Revedores
Barrada
7200 Monsaraz
Alentejo

Tel: (0)66 557385
Fax: (0)66 557485
E-mail: monte.saraz@mail.telepac.pt
www: www.portugalvirtual.pt/monte.saraz

Management: Monique Deckers

Don't miss Monsaraz. This remarkably well-preserved medieval village looks out from behind lofty battlements across the plain below. Arrive by night and you'll see it from ten miles away hovering ethereally in the night sky. Within the walls the silence, narrow streets and herringbone cobbling are bewitching indeed. Down on the plain among a grove of gnarled old olives this cluster of farm buildings is a wonderful retreat from the mundane. Olives were milled here; you can still see the spring which once fed the mill race beneath the main *lagar* (mill). A simple white exterior (windows unusually picked out with plain black bands) belies a wonderfully rich interior, an eclectic mix of Portugal and the Orient with wonderful vaulted brick ceilings. There are rugs, richly painted walls, unusual sculptural flourishes and Monique's paintings. The gardens are just as enticing with hedges and fountains leading naturally on to the orchards and groves beyond. The swimming-pool has a feel of inner sanctum-cum-Roman bath with wrap-around colonnade; to one end is the summer dining room with views up to Monsaraz. In the three self-contained *casas* the emphasis is on a clean, simple and restful mix of whitewashed walls, some antiques, and good bedding. A wholesome breakfast, good restaurants nearby and just the hoot of an owl to break the silence at night. Unforgettable.

Rooms: 1 with bath & wc + 3 suites.
Price: Tw 13000 Esc; Ste 15000 Esc.
Breakfast: Included.
Meals: None available.
Closed: Never.

How to get there: From Évora N258 towards Spain to Reguengos de Monsaraz and here towards Monsaraz. Approx 4km before from Monsaraz left at sign for "Anta" along track. At T junction right and first house is Monte Saraz.

Map No: 17

Casa de Terena

Rua Direita 45
7250
Terena-Alandroal
Alentejo

Tel: (0)68 459132
Fax: (0)68 459155

Management: António and Conchita Pimenta de Castro

Terena is a peaceful hilltop village with tumble-down castle and church bells, and not a bit touristy. It is far enough off the beaten track to ensure that tourists will be a long time in coming. Groups of village ladies were sunning themselves, bent over their lace, the day that we visited and we could see why Conchita and António were inspired to move here from Lisbon. It was a labour of love to nurse this grand old village house back to life. From the inner dragon-tooth patio a grand marble staircase sweeps you up to the bedrooms. Here the ingredients include old dressers, wrought-iron bedsteads (but new mattresses), Alentejo rugs, terracotta tiles, dried flowers and views out to the reservoir beyond — and all sparkling like the newest pin. And there are Casablanca-style ceiling fans to cool things down when the heat sets in. The downstairs lounge has wafer-bricked, vaulted ceilings and a collection of old cross-stitch (some by those village ladies?) gracing the walls. The tranquillity and beauty of Terena and your hosts' enthusiasm make the journey — or slight diversion if en route to or from Spain — worthwhile. Abundant bird life if ornithology is your thing.

Rooms: 6 with bath & wc.
Price: S 10000 Esc; D/Tw 12000 Esc.
Breakfast: Included — buffet.
Meals: Lunch/Dinner 3000 Esc (M).
Closed: Never.

How to get there: Coming from Spain through Badajoz and on into Portugal towards Évora. Terena is half way between Vila Viçosa and Monsaraz. House next to castle in village.

Map No: 17

331

Castelo de Milfontes

7645
Vila Nova de Milfontes
Alentejo

Tel: (0)83 998231
Fax: (0)83 997122

Management: Ema M. da Câmara Machado

Carthaginians, Romans, Moors and even Algerian pirates have all coveted the remarkable strategic site now occupied by the Castelo de Milfontes; you see why when looking out across the river estuary to the Atlantic breakers beyond. The present fort dates from the 16th century and was rescued from abandon by the family some fifty years ago. This is no ordinary 'hotel'; the spirit of (genteel) welcome is captured in the plaque above the hearth which reads *'viver sim amigos não é viver'* (living without friends is not living). Full board is de rigeur at Milfontes and dinner is the occasion to get to know your fellow guests and to meet Ema, who graciously officiates at table. It is an occasion to dress for; at 8 o'clock a maid announces that it is time to pass through to the dining room — silver service and traditional Portuguese cuisine await you. The rooms have views that defy description; we think 'tower room 1' is one of the loveliest we have seen anywhere. The furniture matches the Castle; perhaps an old writing desk, a baldequin bed, original oils — and all poised between vaulted ceilings and parquet floors. The Castelo's fame has spread far and wide and guests return year after year; spend a night here and you will never forget it. *Half board only.*

Rooms: 7 with bath & wc.
Price: S 18500-19500 Esc; Tw 26000-28000 Esc (Full board for two).
Breakfast: Included.
Meals: Picnic lunches 2000 Esc; dinner included.
Closed: Never.

How to get there: From Lisbon, A2 to Setubal, then N10 towards Évora and branch right on N5/N20 toward Grandola. Left on N120 to Santiago and on to Cercal. Here, N390 to V.N. de Milfontes. Castle at edge of estuary by beach.

Map No: 23

Herdade da Matinha

7555
Cercal do Alentejo
Alentejo

Tel: (0)69 949247
E-mail: matinha@aol

Management: Alfredo Moreira da Silva

This a classic Alentejo *monte* (farmhouse); long, low and encircled by the striking russet-brown trunks of the cork oak. Yet though the setting is deeply rural you are close to the wonders of the Alentejo's protected Costa Vicentina and to the towns of Cercal and Vila Nova de Milfontes. Monica works for part of the year as a tourist guide and will help plan your sorties; Alfredo is an artist and looks after the cooking. He loves to chat with his guests in the kitchen while preparing meals, probably to the accompaniment of classical or baroque music. His paintings add life and colour to the lounge which is large, light and comfortable and leads to a terrace where stands of camellias give way to groves of citrus — a lovely spot for meals when it's warm. Central stage at Matinha — unusually for Portugal — is the kitchen and a big wooden table where you eat a generous breakfast *en famille* and where dinner offers "the best traditional dishes but healthier than usual" (in other words, with more and better-prepared vegetables). Bedrooms are large, uncluttered, slate-floored and home to more of Alfredo's paintings; furnishings seem rather Conran in inspiration. Come for the utter peace, an interesting mixture of 'trad' Portugal with more contemporary elements, and to meet your polyglot hosts.

Rooms: 4 with shower & wc + 2 suites.
Price: D/Tw 10000 – 12000 Esc; Ste 10000-12000 Esc.
Breakfast: Included.
Meals: Dinner 3000 Esc (C).
Closed: Never.

How to get there: From Lisbon A2 to Grandola then towards Sines on IP8 then IC4 to Cercal then N390 to Vila Nova de Milfontes. Here, opposite Frezas factory right and follow signs along 3km of track.

Map No: 23

333

Verdemar

Casas Novas
7555
Cercal do Alentejo
Alentejo

Tel: (0)69 904544

Management: Nuno Vilas-Boas and Christine Nijhoff

Although only a short drive from the mighty Atlantic and some wonderful beaches, Verdemar's setting is deeply bucolic. Hidden away among stands of old cork oaks beyond the blue and white main gate a very special country retreat awaits you. Guestrooms are spread around the outbuildings but the focus of life here is the main farmhouse and dining room (see photo). The atmosphere is easy and cosy; a beam and bamboo ceiling, an open kitchen/bar, wooden stools and chairs. You'll share fun and good food around one big table — *al fresco*, of course, in summer. Nuno, a professional chef for 20 years in Amsterdam, loves to have your company as he prepares dinner and likes to exchange a recipe or two. Leading off the kitchen, the lounge is equally cosy — guitar, paintings, an old lamp; a cool place to escape the heat of the summer. And it is heartening to find somewhere so ready to welcome families with young children; they'll meet ducks, chickens, donkeys, cows and sheep. A special children's dinner is even prepared early evening. Bedrooms are just right; no hotelly extras but nothing lacking. A favourite address, our type of idyll — with the true spirit of honest hostelry.

Rooms: 5 with bath & wc + 1 apartment.
Price: D /Tw 7000-9000 Esc; Apt 6500-8000 Esc.
Breakfast: Included (not for apartments).
Meals: Dinner on request 3200 Esc (M). No meals on Sundays.
Closed: Never.

How to get there: From Lisbon A2 then IP1 towards Algarve. 500m after Mimosa right towards Cercal; 7 km before you arrive in Cercal left on track at sign for Casas Novas; house signposted.

334   **Map No:** 23

Quinta do Barranco da Estrada

7665
Santa Clara a Velha
Alentejo

Tel: (0)83 933901
Fax: (0)83 933901
E-mail: lakescape@mail.telepac.pt

Management: Lulu & Frank McClintock

It you love wild beauty, and look for a real hideaway when you holiday, Barranco da Estrada will be ideal. The Quinta's low buildings hug the shore of one of the Alenejo's largest freshwater lakes. The whole area has a microclimate which keeps the water warm enough for a long swimming season and nurtures an amazing range of plant and animal life; visit in spring and the wild flowers will have you in raptures. Lulu and Frank spent a decade renovating the original house and then added a row of guest rooms. They are light, cool and uncluttered and their terraces all look towards the lake. Lounge, dining room and bar share one large room and happily embrace Portuguese and English styles of décor. Beyond huge windows there is a vine-festooned terrace where you spend most of your time when it's warm. Above the lake a series of terraces has been planted with hibiscus, oleander, palm, jasmine, plumbago and cactus. A sinuous path cuts down through all this colour to the jetty where you can canoe, fish for crayfish, sail, water-ski or walk the shoreline, perhaps in the company of one of the McClintock's six dogs. Frank will help with the naming of all those birds and, if you're lucky, you may see mongoose or wild boar.

Rooms: 7 with bath & wc.
Price: S 12000-17500 Esc; D/Tw 13250 – 18500 Esc; Family room (for 4) 25000-35000 Esc.
Breakfast: 1000 Esc (cooked breakfast).
Meals: Lunch 3000 Esc; dinner 4000 Esc (M).
Closed: Never.

How to get there: From Lisbon A2 towards Algarve and after 175km right towards Odemira then left to S. Martinho das Amoreiras; here towards Portimão then (doubling back) to Cortebrique: follow track and after 9km signposted on right.

Moita Nova do Cavaleiro

Cavaleiro
7630
Odemira
Algarve

Tel: (0)83 64357
Fax: (0)83 64167

Management: Ute Gerhardt

If horse-riding and unspoilt beaches are your thing then why not stay a week with Ute and Walter at their Alentejo farmstead? This is an exceptionally beautiful and unspoilt part of Portugal's Atlantic coastline which has recently been designated a National Park; the ecosystem of these coastal dunes nurtures a huge variety of plant and animal life. You can reach them, and hidden coves beyond, by walking just three hundred yards across Cavaleiro's pastures. The original farmhouse has two apartments and a large guest lounge; the other two have been newly built and horse-shoe around a central swathe of green. They are south-facing to catch the sun, each has its own terrace and wood-burner and they have a fresh and uncluttered feel: you are benefitting from architect Walter's professional eye for good use of space. Floors are of terracotta, sheets of good linen, beds of pine and the kitchens have full self-catering kit. The buildings are softened thanks to a riot of climbers, a wonderful spot from which to watch the sun dipping down into the Atlantic. It is nice to come across a place which is so friendly to littl'uns; there's a paddling pool, beach toys and a collection of games. Ride out from Cavaleiro on well-mannered thoroughbreds, but do book your stay well ahead; old fans return again and again.

Rooms: 4 self-catering apartments.
Price: Apt (for 2) 9500-11000 Esc; 55000-85000 Esc weekly.
Breakfast: None available.
Meals: None available.
Closed: Never.

How to get there: From Faro IC4 via Abufeira, Portimão and Lagos to Aljezur. Then N120 to S. Teotónio. Left here via Zambujeira to Cavaleiro. Here towards beach (not Cabo Sardão), and right after bridge to Moita Nova.

Inn Albergeria Bica-Boa

Estrada de Lisboa 266
8550
Monchique
Algarve

Tel: (0)82 912271
Fax: (0)82 912360

Management: Susan Clare Cassidy

Bica-Boa's name was inspired by the many springs that well up on this thickly wooded mountainside above Monchique; winding your way up from the western Algarve the exuberant vegetation of the place takes you by surprise. There are stunning walks galore and, if you venture up here, do stay at Bica-Boa. The hotel stands just to the side of the road but there is little traffic and the four guestrooms are tucked away to the rear of the building. They are fresh, light and simply decorated with wooden floors and ceilings — and all have views across the valley. There is a quiet little guest lounge with the same view; a corner chimney, *azulejo*-clad walls and a chess table give a homely feel. Bica Boa's restaurant is popular with locals and ex-pats up from the coast; fish is the speciality, from sole to stuffed squid to lobster (order ahead). There are terraces for *al fresco* dining when the weather is right and a terraced garden with quiet corners for sitting out. Susie has lived here for many years and has a deep attachment to the area and its people; she will help organise walks for you, can sometimes accompany you herself and is as kind and caring a hostess as you could hope to meet. She is adding more vegetarian dishes to the menu this year.

Rooms: 4 with bath & wc.
Price: Tw 9500-11500 Esc.
Breakfast: Included.
Meals: Lunch/Dinner 4500-5000 (C).
Closed: Never.

How to get there: From Faro take motorway N125 west towards Lagos. Exit for Portimão/Monchique. Climb up to Monchique, then follow signs to Lisboa through town. Bica-Boa is approx. 300 yards after leaving town on right; well signposted.

Map No: 23

337

Quinta das Achadas

Estrada da Barragem
8600-251
Odiáxere
Lagos Algarve

Tel: (0)82 798425
Fax: (0)82 799162

Management: Beatrice and
Willy Hagmann

It took seven long months of work from dawn to dusk for Willy and Beatrice to redecorate/convert the Quinta das Achadas. Hats off to this quiet-mannered Swiss couple for creating one of the very best B&Bs of the Algarve. The approach is a delight: a winding drive through groves of olive, almond and orange trees which then give way to a sub-tropical garden where maguey and palm, geranium and bougainvillea, pine and jasmine jostle for position. The guest bedrooms, each with its own small terrace, look out across the gardens and are in the converted barn and stables; some have modern furniture, others antiques (our favourite is 'Hibiscus') and the innumerable South American bits and bobs are mementoes from Willy's work in those parts. In colder weather you breakfast in a cosy dining room (it doubles as a bar — just help yourself) but most of the year it's mild enough to sit out on the terrace; try the 'gourmet breakfast' and you'll be hooked. If you're in the apartments you can prepare your own food; 'Bougain-Villa' (sic) was our favourite, but all deserve the special etiquette. We're longing to return here!

Rooms: 3 with bath & wc + 3 apartments.
Price: D/Tw £36-56 inc. breakfast; Apt £51-75. *Minimum stay 3 nights.*
Breakfast: Included. £5 extra if in Apt.
Meals: None available.
Closed: End October-mid March.

How to get there: From Portimão, N125 towards Lagos. In village of Odiáxere, right at sign for Barragem. House signposted on right after 1.2km.

338   **Map No:** 23

Quinta da Alfarrobeira

Estrada de Palmares
8600
Odiáxere
Lagos Algarve

Tel: (0)82 798424
Fax: (0)82 799630

Management: Nanette Kant

Quinta da Alfarrobeira stands on a hill just inland from the Algarve coast and is surrounded by six hectares of old fruit groves. Nanette and Theo, a young couple from Holland, fell in love with the place and moved down from Amsterdam to set up their dream home. You might be fired by similar dreams as you sit beneath the enormous *alfarrobeira* (carob) and gaze out across the old olive and almond trees, or watch Tjacco, the couple's young son, playing happily with his adopted pets on a sunny flower-filled patio. Choose between a room in the main house or one of two new apartments built in traditional Algarve style where terracotta, beam and bamboo are the essential ingredients. We loved their light, airy feel and the antique furnishings that have been collected piecemeal from all over Europe. There are biggish bathrooms, private terraces and views — and kitchenettes in the apartments if you plan to cook for yourself. Add to this the lovely walks out from the Quinta (just 1.5km down to the sea), exceptionally kind hosts and you begin to get the measure of this altogether most special place.

Rooms: 1 with bath & wc + 2 apartments.
Price: D 12000 Esc; 'Stable' Apt 8000-13000 Esc; 'Farmhouse' Apt 10000-15000 Esc.
Breakfast: Included.
Meals: None — self-catering.
Closed: Never.

How to get there: From Faro m'way (E1) then N125 to Portimão and on towards Lagos. In village of Odiáxere left at square towards Meiapraia/Palmares. After approx. 1.3 km (cow sign on right) turn left onto dirt track, house on right.

Map No: 23

339

Casa Três Palmeiras

Apartado 84
8501-909
Portimão
Algarve

Tel: (0)82 401275
Fax: (0)82 401029

Management: Dolly Schlingensiepen

The setting is a dream; from Casa Três Palmeiras' perch right at the cliff's edge the view is incomparable, a symphony of sea, sky, and rock — ever-changing according to the day's mood and ever beautiful. The house was built in the sixties, but the 'Zen' design still feels modern three decades on. The house is given a distinctly exotic feel by three enormous palm trees and the simple arches that soften the façade and give welcome shade to the guest rooms once the temperature starts creeping up. Rooms have everything you might expect for the price. There are marble floors, double sinks and big, fitted wardrobes, yet they remain uncluttered. Best of all, they lead straight out onto the terrace whence those heavenly views (and a sea-water pool). There are always freshly cut flowers and a bowl of fruit awaiting guests and it is obvious that Brazilian Dolly is happy in her role of hostess; after years in the diplomatic service, entertaining comes naturally. A path leads from the house straight down to the beach; get up early and even in midsummer you may find you have it to yourself. Book well ahead if you plan to stay in summer. *Reduced green fees and car hire rates available for Três Palmeiras guests.*

Rooms: 5 with bath & wc.
Price: Tw 29900 Esc.
Breakfast: Included.
Meals: Snacks available all day.
Closed: 1 December-31 January.

How to get there: From Portimão take dual carriageway towards Praia da Rocha. Right at last roundabout towards Praia do Vau and at next roundabout double back and turn up track on right after 100m. Right along track at first villa.

340

Map No: 23

Casa Domilu

Estrada de Benagil
Alfanzina
8400 Carvoeiro
Algarve

Tel: (0)82 358404
Fax: (0)82 358410
E-mail: casa.domilu@mail.telepac.pt
www: www.casa-domilu.com

Management: Abilio D'Almeida

Yes, finally a place to stay in Portugal that is less than two hundred years old! Abilio originally designed and built this pinky-beige villa as a holiday home for the family. Then the children grew up and he decided to extend it and this small, special hotel was born. If you wince at anything that smacks of kitsch then this is not for you. But it you don't, and are looking for a comfortable and friendly place to stay on the Algarve, then do give Domilu a go. The décor of lounge and dining room is very pick-and-mix; there are repro antiques, Art-Deco-ish chairs, dragon-tooth floors and modern prints. An enormous sweep of glass in both rooms looks out to the pool, the nerve centre of the place. The bedrooms are big, light, cheerful and marble-floored and have all the swish extras: book the honeymoon suite and you get a sunken whirlpool bath surrounded by potted palms and Doric columns! The breakfast at Domilu is a buffet: big and designed to please a northern European palate, while dinner is resolutely Portuguese. Try the *cataplana*, seafood cooked in a clam-shaped copper pot — one of the Algarve's most delicious dishes. There is tennis, a sauna on the way and mountain bikes. Guests, many of whom are German, return year after year.

Rooms: 24 with bath & wc + 6 suites.
Price: D 8000-15000 Esc; Tw 12000-20000 Esc; Ste 18000-36000 Esc.
Breakfast: Included.
Meals: Lunch 2000-3500 Esc (M); dinner 3000-5000 Esc (C).
Closed: Never.

How to get there: From N125 exit for Carvoeiro and 200m after Intermarché supermarket right at signs for Casa Domilu.

Map No: 23

341

Casa Belaventura

Campina de Boliqueime
8100
Loulé
Algarve

Tel: (0)89 360633
Fax: (0)89 366053
E-mail: belaventura@mail.telepac.pt

Management: Carlos Dias

Belaventua lies tucked away in the Algarve hinterland; in such a pastoral setting you can soon forget that the busy coastal towns of Vilamoura and Albufeira are just a quarter of an hour's drive away. Carlos converted this old farmhouse with B&B and self-catering in mind; as well as a beautifully proportioned sitting room there is a large dining room and fully equipped kitchen. The house is light and airy by the open arches that link the different spaces; a more traditional 'Algarve style' is present in terracotta floor, wafer-brick work and marvellously weathered roof titles. Carlos has given the building extra volume and more modern lines by extending the roof outwards thus creating a shady outside sitting area. By the pool in the garden there's a hammock in the shade of an olive tree and beyond it, through the almond groves, you catch glimpses of the glittering sea. The bedrooms have contemporary paintings (some by Carlos's wife), durries, more traditional beam and bamboo roofs, perhaps a rattan chair or view across the garden. One is more of a suite with its own sitting room and inglenook. Carlos has a boat and will take you for a day's sailing along the Algarve coast.

Rooms: 5 with bath or shower & wc.
Price: S 9000 – 15000 Esc; D 10500 –
17000 Esc. *Public hoildays extra 20%.*
Breakfast: Included.
Meals: None available.
Closed: Never.

How to get there: From Faro towards
Spain on IP1 motorway. Exit for
Boliqueime and after just 250m turn right
and Belaventura signposted on right after approx 750m.

The Garden Cottages
8100
Loulé
Algarve

Tel: UK agent: 0181 3668944

The *Val de Jedeu*, or 'Valley of the Jews', is a lush valley in the Algarve hinterland, just a couple of miles back from the coast; mild winters, long hours of sunshine and rich soil allow nearly everything to grow in profusion. The English owner found this old wine farm in ruins in the early 70s and has put in years of patient restoration and planting. This is a place of peace and privacy; behind the whitewashed outer wall the cottages stand apart from one another facing the gardens and — tucked away beyond — an enormous round swimming-pool. Each cottage has a sun and a shade terrace, a prettily tiled kitchen, a lounge with wood-burner and is large enough for four — though generally only let to two. Dried flowers, eucalyptus beams and terracotta give a 'country' feel, while mementoes from Africa and Turkey add an exotic note. There are magazines and a carefully compiled file with details of restaurants, shops and visits; you'll feel instantly at home. What we remember most are the gardens: olive, pomegranate, almonds and lemon and, beneath them, a profusion of flowers of every hue. The benign climate means that visiting out of season is just as special.

Rooms: 6 cottages with shower & wc + lounge/kitchen.
Price: Weekly £200-£500 (depending on cottage and season). Details on request.
Breakfast: Self-catering, or Continental can be arranged.
Meals: None — self-catering.
Closed: Never.

How to get there: Information will be sent by UK agent (see above) or direct from the owner (phone/fax in Portugal (0)89 328637).

Map No: 23

Monte do Casal

Cerro do Lobo
Estoi
8000 Faro
Algarve

Tel: (0)89 991503/990140
Fax: (0)89 991341

Management: Bill Hawkins

After more than a dozen years at the helm, Bill Hawkins has firmly established Monte do Casal's credentials as one of the Algarve's most special small hotels. This former farmhouse is tucked away in the gentle hills of the Algarve hinterland, a low, white building surrounded by exuberant stands of bougainvillea, mature palms, olives and almonds. Inside, the eucalyptus and cane roofing and the terracotta floor tiles create an unmistakably Mediterranean atmosphere. Food is a cornerstone of the hotel's fame; Bill trained in the kitchens of Claridges and the Savoy and his house specialities and well-stocked wine cellar are a formidable partnership. But if you do fancy a change, ask for his 'cryptic-map-guide to the Algarve'; it will lead you towards treasures you would otherwise miss and picnic hampers can be provided for your forays. The guest bedrooms have fine old brass cornered 'travel' furniture and decent bathrooms; nearly all have private terraces overlooking pool and gardens. But do book early, especially if planning a visit in season. *Children over 16 welcome.*

Rooms: 8 with bath & wc + 5 suites.
Price: Tw 17000-30000 Esc; Deluxe 18800-36000 Esc; Ste 22600-43000 Esc. *Minimum stay 2 nights.*
Breakfast: Included.
Meals: Lunch/Dinner 5100 Esc (M), from 5000 Esc (C).
Closed: Never.

How to get there: From Faro take N2 north towards São Bras. Exit for Estoi. Here at square take road towards Moncarapacho; hotel is approx 2.5km along this road signposted to left.

Quinta Fonte do Bispo

Estrada National 270
Fonte do Bispo
8800 Tavira
Algarve

Tel: (0)81 971484
Fax: (0)81 971484
E-mail: qtfontebispo@mail.telepac.pt
www: www.telenet.pt/-dk1692/Quinta.htm

Management: Jaime da Silva Brito Neto

The benign climate, exceptional vegetation, proximity to the sea and interesting folk architecture means that the gentle hills of the Algarve hinterland remains a good choice for a relaxing holiday. This old farmstead could be a good base for acquainting yourself with the region. It is a long, low white building with pretty chimney stacks and broad bands of blue around doors and windows — typical of the area. Parts of the farm are nearly two hundred years old but it was completely renovated and you might not guess its age. There are just six apartments in the converted outbuildings of the farm — they look onto a cobbled central patio. They have been designed with families in mind: open-plan lounges have two bolstered single beds which double up as sofas and there is a small kitchenette (not really intended for preparing full meals but useful for heating a bottle or making a cup of tea). The style is local and 'country'; the inevitable (herringbone) terracotta floor, beamed and bambooed roof and simple yet adequate shower rooms. There is a large communal lounge in similar style but most of the year you will be out by the pool; find a shady spot in the garden beneath the orange, almond and olive trees. We could see why painting courses are sometimes held here. Faro, Tavira and Vila Real are all close by as are many good restaurants.

Rooms: 6 apartments each sleeping max. of 6 persons.
Price: Apt (for 2) 11000-14000 Esc.
Breakfast: Included.
Meals: On request. Approx. 2500 (M).
Closed: Never

How to get there: From Faro towards Spain on IP1. Pass Loulé then exit for Olhão/Santa Catarina. Arriving in Santa Catarina right towards Tavira. Quinta signposted on left after approx. 1km.

Convento do Santo António

Atalaia 56   **Tel:** (0)81 325632
8800   **Fax:** (0)81 325632
Tavira
Algarve

Management: Isabel Maria Castanho Paes

Monks of the Capuchin order built the convent of Santo António and its diminutive cloister; they chose a wind-swept place of rare beauty. Isabel is almost apologetic that "the home has only been in the family for five generations". A portrait of great-grandmother officiates over one of the vaulted corridors that runs the length of the cloister (Santo Antonio looks benignly on from his chapel at the end of the other) and it was grandfather, much travelled, who planted the exotic garden. Here are rooms to remember; varying in size (and price) they have great charm; here a vaulted ceiling, there a fine dresser; here a seaward view, there a hand-knotted rug. It is a Lusitanian feast of hand-crafted terracotta and ceramic tiles, of rich *alcobaça* fabrics and carefully chosen (often naïve) paintings. We loved the Chapel room (one of two 'specials') with its high ceilings and bathroom sitting snugly inside what once was a chimney breast! Lounge and bar are just as special and it would be heavenly to breakfast in summer with Gregorian chant to accompany your feast. Hardly surprising that the glossies run features on Isabel's creation. And such a PEACEFUL spot.

Rooms: 6 with bath & wc + 1 suite.
Price: D/Tw 16000-19500 Esc; 'Special' D/Tw 18000-23000 Esc; Ste 24000-29500 Esc. *Minimum stay (Oct-Mar) 3 nights; April-Sept 4 nights.*
Breakfast: Included — buffet.
Meals: Dinner on request 3500 Esc.
Closed: January.

How to get there: From Faro, N125 then M'way IP 1 towards Espanha. Exit 7 to Tavira. Here, under archway to r'bout and straight on towards 'Centro Saude'. On, over T-junct and once past church right towards 'Cento Saude'. Bear right past army barracks, then first left, then after 200m fork right to Convento. Or ask a local!!

Useful Vocabulary – Spanish

We hope that the following words and phrases may be of use.

Before Arriving (therefore over the telephone).

Do you have a room for the night?	¿Tiene una habitación para esta noche?
How much does it cost?	¿Cuánto cuesta?
We'll be arriving at around 7p.m.	Estaremos llegando sobre las siete.
We're lost!	Estámos perdidos.
We'll be arriving late.	Vamos a llegar tarde.
I'm in the phone box at.....	Estoy en la cabina en...
I'm in the 'La Giralda' bar in.....	Estoy en el bar 'La Giralda' en...
Do you have any animals? I'm allergic to cats.	Tienen animales? Tengo alergia a los gatos.
We would like to have dinner.	Quisieramos cenar.

On arrival.

Hello! I'm Mr/Mrs X.	¡Hóla! Soy Señor/Señora X.
We found your name in this book.	Encontramos su nombre en esta guía.
Where can we leave the car?	¿Dónde podemos dejar el coche?
Could you help us with our bags?	¿Podría ayudarnos con las maletas?
Could I leave this picnic food/bottles in your fridge?	¿Podríamos dejar esta comida/estas botellas en la nevera?
Could I heat up the baby's feeding bottle?	¿Podríamos calentar este biberón?
Can the children sleep in sleeping bags on the floor?	¿Podrían dormir los niños en sacos de dormir en el suelo?
How much will you charge for that?	¿Cuánto nos cobrará para éso?

Things you need/that go wrong.

Do you have an extra pillow/blanket?	¿Podría dejarnos otra almohada/manta?
A light bulb needs replacing.	Es necesario cambiar una bombilla.
The heating isn't on.	No está encendida la calefacción.
How does the air conditioning work?	¿Cómo funciona la climatización?
We've a problem with the plumbing.	Tenemos un problema de fontanería.
The room smells!	¡La habitación huele mal!
Do you have a quieter room?	¿Tiene una habitación menos ruidosa?
How does the cooker work?	¿Cómo funciona el horno?
Please ask the man in the room next door to stop singing/dancing.	Dígale al hombre de al lado que deje de cantar/bailar.
Where can I hang these wet clothes?	¿Dónde podemos colgar esta ropa?
Could we have some soap?	¿Hay jabón por favor?
Could you give us some hot water to make tea - we have our own teabags!	¿Podría dejarnos agua caliente para hacer un té? ¡El té ya tenemos!
Would you possibly have an aspirin?	¿Tendría una aspirina por favor?
Could you turn the volume down?	¿Podría bajar un poco el volumen?

How the house/hotel works.

When do you begin serving breakfast?	¿A qué hora empiezan a dar el desayuno?
We'd like to order some drinks.	Queremos tomar algo, por favor.
Can the children play in the garden?	¿Pueden visitar la finca los niños?
Is there any danger?	¿Es peligroso?
Can we leave the children with you?	¿Podemos dejar los niños con vosotros?
Can we eat breakfast in our room?	¿Podemos desayunar en la habitación?

Local information.

Where can we buy petrol?	¿Dónde hay una gasolinera?
Where can we find a garage to repair our car?	¿Dónde hay un taller de coches?
How far is the nearest shop?	¿Dónde está la tienda más cerca?
We need a doctor.	Nos hace falta un médico.
Where is there a chemist's?	¿Dónde hay una farmacía?
Where is the police station?	¿Dónde está la comisaría?
Where's a good place to eat?	¿Dónde come uno bien por aquí?
Where can we find a cash-dispenser?	¿Dónde hay un cajero automático?
Could you recommend a good walk?	¿Podría recomendar algun paseo bonito?
Do you know of any local festivities?	¿Hay alguna fiesta local en estos dias?

On leaving.

What time must we leave?	¿A qué hora tenemos que dejar libre la habitación?
We'd like to pay the bill.	Nuestra cuenta, por favor.
How much do I owe you?	¿Cuánto debemos?
We hope to be back.	Esperamos volver.
We've had a very pleasant stay.	Nos ha gustado mucho estar aquí.
This is a beautiful spot.	Este es un lugar divino.
Thank you so much.	Muchas gracias.

Eating out (or in).

Where's there a good tapas bar?	¿Dónde hay buenas tapas por aquí?
Could we eat outside, please?	¿Es posible comer fuera?
What's today's set menu?	¿Qué tienen hoy de menú?
What do you recommend?	¿Qué es lo que Usted recomienda?
What's that man over there eating?	¿Qué está comiendo aquel hombre?
We'd like a dish with no meat in it.	Queremos algo que no tenga carne.
What vegetarian dishes do you have?	¿Qué platos vegetarianos tienen?
Do you have a wine list?	¿Hay una lista de vinos?
This food is cold!	¡Esta comida está fría!
Do you have some pepper/salt please?	¿Hay pimienta/sal por favor?
What tapas do you have?	¿Qué tapas tienen? *see introduction!
We'd like half a plateful of that one.	Una media ración de aquella por favor.
A plate of this one.	Una ración de esta.
Please keep the change.	La vuelta es para usted.
Where are the toilets?	¿Dónde están los servicios?
The toilet is locked!	¡El servicio está cerrado con llave!
It was a delicious meal.	¡Estaba muy rica la comida!
I'd like a white/black coffee/ /weaker coffee.	Un café con leche/un café solo. /un café menos cargado.
Coffee with just a little milk.	Un café cortado.
Tea/camomile tea	Un té/una manzanilla

**remember, the safest way to order tea with milk is to ask for 'un té, y un poco de leche, pero aparte'. It's tempting to ask for 'té con leche' - but you may well end up with a glass of hot milk with a teabag plonked in the top! Milk is nearly always UHT so if you really need your tea we recommend drinking it with a slice of lemon 'té con limón'. Or take your own along and just ask for 'un vaso de agua caliente' in the bar. Your request will rarely be refused.

Useful Vocabulary – Portuguese

Before Arriving (therefore over the telephone).

Do you have a room for the night?	Tem um quarto para esta noite?
How much does it cost?	Quanto custa?
We'll be arriving at about 7pm.	Nós chegaremos por volta das sete da tarde.
We're lost!	Estamos perdidos!
We'll be arriving late.	Vamos chegar tarde.
I'm in the phone box at…	Estou na cabine telefónica em…
I'm in the 'Oporto' bar in…	Estou no bar 'Oporto' em…
Do you have any animals? I'm allergic to cats.	Você tem algum animal? Sou alérgico a gatos.
We would like to have dinner.	Queriamos jantar.

On arrival.

Hello! I'm Mr/Mrs X.	Olá! Eu sou o Senhor/ Senhora X.
We found your name in this book.	Encontramos o seu nome neste livro.
Where can we leave the car?	Onde podemos deixar o carro?
Could you help us with our bags?	Podia ajudar-nos com as nossas malas?
Could I leave this picnic food/bottles in your fridge?	Podia deixar esta comida/garrafas para picnic no seu frigorífico?
Could I heat up the baby's feeding bottle?	Podia aquecer o biberon?
Can the children sleep in sleeping bags on the floor?	As crianças podem dormir no chão em sacos camas?
How much will you charge for that?	Quanto é que você cobrará por isto?

Things you need/that go wrong.

Do you have an extra pillow/blanket?	Você tem uma outra almofada/um outro cobertor?
A light bulb needs replacing.	É preciso mudar uma lampada.
The heating isn't on.	O aquecedor não está ligado.
How does the air conditioning work?	Como funciona o ar condicionado?
We've a problem with the plumbing.	Temos um problema com a canalização.
The rooms smells!	O quarto cheira mal!
Do you have a quieter room?	Tem um quarto menos barulhento?
How does the cooker work?	Como funciona o fogão?
Please ask the man in the room next door to stop singing/dancing.	Por favor, peça ao homem do quarto ao lado para parar de cantar/dançar.
Where can I hang these wet clothes?	Onde posso secar estas roupas?
Could we have some soap?	Queriamos sabonete por favor?
Could you give us some hot water to make tea—we have our own tea bags!	Podia-nos dar água quente para o nosso to chá—nós temos as nossas próprias saquetas de chá.
Would you possibly have some aspirin?	Tem aspirina, por favor?
Could you turn the volume down?	Pode baixar o volume?

How the house/hotel works.

When do you begin serving breakfast?	A que horas começa a servir o pequeno-almoço?
We'd like to order some drinks.	Queriamos tomar algumas bebidas, por favor?
Can the children play in the garden?	As crianças podem brincar no jardim?
Is there any danger?	É perigoso?
Can we leave the children with you?	Podemos deixar as crianças convosco?
Can we eat breakfast in our room?	Podemos tomar o pequeno-almoço no quarto?

Local Information.

Where can we buy petrol?	Onde fica a próxima estação de serviço?
Where can we find a garage to repair our car?	Onde há uma oficina para repararmos o nosso carro?
How far is the nearest shop?	Fica muito longe a próxima loja?
We need a doctor.	Precisamos de um médico.
Where is there a chemist's?	Onde há uma farmácia?
Where is the police station?	Onde fica o posto de policia?
Where's a good place to eat?	Onde há um sítio onde se coma bem?
Where can we find a cash-dispenser?	Onde há uma caixa automática?
Could you recommend a good walk?	Era capaz de recomendar um bom passeio?
Do you know of any local festivities?	Sabe de algumas festividades locais?

On leaving.

What time must we leave?	A que horas temos de libertar/deixar o quarto?
We'd like to pay the bill.	Queriamos pagar a conta.
How much do I owe you?	Quanto devo?
We hope to be back.	Esperamos regressar.
We've had a very pleasant stay.	Tivemos uma estadia muito agradável.
This is a beautiful spot.	Este é um lugar muito bonito.
Thank you so much.	Muito obrigado.

Eating out (or in).

Where's there a good bar?	Onde há um bom bar?
Could we eat outside, please?	Podemos comer lá fora?
What's today's set menu?	Qual é o menu para hoje?
What do you recommend?	O que nos recomenda?
What's the man over there eating?	O que é que aquele senhor está a comer?
We'd like a dish with no meat in it.	Gostariamos de um prato que não seja de carne.
What vegetarian dishes do you have?	Que pratos vegetarianos tem?
Do you have a wine list?	Tem uma lista de vinhos?
This food is cold!	Esta comida está fria.
Do you have some pepper/salt please?	Tem pimenta/sal por favor?
What tapas do you have?	Que aperitivos tem?
We'd like half a plateful of that one.	Gostariamos de meia dose daquele por favor.
A plate of this one.	Uma dose deste.
Please keep the change.	Guarde o troco.
Where are the toilets?	Onde ficam as casas de banho?
The toilet is locked.	As casas de banho estão fechadas.
It was a delicious meal.	Foi uma óptima refeição.
I'd like a white/black coffee/ weaker coffee	Queria um café com leite/café simples/ café fraco
Coffee with just a little milk.	Café com um pouco de leite.
Tea**/camomile tea.	Chá/Chá de camomila

**remember, the safest way to order tea with milk is to ask for 'um chá e um pouco de leite, mas aparte'. It's tempting to ask for 'chá com leite'—but you may well end up with a glass of hot milk with a teabag plonked in the top! Milk is nearly always UHT so if you really need your tea we recommend drinking it with a slice of lemon 'chá com limão'. Or take your own along and just ask for 'jarro com água quente' in the bar. Your request will rarely be refused.

Special Places to Stay in Britain

Can you afford to think of travelling in Britain without this guide? It includes over 620 fascinating places to stay in England, Scotland and Wales - each one chosen because we *like* it.

It might be the stunning, interior, spectacular setting, the amazing garden, an incredible history or a beautiful interior that won us over. A splendid breakfast beside a moat, a bedroom with heart-stopping views, a host so kind and and interesting that you may never want to leave - the book will help you discover all these things and much more besides.

Unlike other guide books that mercilessly squeeze homes and owners to fit their mould, our book allows them to do it their way - with kindness, humour and individuality.

This is the third edition of this much-loved and trusted book.
Price £12.95

Alastair Sawday's
French Bed & Breakfast

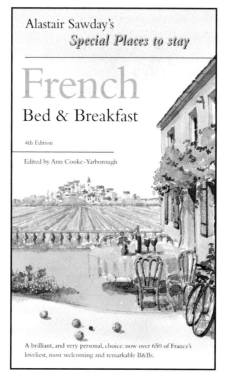

Put this in your glove compartment; no visitor to France should be without it!

It has become a much-loved travelling companion for many thousands of visitors to France. What a treat it is to travel knowing that someone else whom you can trust has done the researching, agonising and diplomatic work for you already. Wherever you are there will be, not too far away, a warm welcome from a French (or even English) family keen to draw you into their home and give you a slice of real French hospitality.

The selection has been honed over 4 editions, and is delectable. We can **almost** guarantee you a good time! And you will, too, save a small fortune on hotel prices.

One reader wrote to tell us that we had changed her life! Well, we don't claim to do that, but it does seem that we have changed the way thousands of people travel.

Over 660 places. Price: £12.95.

Alastair Sawday's Paris Hotels

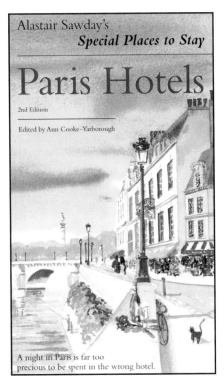

Alastair Sawday's
Special Places to Stay

Paris Hotels

2nd Edition

Edited by Ann Cooke-Yarborough

A night in Paris is far too
precious to be spent in the wrong hotel.

Things change so quickly... how on earth are you to know which hotels are still attractive and good value? Which *quartiers* are still livable and quiet? Where has the long arm of the corporate hotel world NOT reached?

Well, you are lucky to hear of this book... it will rescue your week-end! This second edition follows a successful first edition, still with just a small, select number of our very favourite hotels.

Ann Cooke-Yarborough has lived in Paris for years and has tramped the streets to research and upgrade this second edition. She has chosen with an eagle eye for humbug. Unerringly, she has selected the most interesting, welcoming, good-value hotels in Paris, leaving out the pompous, the puffed-up, the charmless and the ugly.

Trust our taste and judgement, and enjoy some good descriptive writing. With the colour photos, the symbols and the light touch you have a gem of a book. Price: £8.95.

Special Places to Stay in Ireland

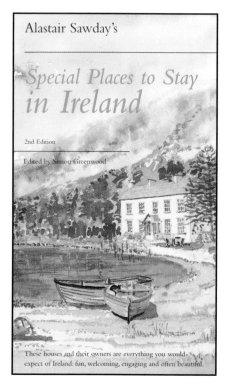

Alastair Sawday's

Special Places to Stay
in Ireland

2nd Edition

Edited by Simon Greenwood

These houses and their owners are everything you would
expect of Ireland: fun, welcoming, engaging and often beautiful.

"This is a corker of a book!" writes the editor himself! Indeed, it is. There is nothing quite like it on the subject of sleeping and carousing in Ireland. If you ever doubted for one moment that the Irish are the most entertaining and sumptuously alive people in Europe, then Special Places will put you right.

But that is not all, of course. The houses and hotels in this book are an architectural feast, a riot of colour and variety, of unexpected comforts and surprising touches of personality. If we ever fail to delight you we will, at least, give you a very good night's sleep.

"... a superb book..., and it's honest-to-goodnesss, top notch. It's only £10.95 and worth at least double that."
John Clayton's 'Travel with a Difference'

This is the second edition of this much-loved and trusted book.
Price £10.95

ORDER FORM for the UK.

All these books are available in the major bookshops but we can send them to you quickly and without effort on your part. Post and packaging is FREE if you order 3 or more books.

	No. of copies	Price each	Total value
French Bed & Breakfast – 4th Edition		£12.95	
Special Paris Hotels – 2nd Edition		£8.95	
Special Places to Stay in Spain & Portugal – 3rd Edition		£11.95	
Special Places to Stay in Britain – 3rd Edition		£12.95	
Special Places to Stay in Ireland – 2nd Edition		£10.95	

Add Post & Packaging: £1 for Paris book, £2 for any other, **FREE** if ordering 3 or more books.

TOTAL ORDER VALUE

Please make cheques payable to Alastair Sawday Publishing

All orders to: Alastair Sawday Publishing, 44 Ambra Vale East, Bristol BS8 4RE Tel: 0117 929 9921. (Sorry, no credit card payments).

Name _____

Address _____

_____

_____ Postcode _____

Tel _____ Fax _____

If you do not wish to receive mail from other companies, please tick the box ☐   SP3

REPORT FORM

If you have any comments on entries in this guide, please let us have them.

If you have a favourite house, hotel or inn or a new discovery in Spain or Portugal, please let us know about it.

Please send reports to: Alastair Sawday Publishing, 44 Ambra Vale East, Bristol BS8 4RE, UK.

Report on:

Entry No _____ New Recommendation ☐ Date _____

Name of owners or hotel/B&B
_____

Address
_____
_____
_____
_____ Tel No _____

My reasons for writing are :
_____
_____
_____
_____
_____
_____

My name and address :

Name
_____

Address
_____
_____
_____
_____ Tel: _____

HOJA DE RESERVA
Spanish Reservation Form

ATENCION DE:
To
DE PARTE DE:
From

NOMBRE DE ESTABLECIMIENTO:
Name of hotel, inn, B&B etc

Estimado Señor/Estimada Señora,
Dear Sir/Madam

Le(s) rogamos de hacernos una reserva en nombre de: _____
Please could you make us a reservation in the name of

	Para _____ noche(s)			
	For *nights(s)*			

Llegando   día _____ (mes) _____ (año) _____
Arriving   *day*   *month*   *year*

Saliendo   día _____ (mes) _____ (año) _____
Departing   *day*   *month*   *year*

Necesitamos _____ habitacíon(es)
We require   *room(s) i.e. how many rooms*
                    you require

* Tick type   Doble   *(double)*   _____
required   Individual   *(single)*   _____
                Triple   *(triple)*   _____
                Quadruple   *(quadruple)* _____
                Tipo Suite   *(suite)*   _____

Apartamento *(apartment)* _____

Requeriremos también la cena: Si _____ No _____ Para ____ persona(s)
We will also be requiring dinner   *yes*   *no*   *for*   *person(s)*

Les rogamos de enviarnos la confirmación de esta reserva a la siguiente dirección:
Please could you send us confirmation of our reservation to the address below
(ésta misma hoja o una fotocopia de la misma con su firma nos valdrá)
(this form or a photocopy of it with your signature could be used)

Nombre:
Name
Dirección:
Address

O pasárnosla por fax en este número:
Or fax it to us at this number

* quitando el primer 0 del prefijo

Muchas Gracias - *Thank you*

(Special Places to Stay in Spain and Portugal)

FORMULÁRIO DE RESERVA
Portuguese Reservation Form

Á ATENÇÃO DE:
To
DE PARTIE DE:
From

NOME DO HOTEL, ESTALAGEM, PENSÃO, etc.
Name of hotel, inn, B&B etc

Estimado Senhor Estimada Senhora,
Dear Sir/Madam

Agradeciamos que efectuassem uma reserva em nome de:
Please could you make us a reservation in the name of

	Para ____ noites			
	For *nights*			
Chegada a	dia ____	mês ____	ano ____	
Arriving	*day*	*month*	*year*	
Partida a	dia ____	mês ____	ano ____	
Departing	*day*	*month*	*year*	
Desejamos	quarto			
We require	*rooms(s) ie how many*			
	rooms you require			

* Tick type   Duplo *(double)*   ____
required   Individual *(single)*   ____
                   Triplo *(triple)*   ____
                   Quádruplo *(quadruple)*   ____
                   Suite *(suite)*   ____

Apartamento *(apartment)* ____

Também desejamos jantar: sim ____   não ____   para ____ pessoas
We shall also be requring dinner   *yes*   *no*   *for*   *person(s)*

Agradeciamos que nos enviassem confirmação desta reserva para o endereço acima mencionado
Please could you send us confirmation of our resevation to the address below
Pode utilizar este formulário ou uma fotocópia do mesmo com a sua assinatura
(this form or a photocopy of it with your signature could be used)

Nome *(name)*
Endereço *(address)*

Ou enviar-nos um fax para o seguinte número
Or fax it to us at this number

* ignorando o primeiro 0 do prefixo

Muito obrigado *(Thank you)*

(Special Places to Stay in Spain and Portugal)

Alastair Sawday's
'Special Places' Walks

Our *walks* are as unusual, different and imaginative as our *books*... and based on the same conviction that people matter as much as places.

If you enjoy walking rather than hiking, if you would like to be guided by an English-speaking local and want to sleep in houses or hotels from *Special Places*, then do join in. We take small groups of 8 to Andalucia, Tuscany and the French Pyrenees.

Our food is terrific, we carry your luggage, we invariably have fun... want to know more?

INDEX OF NAMES

INDEX OF PLACES